WITHDRAWN

Gramley Library
Academy and College
27108

Women Writing Women

ESTIMADO PÚBLICO: HOY DISERTARÉ SOBRE. "LA SOLEDAD DE LA MUJER Y COMO COMBATIRLA"

Ladies and Gentlemen: The topic of my talk is
"Loneliness in Women and How to Prevent It."

SUNY Series in
Latin American and Iberian
Thought and Culture

Jorge J. E. Gracia, Editor

Women Writing Women

*An Anthology of Spanish-American Theater
of the 1980s*

Edited by

Teresa Cajiao Salas
and
Margarita Vargas

Introduction by
Margarita Vargas

STATE UNIVERSITY OF NEW YORK PRESS

Gramley Library
Salem Academy and College
Winston-Salem, N.C. 27108

Frontispiece courtesy of Diana Raznovich.

Production by Ruth Fisher
Marketing by Theresa Abad Swierzowski

Published by
State University of New York Press, Albany

©1997 State University of New York

All rights reserved

Printed in the United States of America

No part of this book may be used or reproduced in any manner
whatsoever without written permission. No part of this book may be stored
in a retrieval system or transmitted in any form or by any means including
electronic, electrostatic, magnetic tape, mechanical, photocopying,
recording, or otherwise without the prior permission in writing of the publisher.

For information, address the State University of New York Press,
State University Plaza, Albany, NY 12246

Library of Congress Cataloging-in-Publication Data

Women writing women : an anthology of Spanish-American theater of the
    1980s / edited by Teresa Cajiao Salas and Margarita Vargas.
        p.   cm. — (SUNY series in Latin American and Iberian thought
    and culture)
        Includes bibliographical references (p.   )
        Contents: Altarpiece of Yumbel / Isidora Aguirre — Yankee /
    Sabina Berman — The great USkrainian circus / Myrna Casas — Evening
    walk / Teresa Marichal — Dial-a-mom / Diana Raznovich — Waiting
    for the Italian / Mariela Romero — Seven times Eve / Beatriz Seibel
    — A woman, two men, and a gunshot / Maruxa Vilalta.
        ISBN 0–7914–3205–X (alk. paper). — ISBN 0–7914–3206–8 (pbk. :
    alk. paper)
        1. Spanish American drama—Women authors. 2. Spanish American
    drama—20th century.   I. Salas, Teresa Cajiao.   II. Vargas,
    Margarita, 1956– .   III. Series.
    PQ7082.D7W6 1997
    862–dc20   96–22946
                                                                    CIP

10 9 8 7 6 5 4 3 2 1

To Alberto for his love and unfailing support

To David, for his love, patience, and incisive comments

Also, to my mother, María M. Vargas

and my children, Isaac, Christopher, and Elena

Contents

Preface

The dearth of anthologies on Spanish-American drama, either in English or in Spanish, was a leading motivation behind this project. The decision to put together an anthology of plays written by women stems from our participation in the First International Conference of Women Playwrights organized by Anna Kay France and held in Buffalo in 1988. Our intention was not to ghettoize women but rather to create a space in which their voices could be heard without being easily dismissed by the dominant presence of male authors.

Aware of the fact that translations can never be an exact reproduction of the original work, we nevertheless undertook this project in order to disseminate among English-speaking audiences different feminist and feminine visions of Spanish-American reality. In selecting the plays, we wanted to represent as many countries as possible to avoid falling into the trap of including only women from countries with a long theatrical tradition. Unfortunately, because it was not financially feasible to publish two volumes, we were forced to omit playwrights from Central America and Brazil. In addition to the above criteria we chose these playwrights because they have all produced at least three plays and have received national and, in some cases, international acclaim. Moreover, they are all presently active in the theater, whether as playwrights, directors, actresses, or critics. We regret that economical restraints prevented us from including Argentina's distinguished playwright, Griselda Gambaro.

As is the case with projects of this scope, we would have been unable to complete it without the assistance, advice, and encouragement of family members, friends, colleagues, and students. Special recognition goes to our respective husbands, Alberto J. Salas and David E. Johnson, for their patience and understanding. To Lalita, whose delicious lunches and *meriendas* provided us with nourishment to maintain the energy level necessary to complete such a task, we will always be grateful.

Our deep appreciation goes to the playwrights, who generously gave us access to their works and permission to translate and publish one of their plays. In accordance to our agreement with them, we alert readers that the playwrights hold all production rights and that permission to perform any of the plays in this anthology should be secured directly with them. To this end, their addresses are included in the first endnote of each play.

Friends and colleagues who contributed to the fruition of our project include Wilma Newberry, Kathleen Betsko, and Darleen Pickering-Hummert. We thank Wilma for her thorough readings of all the translations and her useful comments. Kathleen's expertise in playwrighting proved invaluable in testing the theatrical feasibility of our translations. To Darleen, who performed the mother role in a stage reading of Diana Raznovich's *Casa matriz*, we owe its present English title. To all the students at the University at Buffalo, now too numerous to mention individually, who read the plays in the various typescript versions and made constructive suggestions, *mil gracias*.

We also want to thank David M. Bergeron and David E. Johnson for their meticulous reading of the introduction and their insightful comments.

Last, but not least, we are indebted to the different organizations who sponsored this project. The idea of putting together an anthology was initially supported by the SUNY system, who encouraged collaborative work and granted Teresa C. Salas two successive Graduate Research Initiative Awards from 1988 to 1989. The Lilly Foundation provided Margarita Vargas a fellowship in 1989 to continue working on the anthology with the understanding that the project would lead to the development of a course in English for the Undergraduate College. The Nuala McGann Drescher Award, granted to Margarita from 1990–1991, contributed to the finalization of the anthology. And finally, we wish to acknowledge the Dean's Office in the Faculty of Arts and Letters for funding the artwork in the anthology.

Introduction

by Margarita Vargas

> Despite societal pressures, no longer are women uncritically telling themselves the same story men have told them, and told about them, for centuries, no longer is exploitation by colonial powers the sole measure of oppression.
>
> —Debra Castillo 31

Those not familiar with Spanish-American letters may find the notion of Spanish-American feminism contradictory; yet, feminist ideals can be traced more than three hundred years back to the Mexican writer Sor Juana Inés de la Cruz (1648/51–1695).[1] To those conversant in the field, however, Sor Juana is a household name, singled out whenever women writers are discussed.[2] Nevertheless, because Sor Juana's contribution to feminism is significant, forming a link that needs to be articulated within the context of a general introduction to Spanish American women's writing for an English audience, we must trace and retrace the long line—albeit discontinuous—that ties her to contemporary women writers.

Like Sor Juana, most of the writers in the anthology are involved in the desedimentation and denunciation of male-constructed roles for women. They have abandoned the direct, didactic tone adopted by Sor Juana in her *redondilla* "Hombres necios" (Foolish men), where she admonishes men for erecting idyllic representations of womanhood.[3] Instead, they have pursued the general mode of her "Respuesta a Sor Filotea" (Response to Sister Filotea) in which Sor Juana promotes, though circuitously, the right of women to think out loud, to participate in the making of culture, and to excel intellectually. The following remark by Jean Franco indirectly points to other connections between Sor Juana and the playwrights: "her empowerment by writing led her to understand gender difference as a social construction . . ." (xv). The consciousness of both the power of writing and the constructedness of gender difference are central issues in most of the plays.

1

The 1700s—in part because of the dearth of literature—interrupt the feminist efforts initiated by Sor Juana. To our knowledge, no archival research has confirmed the existence of a literary corpus published during this period. Recent studies, such as Asunción Lavrin's *Latin American Women: Historical Perspectives* and Emilie Bergmann et al.'s *Women, Culture, and Politics in Latin America*, however, do remark on the important roles women played in society through their active participation in the church, in the education of the children, and, if widowed, the administration of property.

Literary histories regard José Joaquín Fernández de Lizardi as the next eminent Spanish-American writer to emerge after Sor Juana. In addition to his famous *El periquillo sarniento* (1816), he authored *La Quijotita y su prima* (1818), which is considered "the first pedagogical novel written in Mexico on the education of women" (Lavrin 29). With its two female characters, "the good and obedient Prudenciana and the evil 'little Miss Quixote'" (Franco 83), the novel can also be credited with prefiguring the two female paradigms common to Spanish-American Romantic literature: angel and demon.

While the 1700s interrupt the dissemination of feminist thought, most male writings of the 1800s openly thwart the possibility of equality between the sexes.[4] During the Romantic period—as many Spanish-American countries were in the process of freeing themselves from colonial rule and involved in the production of a new nation—the political leaders had to figure out a way to quietly suppress half of the population; thus, the angel/demon dichotomy becomes the reigning form of female characterization in the literature. If the readers of the period were to identify with the characters, they had to choose either between the shrewd, dark *femme fatale* or the fragile, blond "good" woman; no middle term existed.[5]

Mexican Romantic literature, for one, captures the ideal feminine by means of the establishment of two religious symbols: the Virgin of Guadalupe and Eve, the first woman. Frequently, though, the *Malinche* (also known as Malintzin and Doña Marina, who served as translator, guide, and mistress to the Spanish conqueror Hernán Cortez) is substituted for Eve, as Elizabeth Ordóñez points out in her essay "Sexual Politics and the Theme of Sexuality in Chicana Poetry" (318 n. 4). Luis Leal corroborates Ordóñez's findings and explains that in *Jicotencal*, an anonymous historical novel published in Philadelphia in 1826, Doña Marina "represents the forces of evil and is characterized as wily, perfidious, deceitful, and treacherous" (228). She is also associated with the serpent, "which placed her under the light of two feminine archetypes, one European and the other Mexican; that is, Eve and Coatlicue, an Aztec goddess" (228). The negative portrayal of these two paradigms makes it difficult for female readers to identify with either, though they may both symbolize the original mother. Instead, as Judith Fetterley has remarked, readers tend to associate with the stronger, more likeable male characters.[6]

These female literary archetypes complemented and extended the limited and sexist education imparted to women. Silvia Arrom cites a paper published in 1852, entitled "Discourse on the Influence of Public Instruction on the Happiness of Nations," which outlines that schooling for girls was "strictly designed to make women 'good daughters, excellent mothers, and the best and most solid support of the goals of Society'" (23). That this essay calls for the repression of women, that it was published in a monthly journal interested in improving society (*Revista Mensual de la Sociedad Promovedora de Mejoras Materiales*), and that it promotes "the happiness of nations" clearly outlines whose interest was at stake. In a continued effort to demarcate a specific place for women, one which excluded them from social decision making, men scorned and labeled women who deviated from the norm. The intellectual woman, "who spent her day reading to the neglect of her personal appearance and home," became a *literata*, and the *talentacia*, "who made a fool of herself with her pedantry (*bachillerías*), was a stock comic character in newspaper satires by the 1840s" (Arrom 24).

Similar negative representations of women during the Romantic period can be found in the literatures of other Spanish-American countries. One has but to glance at any of the major novels of the period, such as the docile character in Jorge Isaacs' *María*. Like most Romantic female "heroines," María—whose life project consists of patiently awaiting her childhood sweetheart—suffers from poor health and predictably dies just before her lover returns.

Spanish-American literary histories, however, can claim (though for a long time they did not) at least two feminist writers: Clorinda Matto de Turner (Perú, 1852–1909) and Gertrudis Gómez de Avellaneda (Cuba, 1814–1873). Even though they do form part of the canon, their feminism, like Sor Juana's, was ignored for over a century. Criticism of their works has focused mainly on their personal lives or on their defense of the disenfranchised—either the Indians in Peru or the slaves in Cuba.

Unlike their male contemporaries, though, Gómez de Avellaneda and Matto de Turner avoided reproducing the angel/demon dichotomy when delineating their characters. In *Sab* (1841), Gómez de Avellaneda endows her male protagonist with traditionally feminine characteristics, and according to Mildred V. Boyer, he "encompasses the author's sentimental experiences" (Torres-Pou, "ambigüedad" 57). The advice that female characters give each other also deviates from that which appears in masculinist Romantic works. While the latter generally suggest that women drown their sorrows in church activities, in *Sab* the female protagonist is told to look for solace in literature (Torres-Pou, "ambigüedad" 60). In another novel, *Dos mujeres* (Two Women, 1842), Gómez de Avellaneda characterizes her male protagonist as "innocent, sentimental and passive"; and in addition to subverting the Romantic dichotomy of good and evil, she also undermines the traditional adjudication of "intelligence and action" to men and "sentimentalism and passivity" to women (Guerra 721).

Joan Torres-Pou shows how in her most popular novel—*Aves sin nido* (Birds Without a Nest, 1889)—Matto de Turner, besides denouncing the perils of the Indians, also creates a female character in search of her subjectivity (Clorinda 4). Even though she constructs her novel well within the confines of Romantic expectations, Torres-Pou asserts that the author "realizes a demolishing criticism of the patriarchy" ("Clorinda" 5).

Alongside these two canonized women writers, the period spawned others who—though they may have not been included in the canon—also produced counterimages of woman. Mary Louise Pratt contends with respect to Argentinean Juana Manuela Gorriti's story "El guante negro" (circa 1850) and José Mármol's *Amalia* (1844) that "at least in some sectors of Spanish American society this postrevolutionary period marked a historical aperture for women . . ." (57). She also sees the period as an experimental moment in which women "could be imaged as players in the drama of nation building" (57). Pratt, nevertheless, neglects to comment on Esteban Echeverría's heavily anthologized "El matadero" (The Slaughter House, 1837–1840), which fails to integrate women in the making of a new nation.

The *modernista* period, traditionally marked by the publication of Rubén Darío's book of poetry *Azul* (1888), reveals an ideological stance similar to that expounded by Romanticism. Sylvia Molloy maintains that this literary period produced "artfully elaborated and culturally convincing clichés—woman as virgin, as child, as toy; woman as demon, as temptress, as witch—" that "were to channel the perception of woman in Latin America and the cultural attitudes toward her for years to come" (109). Some of the most anthologized, and, therefore, most memorable female characters in the poetry of the *modernistas* include Manuel Gutiérrez Nájera's *duquesa Job* (in "La duquesa Job"—Duchess Job), José Martí's *niña de Guatemala* (in "Verso Sencillo IX"—Simple Verse IX), and the various lovers in Darío's "Canción de otoño en primavera" (Autumn Song in Spring). These "women" are either beautiful objects to be exhibited, lifeless adolescents who die from unrequited love, or simpletons who are happy with the morsels of love men might throw their way. Ultimately, they either function as supporting actresses or as the *modernista* version of the Romantics' muse.

The early twentieth century produced two major literary moments: the regionalist novel and avant-garde literature.[7] According to Pratt, both movements "operated to the complete, and often aggressive, exclusion of women" (57). And when they were included, as Francine Masiello has noted, the female characters in the novels "were depicted as uncontrollable and often evil, inclined to wanton aggression or irrational, perilous endeavors" (Women 36). Like the women of the Romantic period, the female characters in the regionalist novel had but two choices: they either "accepted the domestic calling and resigned themselves to a life of subservience or they found themselves eliminated from the scene of narration" (Masiello, Women 36). In avant-garde literature women do not fare any better: the writers (mostly poets) either posit an innocuous image of woman or else—as is the case with Vicente Huidobro—"express an extravagant violence against women" (Masiello, Women 36). In general, Masiello finds overt hostility toward women during this period, but especially in the Argentinean poet Oliverio Girondo, who "describes women's bodies as fragmented limbs or objects to be contemplated by the tourist-poet" (Women 36).

An example of the hollow representation of women can be found in Mexican writer Xavier Villaurrutia. His play *Invitación a la muerte* surrounds the anguished male protagonist with three stock female characters: the adulteress mother, the self-sacrificing wife, and the insipid girlfriend. Pablo Neruda's love poem number 15 also displays an antifeminist viewpoint as it promotes the silencing of women in order to maintain the male's dominant linguistic position. The poem emphasizes the speaker's delight in the woman's silence, her absent presence, by strategically repeating at the beginning, the middle, and the end, "Me gusta cuando callas" (I like it when you are quiet). Thus, these masculinist writers bring female characters on stage merely for aesthetic effect, realistic illustration, or occasionally to help advance the plot.

Fortunately, male avant-garde literature and the regionalist novel make up only part of the canvas. Even though this canonized literature does not reflect it, both political unrest and social reform marked the early twentieth century. As was true elsewhere, in Latin America women were fighting for civil rights, anarchist movements flourished, and workers demanded labor rights (Greenberg 141). Thus, at the same time that men were busily creating disparaging images of woman, women's groups were proliferating all over Latin America and gathering at annual international meetings to discuss women's issues.[8] Moreover, women were writing and publishing their literature in larger numbers than ever before. This historical period witnessed the appearance of four major poets: Delmira Agustini (1886–1914), Gabriela Mistral (1889–1957), Alfonsina Storni (1892–1938), and Juana de Ibarbourou (1895–1979). Though "they were not accepted in avant-garde circles" (Pratt 57), These writers counteracted the female images created by their male cohorts and depicted women's problems from a female perspective.

While all four writers contemplate feminist concerns, Storni's poetry is unequivocally the most committed. Her poem "Hombre pequeñito" (Little Man) alone qualifies her as a radical feminist since it "addresses the question of 'female aesthetic' as well as the desirability of a separate female culture" (Austin 5). Even though Storni denied that she was a militant feminist, she participated in feminist activities, labor rights meetings, and was one of the leaders of the "Asociación pro Derechos de la Mujer" (Association for the Rights of Women) (Kirkpatrick 115). She also wrote and directed feminist columns for *La Nación* and *La nota*, both important dailies in Buenos Aires, that supported many "proposed legal and social changes regarding women" (Kirkpatrick 118).

Perhaps because these poets expressed an aesthetic foreign to masculinist critics, they continue to be "benignly classified in literary typologies as *posmodernistas* distinct from the avant-garde" (Pratt 57). Marking them as other, then, in a way indicates their unequal status among the male writers. Also, unlike male writings, their poetry has been discussed not in terms of its literary quality but in terms of the writers' personal life. Mistral, for example, has always been portrayed as a forlorn school teacher who could never recuperate from the loss of her first love and who spent her entire life exalting in her poetry a motherhood she never enjoyed. Sylvia Molloy reports that Mistral endorsed "this pathetic compensatory image" of herself and, therefore, successfully wrote "her lesbianism out of existence" (116). At present, however, the work begun by critics such as Kirkpatrick, Molloy, Pratt, Castillo, and Castro-Klarén promises the advent of a revisionist literary and cultural history that will not only recognize the experimentalism in their writings but will validate their position within avant-garde literature.

The emergence of the "Boom" writers (which includes, among others, Julio Cortázar, Carlos Fuentes, Gabriel García Márquez, and Mario Vargas Llosa) in the 1960s, with all their innovative narrative techniques, did little to change the image of woman created by their predecessors. With regard to the portrayal of la Malinche, Elizabeth Ordóñez remarks that "Octavio Paz shapes her into a symbol of the violated native woman, '*la chingada*' or the passive woman open to sexual violence," while for Carlos Fuentes, "*Malinche* generates betrayal and corruption in woman" (318 n. 4). Even though the writers of this period did not go so far as to replicate the female portraits painted by previous generations, the female characters depicted by most of them play secondary roles.[9]

Remarkably, although publishing houses had begun in the 1960s to recognize the significance of women writers, none of them were integrated into the so-called Boom. Glaring omissions include María Luisa Bombal, Rosario Castellanos, and Elena Garro. Despite the oversight or, perhaps, intentional exclusion of women from the canon, the number of women writing has increased significantly in the last twenty-five years. The last eighteen years have witnessed the publication of numerous anthologies dedicated exclusively to Latin American and Latina women.[10]

From within this historical literary context—both as involuntary consumers of a masculinist tradition and as legitimate inheritors of Sor Juana's feminist legacy—the playwrights in this anthology emerge to pursue the task of dismantling what Molloy terms the "persuasive icons of femininity" produced by *modernismo* (109), as well as to resume the work done by feminists in the mid 1800s and early 1900s. For the most part, these writers are not interested in re-evaluating or recuperating the language of spaces traditionally considered female. Diana Raznovich's *Dial-a-Mom* approximates this interest; its Spanish title, *Casa matriz*, refers simultaneously to the womb and the headquarters of a business. According to Debra Castillo, texts with such titles "mark the public, philosophical call for legitimation of a space traditionally associated with and denigrated as female" (35).[11] By situating a female icon within a historically male space, however, Raznovich joins the rest of the playwrights in the enterprise of either demarcating new spaces or erasing spatial boundaries based on gender difference.

While each of the playwrights has a specific agenda, they all share the desire to deconstitute existing structures that limit and confine women and they all question the basic gender assumptions grounding their particular cultures. The three main areas that we will highlight are the search for a self-created female identity that includes education, the reappropriation of language, and a capacity for writing; the affirmation of feminine subjectivity; and the denouncing of senseless acts of violence committed in and by society.

The most common topic addressed by the dramatic texts is the search for identity; yet each playwright approaches the issue from different positions. Diana Raznovich, for one, examines the daughter/mother phenomenon in *Dial-a-Mom* from a psychological perspective, while Myrna Casas takes on a more philosophical/cultural approach as a means of confronting self with other in *The Great USkrainian Circus*. In both plays, the characters have reached a crossroads in their lives and are drawn into a self-analytic process. In *Dial-a-Mom* the juncture reached by the protagonist, a literature professor, is related to age. She has turned thirty and has not resolved her identity vis-a-vis her mother. In order to come to terms with herself, she hires an actress from an agency that specializes in training "substitute mothers" to play out several possible mothers.[12] The play begins with the arrival of the substitute mother at the protagonist's home and what ensues is a simultaneous, three-dimensional relationship: mother/daughter, consumer/provider, and director/actress.

The first instance recalls the adolescent stage in which the child vies for her own identity, the second speculates on the rights of the consumer and the integrity of professionals providing a service, and the third stages the negotiations between a director, who shapes the entire play, and an actress, who expects to display her histrionic abilities. The play ends in a stalemate, suggesting that "Subjectivity is never a fixed entity, but rather a constant process of constitution in specific historical and symbolic networks" (Kristeva in Castro-Klarén, Situations 29), or that identity is never stable but, rather, comprises multiple and shifting relations of power.[13] Nevertheless, the play also hints at the possibility of creating oneself through acting, writing, and directing.

The characters in *The Great USkrainian Circus* are all professional actors searching for their identity through role playing. They constitute a vaudeville-type theater group—owned by a woman—that travels from town to town with the supposed purpose of functioning as a mirror to society. To carry out their mission, they gather information about the town and then proceed to re-enact the various local events and recent occurrences. In the process of lifting a mirror to the audience, the performers end up seeing their own reflections and thus have to confront their identities. Unlike the protagonist in *Dial-a-Mom*, the characters have reached the crux of their lives not primarily through age (though it is significant), but because they are in a town they had visited before. The return to a place from the past and the representation of current events summon old memories and force the thespians to examine themselves. The owner of the theater group, for one, confesses that she was forced to abandon her son to pursue her career. But since the process of self-analysis occurs while they are acting a specific role, and the information provided when they are out-of-character contradicts what the role has revealed, their "true" identities remain enigmas. Thus, the inability to discern between truth and fiction evokes once again the impossibility of ever knowing who we, and much less others, are.

In *7 Times Eve* the search for identity is gender specific. Beatriz Seibel conducts a historical survey to map the experience of the Argentinean woman from the 1600s to the 1970s and defines her identity in terms of the duality mind/body and the burden of the male tradition. Seibel shows that woman develops as she questions and modifies the roles imposed on her. The development occurs as the female characters move from a sense of self directly tied to the social function of their bodies to a self that has integrated body and mind via the acquisition of voice.

As a person dependent on her body for an identity, woman is relegated to the position of object, useful only for men's sexual pleasure or as a receptacle charged with reproduction. Also, her voiceless body ties her identity to her lineage, whether by blood or by trade. Thus, in order to avoid the mistakes of her ancestors—the convictions that a woman can only aspire to an inferior position within the public sphere or that she is at her best when procreating or serving and caring for others—a woman must interrupt the line and acquire a voice. The narrator is the first one who succeeds in breaking the line of tradition by modifying the profession that had been in her family for several generations. The last character, an actress who reaches stardom through unconventional means, exemplifies the acquisition of voice. Once she surmounts the hurdles imposed on women in the theatrical field, the next step is to overcome stagefright (a metaphor for losing the fear of being in charge). She shows how to acquire voice (subjectivity) through an erotic (bodily), though completely mental (linguistic), experience that occurs during the performance. However, the unity of self, accomplished through the confluence of body and language, creates another dilemma that remains unresolved: like the colonial woman who awaits the return of her husband until she dies, the modern woman finds herself alone, albeit on center stage.

The break with tradition exemplified in *7 Times Eve* is even more radical in *Evening Walk*. Teresa Marichal, determined to topple masculine hierarchical structures in order to begin with a clean slate in the search for identity, defies Otto Rank, who said to Anais Nin: "to create it is necessary to destroy. Woman cannot destroy . . ." (Russ 14). Marichal's play is entirely about destruction, from the obliteration of the female figure as object of desire to the rewriting of the canon and the eradication of society's construction of feminine roles. The play initially provides a conventional representation of two typical figures: the mother and the writer who are, nonetheless, problematically located in front of a stage backdrop depicting a woman in a sudsy bathtub who has slashed her wrists. The two characters set out to bring about social change either through physical or intellectual dissension. The mother challenges her socially imposed role by killing her son, and the writer defies the category "female writer" by rewriting the children's canon and appropriating what has been considered a male genre, the adventure story. The play, then, summons women to participate in the act of creation, which goes beyond procreation, in order to guarantee the construction of a self-identity, one not hegemonically determined or decided beforehand by masculinist writers.

Though in more recent works, Sabina Berman displays a search for identity similar to the one exhibited by the plays already outlined, the female character in *Yankee* is in the initial stages of recognizing her culturally constructed position. Blinded by tradition and social expectations, the protagonist appears never to have questioned her role as housewife and mother, and never to have thought about her husband's language, except to remark on its beauty within the context of his poetry. However, the loneliness experienced at the beach—where her husband has taken her so he can write—and the presence of a North American man, eventually encourage her to contemplate her social position and analyze herself. The moment of recognition comes after the third time she hears her husband pronounce the words *puta madre* (literally, mother whore). When she asks him to repeat what he has said, he dismisses the importance of his words by calling them a mere expression. She retorts with silence; but towards the end of the play she consciously rejects the virgin mother image with which the "intruder" had imbued her[14] and embraces, in order to redefine, her husband's "puta madre" (53). The ability to murmur "puta madre, sí" (mother whore, yes) is, according to Monique Wittig, an affirmation of the self because "when one says 'I' and, in so doing reappropriates language as a whole, . . . it is then and there, . . . that there occurs the supreme act of subjectivity" (66).

What the protagonist will do with her newly acquired subjectivity remains unresolved; but within the context of Berman's *oeuvre*, it marks the beginning of a continuous search for identity and the initial step toward an ongoing exploration of feminist and lesbian issues.

Unlike the female characters in the above texts, Mariela Romero's women are for the most part beyond the search of identity; in fact, they seem to have an answer to Freud's dilemma concerning women's desires. The women in *Waiting for the Italian* know exactly what they want. They are four women in their mid fifties who have complied with society's demands (most of them have married, had children, and grandchildren), and now they want to fulfill their own needs. They refuse to succumb to the traditional roles assigned to women their age by trading their white hair, sagging breasts, rockers, and grandchildren for more gratifying bodily pleasures. To accomplish their goal they have formed a co-op to hire a young Italian who will satisfy their sexual desires and not compromise their social position.

By affirming what they want, as opposed to what society expects from them, they have destroyed long-held myths advanced in masculinist literature. This literature, intent on preserving the image of the lady-in-waiting, has been entirely self-serving for it has guaranteed the preservation of the public/private dichotomy: women enclosed at home and men free to assume positions of power out in the "real" world. While Judith Butler, for one, maintains that "the search for woman is still an on going enterprise" (Castro-Klarén, "Situations" 29), Romero shows that the experience acquired with age does potentially provide women with a better understanding of who they are and what they want.

In *Altarpiece of Yumbel* Isidora Aguirre depicts the story of a group of actors who arrive in the town of Yumbel to re-enact the martyrdom of St. Sebastian. Since St. Sebastian's predicament parallels their own, the actors take the opportunity to relate indirectly their personal story. Aguirre, then, uses both accounts to honor those who have suffered political retribution throughout South America, but particularly in Chile.

Even though Aguirre is predominantly interested in denouncing acts of political injustice committed upon both men and women, she, nevertheless, grants women key positions in her play. One of the female characters performs the role of narrator, and thus guides our reading as she provides historical information about either St. Sebastian or the political prisoners. One of the actresses relates how she was abducted and tortured during Argentina's Dirty War. Her recounting is a cathartic experience, a questioning of gender difference, and a criticism of her society. That the government made no distinction between the magnitude of torture imposed on and suffered by either men or women shows how society is willing to grant equal status only at those moments when there is no regard for human life whatsoever. Torturers made no sexual distinction when they treated both women and men with equal brutality and gave both the opportunity to reveal their fears, physical endurance, and psychological strength. Aguirre ends her play with the presence of five women who take to the streets—in a fashion that recalls the Mothers of the Plaza de Mayo in Argentina—demanding information about the disappeared. By having them confront the authorities, despite the possibility of reprisal, Aguirre underscores the power potential in women.

For her part, Maruxa Vilalta, in *A Woman, Two Men, and a Gunshot*, participates in the destruction of male forms by satirizing subgenres such as melodrama, surrealism, the theater of the absurd, and the musical. She writes a play in which three actors and two actresses rehearse

Gramley Library
Salem Academy and College
N. C. 27108

four mini-dramas that ridicule these subgenres and subvert social stereotypes, including traditional views of the feminine, of homosexuality, and even the theater. By resorting to metatheatrical devices, especially the play within the play, Vilalta also exposes the tenuous relationship between the director, the actors, and their financial supporters.

Though neither Casas, Vilalta, nor Aguirre outlines female concerns specifically, they are involved in challenging current discursive forms, whether literary, theatrical, or political, which continue to be dominated by men.

Because all the plays included in the anthology were written in the same decade (the 1980s) by women born on the same continent, one might presume a homogeneous *corpus*, but that is far from true. The conflicts and concerns, as well as the theatrical techniques, evident in the works are as diverse as the society each of the playwrights scrutinizes. However, a similar historical background—encompassing conquest, colonization, independence, and the prevailing cultural imperialism—and their need to further women's issues, provides their theater with continental cohesiveness. Their countries appear unified by their negative reaction against foreign influence and the positive embrace of a common Spanish American culture disseminated through the arts, sports, cinema, radio, and television. Thus, the final mural composed by this collage of writers offers a symbiotic Spanish America whose theater constitutes an integral part of contemporary world drama.

Notes

1. Sor Juana Inés de la Cruz wrote mystical and cloak-and-dagger plays, short dramatic panegyrics, and farces. Her two most famous plays are *Los empeños de una casa* (a cloak-and-dagger play) and *El divino narciso* (a mystical play). Her poetry, especially her sonnets, has appeared in every major anthology of Spanish American literature.

2. See for example, Emilie Bergmann et al., *Women, Culture, and Politics in Latin America*; Sabina Berman, "La mujer como dramaturga"; Jean Franco's *Plotting Women: Gender and Representation in Mexico*; Magdalena García Pinto, *Women Writers of Latin America*; and Gerda Lerner, *The Creation of Feminist Consciousness*, among others.

3. A *redondilla* is an octosyllabic quatrain rhyming abba. In this poem Sor Juana reprimands men for defiling women and then

demanding virginal spouses. She advices them: "Queredlas cual las hacéis, / o hacedlas cual las buscáis" (Love them as you've made them / or make them as you'd like them).

4. As we all know, literary histories have neglected the contribution of women writers; thus, the prevailing images of women in literature have been those advanced by men.

Except for the recognition accorded Clorinda Matto de Turner (Perú, 1852–1909) and Gertrudis Gómez de Avellaneda (Cuba, 1814–1873), little is known about female writers of the period. The works of playwrights such as Carmen Pérez de Rodríguez (1828–1898) and Mercedes González de Moscoso (1860–1911) from Ecuador; Vicenta Laparra de Cerda (1834–1905) from Guatemala; María Bibiana Benítez (1783–1875), Carmen Bozello (1850?–1882) and Carmen Hernández de Araujo (1832–1877) from Puerto Rico have received marginal attention.

5. The section on the representation of woman during the Romantic period in Mexico comes from Margarita Vargas's essay in David William Foster's *Mexican Literature: A History*.

6. The lack of positive female roles is neither site specific nor exclusive to a literary period. In "Palpable Designs: An American Dream: 'Rip Van Winkle,'" Judith Fetterley points out that in early nineteenth-century American literature the female characters could be so inane that women readers had to side with the male protagonist and consequently against themselves (Warhol 507).

7. The two canonized regionalist novels are Rómulo Gallegos, *Doña Bárbara* (1929) and Ricardo Güiraldes, *Don Segundo Sombra* (1926). The avant-garde literature produced mainly poets, among them the renowned Pablo Neruda.

8. The First International Feminine Conference was held on 10 May 1910 in Buenos Aires. Over two hundred women from Perú, Chile, Uruguay, Paraguay, and Argentina attended (Francesca Miller 12). Some of the groups active during this period were the Consejo Feminista Mexicano, the Women's International League for Peace and Freedom, the Federaçao Brasileria pelo Progresso Feminino, the National Woman's Party of the United States, the Ligue Feminine Haitienne, the Club de Madres of Buenos Aires, etc. (Francesca Miller 15).

9. García Márquez's Ursula Buendía is an exception.

10. We mention anthologies because of the crucial role they play in the canonization process. Thus far, in drama at least two have

appeared in Spanish, but none in English. There are several on fiction, including Alma Gómez, Cherríe Moraga, and Mariana Romo-Carmona, *Cuentos: Stories by Latinas* (1982); Alberto Manguel, *Other Fires: Short Fiction by Latin American Women* (1986); Evelyn Picon Garfield, *Women's Fiction from Latin America: Selections from Twelve Contemporary Authors* (1988); as well as others in Spanish. While *Hispanic Feminist Poems from the Middle Ages to the Present: A Bilingual Anthology* (1986), edited by Angel and Kate Flores, is exclusively dedicated to poetry, Evangelina Vigil's *Woman of Her Word: Hispanic Women Write* (1984) and María del Carmen Boza, Beverly Silva, and Carmen Valle's *Nosotras: Latina Literature Today* incorporate both poetry and fiction. Sara Castro-Klarén, Sylvia Molloy, and Beatriz Sarlo's *Women's Writing in Latin America: An Anthology* (1991) contains both poetry and essays. Alicia Partnoy's *You Can't Drown the Fire: Latin American Women Writing in Exile* (1988) includes testimonies, narrative, essays, poetry, and letters.

There are also collections of interviews by Magdalena García Pinto, *Women Writers of Latin America: Intimate Histories* (1988) and by Evelyn Picon Garfield, *Women's Voices from Latin America: Interviews with Six Contemporary Authors*, as well as bibliographical references such as Lynn Cortina, *Spanish-American Women Writers: A Bibliographical Research Checklist* (1983); Margery Resnick and Isabelle de Courtivron, *Women Writers in Translation: An Annotated Bibliography, 1945–82* (1984); Diane Marting, *Women Writers of Spanish America: An Annotated Bio-Bibliographical Guide* (1987); and Sandra Cypess, David R. Kohut, and Rachelle Moore, *Women Authors of Modern Hispanic South America: A Bibliography of Literature, Criticism, and Interpretation* (1989).

Finally, some of the most influential critical studies on women's writings include Yvette Miller and Charles M. Tatum, *Latin American Women Writers: Yesterday and Today* (1977); Doris Meyer and Margarite Fernández Olmos, *Contemporary Women Authors of Latin America: Critical Essays* (1983); Beth Miller, *Women in Hispanic Literature, Icons and Fallen Idols* (1983); Sharon Magnarelli, *The Lost Rib: Female Characters in the Spanish-American Novel* (1985); Carmelo Virgillo and Naomi Lindstrom, *Woman as Myth and Metaphor in Latin American Literature* (1985); Jean Franco, *Plotting Women: Gender and Representation in Mexico* (1989); Emilie Bergmann et al., *Women, Culture, and Politics in Latin America* (1990); Debra A. Castillo, *Talking Back: Toward a Latin American Feminist Literary Criticism* (1992); and Francine Masiello, *Between Civilization and Barbarism: Women, Nation, and Literary Culture in Modern Argentina* (1992).

11. Castillo alludes directly to Patricia Elena González and Eliana Ortega's *La sartén por el mango* (The Pan by Its Handle, 1985), but one could also include in this definition Laura Esquivel's novel *Como agua para chocolate* (Like Water for Chocolate, 1989), Dolores Prida's play *Coser y cantar* (As Easy as Sewing and Singing, 1991), and even Castillo's own text, since she incorporates cooking terminology in her study, though her title does not reveal it.

12. It is important to note that the actress's rebellion as well as the variety of mother roles she plays—from the most submissive to the ultra sophisticated and worldly mother—help to dismiss the conventional image of woman as subservient being.

13. For a thorough description of the theory of power relations see Michel Foucault, *History of Sexuality*, especially volume I. On Foucault, see Hubert L. Dreyfus, *Michel Foucault, Beyond Structuralism and Hermeneutics* and Paul Rabinow, *The Foucault Reader*.

14. Bill, the "intruder," claims, "Cuando la vi en el mercado, el bebé en brazos . . . me pareció una madona . . . usted era una aparición . . . La virgen de Guadalupe" (When I saw you at the market, with the baby in your arms . . . you looked like a Madonna, . . . You were a vision . . . The Virgin of Guadalupe," 15).

Isidora **Aguirre** (Chile, 1919), though primarily recognized as a play-wright, has also published short stories and novels. In addition to the myriad national awards her plays have received, *Retablo de Yumbel* (Altarpiece of Yumbel), included in this anthology, was awarded the Cuban "Premio Casa de las Américas" in 1987.[1]

Even though Aguirre's first plays mainly comprised light musical comedies or humorous portrayals of local characters, her concern for social problems is already evident in her most famous play, *La pérgola de las flores*, first staged in 1960. Because it is a musical comedy, the audience can easily get wrapped up in the beauty of the costumes, the colorful flowers, the pleasant music, and the light humor. However, there is an underlying theme that reveals a concern with the plight of the proletarian group of flower vendors.

While several of her plays emphasize the light tone generally associated with *La pérgola de las flores* (The Flower Stand) and focus primarily on failed relationships, others concentrate on social issues. Thus, her dramatic career develops along two parallel veins: the intimate and the social. After the 1980s, however, she examines almost exclusively the ills of society, as elucidated in *The Altarpiece of Yumbel* and *Diálogos de fin de siglo* (Dialogues at the End of the Century, 1988.)

Aguirre, also interested in preserving the cultural and historical traditions of Spanish America, has incorporated national heroes, folkloric elements, and religious practices in the writing of her plays.

Retablo de Yumbel, through the reenactment of Saint Sebastian's martyrdom by a troupe of actors, establishes a parallel between the Saint's tribulations and the murder of nineteen political activists who disappeared in 1973. The unearthing of their bodies from a site near Yumbel, the city which annually celebrates Saint Sebastian's Day, motivated Aguirre to write this play. The personal stories of the actors emphasize the horror of political persecution suffered in Chile and Argentina in the mid 70s and stress the self-reflective nature of the play.

Notes

1. The most noted national awards include "Laurel de Oro" for *Población Esperanza* (Hope Village), "Premio de la Crítica" for *La pérgola de las flores* (The Flower Stand), and "Premio Luis Alberto Heiremans" for the wide acceptance of her plays.

The Altarpiece of Yumbel

BY ISIDORA AGUIRRE[1]

Casa de las Américas Prize 1987
Translated from *El retablo de Yumbel*
by Teresa Cajiao Salas and Margarita Vargas

To José Manuel Parada Maluenda
(1985)

Ximena Ramírez's theater group "El rostro," from Concepción, Chile asked Isidora Aguirre to write this play in honor of the people who disappeared in the southern region of Chile. It was premiered by the group in August 1986 under the direction of Julio Muñoz.

    Altarpiece of Yumbel takes place in January 1980 in the town square of Yumbel, on the eve of Saint Sebastian's Day, the town's patron saint.

Characters

The Actors

Alejandro (mid 30s)	portrays emperor Diocletian; Roman Proconsul
Marta (early 30s)	(Alejandro's sister-in-law) portrays Torquatus the centurion; a Roman horseman
Eduardo (early 30s)	(a friend of Alejandro and Marta) portrays Saint Sebastian; the Tribune
Magdalena (late 20s)	(Argentinean wardrobe mistress; Mother 5)
Actor (early 30s)	portrays Galerius; functions as stage manager; organ grinder

The Townspeople

Juliana (18)	a candle and flower vendor
Chinchinero[2]	Juliana's father; the one-man orchestra.
Five women	portray the roles of wives or mothers of the disappeared men
One man	portrays a street vendor with a cart at the end of the play

Stage Setting: A town square with a platform; an altarpiece with three arches for the Roman "Episodes." Initially, the altarpiece appears covered with a curtain. The workshop, where the actors stand when they are not performing, is highlighted by a spotlight and some simple props, a table with a mirror, benches, coat rack. *Arpilleras*,[3] depicting scenes of the martyrdom of Saint Sebastian; a banner with his image; and red and yellow flags. A small, cute, rag pony with scarves and Roman ornaments that Marta will tie around her waist. A flying cloth angel is on one of the arches.

Music: Aside from the incidental music for the Roman episodes, we recommend the use of the Gavotte No. 6, English suite by Bach played with Andean instruments, to suggest the Chilean northern folklore (dances from the Tirana and the Coast.) Some of the ten-line stanzas are taken from those found in the Church of Yumbel between each of the images that narrate the life and martyrdom of Saint Sebastian.

Part One

Introductory, dramatic orchestral music in blackout. Music fades to silence. Beat.

ACTOR: And the Lord said unto Cain . . . "Where is thy brother Abel?" And he said, "I know not: am I my brother's keeper?" And He said, "What has thou done? The voice of thy brother's blood crieth unto me from the ground."

SCENE I

The music changes into a lively cueca[4] *for the entrance of the dancing couple—Juliana, who is carrying the banner or flag of Saint Sebastian, and her father, Chinchinero, who is playing his instruments. Then the mothers appear, as if coming out of church. The mothers go around the town square once, following Juliana and Chinchinero. The latter continues to mark the rhythm as soon as the dance stops. Juliana recites:*

JULIANA: To the town square of Yumbel,
                    With a candle and a carnation
                    We come to visit you,
                    Dear Sebastian.
                    Sebastian is the young nobleman
                    To whom the pilgrims sing
                    And the larks praise with their trills
                    With tender devotion:
                    "Carry out your mission by
                    Conceding divine favors!"

CHORUS: "Grant us your favors, Saint Sebastian!"

CHINCHINERO: (*To the audience.*) In case you don't know, the image of this saint we worship in the church of Yumbel is very old: it should suffice to say that it was brought here by the Spanish conquerors. Come on Juliana, recite the poem.

JULIANA: This most worshiped image,
Came to Chillán from Spain
It anchored here,
Miraculously, in this church.
God allowed this feat:
A Colonel, fleeing the war
Was carrying it
When he was passing by Yumbel
He buried it in the sand
And then forgot about it!

CHINCHINERO: Later on, when the people from Yumbel
Dug in the sand,
They found the sacred image.
From Chillán they demand his return,
The people from Yumbel respond:

JULIANA: "We don't want to lose the saint,
And we won't let anyone take him."

CHINCHINERO: Not even with two pair of oxen
Were they able to remove the image!

MOTHER 2: Fulfill our requests, Saint Sebastian!

MOTHER 3: Yes, fulfill them, miraculous saint . . .

CHINCHINERO: (*To mothers.*) Be careful: he's miraculous but very cunning. He grants wishes only if his wishes are fulfilled in return. And if you fail to keep your vows, he punishes you.

He happily turns around once, playing his instruments. He watches the actors advancing toward the stage and points them out to Juliana.

The actors.

JULIANA: (*She advances toward them and announces.*) The actors are coming! They will rehearse in the town square.

She goes toward them and helps them with some of the props they are carrying toward the back of the stage. While Alejandro, Marta, Eduardo and Magdalena—the latter always wears sunglasses—put down a basket full of costumes in the workshop section, she returns, accompanied by the drum and cymbals being played by Chinchinero, to announce to the audience:

JULIANA: The twentieth of this month of January is the celebration of our patron, Saint Sebastian. The actors are going to stage a play entitled . . . (*She and Chinchinero move.*) . . . (*Drumrolls.*) Altarpiece of Yumbel!

Juliana, Chinchinero, and Mothers 2 and 3 have stepped up to the foreground. Mother 1 and Magdalena stay back helping Marta to fasten the pony around her waist. The other actors are preparing the wardrobe and props in the background.

CHINCHINERO: It is a performance which narrates the cruel martyrdom of the young nobleman Sebastian:

MOTHER 2:   It is true, and it's not fiction!

MOTHER 3:   There's abuse and there's no sanction!

CHINCHINERO: You will notice during this celebration that this world is still the same:

JULIANA: The criminals are calm and free

MOTHER 2:   And the innocent are in prison

ALL THREE: There's abuse and no sanction!

Drum and cymbals.
They freeze in this position, the light switches to the foreground. Brief incidental music.

ALEJANDRO: (*In the foreground, as narrator.*) Summer of 1980. It was Marta's idea. The idea of writing the play and staging it in the town square for Saint Sebastian's celebration. (*Pause.*) I loved Marta. But she continued to love her companion, my brother Federico, who was killed in 1975. Eduardo chose the role of Saint Sebastian. We recruited another actor in Yumbel. And the women of . . . the "Association of Relatives" sent us Magdalena, a young Argentinean who is in charge of the wardrobe. (*At the back of the stage, these actors are getting ready in semidarkness.*) (*Hurdy-gurdy music.*) They lent us a workshop next to the church. It was always open, as if inviting the people from Yumbel to participate. The people circulating around the town square looked happy. It was a nice place with majestic trees and chirping birds. Nevertheless, not long ago, the earth in Yumbel had parted to accept the remains of nineteen men who had been shot, and whose names had been on the list of the arrested and disappeared since the military coup.

He exits taking clothes from the basket and enters into the covered altarpiece. The light now illuminates the other front side of the stage, where Mother 1 speaks:

MOTHER 1: Nineteen leaders were shot for no reason at all—as was proven in the trial—a few days after the military coup, during a transfer from Laja and San Rosendo to the barracks in the city of Los Angeles. Even though there were claims, appeals for assistance, countless requests, and the long pilgrimage of mothers and wives, it was not possible to find out what happened to the group of arrested men whose personal records were lost early in the morning of September 17, 1973. The identity of each of the victims and that of their executioners was established during the trial. But as it happened in Lonquén, in 1979, the executioners were pardoned by an amnesty law formerly decreed by the Military Junta. (*She exits, the light returns to the center, those who had remained still come to life.*)

Brief incidental music. Chinchinero beats his drum as he turns around and recites:

CHINCHINERO: In the play
About Saint Sebastian
He who wants to see will see
Exactly what happened in Yumbel
When the earth parted.

MOTHER 2:   They persecuted innocence
And this land in its mercy
Wanted to free our beloved
From oblivion:

MOTHER 3:   From heaven came the sentence!

Chinchinero pounds a few beats, they exit as the Actor appears in the background:

ACTOR: The rehearsal begins: first episode. Lights out! (*The stage is in darkness.*) Music! (*The cheery Gavotte begins. After the first measures, whistles and drums join in. The stage remains dark.*)

Episode 1 of the Altarpiece

Bright and warm light over the golden parts of the altarpiece, now without a curtain. Motionless like two statues, Diocletian, stands with his hand raised, Sebastian is in front of him with a knee on the ground, dressed in his legionnaire's cuirass and helmet. Chinchinero, Juliana, with a banner or a flag, and Marta, as a Roman horseman with a mask and the pony tied around her waist, enter spinning, dancing to the Gavotte. The music stops.

JULIANA: The august emperor, Diocletian,
Called Sebastian, the legionnaire,
And bestowed upon him his favor.
However,
Sebastian was a Christian.
People already knew
That in those days
Cruel persecution existed
And death was the fate
Of the Christian!

They exit dancing. The characters in the altarpiece come to life,
maintaining the posture they had while they were motionless.
Sebastian, knee on the ground, the emperor standing in the center.

DIOCLETIAN: I greet you, legionnaire.

SEBASTIAN: Oh holy one! (*He bows.*)

DIOCLETIAN: (*Stopping his movement.*)
You need not bend your knee
nor kiss the fringe of my robe.

SEBASTIAN: (*He stands up.*) Lord, may the heavens grant you a
long life.

DIOCLETIAN: (*He laughs.*) So be it. The higher you rise
The more your existence is in danger.
And power
Obtained with violence, Sebastian,
Is usually lost with violence . . .
But now the Empire is at peace.
I hope the pomp of the palace doesn't dazzle you:
Tonight share supper with me.

SEBASTIAN: Lord, I'm not your equal . . .

DIOCLETIAN: My sanctuary intimidates you?
As loot from war we bring captive
Exotic gods from the conquered nations.

SEBASTIAN: The emperor doesn't honor the gods of Rome?

DIOCLETIAN: They provide little consolation and no hope.
Enjoy the pleasure that luck grants you, my son,
Because nothing lies beyond death.
I, the August invite you: drink from my cup.

SEBASTIAN: Forgive my being frugal.

DIOCLETIAN: Beware! You're behaving like a Christian:
They fear pleasure and riches,
Since "It is easier for a camel," their doctrine
preaches,

"to go through the eye of a needle
than for a rich man to enter into the kingdom of
    God."
Tell me, what happens upon entering that
    kingdom?

SEBASTIAN: At the end of time, we shall be judged.

DIOCLETIAN: (*He smiles.*) Judged, by whom?

SEBASTIAN: By the Christian god.

DIOCLETIAN: They say he's strict, that he inspires fear . . .

SEBASTIAN: He sent Jesus Christ, his son, to this world to teach
               men about love.

DIOCLETIAN: (*Cunning.*) Do you love me, Sebastian?

SEBASTIAN: Yes my Lord. You and all those who serve you.

DIOCLETIAN: I, without being a Christian feel love for you who
               serve me.

SEBASTIAN: (*Pointing outside.*) And for him, your slave?

DIOCLETIAN: Of course not. Am I a cruel man, then?

SEBASTIAN: He who is served ignores the sufferings of those
               who are forced to serve him.

DIOCLETIAN: And I? Am I not always serving you?
               I was forced, Sebastian, to make war.
               I conquered lands with suffering
               I was forced to straighten out what was crooked in
                   this
               Empire and to put an end to anarchy.
               I was forced to build my beautiful city of
                   Nicodemia.
               How can the Christian god reproach me!
               Or will he condemn me, the Emperor, for living in
                   luxury?

SEBASTIAN: Oh, sacred one . . .

DIOCLETIAN: Speak!

SEBASTIAN: My lord, your jewelry, your crown . . .
                You wear them without wondering about
                The sufferings they cost the miserable slave
                Who seeks each gem risking his life
                For your embroidered robe,
                How many sleepless nights! And for the rich loot
                You have brought from war, so much blood!
                So much whipping and punishment
                Just to wear on your finger . . . an emerald!

DIOCLETIAN: Enough! Now in everything that surrounds me
                I will see only hard work and fatigue.
                You have courage, Sebastian, to remind me
                That those who serve are never served.
                (*Calling.*) Slave! Have supper with me. (*Pause.*)
                It's an order! No, I beg you.
                (*Pause. He points.*): See . . . he vanished.

SEBASTIAN: For such a sacrilege, he fears to lose his life.

DIOCLETIAN: That's the way it is. So what is the purpose of
                Your speech?
                Do you want Diocletian to sign a decree
                To order the rivers to change their course,
                The lion to become tame, and the lamb, fierce?

SEBASTIAN: No, my Lord. But you can sign a decree that stops
                the persecution of Christians.

DIOCLETIAN: (*Serious.*) Whatever a decree says, no other can
                retract!
                But if you have a friend in the dungeons,
                I will pardon him, if you prove his innocence!

SEBASTIAN: Your jails are full of innocent people!
                I'm speaking, sir, of justice, not mercy.

DIOCLETIAN: Careful, Sebastian: there's arrogance in your voice.
                I delegated this issue to my Caesar Galerius.

| SEBASTIAN: | Galerius is unjust and cruel to Christians. |

| DIOCLETIAN: | And they? Aren't they rebels? Aren't they impious? The teachings of the one they call "Jesus" have endangered the peace of the Empire. Enough of that! (*Melancholy.*) Discussing Christians irritates me. Sebastian, do you know I have a daughter who secretly makes the sign of the cross? And Galerius should be feared. |

| SEBASTIAN: | Sir, your word is the law! |

| DIOCLETIAN: | I can't take away the power I've granted him. (*Pause.*) Sebastian, stay away from the Christians, Get closer to me! And give me your love, Because I prefer you over others. Today I make you Captain of my Pretorian Guard! *Silence.* |

| SEBASTIAN: | Sir, I'd serve you better as a legionnaire. |

| DIOCLETIAN: | I want you here, in my palace, always beside me. With your words you wanted to take care of my soul: take care, then, of the body my soul inhabits. |

| SEBASTIAN: | But I, sir . . . |

| DIOCLETIAN: | No! I do not accept your rejection: Come. Bend your knee. (*Sebastian hesitates.*) Do as I say! (*Sebastian obeys, and Diocletian touches his shoulder.*) More than captain of my Guard I shall name you, Sebastian . . . my most faithful friend! |

The light dims with the figures remaining motionless for a moment as in the beginning of this episode, as if they were returning to the stillness of statues. Music to end the scene.

SCENE II

Lights gradually transform the shadowy workshop area, where the actors have left the basket, into an intimate place. Alejandro, taking off his wig and robe, walks in that direction. Marta and Magdalena, the latter still wearing her sunglasses, are already laying out the costumes. When she sees Alejandro approaching, Magdalena exits; she moves in silence. Marta is leafing through a book.

ALEJANDRO: (*To Marta, alluding to Magdalena.*) She's still not talking? (*Marta nods.*) What do you have there? (*Marta hands him the book.*) Roman History . . .

MARTA: I marked something for you on Diocletian. (*She sits down to sew her tunic.*)

ALEJANDRO: (*Reading.*) "He establishes an ironclad military bureaucracy, he undertakes reforms to alleviate the economic crisis . . . (*He skips something.*) In a Junta made up of four, two Augustus and two Caesars, who were to succeed the previous rulers, Diocletian maintains absolute power. (*Pause.*) He rules without limits or restrictions." (*Marta is engrossed in her sewing.*) Marta, did you hear that?

MARTA: Yes, Alejandro. Is it true that Diocletian had a Christian daughter?

ALEJANDRO: It's a historical fact.

MARTA: That's probably why Sebastian hoped to convert him to Christianity.

ALEJANDRO: But Caesar Galerius kept him from doing so. (*He reads.*) According to Gringberg: "The measure adopted by Galerius is an insensitive measure, a methodically calculated decision to exterminate the Christians. Because they had come to form a power within the State." (*Addressing Marta.*) Marta, you are not listening.

MARTA: Yes, Alejandro.

ALEJANDRO: I love you. (*She stares at him fixedly.*) I remind you of Federico, don't I?

MARTA: You look very much like your brother.

ALEJANDRO: (*Upset.*) But I'm not. (*He arranges the costumes for the next scene in which he will be Proconsul, while saying:*) Marta, you look without seeing, you hear without listening, as if you weren't entirely alive.

MARTA: Then we're the same: we both love a being who barely exists.

ALEJANDRO: My brother barely exists? Federico exists much more than I.

MARTA: He used to say, "He who gives his life for an ideal only absents himself."

ALEJANDRO: He didn't even leave. You have the gift of reviving the past as if you were recovering it for the present. All of a sudden, something brings back memories, and you take off . . . with him, I suppose. Your companion was an exceptional human being, but he's no longer with us. (*She looks at him.*) Well, I mean, even though he appears on these lists of "disappeared men," we know he's not going to return. (*She remains silent.*) You know, don't you? (*She agrees.*) Then, it is time to think . . . about getting on with your life. I wish you would, because . . . (*He stops talking.*)

MARTA: Because . . .

ALEJANDRO: Because I love you.

MARTA: Yes. You already told me so. (*She smiles at him.*) I'm sorry, Alejandro.

ALEJANDRO: "I'm sorry, Alejandro . . ." (*He picks up the book again, annoyed. He reads.*) "In the year 313, Caesar Galerius is struck by a terrible pain. Fearing that he is being punished by the god of the Christians, he makes peace with them. They are seen, then, coming out of prisons and catacombs, like an army of ghosts. They gather strength and sing their hymns . . . they seem encircled with light . . ." (*He sets the book down.*) (*Dreamy.*) Our Sebastian didn't get to see his hope fulfilled.

MARTA: Neither did Federico. (*Pause.*) It's not fair. His faith was so beautiful.

ALEJANDRO: Don't be sad. (*He touches her hand, then they turn their attention to the costumes.*) Marta, what made you join us?

MARTA: My reasons . . . are very simple.

ALEJANDRO: What are they?

MARTA: I can't stand to see children begging.

ALEJANDRO: Okay. The truth is that we're always shuffling concepts, tied up in catchwords and slogans . . . and we often forget the most essential things. Children begging? Why not? Injustice has many names. Did you know that in the Caribbean there are twelve-year-old boys who take up rifles? Those of their fathers fallen in action. I guess it's their right to go on living. (*Pause.*) "No more children begging, no more children with rifles."

MARTA: "No more torture."

ALEJANDRO: When we were in prison, Federico told me: "What distresses one more than the physical pain, is . . . the cruelty of one's torturers."

MARTA: How long is it going to last, Alejandro? Death, persecution . . .

ALEJANDRO: Who knows? (*Cheering her up.*) Marta, we don't know anything about the future. It could be the bomb: an explosion, and it's all over! But, it could also be . . . the opposite!

MARTA: And what's the opposite?

ALEJANDRO: Well, men have always believed in great values,
                    haven't they?

MARTA: (*Adjusting her stuffed pony.*) Yes, I suppose so.

ALEJANDRO: Then it's not impossible that one day they'll
                    decide . . . to put them to practice! Or we could
                    count on a "hope of galaxies," as Federico used to
                    say. Travellers from other worlds will come to
                    restore our sanity. Let's dream on, Marta. Who's to
                    say that our children won't start training, won't
                    run morning races in the parks, exercise daily to
                    become the best? In a great championship! A world
                    championship to end injustice! (*He looks at Marta
                    very tenderly.*) No, this time you don't go out with
                    the pony: you will play the centurion Torquatus.
                    (*He helps her take off the pony and hands her the chains
                    in the basket. While she puts them on, he tells her:*)
                    Marta, I would marry you, even though I realize
                    you can only love Federico . . . (*Marta turns around
                    starting a gesture of protest, Alejandro adds, smiling
                    slyly.*) To take care of you, see what I mean?

*They both go over to the altarpiece wearing their masks. The light dims
till it is dark, while the Gavotte begins.*

A brilliant spotlight on the altarpiece:

Episode 2 of the Altarpiece

*Marta and Alejandro are on the platform. Alejandro, as Proconsul, is
dressed in white and wearing a mask; Marta, as Torquatus, is dressed
in a short tunic and also wearing a mask. She is chained as if she were
hanging in a torture chamber. On one side there is a curtain or a poster
depicting torture instruments. The Proconsul has a parchment. When
the light comes back on Juliana, carrying the banner, and the one-man
orchestra enter. They perform a brief dance and then Juliana recites:*

JULIANA: By decree, Diocletian,
                    In a horrible and frightful trial,
                    Had Torquatus, saintly man,

Tortured by the Romans.
Using refined means of torture,
They bled the heart
And mutilated the body
Of this noble centurion.
They cruelly tortured him
For believing in his religion!

They exit, dancing in circles. The actors in the altarpiece come to life.

PROCONSUL: Being the 8th day of April, before the calends, in this honorable court appears before me, the Roman Proconsul, a centurion accused of committing actions punishable by the law. Identify yourself!

TORQUATUS: Christian.

PROCONSUL: Blasphemous word! Say your name.

TORQUATUS: Christian.

PROCONSUL: Hit him on the mouth so that he won't say one thing instead of another. (*Spotlight on symbol of torture.*)

TORQUATUS: Christian is the name I hold as mine. But, my parents called me Torquatus.

PROCONSUL: I read from these writings that were confiscated from you: (*He reads from a parchment.*) "The princes of the priests meeting in Council said: 'What will we do with this man Jesus? He performs many miracles. If we continue to let him preach his doctrine, the whole nation will believe in him . . .'" (*To Torquatus.*) Don't you know that those who hide such writings are punished by death? The imperial proclamation says: "Secret Christian gatherings and the possession of writings that refer to their impious doctrine are prohibited." Did you know about the proclamation?

TORQUATUS: Yes, I did.

PROCONSUL:	You tore your military insignia and disposed of your arms!
TORQUATUS:	My doctrine says "thou shalt not kill."
PROCONSUL:	Your crime is high treason. Jesus was a rebel who pretended to turn the Jews against the Roman. Your duty was to surrender these writings to be burned.
TORQUATUS:	Burn me first!
PROCONSUL:	Torture him! (*Loud sounds. Spotlight on symbol of torture.*) Enough. To whom did you read these writings?
TORQUATUS:	To my brothers in the Christian faith.
PROCONSUL:	Turn in your brothers and you can go free.
TORQUATUS:	I'm not an informer.
PROCONSUL:	Put him on the racks, until he tells us all their names! (*Spotlight on the symbol of torture.*) Enough! Torquatus, I officially order you to offer sacrifices in front of Jupiter's altar as do the emperors, to whom you owe honor and obedience.
TORQUATUS:	The emperors are wrong.
PROCONSUL:	Burn his feet and hands for blasphemy!
TORQUATUS:	Why do you torture me so? I'm only praising the true God!
PROCONSUL:	Pour salt on his wounds for saying "god" and not "gods!" Torquatus, even knowing that they will continue to torment you, do you still uphold what you said?
TORQUATUS:	I do.
PROCONSUL:	You fool, you crazy Christian, do you happen to love death?

TORQUATUS: I love life, but I don't fear death.

PROCONSUL: (*He yells toward the executioner.*) Scrape his ribs with
              sharp shells, hang him from his feet and put him
              over the fire, let his body burn, but don't let him
              die . . . ! (*The symbol of torture is still under the
              spotlight.*) I'll force you to waste away slowly before
              I have you beheaded! And don't expect
              posthumous glory, because I will not allow those
              whores to cover you with balsams and ointments
              to give you an honorable burial. I'll see to it that
              your remains be discarded where they cannot be
              found, as well as with those of all the damned
              Christians. Take him back to the dungeon!

Darkness. Music to end the scene.

SCENE III

*Light on the foreground section which represents a corner of the town
square. Woman 1 is there and Woman 2 approaches her.*

WOMAN 1:   (*She sits on the bundle she is carrying, and addresses
              Woman 2 who is sitting on the floor with her basket of
              goods.*) I was taking food and clothing to the
              prisoners at the jail of Concepción, but I came back
              with everything!

WOMAN 2:   Why?

WOMAN 1:   Guard González chased me away, "for talking such
              nonsense," he said.

WOMAN 2:   You don't say. And what did you tell him?

WOMAN 1:   I asked him how he could work in a place like that,
              a place where they torture innocent young people.
              And he said: "They're not innocent. And even
              though the job is ugly, someone's got to do it."

WOMAN 2:   And what did you answer?

WOMAN 1:   "If the job is so ugly, look for another one." And he answered, "With so many people out of work? Besides, since I wear a uniform, my children will never lack anything." So I asked him, "And if they take one of your boys and they starve him to death, what will you do?"

WOMAN 2:   And what did he say?

WOMAN 1:   "I'll kill them," he said. Using these very words: "even if they shoot me afterwards." "You see," I said, "that's the difference! You worry only about your own children. While the men they have arrested worry about all the children, everybody's children." "You really think so?" he said, as if making fun of me. And I replied: "Don't you know that those young people are fighting so that every child can eat and go to school? And shoes. Shoes are important to children!" That's what I told him.

WOMAN 2:   What did he say, then?

WOMAN 1:   He said, "All you talk about is children." This is a war between grown-ups. Children have nothing to do with it."

WOMAN 2:   My goodness! Listen to that!

WOMAN 1:   "Children *are* involved," I said, "since all of them start life hungry and barefoot, sleeping in doorways and sniffing glue. (*Looking up.*) There's the bus . . . (*She gets up.*) Let's see if this time the guard will let me in. (*She exits followed by Woman 2.*)

Darkness.

SCENE IV

Light on the altarpiece. Torquatus is under an arch. He is imprisoned and chained; at one end, hanging above is the cloth angel. Juliana, with the banner, and Chinchinero enter and perform a brief dance.

JULIANA: Sebastian, pious soul
                      Suffered when he saw so many
                      Of his brothers being tortured
                      In the darkness of the dungeons . . .

Alejandro enters and stops her with a gesture.

ALEJANDRO: —Wait, Eduardo's missing.

Juliana exits and runs into Eduardo who is dressed as Sebastian. He is holding his helmet and a script in his hand. Marta descends from the platform.

EDUARDO: (*Very upset, he reads from the script.*) "Turn in your brothers and you will be free." Marta, Alejandro, I never told on Federico! Even though they asked me about him all the time! I gave only some false addresses. (*He flops depressed on the edge of the platform.*) And then . . . a real one, according to what we agreed on.

MARTA: Eduardo, what are you talking about? (*She approaches him, affectionately.*)

EDUARDO: About torture. You can tolerate the electric spur, the blows, the mock executions, but not suffocation, no! (*Aggressive.*) Alejandro, when you wrote the play, you forgot "suffocation" in the torture scene!

ALEJANDRO: (*He calms him with a gesture.*) Calm down, Eduardo.

MARTA: No one has ever said that you turned him in!

EDUARDO: I shouldn't be here playing the role of a hero . . . Federico would have done it with more conviction; he never opened his mouth!

ALEJANDRO: Listen . . .

EDUARDO: And don't tell me that I'm not to blame!

MARTA: But, blame for what?

EDUARDO: (*Excited, pointing at the script.*) And here is another speech by Sebastian, about those who deny their faith. (*He reads.*) "they curse their weakness and are never able to find peace . . ." (*To Alejandro.*) Did you have me in mind, Alejandro?

ALEJANDRO: Eduardo, that was written in the third century.

Alejandro and Marta watch Eduardo, who seems confused. Silence.

EDUARDO: (*He hesitates, then livens up.*) Okay. Don't worry. Let's continue with the rehearsal. (*He becomes quiet.*) And on with my role . . . as a fantastic guy.

He approaches the platform, but Marta stops him.

MARTA: No. Eduardo, all the time you were in exile you kept tormenting yourself for no reason. The agreement was to wait two days before talking.

EDUARDO: (*Cutting her off.*) I didn't wait that long!

MARTA: Well, you waited as long as you could. It's the same thing.

EDUARDO: How can it be the same thing!

MARTA: We said it was impossible to judge what one can or cannot endure when being tortured. No one has the right to judge anybody's behavior.

EDUARDO: Except for the one who was tortured. He certainly has the right.

ALEJANDRO: Enough, Eduardo, you had nothing to do with what happened to my brother. He was caught because someone denounced him. (*Eduardo looks at him doubtfully.*) (*To Marta.*) Eduardo refuses to believe it. He wants proof, but there is no proof.

EDUARDO: Then, whose fault was it?

MARTA: (*She stands between the two of them.*) I know!

EDUARDO: (*Pointing at Marta.*) She says that only to bring peace back to me.

ALEJANDRO: (*To Marta.*) What do you mean by "you know whose fault it was?"

MARTA: There you are, blaming and excusing yourselves! Don't you remember that the only ones to be blamed are "the others?" Those who torture and kill! "Guilty are those who persecute as if the worst crime was man's hope to live in justice and with dignity." (*Pointing to the script.*) Isn't that what you wrote here, Alejandro? (*To Eduardo.*) These are the words of the tribune.

Eduardo, changing his attitude, hugs Marta and approaches Alejandro affectionately. They remain silent for a few moments.

EDUARDO: (*To Marta.*) Come on, "Torquatus," put on your chains. (*He helps her. Alejandro exits.*) Where's Juliana? (*Juliana peeks in, this time with the rag pony tied around her waist and with the banner.*) The scene at the prison begins again. (*He speaks while he and Marta take their positions on the platform.*)

Darkness.

Brief music of the Gavotte.

Episode 3 of the Altarpiece

Juliana and Chinchinero dance briefly. The music stops.

JULIANA: Sebastian, pious soul,
Suffered when he saw so many
Of his tortured brothers
In the dark dungeons.
Secretly and cautiously
Outwitting the guards
He visited the prisoners
To soothe their pain:
He gave them consolation and prayer,
True and saintly love!

They exit. In the altarpiece, the imprisoned Torquatus and Sebastian come to life.

TORQUATUS: A captain from the Emperor's Guard! What do you want?

SEBASTIAN: To comfort you, brother.

TORQUATUS: Brother?

SEBASTIAN: I only wear the soldier's uniform to help the Christians. You were courageous, Centurion.

TORQUATUS: There's light in your face!

SEBASTIAN: It's your soul that brightens this dark place!

TORQUATUS: Oh, what will become of me!

SEBASTIAN: Tomorrow the Proconsul will interrogate you again.

TORQUATUS: I won't be able to endure it! What's your name?

SEBASTIAN: Sebastian.

TORQUATUS: Sebastian, brother in arms, since you're carrying a sword, kill me!

SEBASTIAN: I came to give you life, not to take it away.

TORQUATUS: You will lose yours if they catch you in the dungeon.

SEBASTIAN: Say the Scriptures with me: "May your heart not worry or be frightened, as I will not abandon you . . ."

TORQUATUS: "Because there is no finer way of showing love than by risking your life for your brothers." I no longer feel the weight of my chains! Your strength fortifies me.

SEBASTIAN:	Repeat with me: "If they have persecuted me, they will persecute you."
TORQUATUS:	"They will persecute you . . ."
SEBASTIAN:	"But if they have minded my word, they will also mind yours."

Brief music, a light shines in front of the platform, Sebastian exits.

SCENE V

Marta, taking off her mask and chains, sits on her heels, at the front of the stage. Spotlight on her.

MARTA: (*Solemnly, taking a folded letter from her bosom.*) "If they have kept my word, they will also keep yours . . ." Your words, Federico. (*She opens the letter and reads.*) "Marta, my love, don't be sad. Don't remember me wrapped in blood and pain. There can be much light behind the walls of a dungeon! Even though you are living with death, you learn to love life." (*She puts down the letter and whispers*): After midnight I think of you, Federico. But it's not only that, "thinking." I pick up the threads of your memory . . . and then you're there, your presence once again envelops me. As if you had never died. Perhaps because it is an illusion, the bond between us is so strong! (*Pause. She continues reading the letter.*) "Even though you are living with death, you learn to love life. One's words pass on from mouth to mouth, from cell to cell, and escape out of the prison through long and secret roads until they reach our people. Nothing is lost. Neither the great gestures, nor the small sacrifices. And now let me tell you that I passed the test. I'm talking about that dark tunnel . . . Marta, I succeeded, I survived. If you can call this meager existence living. And what I now dictate will reach you . . . some day." (*She raises her head and talks to Federico's ghost.*) No, you haven't died. I imagine you walking through a foreign, unreachable country. Or perhaps you're so close that I could touch you with my hands. (*She remains quiet, Alejandro enters from behind, she knows he is there without turning around. She resumes the reading of the letter.*) "I crossed the last threshold and my lips didn't open. You know why? Because the only word I wanted to say, that I would have wanted to shout at them, was not in my memory!"

She breaks down, she remains shrivelled up on her knees. Alejandro, who is behind her, leans over to pick up the letter.

ALEJANDRO: (*Reading.*) "Because when they stick knives deep into your body, when you're nothing more than wounds and torn flesh, then, you look desperately for a word . . . a single word that contains your struggle . . . that gives you the strength to resist. It must be a simple but yet violent word: stronger than hatred, as quick as lightning which illuminates without hurting, straight as the blade of a sword, capable of ending all the cruelty of the world. It exists . . . right? Look it up for me, will you? I suppose the word is written in the galaxies, from where other beings must be looking at us with infinite compassion." (*He gives the letter to Marta.*)

MARTA: (*Getting up.*) He was always talking about the galaxies.

ALEJANDRO: (*Smiles at her.*) That's probably where he is, don't you think?

MARTA: Then, he must have already found the word.

ALEJANDRO: Do you know it?

MARTA: No.

ALEJANDRO: (*Pause, while he puts on the wig and robe.*) Yes. You do. (*With tenderness, moving closer.*) The word is "Love."

MARTA:　　　　　　　How do you know?

ALEJANDRO:　　　　Because love was the only feeling those men who
　　　　　　　　　were torturing him didn't have! (*They remain still
　　　　　　　　　for an instant, looking at each other as the light dims
　　　　　　　　　and finally goes out.*)

The Gavotte begins.

Episode 4 of the Altarpiece

*When the light comes back on, Juliana enters with the pony, spinning
and dancing, followed by the Chinchinero. When they end the brief
dance and the music stops, Juliana recites:*

JULIANA:　　　　　Without restraint,
　　　　　　　　　In the times of Diocletian,
　　　　　　　　　Those who stood by their Christian faith
　　　　　　　　　Were persecuted by the Roman Caesar.
　　　　　　　　　A Roman Tribune,
　　　　　　　　　Willing to defend the Christians,
　　　　　　　　　Demanded mercy for them.
　　　　　　　　　The Tribune lost his life
　　　　　　　　　For pleading against their death!

*Juliana exits. At the altarpiece, the following come to life: in the center,
Diocletian; on one side, Actor—wearing a mask—plays Galerius; on
the other side, Eduardo—also wearing a mask and different clothes than
when he plays Sebastian—plays the Tribune.*

DIOCLETIAN:　　　You two have come: one to accuse and the other to
　　　　　　　　　defend the Christians. Galerius, you are higher in
　　　　　　　　　rank, speak first.

GALERIUS:　　　　Sir, the actions of this sect are such that they're
　　　　　　　　　encouraging anarchy! They preach that all men are
　　　　　　　　　equal, that wealth is a vice and poverty a virtue;
　　　　　　　　　they condemn slavery as unjust. In sum, we are
　　　　　　　　　dealing with an internal enemy, hidden and tame,
　　　　　　　　　but more dangerous than the Barbarians you fight
　　　　　　　　　at the borders. They invade Gaul, Carthage, the
　　　　　　　　　Orient. In Rome they have undermined the ground
　　　　　　　　　you step on; like moles they excavate their

catacombs! You should aim at the very heart of their sect or soon a Christian will rule the Empire! You can find them among the nobles and patricians and, according to gossip, even in your own palace . . .

DIOCLETIAN: Galerius, speak wisely and slowly! Don't make a mistake if you're accusing someone.

GALERIUS: May the gods keep me from being an informer. But, if there's someone who abuses your trust, watch out for him, my lord . . .
Silence.

DIOCLETIAN: Speak, Tribune.

TRIBUNE: I want to remind you, oh sacred one, that in the times of Nero, the Roman people used to clamor, "Christians to the beasts." Back then, Christians were killed without trial or sanction only to amuse the people with their blood. And why were they persecuted and condemned? Only because they refused to worship some gods in which no one believed any more, gods who fought, devoured, and killed each other for the beauty of a queen. (*Pause.*) Lord, the "moral strength" of the Christians is not harmful to the Roman people, but rather a benefit to them!

GALERIUS: (*Mockingly.*) What is it that you call "moral strength," Tribune?

TRIBUNE: Remember that in the past, in the circus arena, when the wild beasts saw the Christians they stood still, without harming them.

GALERIUS: (*Accusing him.*) You admire these people!

TRIBUNE: Must I die for that?

GALERIUS: Not without being judged first: one does not condemn a Christian without a trial.

TRIBUNE: I protest! They're not properly interrogated, nor are
                        they judged in court. The law of Rome is not
                        applied to them as it is to criminals.

GALERIUS: Because a thief, or even a murderer, compared to a
                        Christian, is shown more mercy! They attempted to
                        burn the imperial palace and desecrate the temple
                        of Juno!

TRIBUNE: That's a lie! The guilty one is he who sends his
                        slaves in the darkness to carry out such misdeeds,
                        merely to rouse the people against the Christians!

DIOCLETIAN: Can you prove it, Tribune?

TRIBUNE: No my lord. Can anyone testify against the actions
                        of those who are so highly placed? And if they
                        can—I mean, with your permission—there is
                        always somebody higher to cover their actions!

GALERIUS: He is insulting us, Diocletian!

*Diocletian looks at both of them, hesitant, wishing to protect the
Tribune.*

TRIBUNE: Neither lies nor false accusations justify the
                        violence of the punishment. Would they be able to
                        resist the power of your legions? When the
                        Emperor Adrian ruled ten thousand innocent
                        people were massacred. Their only crime was their
                        doctrine! Then, to say "Christians," is to say
                        "criminals?" And now, before you, I accuse
                        Galerius of having had the temple of Juno burned
                        in order to blame the followers of Christ!

DIOCLETIAN: (*Authoritarian, curt.*) Answer, Galerius.

GALERIUS: Even if it were so, disobedience of your
                        proclamations is enough reason to be condemned.
                        Thus, you should give stricter sentences and judge
                        the Tribune for what he has said here!

DIOCLETIAN: That's what Galerius requests. What do you request, Tribune? Be brief.

TRIBUNE: To be brief, lord, no more deaths, no more persecution, no more torture! You are persecuting innocence, justice, and dignity. And now, allow me once again to plead for mercy before I leave! (*After saying it, he makes a motion to exit.*)

GALERIUS: Don't let him go! He has given himself away: he is a Christian! Guards, after him! (*Shouting.*) Arrest him before he escapes!

He moves back to go after the Tribune, Diocletian stops him.

DIOCLETIAN: Wait: whom shall I watch out for in my palace?

GALERIUS: (*Defiant.*) He who looks after you!

Brief music. Darkness.

INTERMISSION

Part Two

SCENE VI

When the light comes on after the intermission, all the actors are on stage arranging the altarpiece for the next episodes. Chinchinero, Alejandro, and Eduardo work on the altarpiece. Juliana is holding her basket to sell flowers and candles; Magdalena, still wearing her sunglasses, is busy in a corner with a costume. In the center foreground, separate from the other groups, the four mothers work on an arpillera. *The Actor is playing the hurdy-gurdy. Marta is fastening her rag pony, close to Magdalena.*

CHINCHINERO: (*To Alejandro.*) Did you know that the statue of the saint worshipped here was almost burned? They wanted to desecrate it. That happened a hundred years ago.

ALEJANDRO: How did it happen?

CHINCHINERO: They say that some "perverse" young men, angry because of so much devotion for the saint, stole the statue from the church and . . . you know the poem, Juliana. Recite it!

JULIANA: Some mischievous young men
Stole it from the altar.
They desperately searched and searched,
But continuously faltered.
And there, buried in the sand,
A shepherd found it.
Those people tried in vain
To burn it during a spree,
But the ancient wood, hard as stone,
Did not give and the statue was set free!

ALEJANDRO: So tell me, is it true that Saint Sebastian of Yumbel was buried, unburied, and that during the last century was buried again in the sand and unburied once more? It's strange, because in Rome, after his martyrdom, Saint Sebastian was hidden but his followers found his remains and gave them a Christian burial.

JULIANA: The same thing happened to the 19 leaders they arrested in Laja and in San Rosendo. Twice they were buried and unburied.

Hearing this, the four Mothers turn their heads toward them.

CHINCHINERO: Well, yes. First they buried them in the pine forest, where they shot them . . . also during a spree. Don't you know they found empty liquor bottles buried there also?

The Mothers make a motion as if evidencing their shock and they keep working.

It happened in September, just before the National holidays. But a few days later, some dogs started digging, so they had to get the bodies out of the pine woods. At night they threw them over the

cemetery wall and buried them again. (*Pause.*)
Here in Yumbel. (*Leaving with Alejandro and
Juliana.*) And there they remained, for six years. No
markers, no crosses . . .

Light over the Mothers.

MOTHER 1:   Six years. Without markers or crosses.

MOTHER 2:   Six years of wondering.

MOTHER 3:   It was painful to find them in that state, but we
               were able to give them a Christian burial.

MOTHER 2:   That was comforting.

Brief incidental music. Marta and Magdalena listen without moving.

MOTHER 4:   Many people who haven't found their relatives still
               hope to find them alive.

MOTHER 1:   "Alive they took them, alive we want them" is the
               slogan in other countries.

MOTHER 2:   Other countries?

MOTHER 1:   People disappear in Argentina, Uruguay, Bolivia,
               Salvador, Guatemala, Colombia . . . all over Latin
               America.

MOTHER 3:   They say that the Mothers of the Plaza de Mayo, in
               Argentina, write the names of their loved ones on
               posters and march hoping to find them . . .

Brief incidental music.

MOTHER 2:   I ask for justice because for six years we have been
               deceived. They lied to us when they said that no
               one had died here.

MOTHER 4:   I pray to God that the children of those who shot
               them, don't suffer for their parents' sins.

MOTHER 2:   When I realized my husband wasn't returning I
             looked for him at the police station. There I found
             out he was one of the leaders and had been
             fighting for the labor union.

MOTHER 3:   I also went to the police station, but by the second
             day he was no longer there. They had transferred
             him, they said, to the Army barracks in Temuco. I
             went there. They denied he had been detained:
             "See, ma'am, his name is not on the list of
             prisoners." "Look closer, he has to be here," I said.
             "Please ma'am, get out of here," an angry man told
             me. In any case, they bullied me, so I had to leave.

MOTHER 2:   I also went to Temuco. And from there I went to
             Concepción . . . to Talcahuano, I went everywhere.

MOTHER 4:   I presented all the legal documents, I did
             everything they advised me to do. Six years
             looking for him!

MOTHER 2:   Six years without knowing anything about them!

Music. They keep working in silence.

MOTHER 2:   I knew inside of me that he was dead because I saw
             him in my dreams. "Why are you looking for me so
             far away when I'm here?" he would say. (*Pause.*)
             When they buried him I dreamed about him again.
             He would put his hand kindly on my face and say:
             Take care of my children!" I woke up crying. And I
             shouted to him: Here are all your children . . ."

MOTHER 3:   I didn't have any trouble recognizing him: Look
             carefully," the doctor told me. Once I saw his
             dentures I knew he was my husband!

MOTHER 2:   I went to the court for the proceedings. It was
             awful! The same ones who arrested them, before
             our very eyes, denied everything. Just like that,
             everything!

MOTHER 3:   In any case, the guards weren't upset; they knew
                     beforehand that they would be granted amnesty.

MOTHER 2:   But it was a consolation to finally hear the truth,
                     there, publicly, in the Court of Justice.

Brief transitional music. The four mothers exit with the arpillera. *The
Actor enters to place the golden angel for the next scene. He signals
Magdalena, who is about to exit.*

ACTOR: Magdalena, can you help me with this? (*He points
                     to the angel.*)

MAGDALENA: Yes, of course.

ACTOR: Do you have to wear these sunglasses?

Silence. She looks at him hesitantly.

MAGDALENA: Over there, they covered our heads with a hood,
                     we were always blindfolded. (*Pause.*) In the prison
                     camp.

Marta has entered.

ACTOR: Do you often think of those days?

MAGDALENA: I feel like I'm still in that darkness.

MARTA: The women of the Association told me you had a
                     son.

MAGDALENA: Yes. I left him in Concepción with his
                     grandparents. (*Pause.*) My parents are Chilean.

MARTA: Magdalena, this is the first time you've talked
                     about your imprisonment.

ACTOR: (*Coming closer.*) It would do you good to talk, don't
                     you think so?

MAGDALENA: To talk . . . (*She stops and becomes pensive.*)

ACTOR: About the military coup in Argentina.

MAGDALENA: (*As if it didn't concern her, in almost an impersonal voice.*) March 1976. We noticed a very obvious change in values. A total change. You always heard the same words on the radio and television: "The nation's security, the nation's order. We are here to save this country from chaos and foreign doctrines. The security of the Argentinean citizens . . ." Repeated until you were fed up. (*Pause.*) I thought nothing would happen to us, there was a feeling of reassurance in the media . . . (*She looks at them.*) And you want to believe everything they say. Even though you're seeing the crimes, the impunity . . . (*She stops talking when Juliana enters with the banner.*)

JULIANA: We're going to start. (*To Marta.*) Fifth episode.

Magdalena exits, Actor finishes fastening the angel to the altarpiece. Chinchinero enters. The light fades to a semi-penumbra, and this time we see how Diocletian and Sebastian position themselves on the platform.

Episode 5 of the Altarpiece

Bright, intense light on the altarpiece. Sebastian wearing a tunic, chained; Diocletian without the symbols of his rank. Juliana and Chinchinero enter dancing the Gavotte. Then Juliana recites:

JULIANA: Sebastian, accused of treason,
Is, in chains,
Taken to prison
And sentenced to death.
Diocletian visits him
And begs him with fervor
To renounce his beliefs
In exchange for freedom:
"If they kill you, Sebastian,
I will be the one who grieves!

Juliana and Chinchinero exit.

DIOCLETIAN: The captain of my guard
Has been accused of treason!

SEBASTIAN: Being a Christian, isn't it
                The worst of all crimes?

DIOCLETIAN: You visited the dungeons
                And encouraged your brothers
                To deny our gods!

SEBASTIAN: Haven't you come to this dungeon
                To ask me to renounce my God?

DIOCLETIAN: Filled with sorrow,
                I approach you like a thief in the dark . . .

SEBASTIAN: You ordered my chains.
                What does the emperor want?

DIOCLETIAN: To hear from your lips the truth!

SEBASTIAN: What you heard is the truth.

DIOCLETIAN: You were my favorite one,
                I treated you like a son . . .

SEBASTIAN: You knew I was a Christian
                With duties to fulfill.

DIOCLETIAN: The Captain of my Guard
                Should only serve his Emperor!

SEBASTIAN: I don't serve anyone who sends
                My brothers to death.

DIOCLETIAN: I bestowed upon you my favors
                And the greatest was my friendship!

SEBASTIAN: And for that I am indebted to you.

DIOCLETIAN: (*Begging*) You wouldn't offend your God
                Pretending to sacrifice
                To our Roman gods . . .
                I beseech you, Sebastian!
                Do it for me!
                Many who have done so
                Have won their freedom.

SEBASTIAN: For that they curse their weakness
               And they never find peace.
               Stop persecuting them!

DIOCLETIAN: Sebastian, your persistence is useless:
               Galerius will rise up in arms.

SEBASTIAN: Aren't you the August and the "Master"?
               Does Caesar have more power than you?
               Peace is what your people want.
               You don't give them life
               By planting death on the fields!
               Not in hatred, but in love
               Will you find true peace.
               In your laws you must decree:
               "Yes" to life, "No" to death!

DIOCLETIAN: (*Angry.*) Our law is our law!
               I don't know of a better one!
               Rome owes its grandeur
               To the courage of its legions,
               Not to peace, but to war,
               And to its code of honor!

SEBASTIAN: There's a man who didn't need a sword
               For the crowds
               To hail him as their lord.
               He came to show the way
               To our salvation.

DIOCLETIAN: If you're referring to your Master
               —the one they call Jesus Christ—
               No one could save him
               From his crucifixion!

SEBASTIAN: His word is still alive,
               His word gives us light.
               His followers preach
               Virtue, hope, and justice.

DIOCLETIAN: (*Overwhelmed.*) What should I do with you?

SEBASTIAN:	(*Ironic.*) Make me die on the cross, And thus save the Empire!
DIOCLETIAN:	Oh, you stubborn man, you're making fun of me!
SEBASTIAN:	Didn't you send your archers To take away my life?
DIOCLETIAN:	If I order them to wound you with arrows I will feel your pain, Sebastian. Besides, I have no reason To order your death!
SEBASTIAN:	Because of my beliefs I know They will take my life away. Whereas you, my executioner, you don't know Why you're sending me to death![5]
DIOCLETIAN:	(*Hurt.*) For calling me your executioner, Consider yourself lost!
SEBASTIAN:	What is lost on earth Is gained in Heaven. My God looks after me. He who speaks through my mouth Has greater power than you.
DIOCLETIAN:	You have signed your sentence! And I challenge that powerful God, To save you from martyrdom and death! Come take him away, archers! My guards, come! Give death to your Captain!

Darkness.

SCENE VII

Brief transitional music as the light comes back on. Magdalena, wearing her sunglasses, is sitting on a bench. She will give her testimony using an impersonal voice.[6]

MAGDALENA: "They arrested me in Buenos Aires, in April 1977. I was two months pregnant. On the same day, they arrested my husband, in the street. They took me out of my house violently and threw me on the floor of a car. Once we got to the prison camp, they pulled me out of the car, screaming at me and beating me. Blindfolded, they forced me to run in all directions, making me crash against the walls and trip over the prisoners lying on the floor. For five days they kept me tied to my husband; every single day they tortured him with an electric prod . . . and I can't even remember now how many times I was abused . . . raped."

Brief transitional music.

The light on the altarpiece shows Juliana reciting the martyrdom of the saint—alternating with Magdalena's testimony—and two mothers hanging the arpillera *which illustrates the martyrdom of Saint Sebastian as depicted in the poem: "To a Tree He Is Tied."*

JULIANA: Moved and with grief,
Diocletian orders:
"Tie this man to a tree,
He, who was once my guard of honor."

Music.

MAGDALENA: "A year later they transferred my husband. Being 'transferred' was synonymous with dying: it meant to be led to a lime pit and receive a burst of gunshots that would make you fall inside. They 'transferred' him along with sixteen other prisoners who are still on the list of the disappeared."

Music. A curtain falls: an embroidered arpillera *which represents the archers.*

JULIANA: And the Emperor orders
The seven fiercest archers
To take Sebastian's life
Without showing any mercy.

Music.

MAGDALENA: "Shortly after my release, my son was born. Soon I
                 will have to explain to him that his father was
                 kidnapped in his own country, his own native
                 land. His only crime was to fight for justice, for a
                 better way of life."

Music.

JULIANA: Instead of seven wounds
                 Seven stars
                 Shined on him!

*In the central arch, lights in the shape of stars appear on Saint
Sebastian's image.*

Music.

MAGDALENA: "When you enter a secret jail you find yourself
                 suddenly stripped of all your defenses. It means to
                 be flung to the bottom of an abyss. But suffering
                 the agony of waiting for death day after day is not
                 so hard if we are sure of our hopes and ideals!"

*The Mothers approach Magdalena, who has taken off her sunglasses.
They give her a veil like the ones they are wearing and exit with her.*

Episode 6 of the Altarpiece

*This time the last Roman Episode begins without transition. The
characters, Diocletian and Sebastian are already on stage at the
altarpiece where the* arpilleras *are hung. Diocletian is wearing his
purple robe and his crown and Sebastian is covered with a cape with a
hood, similar to a monk's habit. The scene takes place on the palace
stairway. Sebastian will be seated at the edge of the platform and
Diocletian enters and goes up to the altarpiece. Magdalena's exit is
simultaneous with the action. Juliana has remained on the altarpiece
and descends to recite.*

JULIANA: And lying in that orchard,
                 They left him, by seven arrows,
                 Badly wounded.

Taking him for dead
The seven archers left.
Two saintly Christian women
Healed his wounds and
Sebastian came back to life!
What he had promised, he didn't forget:
To plead for his Christian brothers.

Juliana exits.

DIOCLETIAN: *(When Sebastian raises his hood.)* Sebastian . . . I ordered your death!

SEBASTIAN: And you challenged my God to preserve my life.

DIOCLETIAN: What witchcraft did you perform? With your preaching you turned my archers into cowards! They will pay for their disobedience.

SEBASTIAN: They carried out your orders. Look at my scars. *(He opens his cape.)*

DIOCLETIAN: My stars! Who was able to heal incurable wounds?

SEBASTIAN: Two saintly women who found me in the orchard. Don't blame your archers, they thought I was dead.

DIOCLETIAN: If he has enough power to save you from death, why doesn't he turn me into a despicable slave, or into a pious Christian, and thus spare you so much effort?

SEBASTIAN: You'll see the light only if you want to see it; man has free will.

DIOCLETIAN: But you don't; you came to me "sent" . . . by your God.

SEBASTIAN: I am his servant, but I freely chose whom I wanted to serve. Faith in his beliefs doesn't enslave man. You too, Diocletian, are free to order that Christians die, or live!

DIOCLETIAN:	(*He turns his back.*) Enough! I don't want to hear any more. (*Pause.*) Why do you continue to torment me? Why did you come to the palace?
SEBASTIAN:	To plead for my brothers! And to save you, Diocletian.
DIOCLETIAN:	Why?
SEBASTIAN:	Because I love you, sir.
DIOCLETIAN:	(*Hurt.*) And I, because of the love I gave you, and the love you gave me, Sebastian, must I sign your death sentence twice? (*They look at each other in silence.*) Will your God save you once again?
SEBASTIAN:	I won't have another opportunity to talk to you. (*Pause.*) Give your pardon, I beg you, Diocletian. Stop this unjust persecution; otherwise, your tenure will be very difficult.
DIOCLETIAN:	(*Ironically*) Can you predict the future? Can you read the stars like the fortune tellers? (*He smiles.*) What do you see in the days to come?
SEBASTIAN:	(*Serious*) Grief, sorrow. Your Caesar Galerius will betray you.
DIOCLETIAN:	He will be my successor. Why stain himself with my blood?
SEBASTIAN:	He will spill your blood, but it will not flow from your body.
DIOCLETIAN:	From my lineage, then? (*Sebastian nods.*) My daughter! No, I don't believe in your predictions.
SEBASTIAN:	Before dying, you will see everything you built with love and effort collapse.
DIOCLETIAN:	(*Incredulous.*) My beautiful city of Nicodemia?
SEBASTIAN:	The Empire.

DIOCLETIAN: *(He explodes.)* You are lying! All my deeds will remain in the memory of men. They will recognize my merit and sing my glory.

SEBASTIAN: They'll curse your name for persecuting Christians.

DIOCLETIAN: None of them will be left on earth to curse it!

SEBASTIAN: *(As though illuminated, looking in the distance.)* There will be thousands and thousands . . . I can see them coming out of jails, out of the darkness of mines and catacombs, stumbling, thin, pale like a ghostly army. I see them gathering strength, singing their hymns, rebuilding their temples, taking the Gospel to all corners of the Earth . . .

DIOCLETIAN: *(After hearing the sound of a trumpet.)* Flee, Sebastian! Galerius is approaching. Go into the palace and I will arrange for your escape!

SEBASTIAN: If I escape you will say: "He was a coward, he didn't have the strength to stand by his convictions." If I die, perhaps you will remember my words. Perhaps the seed will bear fruit.

DIOCLETIAN: *(He urges him.)* Go, Sebastian! I want to save you!

SEBASTIAN: And who will save those who die because of your decrees?

DIOCLETIAN: *(Hearing the trumpet again.)* Please go! Only you matter, Sebastian. I consider you my son!

SEBASTIAN: You say "only my son matters" and you are not ashamed of it. To those you unjustly persecute, the sons of everyone, all the sons, matter. *(He turns, hiding his face because Galerius has entered.)*

GALERIUS: Hail, Diocletian. Who dares to bother you on the stairs of your palace?

DIOCLETIAN: *(Hiding his fear.)* A fortune teller who reads the future.

GALERIUS: What has he predicted?

DIOCLETIAN: (*He hesitates, then speaks aggressively.*) That my
                    Caesar Galerius will spill the blood of my lineage.

GALERIUS: I see! (*Addressing Sebastian.*) And what lies do you
                    have for me? Speak!

SEBASTIAN: (*He uncovers himself, Galerius looks at him surprised.*)
                    You will fall victim to an illness that will make you
                    curse life for your suffering. Then you will sign the
                    peace with the Christians, hoping that their God
                    will cure you.

GALERIUS: It is you who's going to die cursing life for your
                    suffering, treacherous captain! (*To Diocletian.*) You
                    had ordered his death!

DIOCLETIAN: My archers pierced his body, but the wounds
                    healed!

GALERIUS: Christian and sorcerer . . . (*Shouting*) To the stake!
                    Burn him! No. Your god could save you from the
                    fire . . . you'll be mutilated and beheaded! Let's see
                    if your god can join what I have separated! Your
                    remains will be thrown into the Roman sewer
                    where no one will ever find them to pay you
                    homage as a martyr. Arrest him! I condemn you,
                    Sebastian, to eternal oblivion!

Brief music. Juliana enters with the banner depicting Saint Sebastian's
martyrdom.

Diocletian and Sebastian exit.

SCENE VIII

The four mothers, whom Magdalena joins as Mother 5, wearing black
transparent veils over their faces, act now like a folk chorus, while
Juliana on the platform continues reciting the poem which ends the
story of Saint Sebastian.

JULIANA:	And Galerius, enraged, took out his sword and ordered: "Behead him and throw him in a filthy sewer!"
MOTHER 1:	How strange! It seems to happen over and over again!
MOTHER 3:	Always the same.
MOTHER 5:	How can men do that to other men? Always the same thing.
MOTHER 2:	The flesh adhered to their clothes
MOTHER 4:	Their bones tied with wires.
MOTHER 1:	In a deep oven full of lime
MOTHER 2:	In the secret land
MOTHER 5:	In the scoria, where those who had a name, lost it.
MOTHER 3:	In a well.
MOTHER 1:	Going back centuries you'll find men torturing Christians and hiding their remains
CHORUS:	How strange! It seems to happen over and over again!
JULIANA:	(*With the banner.*) They condemned Sebastian And the order was fulfilled: Surrounded by light, Bleeding from his thousand wounds, With the sign of the cross Sebastian gave up life!
MOTHER 2:	It's hard for a mother to lose a son.
MOTHER 1:	It's even harder to find him and then learn how he lost his life.

MOTHER 3:   Better not to have found him!

MOTHER 1:   (*She moves forward a little, becoming more
                    conspicuous.*) No! Nothing is better now!
                    Everything is worse: to know or not about a
                    missing son, to find him dead, and to see what
                    they've done to him!

*Mother 1 bends forward in grief, the others speak as if reciting a
scripture.*

MOTHERS 2, 3, 4,
and 5:   He had his feet . . . his hands . . . his throat, his feet,
                    his hands, his throat, his organs, his feet, his
                    hands . . . mutilated, mutilated, mutilated . . .

MOTHER 1:   Beheaded!

Silence.

JULIANA: They took his sacred remains
                    To a hidden drain pipe,
                    Assuming that, buried there,
                    He would be left in oblivion.

MOTHER 4:   We cannot forget!

CHORUS: We must not forget!

MOTHER 4:   These horrible events, with the passing of time,
                    may seem less horrible to us.

MOTHER 2:   We could get used to taking in our hands a
                    jawbone and then saying, "Yes, it's him, my son, he
                    was so good."

MOTHER 3:   Or when seeing a skull full of holes coming out of
                    the earth, whisper: "My son never hurt anybody."

MOTHER 2:   Or when we see a torn piece of material and
                    recognize it as something we knitted with our own
                    hands for our husbands when sitting by the fire
                    while the bread was baking, we'll say: "He was
                    peaceful, he always fulfilled his duties . . ."

MOTHER 1:   (*She takes off her veil and walks to one end of the platform before speaking.*) My son, with your death, I lost my life! No one should allow these events to fall into silence, to fall into oblivion . . .

Silence.

JULIANA: They had hidden his remains
But their effort was in vain.
He informed a Christian woman
Of his secret burial:

CHORUS: Now the pilgrims know
Where Sebastian lies!

The Mothers, following Juliana with the banner, move about in a circle, Mother 1 remains in her place. Taking turns, they speak:

MOTHER 1:   We want neither revenge nor oblivion.

JULIANA: Don't call them "the nineteen from Yumbel."

MOTHER 2:   Or the fourteen from Lonquén.

MOTHER 3:   They can't be just numbers . . . only numbers.

MOTHER 4:   Behind numbers there are only names, and there's no place for men,

MOTHER 5:   And no place for the grief of those who loved them.

MOTHER 1:   We want to feel their presence,

MOTHER 2:   To call them by the name with which we greeted them every day.

MOTHER 3:   To talk about what kind of people they were, what they said.

MOTHER 4:   To talk about their sorrows,

MOTHER 5:   Their hopes . . .

MOTHER 1:   Son, since I resumed my normal life, there is not a
                   single day that I don't feel your presence and hear
                   the sound of your voice!

JULIANA: What a sad fame,
                   Diocletian, persecutor of Christians, had.
                   Sebastian predicted it!
                   In his old age, Diocletian said,
                   "My empire collapsed,
                   My glory was extinguished,"
                   And while saying it, he would cry.
                   "Oh, Sebastian," he clamored,
                   "Only you gave me love!"

MOTHER 1:   Son, where did they take you? What did they do with
                   you? (*Pause, as son.*) "It's dark, mother; I open and I
                   close my eyes and it's dark. It's cold, my hands are
                   tied, my body is bent and I feel cold." (*Pause.*) Son, we
                   will never stop looking for you, even though they
                   always give us the same answers: "The legal process
                   is extremely slow; see pages such and such; we have
                   to check up on several things; he has not been
                   arrested; we don't know anything about him;
                   nothing can be done; the *Habeas Corpus* doesn't save
                   anyone from torture!" (*Pause, as son.*) "Mother, a river
                   doesn't end; if I can leave you dignity forever you
                   will continue to believe in what is worthwhile and to
                   build a future with your hands!" (*Pause.*) Son, they
                   want to tear you to pieces, denying you life, without
                   giving you death either . . . And the judges write
                   calmly, "Add it to his file. Take care of it. File it. Forget
                   it." Because for some people, what's important is
                   that petitions merely go through the legal
                   procedures . . . that appeals be used up even if life
                   runs out much earlier! (*Pause, as son.*) "Mother, I feel
                   like dying at every moment, my victory is in
                   remaining silent, in fainting. The moment I can rest,
                   I struggle with the staunch decision of not speaking,
                   but I want to assure you that I haven't changed. After
                   all, our hearts get tired, and there's a lack of air, a lot
                   of thirst, and even more hunger. But do not let them
                   kill your soul!"[7]

Brief incidental music.

The other Mothers and the Actors, Chinchinero, and Juliana move about and Mother 1 joins them, in a procession. Alejandro and Marta offer them some candles placed in red paper carnations which look like small chinese lanterns and they also give them a sheet of paper with the names of the 19 leaders found in the cemetery of Yumbel that they will read later.

MOTHER 2:	Don't allow us, Sebastian, to forget those who are absent.
VOICES:	Do not allow it.
MOTHER 3:	Life is hard and we are so prone to forgetfulness.
MOTHER 4:	If we forget the past, we'll be condemned to repeat it!
VOICES:	Don't allow it, Sebastian.
MOTHER 1:	Thus, when we remember them, we'll say, "Never more!"
VOICES:	Never again . . . never again . . .

The procession can descend into the theater and return to the stage, preceded by Juliana, who is carrying a banner, and they all name the dead. In chorus, and in unison they say the litany.

ONE:	Juan Acuña
CHORUS:	Pray for him
ONE:	Luis Araneda
CHORUS:	We entrust him to you, Sebastian
ONE:	Manuel Becerra
CHORUS:	Look after him, beloved Saint
ONE:	Rubén Campos, Dagoberto Garfias

CHORUS:	Pray for their souls
ONE:	Juan Jara, Fernando Grandón
CHORUS:	Take our love to them
ONE:	Jorge Lamaña, Heraldo Muñoz, Federico Riquelme
CHORUS:	We entrust them to you, Sebastian
ONE:	Oscar Sanhueza, Luis Ulloa, Raúl Urra
CHORUS:	Take care of them in the Holy Kingdom
ONE:	Juan Villarroel, Jorge Zorrilla, Eduardo Gutiérrez
CHORUS:	Look after them, beloved Saint
ONE:	Mario Jara, Alfonso Macaya, Wilson Muñoz
CHORUS:	Take our love to them
JULIANA:	From your sanctuary in Yumbel, protect us so that we can build a free country, where justice reigns!

MOTHERS 2 and 3: Give us that hope, miraculous Saint!

A polka is played by the actor who plays the role of the organ grinder. Chinchinero accompanies him.

JULIANA:	Today is Saint Sebastian's Day!
EVERYBODY:	We are here to rejoice with the saint!
CHINCHINERO:	The pilgrims are here!

There are balloons and a vendor pushing his cart in the town square. Unexpectedly, a folk pageant begins with a couple wearing amusing masks crossing the stage and dancing first a polka and then some cueca steps. Other options for this scene may include: a puppet show of folk marionettes or an actor on stilts holding paper dolls representing Diocletian and Sebastian. The Mothers have taken off their veils and gotten rid of the candles. They join the pilgrims' celebration.

CHORUS:　　　　　Here we are, in Yumbel.
　　　　　　　　　We come to pay you homage,
　　　　　　　　　Our beloved Sebastian,
　　　　　　　　　With a carnation and a verse.

SEVERAL PEOPLE:　Long live the Saint! Don't forget your pilgrims!

Some are carrying flags with the saint's colors, red and yellow. After Chinchinero parades around, playing the drum and cymbals, Juliana gets up on the platform and turns to audience:

JULIANA:　　　　Attention! (*Drumroll.*) Today, January 20, the feast
　　　　　　　　of our patron Saint Sebastian, the actors have just
　　　　　　　　performed for you the play that tells of his life and
　　　　　　　　martyrdom, called . . . (*Drumroll and cymbals.*)

EVERYBODY:　　　Altarpiece of Yumbel!

Music for the final song, a march. Everyone lines up in single file, facing audience:

> Today they invoke you in Yumbel;
> Your sanctuary is now famous.
> Throngs of pilgrims
> Pay you pious homage.
> First in Rome,
> and later,
> The dancer and the singer
> Say happily and with fervor:
> Between Heaven and Earth,
> Injustice is a scourge,
> And its remedy, love!

They repeat, moving forward:

> Between Heaven and Earth,
> Injustice is a scourge,
> And its remedy, love!

THE END
Isidora Aguirre
Santiago, Chile, 1985–86

Notes

1. For permission to stage the play, the author must be contacted directly: Rengo 1029-c, Nuñoa, Santiago Chile. We want to warn the readers that, in collaboration with the playwright, we made substantial revisions and that, therefore, in many instances the English version will not concur with the original.

2. A one-man orchestra is our translation of the Chilean nickname *chinchinero*. He is a folkloric figure found in the countryside or in urban parks who carries a bass drum and cymbals on his back and wears bells on his ankles. He generally makes music accompanied by an organ grinder.

3. The literal translation of *arpillera* is sackcloth or burlap. Nevertheless, in Chile, the word has acquired an extended meaning. It is now the name given to the handcrafts originally produced by poor Catholic women's groups who used this material to embroider everyday-life scenes that carried sociopolitical messages. This type of naive, folkloric art became a means of sustenance for needy families when the main breadwinner was a political prisoner. The successful exportation of arpilleras by the Catholic Church has not only popularized this type of art abroad, but has continued to offer economic support to those who have suffered most under the dictatorship.

4. The *cueca* is the national folkloric dance of Chile.

5. These were the words Isidoro Carrillo uttered before his execution in Lota, Chile.

6. All of Magdalena's speeches in quotation marks in this scene are fragments taken from the written testimony of an Argentinean woman.

7. Mother 1's monologue is based on a poem by José Manuel Parada, one of the three professionals found beheaded in March 1985. He wrote the poem in 1976 immediately after the arrest and disappearance of his father-in-law, Fernando Ortiz.

Sabina Berman (Mexico, 1955?)—playwright, poet and novelist—began writing for the theater in 1974 with *Mariposa* (Butterfly), a play she directed and in which she also acted. She achieved national recognition early in her career, winning Mexico's National Award for Theater in 1979 and three other times thereafter.[1] In 1986 *El árbol de humo* earned her the Celestino Gorostiza Award for Children's Theatre.

In 1985, several of her plays were published in a volume entitled *Teatro de Sabina Berman* (Sabina Berman's Theatre). Subsequently, three other plays have appeared: *Muerte súbita* (Sudden Death, 1988), *La grieta* (1990), and *Entre Villa y una mujer desnuda* (Between Villa and a Naked Woman, 1992).

Five of the six plays included in her first book result directly from scholarly research; whereas the rest of her work moves closer to the realm of the personal, even though it may be but a rhetorical strategy. In the realm of the personal, what Berman examines is the role of women in a man's world. Ultimately she obfuscates gender difference, challenges historical truths, and tests to the limit any and all fixed notions of identity.

In addition to writing and directing plays, Berman has authored movie, television, and dance scripts.[2] She has also published two books of poetry, a novel, several short stories, and a collection of newspaper articles on levitation.[3]

Notes

1. She first got the award for *Yanqui* (Yankee), then subsequently for *Rompecabezas* (The Puzzle, 1981), *La maravillosa historia de Chiquito Pingüica* (Chiquito Pingüica's Wonderful Story, 1982), and *Herejía* (Heresy, 1983).

2. In 1979 she received the Ariel Award for the year's best movie script *Tía Alejandra* (Aunt Alejandra), co-authored with Delfina Careaga. The dance scripts *Una luna una* (One Moon, One) and *Ni puertas ni ventanas* (Neither Doors Nor Windows) were staged in 1987.

3. Her poetic production includes two volumes: *Poemas de agua* (Water Poems, 1987) and *Lunas* (Moons, 1988). Individual poems have appeared in *Uno más uno*, *El zaguán*, *Aquí estamos*, *Comunicación*, *El cuento*, *Punto de partida*, and *Espera ocho*. In 1990 she published her first novel *La bobe* (*Grandma*), a recollection of her childhood memories and Judaic family traditions. Her short stories have been published in Mexican journals and newspapers. She co-authored the articles on levitation entitled *Volar* (Flying) with José Gordon.

Yankee

(originally BILL)
BY SABINA BERMAN[1]

Translated into English
by Teresa Cajiao Salas and Margarita Vargas
First produced by José Hernández at Teatro Granero
Directed by José Caballero

Cast

BILL:	Héctor Beacon
ALBERTO:	Carlos Cruz
ROSA:	Diana Mariscal
THE LIEUTENANT	

Yankee

Second production by Compañía de Shakespeare. Direction and staging by Abraham Oceransky.

Cast

BILL:	Horacio Salinas
ALBERTO:	Fausto Rocha
ROSA:	Rocío Flores
THE LIEUTENANT:	Ari Tach

Characters

BILL:	Tall, strong, solid, about thirty-two years old. His hair is carelessly cut, almost shaved in some spots and in others long and bristly. He speaks Spanish with a slight American accent. Whenever he speaks English his tone is angry and vehement. Occasionally he bursts out in laughter and quits just as unexpectedly.
ROSA:	Alberto's wife. A pleasant-looking mestiza.
ALBERTO:	Indian. Approximately the same age as Bill.
THE BABY	
THE LIEUTENANT	

The action takes place in Puerto Vallarta. The house is the only one on the beach. The study, located on the first floor, opens onto the road, the master bedroom, the kitchen, and the narrow staircase. The balcony and Bill's bedroom are on the second floor. There is very little furniture, only the most indispensable items: in the study there's a table—which Alberto uses as a desk—a lamp, an armchair, and several chairs; in Bill's bedroom there's a cot; on the balcony two wicker armchairs. The walls are impeccably white.

SCENE I

The balcony. Bill is sitting in a wicker chair. It is late afternoon: during the scene the light gradually dims to indicate nightfall. In the study on the first floor Alberto's silhouette can be seen through the closed blinds. He is writing.

BILL: When I saw her at the market, the baby in her arms . . . She was selecting each fruit, each vegetable with extreme care, testing its ripeness . . . Amid the noise, the Indian vendors, the white buyers, the hustle-bustle, haste . . . Strange idea, haste, the idea that one can arrive at a place earlier . . . She went from stand to stand searching for the best fruit, the best vegetables, she felt them to see if they were ripe! She looked like a Madonna, the baby in her arms, the Indian boy carrying her basket . . . But we're always at the same place. Here. I have been in these ruins for two hundred years . . .

Rosa enters with the baby in her arms. She paces up and down the balcony.

BILL: When I saw you at the market . . . I couldn't keep from following you, you know? I followed you as if in a dream. You were a vision . . . The Virgin of Guadalupe . . .

Rosa laughs softly.

BILL: I heard the handyman didn't want to come all the way out here to fix your roof. I sold my watch; with the money I bought tools.

ROSA: The ship sailed at noon today.

BILL: So what? Am I a Marine? Is that what you think?

ROSA: That's what you told me, Bill.

BILL: What else did I tell you? For example, that I was in Vietnam?

ROSA: No. You didn't tell me that.

BILL: That was an unjust war and I wasn't there. Period. Let's change the subject, huh? How old is the baby?

ROSA: Five months old.

BILL: Who would even think of bringing a baby to Puerto Vallarta?

ROSA: Alberto needs to be near the sea in order to write. That's why we came here as soon as our son was born.

BILL: *(Doubtful.)* Why does he need to be near the sea to write?

ROSA: He says listening to the sea gives him a sensation of eternity. *(Pause.)* Alberto's first book is a collection of songs to the sea. It is his most sincere and melodious book. He swears that before dying he will return to the sea to write a farewell hymn. It will also be a hymn of gratitude.

BILL: Nuts. The sea is a cruel monster. I've seen it swallow a man in one gulp. Of course, from the shore it looks like a puppy. Well, your husband hasn't been in a storm, how nice! And the sea inspires him, that's very nice.

ROSA: Perhaps by the time he finishes his last book he will have lived through a storm.

Bill looks at her with disbelief. Then he looks at the child.

ROSA: His name is Alberto.

BILL:	Oh yes, like your husband. I hope he doesn't get any teeth.
ROSA:	What? I hope they come in soon.
BILL:	Then he'll bite you.
ROSA:	Softly . . . It will be a very intimate pleasure. I imagine.
BILL:	You imagine. Okay. Henry was born when I was five.
ROSA:	Your brother?
BILL:	Yeah, I'd chosen a name for him: Ruth. I wanted a sister, understand? I was afraid another boy would steal my mother's love. That's natural. Dr. Spock says so in his books. I've read Dr. Spock's books one by one, where he explains how this and my other crazy ideas are perfectly normal. Anyway, when I got to the hospital, my mother was in bed. I went to her and kissed her on the forehead, you know?, just like in films—a father, whose wife has just given birth—kisses her on the forehead. Very much like a little gentleman, I leaned over and kissed her. The room was full of visitors, presents, flowers. The nurse came in with the baby, a small bundle, and she gave him to my mother. "How's Ruth Mommy?" "Fine, Bill." "Looks exactly like his father," somebody said behind my back. What, his father? His father? I jumped out of the window. I ran through the dark garden; it was nighttime, it was drizzling, the tears . . .
ROSA:	The room was on the ground floor, then.
BILL:	Yes. But I didn't know. Besides, I was waiting for you to tell me my mother was so mean for having lied to me.
ROSA:	She didn't want to lose your love, Bill. What she did wasn't right but . . . it's understandable.

BILL: Hmm. My love. Does she care? "Your grandfather died while landing in France," she used to tell me, "he died to defend our right to progress. And we have progressed. You never lacked education, food, entertainment. I, on the other hand, was a poor little orphan at twelve. So, you should go defend our liberty. So, you should go! Don't expect me to love a traitor. Big Sam needs you!" (*As if hallucinating, surrounded by Uncle Sams pointing at him.*) He is pointing at me from every poster! You son of a bitch, you! (*He begins to march.*) Left-right, left-right, left-right. Stop! This little oriental is your enemy. Prepare arms! Aim! (*He imitates the report of a machine gun.*) Ratta-ta-ta-ta-ta-ta-ta-ta-ta. How can a burst of fire be stopped once you've pulled the trigger? Rosa, I ask you! Ratta-ta ta-ta-ta.

ROSA: I don't know.

BILL: You can't. Period. Let's change the subject. No, it's not so easy. After the first dead man . . . after the second one . . . After the first war . . . The subject becomes obsessive. Vietnam has turned into a weaving full of holes, but we will eventually find another legacy to destroy. It's impossible to stop . . . "and they left us as legacy a weaving full of holes," it's an Aztec poem. "And there's no place to protect ourselves from our solitude." When I returned home Henry's hair came down to here; his gaze and his hair were like Christ's. "Doesn't it infuriate you to have been so basely deceived?" he asked me. "You went to Vietnam as a watchdog for transnational interests, we know it, brother. Peace and love, brother." We white men are fucked up. Period. The fishermen and the farmers of Puerto Vallarta . . . Now that we have turned your paradise into a tourist attraction, many dollars, huh? But nothing can pay them for the dignity we white men have taken from them. We have turned them into boatmen, waitresses, pimps, and whores. We have filled in the holes of their legacy with drugs and syphilis and haste. Period, I said! Did I wake up the baby?

ROSA: No, he's asleep.

BILL: Could it be he . . . died? No, huh? Go check on him,
                   please.

Smiling, Rosa goes to see the baby.

ROSA: Listen how he's breathing. Little angel . . .

BILL: Do you love him for no particular reason? I mean,
                   do you love him only because he exists?

Still laughing, Rosa agrees.

BILL: When I saw you at the market . . . When I saw you
                   with the baby in your arms I felt like . . .

ROSA: Being the baby.

BILL: (*Frightened.*) You're a psychiatrist.

ROSA: No, how can you say that.

BILL: Witch.

ROSA: No.

BILL: But you read minds.

ROSA: I swear I don't.

BILL: But your husband promised me a portrait. Could I
                   rest my head on your lap?

ROSA: Come here, Bill.

*Bill rests his head on Rosa's lap. He talks while waiting for sleep to
come.*

BILL: It's not right, but it's understandable, isn't it?

ROSA: Yes.

BILL:	And you'll cure me, won't you?
ROSA:	Yes.
BILL:	You alone.
ROSA:	Alberto and I.
BILL:	When I saw you at the market I wanted to kill the baby because you don't love him disinterestedly. You love him because he's yours. Because he makes you feel like a goddess; if you nurse him, you give him life and if you don't, you kill him.

Pause.

BILL:	But you're gonna nurse him, right?
ROSA:	When he wakes up. Now he's about to fall asleep.
BILL:	Right?
ROSA:	Yes.

Pause.

BILL:	(*Half asleep.*) Right?
ROSA:	Yes.
BILL:	Right?

Pause.

ROSA:	Yes.

Darkness.

SCENE II

The stage is dark. Loud steps are heard. Bill kicks open the door to his room and remains at the faintly lighted doorway. Moonlight. He carries his machine gun ready to shoot.

BILL: Anybody here? Anybody here?

A sound reveals somebody's presence.

BILL: Who's there? Answer! Who's there?

WOMAN'S VOICE: (*Shrill, with a Vietnamese accent.*) Woman . . .
                         woman . . .

BILL: North or south? Answer!

WOMAN'S VOICE: Woman . . . woman . . .

BILL: Answer! North or south?

An unexpected child's cry makes Bill lose control and he discharges his machine gun. A woman's scream, and the thump of her fall are heard. The crying does not stop and Bill turns around and around shooting. The crying has ceased when the shooting stops.

SCENE III

There's an abrupt change from darkness to the tenuous light of daybreak: Bill wakes up suddenly from his nightmare. Rosa runs in with the baby in her arms.

BILL: I pissed . . . I shit on the sheets. (*He sits up with the sheets wrapped around him like a big diaper.*) Forgive me, forgive me, I'm very sorry. I gotta go. The ship sails at dawn.

ROSA: Bill, wait. Calm down. Your ship, the Marines' ship left a week ago. Don't you remember? You have stayed with us to help us fix the house. Yesterday you painted the front walls, don't you remember? You put the furniture in place, you fixed the plumbing.

Bill looks at her wildly. Then he looks around. He sits on the edge of the bed with his head in his hands.

BILL: I'm sick.

ROSA: It was only a bad dream.

BILL: Where's your husband?

ROSA: He's asleep.

BILL: Did I wake you up? Is it very early? The sun hasn't come out yet.

ROSA: It must be around four. Alberto went to bed a few hours ago. He had been working since noon. He didn't hear your screams . . .

BILL: Did I scream? I'm sorry. I'm worse than a child. I give you a lot of trouble, don't I? A child has the excuse of . . . being a child.

ROSA: You're sick, calm down.

BILL: I'm a big, stupid baby. I realize that. It hurts me to realize that. I'm sick. No one has to put up with a sick person. It hurts me to realize that. If I were a total idiot . . . But an intelligent part of me watches me making a fool of myself, to be a burden, to be a big idiotic baby. The ship is gone? A week ago? I should have gone on the ship.

ROSA: You didn't want to go back to the ship, remember?

BILL: On the ship at least they have to tolerate me because the big, idiotic baby is a good Marine. Besides, I didn't care what they thought of me. Your husband sleeping?

ROSA: Yes.

BILL: I didn't go. I went A.W.O.L., right? Now I'm a traitor.

ROSA: Yes, Bill.

BILL: If I'm a traitor, I'm good. If I'm not a traitor, I'm bad. It's very confusing, isn't it? It's exactly the opposite of what I learned when I was a kid. I no longer believe anything they taught me. My head's a weaving full of holes. But I should've returned to the ship because I keep on being bad.

ROSA: No, Bill. Now, you're a traitor.

BILL: Do you really believe that? I went A.W.O.L., right? That proves I'm a traitor, doesn't it?

ROSA: Yes, Bill, you're a traitor.

BILL: (*Happy.*) I didn't go to Vietnam, right?

ROSA: You're a traitor.

BILL: Repeat it. I like to hear it from you.

ROSA: You, Bill, are a traitor.

BILL: But I keep on being bad. Rosa, I wanna confess to you how bad I am.

ROSA: It isn't necessary Bill. That's all over now. You couldn't avoid doing what you did in Vietnam. You had to survive.

BILL: (*Defiant.*) I didn't go to Vietnam. I'm a traitor. I spent the war years in Quebec.

Pause.

ROSA: Yes, Bill.

Pause.

BILL: Yes, I was in Vietnam. But that's over Rosa, right?

ROSA: Yes, Bill.

BILL: I wanna tell you what I did in Vietnam.

ROSA: You don't have to tell me, Bill.

BILL:	Yes, I'm gonna tell you so you can forgive me for what I did.
ROSA:	I forgive you. You don't need to tell me what you did. It's enough to see how kind and sensitive you are, to know that now you're a good man. You're a good man, now, Bill; what you did before doesn't matter.
BILL:	(*Defiant.*) I killed a defenseless woman and her baby.

Pause.

ROSA:	You're a good man, Bill.
BILL:	You're very warm, very soft. Is the baby hungry? He was crying.
ROSA:	Your screams frightened him.
BILL:	I'm sorry.
ROSA:	He's asleep already.
BILL:	I'm gonna clean this now, right? (*He shows her the dirty sheets.*)
ROSA:	Yes, Bill.
BILL:	Would you clean this for me?

Pause.

BILL:	You're nauseated by my shit, aren't you?

Pause.

ROSA:	Hold the baby. I'll bring some rags to clean up.
BILL:	Aren't you afraid I'll drop him?

Pause.

ROSA: No.

Pause.

Rosa gives him the baby. He takes the baby very carefully.

ROSA: I'm going to get the rags. (*She walks to the kitchen.*)

Bill is feeling more confident holding the baby. Finally he holds him with the tenderness of a madonna, watching him sleep in silence.

Darkness.

SCENE IV

In the study Alberto is sitting at the desk writing. It is daytime. Rosa enters through the front door with the baby in her arms and her purse. An Indian boy carrying her shopping basket follows her.

ROSA: Hi!

ALBERTO: (*Absentmindedly without looking up.*) Hi!

ROSA: I thought you would be asleep. You wrote all night . . .

Rosa shows the boy to the kitchen so he can set the basket down. On her way to the bedroom to put the baby in his crib she says:

ROSA: Beto fell asleep on the bus in spite of the noise and the bumpy ride. How I envy children! They suddenly feel like sleeping and that's it; they ignore everything and they fall asleep.

Alberto raises his head and mumbles: You envy children? He nods and goes back to his writing. Rosa returns at the same time the Indian boy comes out of the kitchen, she tips him. The boy thanks her with a nod. Rosa pats him on the head. The boy leaves the house closing the door behind him.

ROSA: Do you want a cup of coffee?

ALBERTO: No. Not now.

ROSA:	Something refreshing, then? Some juice?

Pause.

ROSA:	How lucky the house is air conditioned. Bbrrr. It's even cold in here. If you only knew how hot it is outside.

Pause.

ROSA:	How's it going?
ALBERTO:	(*Without taking his eyes off his work.*) Fine. (*Pause.*)

Rosa is about to say something, but before she can do it, Alberto startles her with a shout.

ALBERTO:	What?
ROSA:	What about what?
ALBERTO:	What were you going to ask me now? I don't want coffee. I don't want something cold. I don't want anything. I only want you to let me concentrate. The novel's going well. It'll go better without interruptions.
ROSA:	I only wanted to tell you I couldn't find a handyman willing to come out here. They say the house is too far from town and that they would waste too much time.
ALBERTO:	Too bad.
ROSA:	The roof will end up rotting away completely.
ALBERTO:	Too bad.
ROSA:	Okay. One of these days it'll fall on top of us.
ALBERTO:	Sure.
ROSA:	You don't care?

ALBERTO: As far as I'm concerned, the sky can fall, until I
                finish my novel.

ROSA: Very funny. I was talking about the roof in our
                bedroom.[2]

Pause.

Rosa walks to the door. Alberto takes his eyes off his writing.

ALBERTO: Rosa . . . Rosa, come back. Please understand. I
                came here to have peace. I need absolute silence to
                be able to write. If someone had loaned us a house
                even farther away I would've gone there. It takes
                me hours to distance myself from the world that
                surrounds me and slowly enter the world of my
                novel. Little by little I disconnect myself from all of
                this and when I finally succeed, it's irritating to
                have to connect myself with the exterior again. It
                means I have to repeat the process. And I can't be
                in two worlds at the same time. Why am I
                explaining this to you? It's not the first novel I've
                written since we've been together.

ROSA: But we had never been so isolated.

ALBERTO: Right. That's why this will be a better novel than
                the other two.

ROSA: I feel very lonely.

ALBERTO: I've told you to go to town and enjoy yourself at
                the hotels. Now that it's the tourist season you can
                meet interesting people . . .

ROSA: In a luxury hotel in Puerto Vallarta, a woman alone
                can only be looking for an affair. Men approach
                you openly to propose it, and women are too busy
                looking for men to waste their time making friends
                with women.

ALBERTO: Couples . . .

ROSA:	Sure, I'm going to approach a couple and say: "Hi, my name is Rosa. I'm lonely. Do you mind if I impose on you?" Besides, there's the baby, Alberto. I can't even go to the movies with the baby.
ALBERTO:	I can't promise to hurry. You know I work every day until I'm exhausted, but these things, creative works, take time to materialize and you can't rush them. They have their own rhythm.
ROSA:	"As in flowers, beauty grows slowly, silently in the poet." Alberto Icaza. I know your verse by heart.

Pause.

| ALBERTO: | I'm planning to finish it before the deadline for submissions to the contest. With the prize money we'll go to Europe. Imagine: the two of us sight seeing in Paris, not caring about schedules or clocks, spending money on whatever we want, Rosa. Why save? Our treasure is here (*He points to his head.*) Our treasure, you hear? Ours: yours and mine. |
| ROSA: | You don't know if you'll win the prize. |

Pause.

ROSA:	You don't have to finish the novel before the deadline for submissions. Take all the time you need to write a good novel. A work of art. I understand. I want you to do it. It makes me happy for you to do it. I believe in what your verse says, that beauty grows slowly. I love you because you're able to create beautiful things. I was angry because I couldn't find a handyman to help us, that's all.
ALBERTO:	I have to finish it before the deadline. If I continue working intensely, I can make it, I know.
ROSA:	Don't exert yourself too much.

ALBERTO: What does it mean to exert yourself too much? We
                     have more energy than we can use. But to create
                     you need more than energy, you need peace, you
                     need patience, you have to follow the rhythm of
                     the poetry inside you in order to let it out. The sea
                     calms me down.

Pause.

Rosa sits on Alberto's lap. She hugs and caresses him.

ROSA: What can I do to help you?

ALBERTO: Just keep on being so understanding.

ROSA: Nothing else?

ALBERTO: What else could you do? You can't write for me. I
                     wish you could. Sometimes I feel overwhelmed by
                     the loneliness of this work.

The baby cries.

ALBERTO: (*Mumbling.*) Oh bitch . . . the baby.

*Rosa runs to take care of the baby. Alberto concentrates on his writing.
There is a knock at the door. Rosa runs back to open it. Bill is at the
door. He is wearing shorts and a beach shirt, tennis shoes, he has a
trowel in one hand and in the other a cement bag with several tools
sticking out. Even though it is obviously a heavy load, he carries it
effortlessly. The baby's crying continues.*

BILL: I'm a handyman.

Alberto and Rosa look at him in surprise.

BILL: A baby's crying.

Pause.

BILL: A baby's crying. Isn't it your son?

ROSA: Yes . . .

BILL:	Why don't you go check on him?
ALBERTO:	Who are you?
BILL:	I'm a handyman. Mr. Olvera sent me. He told me you needed a handyman. And since I'm a handyman who needs work . . .
ALBERTO:	Are you an American?
BILL:	Yeah, a *gringo* handyman. Something wrong with that?
ALBERTO:	What?
BILL:	That I am a *gringo* handyman.
ALBERTO:	No, I suppose not.
BILL:	In the States there are handymen, right?
ALBERTO:	Yes, I suppose so. But a *gringo* handyman in Puerto Vallarta is strange.
BILL:	I came as a tourist, but I ran out of money. A baby's crying.
ROSA:	It's my son.
BILL:	Aren't you gonna go check on him, to stop his crying?
ROSA:	Yes, of course.

Rosa goes to look after the child. In the next few minutes his crying will gradually diminish until it stops.

BILL:	Thank you.
ALBERTO:	Thank you?
BILL:	You're an artist, right? Your wife told Mr. Olvera that. She told him that because you were an artist you couldn't repair the roof in your bedroom.

ALBERTO:	You speak Spanish very well.
BILL:	There are *gringos* who speak Spanish very well, right?
ALBERTO:	I suppose so.
BILL:	I'm a *gringo* who speaks Spanish very well; something wrong with that?
ALBERTO:	No, of course, not. It's okay, I only mentioned it because I was a little surprised. There aren't too many Americans who can speak our language well.
BILL:	But it's not bad, is it? Could you paint a portrait of me in exchange for my work?
ALBERTO:	Who me?
BILL:	Don't get upset. Maybe you're a very expensive artist, but it would be a charitable act on your part to paint my portrait in exchange for my humble work.
ALBERTO:	I don't paint.
BILL:	Aren't you an artist? Your wife lied to convince Mr. Olvera, huh?
ALBERTO:	I'm a writer, not a painter.

Rosa returns.

ROSA:	Come in, I'll show you where the roof has rotted.
BILL:	Maybe later on we could talk about my portrait, okay? (*To Rosa.*) Your husband is gonna do my portrait, that bother you?
ROSA:	Are you going to paint him?
ALBERTO:	(*Amused.*) That's what he says.

BILL: Really, it doesn't matter if you don't do it. You can pay me cash, even though I'd be more grateful if you'd do my portrait.

ROSA: But my husband can't draw.

ALBERTO: Yes, but perhaps I could make a composite picture. (*He laughs, but since neither Bill nor Rosa laughs, he stops.*) A composite picture, do you know what that means?

BILL: A portrait made with words, right? Are you saying you could write a story about me?

ALBERTO: Well, yes. But the funny thing is I've just made a play on words. A composite picture, in police jargon, is the tentative sketch a draftsman makes of a criminal, based on the descriptions given by the witnesses of a crime.

BILL: I'm not a criminal.

ALBERTO: I was explaining to you the play on words . . .

BILL: I know what that means. That's why I'm telling you I'm not a criminal.

The three of them remain silent for a moment without knowing what to do.

ROSA: Follow me, I'll show you the roof.

Rosa exits followed by Bill. Alberto smiles while he goes to his desk to put some papers in order. Rosa returns.

SCENE V

ROSA: Alberto. Don't get upset because I'm interrupting you, but . . .

ALBERTO: What is it?

ROSA:	The handyman has already started working. But when he saw the broken pipe, he said he could also fix that.
ALBERTO:	Wonderful!
ROSA:	What if we allow him to sleep here, because he doesn't have money for lodging; he could repair everything that needs to be fixed.
ALBERTO:	We couldn't have had better luck.
ROSA:	Doesn't he seem strange to you?
ALBERTO:	The *gringo?* Extremely strange.
ROSA:	His attitude is strange also. He seems to be . . . I don't know . . . too . . . nice.
ALBERTO:	He came to Puerto Vallarta as a tourist, he ran out of money, he needs work. Of course, he's not a handyman; I'm saying this because of his education, his Spanish is flawless. He must be a university student and is too embarrassed to admit it. It's strange, but understandable. Oh, Rosa: you have to learn how to tolerate and respect people's idiosyncracies. Why do you care who the guy is as long as he repairs the roof? You must have also seemed strange to Mr. Olvera, telling him our life story to convince him to come.
ROSA:	Did I do wrong? I thought that if he understood . . .
ALBERTO:	Most people are not as understanding as you are. Everyone looks after himself.
ROSA:	How awful!
ALBERTO:	Why is it awful? That attitude has its advantages. Everyone can do as he pleases as long as he fulfills his obligations.

Rosa goes to the door facing the staircase. At the doorway she stops. She turns around.

ROSA:	I'm so stupid. You always have to explain everything to me.
ALBERTO:	You're innocent, that's all.
ROSA:	You mean stupid.
ALBERTO:	No. Innocent. You're not corrupted, hardened. (*He goes over to her.*) Do me a favor, child: don't ever change.
ROSA:	Wouldn't you like for me to depend less on you? I don't know what I would do without you.
ALBERTO:	If I had wanted a clever companion, a worldly woman, I would have married one. But I fell in love with your innocence, sweetheart. (*He gives her a quick kiss on the mouth.*) Now let me write, will you? (*He dismisses her with a pat on the rear and closes the door behind her.*)

Darkness.

INTERMISSION

SCENE VI

Bill, Alberto, and Rosa are in the study. Alberto is reading a manuscript.

ALBERTO:	" . . . He looked at the papers scattered out on the floor. He gathered them one by one, but once he had picked them all up, he threw them down again. He looked at the papers spread out on the floor. He thought, if he could at least reach the bottom of something, of anything, answer all the questions . . . but behind each layer of understanding, regardless of how deep it may be, there's always a deeper layer, and behind that one, another, and another, and another. Nevertheless he told himself, I'm sure the bottom of something is identical to any bottom. Then, he thought of the sea." Well, this is the end of the chapter.

ROSA: It's very beautiful, Alberto.

ALBERTO: It may require further revision.

ROSA: It seems . . . magnificent. It's the best you've
                    written.

ALBERTO: I think so. Nevertheless, perhaps I could improve
                    it. There are certain parts that seem weak. The
                    repetitions worry me. They're done on purpose,
                    but I don't know . . . Perhaps they're too
                    irritating . . . Even though I do want to irritate the
                    reader, I don't want to go so far that he tosses the
                    book in the garbage, of course. Not that far . . . This
                    insecurity is so awful: how will the reader react?

ROSA: Well, insecurity is unavoidable.

ALBERTO: You spend days and days revising a text. You end
                    up fearing no one except you will understand it.
                    And you feel tempted to rewrite it in a style that
                    you know people generally accept.

ROSA: I know you could do it. But you would lose your
                    originality.

ALBERTO: Yes, that's the price. What about you, Bill, what did
                    you think of it? (*Condescendingly.*) Did you
                    understand anything?

BILL: It seems too intellectual to me.

        Pause.

ALBERTO: What?

BILL: The character in your novel seems too intellectual
                    to me.

ALBERTO: What do you mean "too intellectual"?

BILL: I mean your main character's concerns are too
                    intellectual for any reader to identify with them.

Most people are concerned with concrete problems, not abstract dilemmas.

ALBERTO: I don't write for most people. I don't intend . . .

BILL: People worry about what they're gonna eat the next day.

ALBERTO: I agree. But the people you're talking about don't even know how to read.

BILL: You don't know your country: I'm not talking about the poorest class.

ALBERTO: The extremely poor.

BILL: The extremely poor. I'm also referring to the working class, and to the middle class. When was the last time you went to the market? People worry about meat prices going up every week. You know how much a pound of beans costs now?

ALBERTO: Why is it precisely foreigners who accuse us, the Third World intellectuals, of not worrying about the problems peculiar to the Third World? Could it be that it bothers them that in spite of all our poverty, we have today the most dynamic artistic forces? Don't I have the right, because I come from a poor peasant background, to be concerned with the same themes as Hegel and Nietzsche? Why do I have to produce art that reflects poverty?

BILL: I said that because I thought you were concerned with your potential readers. I realize you don't have to write about the price of beans . . . but, anyway, common people in Mexico or in Yugoslavia or in the States, have problems that are not intellectual: they wanna know how to love somebody, they wanna know how to educate their children, they wanna know . . .

ALBERTO: I have never heard you talk so much, Bill. You're intelligent, in spite of all appearances. I'm surprised you don't recognize yourself in my character. I'll bet you've also approached the edge of consciousness where questions about specific, everyday matters vanish, springing up in their place bonds that unite human beings throughout the centuries and continents: "what am I?" my character wonders; "what am I? I'm a tunnel," he says, "but from where, to where, and what for; what do I convey if, in truth, I'm conveying something that will outlive me?"

BILL: I've asked myself those questions, sir, and the answers I found were proven false later. I asked myself, for example, if man was good or bad and I answered that basically he was good because he can love. And in Vietnam I saw things that showed me all you have to do is loosen the reins and people will behave like animals. I myself . . . I myself killed, I, the good one, who went to church every Sunday.

ALBERTO: You had to defend yourself, didn't you?

BILL: You don't know who you are until you're put to the test. What's the point of asking yourself about abstractions? Right now I'm a person with good intentions.

ALBERTO: I believe so, Bill. You have helped Rosa and . . .

BILL: Don't mention it, please. Your wife's been nicer to me than I've been to her. You, too.

ALBERTO: That means a man changes according to his circumstances.

BILL: If that's what you get from what I'm telling you about me, okay. But then, what's the point of asking yourself questions outside a real context?

ALBERTO: My character is placed in a real context, Bill.

BILL: But it's a unique context. And you want others to identify with him and to learn from his experience.

ALBERTO: Of course.

BILL: Your book is, and will always be, ink and paper. And the experience of reading it will be the experience of reading it. Nothing else.

ALBERTO: With that type of logic you're denying any validity to any type of literature, including literature that concerns itself with entirely concrete problems. Are you aware of that?

BILL: I realize that. That's why I don't ask myself any longer who I am or who I'm not, and also why I've stopped reading. Alberto, you like to come up with clear answers to questions without answers. I mention that because of what you told me about man changing according to his circumstances. Again, I'm gonna contradict you: I've seen, here in Mexico, your country, Indians who've been deprived of everything, humiliated, whose inheritance has been . . .

ALBERTO: Don't say it: turned into a weaving full of holes. The other day you expressed to me your feelings about what the white man has done to the Indians. It obsesses you, huh?

BILL: Yeah . . .

ALBERTO: Why?

BILL: Let me finish what I was gonna tell you: I've observed that those people never lose their sense of what is right even in the worst situations. I witnessed the interrogation of an Indian farmer, a Cora, in San Blas. He certainly knew who'd set fire to the military headquarters. Even though they tortured him, he didn't open his mouth. They beat him up for an hour, two hours, three hours. They yanked out his fingernails, they hung him by his feet under the burning sun. The Indian cried silently, that's all he did. Finally, they let him go, physically crushed, but with his dignity intact.

ALBERTO:	I'm aware those terrible things happen, but nevertheless . . .
BILL:	You're aware? You would have to witness them!
ALBERTO:	From the beginning you have implied you know my people better than I do.
BILL:	Perhaps I've been closer to your people than you, at least lately. Perhaps the time you don't devote to writing, behind these four walls, you spend with a few intellectuals who also spend the rest of their lives writing enclosed in four walls.
ALBERTO:	What were you doing in San Blas, Bill?
BILL:	What was I doing? I went to Manzanillo on vacation and on the way I stopped in a town where I saw what I just told you. I was living in Mexico City at the time.
ALBERTO:	Are you sure?
BILL:	What do you mean, sure? If you want I can give you my exact address.
ALBERTO:	What were you doing there, in Mexico City?
BILL:	I worked at the U. S. Embassy.
ALBERTO:	At the United States Embassy? And there you were close to the people, in those marble rooms with comfortable armchairs?
BILL:	I lived in a working-class neighborhood; I shopped at the market; I travelled to the provinces during my vacations; I studied Mexican history.
ALBERTO:	What was your position at the United States Embassy?
BILL:	A guard at one of the gates.

ALBERTO: Don't make me laugh. A guard, with your talent?

BILL: For a while I was an office boy.

ALBERTO: Office boy? Yeah. Are you sure you weren't working for the CIA?

BILL: You've got quite an imagination.

ALBERTO: Not really. I can draw conclusions. You were a Marine, you know a lot about my country, you were in Nayarit. No one is allowed to witness torture, much less a foreigner, unless the foreigner . . .

BILL: What?

ALBERTO: You worked as a technical advisor to the Mexican Army.

BILL: That's not true.

ALBERTO: I believe it is, and if I'm wrong, I'm not that far off. You were in my country training murderers of the people.

BILL: I was an English teacher.

ALBERTO: Fuck you! You trained murderers of my people.

Bill runs out. Rosa gets up to follow him, but Alberto stops her at the doorway.

ALBERTO: Wait. What I said must be true. That *gringo* . . .

Rosa exits behind Bill.

SCENE VII

Bill goes upstairs. Rosa, at the foot of the steps, calls him.

ROSA: Bill.

BILL:	Don't you realize the world is falling apart? Breaking down like the sky and the sea in a storm. What's the point of talking in the midst of a storm, with the sky and the sea collapsing together and you in the middle? Yet he writes poetry to the sea. (*He spits.*) Poetry from his house on the coast. (*He spits.*)
ROSA:	Calm down, Bill.
BILL:	I don't know how he can do it. I struggled like a bastard to follow the logic of the conversation. Only because of you, Rosa. To show you I can behave, that I can pretend to be logical.
ROSA:	He treated you as an equal.
BILL:	But we're not equal. I pretend to be logical. He suffers from too much logic.
ROSA:	He told you you were intelligent.
BILL:	Logic blinds him. It blinds him. I swear I'm not a CIA agent.

Rosa smiles at him. She gets close to him. She caresses his hair.

BILL:	The sea calms him down. (*He spits.*) The world is a weaving full of holes. The holes get larger each time. The whole world will end up as a single, black hole. Hope he finishes his novel before then. (*He smiles.*)

Rosa smiles. Bill gets angry when he sees her.

BILL:	I'm leaving. I'll paint the front of the house and then leave. I'm not a military advisor, but if he believes it, I'll leave.
ROSA:	Where to, Bill?

Bill looks at her confused. He seems to be on the verge of crying, but he recovers and continues talking even more angrily.

BILL: His turn will come. He'll be writing when the guerrilla jumps through the window and points his gun at his temple. "Wait a minute," your husband will say: I'm in the middle of the most thrilling part of the chapter. The main character is facing the sea and he's asking himself: "Is there a God? Does God exist?" (*He laughs.*) But the guerrilla knows that if God exists, God's too busy to answer stupid questions. Bang. Goodbye, goodbye, dear Alberto. There where you sink, you'll finally have silence. (*He laughs.*)

Rosa laughs. Bill becomes furious.

BILL: Why are you laughing? Do you think I'm talking nonsense? Doesn't your husband want peace? Isn't he nuts for wanting peace in this world? Shut up world, the writer needs absolute silence to write. Ready, aim, fire. They're giving that order everywhere. Somewhere every minute. (*He pushes Rosa aside and presses her against the wall.*) Women and men up against the wall! Ready, aim, fire. (*He mimics the action of shooting her with a machine gun.*)

Rosa is dumfounded by the liveliness with which Bill mimics the execution. Bill laughs and goes up to his room.

BILL: His turn will come. No one will be exempted. No one. The sea calms him down. Fool. The sea. I'll paint the front of the house and then I'll leave, Rosa. Rosa? She's gone. She went to him. God doesn't have time to answer stupid questions. (*He looks down from the top of the stairs.*) Rosa? If I could at least break down once and for all . . . The thinner. (*In the corner, among the equipment he finds a small bottle. He removes the cap and, sitting on the floor, he inhales.*)

Light diminishes and brightens in the study where Alberto is thinking outloud.

ALBERTO: Sometimes I fear I only write . . . to start spinning my thoughts outside of me. And I spin them with only enough force to be able to give them at least the weight of the paper that receives them. Shut up, Alberto. The voice is more fleeting. (*He bends over the typewriter; he types while reading.*) I only write . . . I only write . . . I only write . . . I only write . . .

His voice fades away and Bill's returns between his inhalations of thinner.

BILL: The sea calms him down. He's never been in a storm. He's never seen an execution. Huh! The bodies falling down. The sea calms him down. Huh! The sea is a savage mouth. A mouth full of anger. Eat him up. Eat him up. Eat him up.

The light becomes dimmer. It is replaced by a bluish light. A guard and a prisoner enter as dreamlike figures. The role of the prisoner should be performed by Alberto. Bill gets up slowly while the guard sits the prisoner in a chair, under a lamp hanging from the ceiling, and ties him up. The lamp is turned on and gradually its light becomes as intense as the ones used during interrogations. The guard leaves. Bill slaps the prisoner with force, laughing. But soon his pleasure is ended by fatigue and the pounding becomes monotonous, routine. The door opens and the lieutenant appears at the doorway. His shadow falls on Bill. Bill stands at attention.

SCENE VIII

LIEUTENANT: He hasn't talked yet?

BILL: No, sir.

LIEUTENANT: You mean you've been at it all night?

BILL: Yes, sir.

LIEUTENANT: Well, keep on.

BILL: Yes, sir.

LIEUTENANT: Until he talks.

BILL: Yes, sir. Sir . . . maybe he won't talk at all.

LIEUTENANT: Bull shit. Every man has his limit.

BILL: Yes, sir.

The lieutenant leaves. Bill continues slapping him almost effortlessly. His blows become fewer and softer until they turn into mere pats on the prisoner's cheeks.

BILL: Speak. Please . . . Please . . . Please . . .

The lights become dimmer until it is dark on stage.

SCENE IX

In the study. Rosa is talking to Alberto. He seems impatient.

ROSA: He has fallen apart. He wants to leave. I asked him not to go. I explained to him he hurt your feelings. You have worked so hard on the novel and it was insensitive on his part . . . He wants to leave, Alberto, and he doesn't know where to go. He doesn't have a place he can call his own. Even now in his country, he feels threatened. It isn't fair. He went to Vietnam believing he was defending his country.

ALBERTO: Who threatens him? He's trying to win your sympathy. Do you think out on the streets they shout as he passes by: "Marine"? He should let his hair grow long and no one will suspect his past.

ROSA: But the mass media threatens him. He's hypersensitive, don't you realize? If you believe what you told me, that you are interested in the human condition, independent of . . .

ALBERTO: (*Interrupting her.*) I know what you're thinking. It's true: I'm interested in the human condition independent of . . . Let's stop talking in abstractions: I forgive Bill even though he doesn't like my novel.

ROSA: What do you mean, you forgive him? You also hurt
                         his feelings.

ALBERTO: Let him stay if he wants to. I'm even going to try to
                         forget my suspicions regarding his activities in
                         Mexico.

ROSA: Will you go and talk to him?

ALBERTO: Me? (*He picks up his notebook and a pen.*) I have to jot
                         down some notes for the next chapter. You liked
                         what I read, didn't you? You told me it was the best
                         I have written. It's true. But perhaps I could
                         improve it, I could polish certain rough spots in the
                         language.

Rosa moves towards the door.

ALBERTO: Tell him I want him to stay, please. I'm grateful for
                         his help, the way in which he keeps you company,
                         and how he looks after the baby. Tell him I like
                         him. Tell him I got carried away with my
                         assumptions. If he says he simply was a guard at
                         the embassy, I'll take his word for it. (*Rosa opens the
                         door ready to leave.*) Tell him that even though I was
                         hurt by what he said about my novel, I appreciate
                         his opinion because he's intelligent.

ROSA: Is that all?

ALBERTO: Perhaps when I finish the next chapter I will take a
                         break. Would you like to go dancing next . . . (*Rosa
                         leaves.*) Bitch.

Darkness.

*In the study Alberto is putting some papers in order. Bill enters,
crestfallen. Alberto listens without interrupting his work.*

BILL: Alberto, I came to tell you . . . I couldn't before . . .
                         you didn't give me a chance . . . I don't think as fast
                         as you do, I get confused . . . I'm . . . I was just a grunt
                         in Vietnam. What I told you about the Coras in
                         Nayarit . . . I was never in Nayarit. What I told you

about a man who in spite of torture never betrayed . . . was never disloyal . . . happened in Vietnam, not in Mexico. In Mexico, like I told you, I was a guard at the U.S. Embassy. I took applications, carried messages . . . After Vietnam I felt torn up inside. And yeah, you're right: I don't know anything about your country first hand. I shouldn't argue with lies. Everything I know about the Indians I read. I was very lonely in Mexico City, and I read a lot. Nahuatl poetry, have you read Nahuatl poetry?

Alberto stops putting his papers in order. He looks at Bill straight in the eye. He lights a cigarette.

BILL: (*Shouting.*) You don't believe me, do you? Say it once and for all. You're a liar, Bill. (*He calms down.*) Forgive me. Will you forgive me?

Alberto remains silent. Bill cannot sustain his stare, he lowers his eyes, and continues:

BILL: When they discovered what you call my "talents" at the embassy they wanted to promote me, so I quit. I worked as an English teacher in an academy. I wanted a peaceful life, without worries, without failures or successes, peaceful . . . Three or four hours of class a day, meals at a cheap restaurant, reading in the afternoons, a little television before going to bed . . . cartoons, you know? (*He laughs like a child.*) Cartoons in order not to think, so I could go to bed like a zombie. For the last few years that was my routine.

ALBERTO: You are, let's say, a dull man.

BILL: Yeah . . .

ALBERTO: Shy. Insecure. Despicable. No one could envy you anything or demand anything from you. You don't bother anyone. You have freed yourself from the competitive world. You don't owe anyone anything and no one owes you anything. You don't run the risk of being threatened.

BILL: Do you really understand me?

ALBERTO: You arrived in Puerto Vallarta on a U.S. Navy ship.
                    You, Bill, are a liar.

        Pause.

BILL: Wait. Let me organize my thoughts . . . That's not
                    true, either. Your wife believed right from the
                    beginning I was a Marine, that I arrived on a ship
                    and . . . I didn't set her straight, first because I
                    assumed it didn't matter to her as long as I fixed
                    the roof and then, when I started . . . a friendship
                    with her . . . because to tell her about my problem
                    didn't matter, how can I put it . . . ? It doesn't
                    matter if my problem is whether to rejoin the navy
                    or the Marines, you see? It doesn't matter whether
                    I was a Marine or a private in Vietnam, whether or
                    not I arrived in Puerto Vallarta on a ship. When I
                    arrived here, it didn't matter. If she . . . if you
                    understood my problem, why should I be so exact
                    when telling the reasons for it? You believe me
                    now? After Vietnam I spent half a year in the States
                    at my mother's house and I couldn't stand it. I
                    came back to a country that didn't want me, that
                    felt ashamed of me, that made fun of me . . . I
                    realized that to forget Vietnam I had to get out of
                    there. Daily on TV, in the newspapers, in
                    conversations: "Was it a fair war or wasn't it?"
                    They told us it was moral but was it moral? How
                    many things did they do they didn't tell us about?"
                    They talk about us, the GIs, as if we were
                    foreigners . . . We were the ones who'd lost the war.
                    Because, do you know what really bothers the
                    gringos? To have lost the war. That's why they
                    neglect us. We lost, they didn't. The most
                    important thing for them is to be winners, winners,
                    wiiiin . . . (*He laughs.*) I wanted a quiet life without
                    successes or failures. I came to Mexico. I didn't
                    accept the promotion at the embassy. I'm boring
                    you. I'm a dull guy. Inocuous. You said it yourself:
                    despicable. Who wants to paint a picture of a guy
                    like me? My stories don't interest you. They don't

impress you as hot topics for a novel. I'm a loser. I repeat everything ten times. I'll leave you alone, now. You wanna write a novel about a guy who ponders metaphysical questions. I killed the animal in me, I didn't feed him, I turned my back on the struggle, there are no sacrifices left for the animal in me nor will there ever be. I'm leaving now. I arrived in Puerto Vallarta by bus, from Mexico City. Too bad, if I were a Marine or a CIA agent you'd be interested in doing a composite sketch of me.

ALBERTO: I would draw a composite sketch of you to denounce you. I prefer you to be who you are.

BILL: But I bore you.

ALBERTO: You don't bore me.

BILL: (*Excited.*) I met the Marines in a restaurant. They invited me to this bar. I liked those noisy guys, anxious to have as much fun as possible while they were on leave. We drank. We talked. I told them what I felt, that I felt like an alien in the States, an undesirable alien, and in fact, in Mexico I was a foreigner, as you were right in pointing out, an undesirable foreigner. They advised me to rejoin the army, this time as a volunteer. The pay's good and with a little plotting I could end up stationed in West Germany, among people like me. I liked the idea. I was drunk. I even believed my true country was the U.S. Army, far from the States. But while I was becoming sober and getting a hangover . . . I got upset, do you understand? It upset me to realize what my choices were, to realize I was still searching for a place where my body wouldn't bother anybody. I walked real fast along the streets almost running, stepping forcefully, stepping as if I wanted to sink into the ground, disappear . . . The sun came up. The streets started getting crowded. I followed the crowd. I arrived at the market . . . I saw your wife, Rosa, among the people, with the baby in her arms, asleep, calm, warm . . . (*As if suddenly coming out of a dream.*) But these days in your home have helped me think things over and I've made a decision: I'm gonna enlist. Today, this evening, I'm going to town to mail my application. I'm going back to the Navy, right? It's the most sensible thing to do. I could have left without any explanations, but . . . you've been very good to me. You and your wife. You've allowed me to live in your house for free. You've fed me. You've given me everything free, free. That's why I wanted to give you an explanation.

ALBERTO: It hasn't been free, Bill. We haven't given you anything for free.

BILL: Yes, everything's been free.

ALBERTO: You earned it with your work. You don't owe us anything.

BILL: You've given me everything free.

ALBERTO: But, what do you mean free? I even feel like we've exploited you. The cost of the food you ate and the shelter you received is not enough to pay for what you did. You worked from dawn to dusk, man.

BILL: It's been free.

Rosa enters from the bedroom. She listens to the conversation.

ALBERTO: Do you know how much a handyman would have charged?

BILL: Free.

ALBERTO: No way. Tell me how much I owe you. (*He takes out his wallet.*)

BILL: Free, what you've given me, has been free.

ALBERTO: But Bill.

ROSA:	Free, Bill, we've given it to you for free.
ALBERTO:	Rosa!
ROSA:	Stay out of this, will you? Free, Bill.
BILL:	That's right, isn't it? Everything was free.
ROSA:	Everything.
BILL:	Free.
ROSA:	Free.
BILL:	Thank you . . . thank you very much. I'll go to town tonight.
ROSA:	No Bill, you will not mail that application. Right Alberto? We're not going to allow it, are we?
ALBERTO:	No, of course not. I have a great idea. You stay here with the baby and Rosa and I will go to town and enjoy ourselves at a nightclub. On the way we'll mail your letter.

Bill runs out. Alberto stops Rosa who was going after Bill.

ALBERTO:	What did I do wrong this time?

Rosa frees herself and exits behind Bill. Alberto mumbles:

ALBERTO:	Bitch . . .

SCENE X

Alberto sits at his desk trying to concentrate. After a while, showing his irritation at his inability to work, he gives up and goes to the bedroom. Simultaneously, on the terrace, Bill and Rosa have fallen asleep in the position of the Pietá—he is lying on her lap. The lights have been dimmed to almost total darkness when Bill stands up and stealthily goes to the bedroom. He comes out of the room with the baby in his arms and walks nervously to the beach. Rosa wakes up startled. She calls Bill, increasingly worried. She looks for him in his room, in the study, and finally, in the bedroom. She realizes the baby is not in his crib. She runs toward the beach, terribly excited. The sound of the waves of a stormy sea is distorted to the point of sounding like two choruses.

CHORUS 1:   For your affections . . .

CHORUS 2:   For your imperfections . . .

CHORUS 1:   For your affections . . .

CHORUS 2:   For your imperfections . . .

Etcetera.

SCENE XI

The light becomes brighter; the day is breaking. Alberto leaves the bedroom and starts writing. At the beginning, when the light is subdued, he turns on the lamp. Then, when the light becomes more intense, he turns it off.

Rosa comes out of the bedroom. She is obviously distressed.

ROSA: Alberto, the baby. He's not in his crib.

Alberto shows his annoyance. He speaks harshly. His speech is slurred.

ALBERTO: Bill took him out to the beach.

ROSA: Did you let him take him?

ALBERTO: At least you could say good morning. He took him
                 so you could keep on sleeping and I could have
                 silence. Obviously, it didn't last long. (*He gets up
                 and goes to the kitchen. Even though Rosa has run
                 toward the beach, he keeps talking.*) I'm gonna make
                 some coffee. Do you want some?

                 (*Pause.*) The chapter isn't going that well. I have
                 problems. I'm stuck with the plot. The damn
                 character doesn't know what to do. He stands on the

seashore. He speaks aloud: "All my beliefs are replaceable," he says. "Like the waves, the beliefs of one generation come, saturate the sand, and leave. Another wave comes. And goes. And another one comes. Aren't there any absolute beliefs?" And then he realizes that the sound of the sea is erasing his words as soon as they hit the air. The more man expresses himself, the more he turns into himself and makes intelligible the beliefs on which he bases his being, the less he believes in them. The intellect dissolves all it reaches. As does the air with words. Even so it is necessary to speak. To listen to oneself. To reckon with oneself. To be heard. To be recognized. Of course. That's it. He would have to tell someone what he is thinking. Not the sea. The sea doesn't stop to listen. Do you understand? Okay. Okay, I've untangled myself. Your coffee's ready, Rosa. Two teaspoons of sugar? I'll have to write it now. (*He exits with two cups of coffee.*) When you come out of the bedroom drink it. I'll leave it on my desk. Rosa? Did you go back to sleep? (*He looks into the bedroom.*) Rosa, sweetheart? (*He goes upstairs. He shouts.*) You left me talking to myself! (*He opens the door to Bill's room.*) Shit! (*He opens the other door.*) Bitch! (*He kicks the door.*) It burns me up to talk to myself. It burns me up to have my words disappear into thin air! Are you listening, Rosa? (*His voice is heard echoing through the empty house.*) Bitch! (*He goes downstairs with such anger that upon entering the room he trips over a piece of furniture. He kicks it. He kicks the waste basket. He kicks the desk. The coffee spills. He runs to save his manuscript. He finally sits down to write.*)

SCENE XII

Rosa, with the baby in her arms, and Bill laughing. They stop laughing when they get closer to where Alberto is working. They tiptoe so as not to distract him. They seem to fear being seen. Alberto sees them out of the corner of his eye.

ALBERTO: Why so happy?

Rosa and Bill stop frightened.

ROSA:	We were talking about the castle. Bill built a sand castle.
ALBERTO:	You don't say.
ROSA:	A beautiful castle. With towers and everything. A door made out of sticks. A wall and then a moat around it. To protect it from the enemy, you know?
ALBERTO:	Marvelous!
ROSA:	And he made a garden inside the wall with palm leaves.
ALBERTO:	With palm leaves!
ROSA:	I was telling him he has a gift for architecture.
ALBERTO:	No doubt, no doubt. Would you like to be an architect, Bill, I mean, when you grow up? (*Pause.*) I'm joking, I'm sorry if I offended you.

Bill lowers his head. He leaves, crestfallen, and goes up to his room slowly. Rosa looks at Alberto reproachfully. She goes toward the door.

ALBERTO:	Rosa, wait. I want to talk to you.
ROSA:	What do you want?
ALBERTO:	I don't like for you to spend so much time with the *gringo*. The two of you become childish. You talk to him as if he were a child.
ROSA:	He is like a child, don't you realize? He's learning to play, to enjoy life. (*She leaves.*)

SCENE XIII

Alberto follows Rosa to the stairs.

ALBERTO:	Rosa.

ROSA:	What do you want?
ALBERTO:	I finished another chapter.
ROSA:	Good.
ALBERTO:	Do you want me to read it to you?
ROSA:	Do you want me to hear it?
ALBERTO:	Me? (*Annoyed.*) If you're not interested, forget it.
ROSA:	Fine. (*She goes up two steps.*)
ALBERTO:	Rosa.
ROSA:	What?
ALBERTO:	Don't you want to hear it? It's good, I think.
ROSA:	Do you want me to hear it?
ALBERTO:	What's wrong?
ROSA:	God, why is it so difficult for you to admit you need to read it to me?
ALBERTO:	I don't need anything. The chapter's already written. It doesn't matter if you hear it.
ROSA:	Okay. (*She goes up two steps.*)
ALBERTO:	Rosa! It's our novel, yours and mine.
ROSA:	How strange! I don't recall having written a single line. All I remember is having washed diapers, floors, and walls. If it weren't for Bill I would've gone months without talking to a man. Without receiving a caress.
ALBERTO:	(*Upset.*) You don't mean you and Bill . . .
ROSA:	It's none of your business!

ALBERTO: What do you mean none of my business. If the two of you are lovers . . .

ROSA: Bill caresses me as if I were his mother. He couldn't do more than that even though, for me, a lover would be a good pastime.

ALBERTO: Rosa . . . You know that when I'm writing I can't waste my energy on other matters. But if you want . . .

ROSA: I'm tired. (*She goes up two steps.*)

Bill's voice can be heard from his room.

BILL: Rosa? Rosa.

ALBERTO: Rosa!

BILL: The baby . . .

ALBERTO: I forbid you to go with the *gringo*!

BILL: The baby is . . .

ALBERTO: It's incredible that in my own house a stranger gets more attention than I. From my own wife.

BILL: Rosa!

The baby's cry can be heard. Bill comes out to the landing of the staircase.

BILL: He's screaming!

ALBERTO: Bitch.

Rosa turns to see Alberto with a strangely calmed expression.

ROSA: Repeat it.

ALBERTO: What?

ROSA: That. Bitch.

ALBERTO: It's just an expression.

BILL: What do I do? With the baby?

Rosa goes downstairs in silence.

ALBERTO: Aren't you going to look after the child?

ROSA: Which of the three? (*She laughs softly. She keeps going down the stairs. The crying becomes more intense. Before leaving for the beach, Rosa mumbles:*) Bitch, yes!

ALBERTO: Damn *gringo*, it's all your fault. She's tired of looking after you on top of having to take care of the baby.

BILL: She said, which of the three children? You're a child, too. The baby sleeps almost all day, he wakes up wanting to be nursed. You write and wake up wanting applause.

ALBERTO: I won't let you . . . (*He goes to the stairs until he is face to face with him.*) Get out of here, Bill. Get out of my house.

BILL: Let's ask Rosa if she wants me to leave.

ALBERTO: Very tough, huh, white boy? (*He shoves him into the room.*) Listen carefully. Hear this: you're not going to leave here until you tell me who you are. Sit down. This time, I'm going to make a composite sketch of you. And maybe I'll give it to the police, do you understand? At least so that Rosa realizes who she's been spoiling like a child.

Bill stands up.

BILL: Rosa!

ALBERTO: Sit down! (*He walks around him.*) Are you a Marine, Bill? an English teacher? a tourist? an employee at the American Embassy? a CIA agent? a psychopath? a schizophrenic? Who the hell are you, Bill?

BILL: The baby . . .

ALBERTO: The baby will stop crying by himself. Sit down!

BILL: I didn't go to Vietnam. When I got the draft notice,
                  the idea made me sick, it broke me down. I
                  couldn't go against my mother, but it scared me. I
                  spent the war years in a psychiatric hospital in
                  Quebec. I only got out a month ago . . .

Alberto is disconcerted. Then he stares attentively at Bill.

ALBERTO: I don't believe anything you say any more. Not
                  even that you're crazy.

BILL: I don't know who I am. I don't remember. I don't
                  wanna remember. Now I'm good. Rosa appreciates
                  me. I'm her handyman.

ALBERTO: Bill . . . (*He points to Bill's crotch.*) Have you just wet
                  your pants to convince me you are an inoffensive
                  child? You are no longer a child, Bill. You should
                  accept responsibility for what you've done. (*He
                  laughs. Suddenly, he threatens him aggressively.*) I'm
                  going to take you to the police so they can tell me
                  who you are.

BILL: I don't have documents. They'll kick me out of the
                  country. Back to the States. Don't take me to the
                  police.

ALBERTO: Yes, yes. That's where we're going, to find out once
                  and for all who you are.

BILL: Please. I don't wanna go back.

ALBERTO: Come on, get up. Get up, Bill, get up.

*Bill makes a pleading gesture. Some time goes by until Alberto becomes
exasperated.*

ALBERTO: Come on, get up.

*Bill closes his eyes and becomes so tense he starts shaking. He bends
over. Suddenly he jumps from the chair. He lands on one foot and with*

the other he kicks Alberto on the jaw. Alberto is propelled backward and crashes against the wall. Slowly he slides to the floor, lifeless. Then Rosa's steps are heard at the foot of the stairs. She talks as she gradually climbs the stairs, while Bill approaches Alberto's body; he lifts it and places it astride the chair. Bill slaps Alberto's face, forcefully at first, then softly, powerlessly, thus reenacting the last image of the scene in which Bill tortures the prisoner of war.

ROSA: Bill. Alberto.

BILL: Speak. Please.

ROSA: Did my baby go to sleep?

BILL: Please . . . Please . . .

ROSA: Did he go to sleep?

BILL: Please.

ROSA: Bill? Alberto?

BILL: Please.

Before Rosa turns the doorknob, it gets dark.

Notes

1. For permission to stage the play, the author must be contacted directly: Avenida México 85, 6o piso, Colonia La Condesa, 06100 México, D.F.

2. While Rosa is referring to the roof, which is *techo* in Spanish, Alberto refers to the *cielo*, which means both ceiling and sky.

Myrna Casas (Puerto Rico, 1934)—dramatist, director, actress, and stage and costume designer—belongs to the "sixties generation" along with Luis Rafael Sánchez and Gerard Paul Marín. One of the main concerns of these writers is the question of national identity.[1]

In one of her first plays, *Eugenia Victoria Herrera* (1964), Casas contemplates the issue of national identity through the emphasis placed on the value of patrimony and the importance of lineage. *Cristal roto en el tiempo* (Glass Broken in Time, 1961), unfolds the loss of traditional values and the constant anxiety about money to reflect the Puerto Rican reality. During this same period, Casas wrote two absurd plays: *Absurdos en soledad* (Absurdities in Solitude, 1963) and *La trampa* (The Trap, 1964). In addition to thematizing the inability of human beings to communicate, *Absurdos en soledad* examines the relationship between fiction and reality and highlights the use of drama to stage the search for a personal and national identity. *La trampa* presents two married couples from two different generations who find themselves trapped by the institution of matrimony. Through situations that oscillate from the real to the absurd, Casas portrays the tedium and disillusionment of life. The only character with enough courage to escape her condition of entrapment is the young bride. The men, on the other hand, assume passive roles and live in fear of the women's rebellion.

Casas continues the absurdist line in *Tres* (Three, 1974), but in addition criticizes specific social problems. Her piercing criticism is directed against bureaucracy, materialism, and an advanced technology that has interfered with the ecological system.

In the seventies, Casas discontinues the absurdist vein and moves toward direct confrontation of sociopolitical issues.[2] Her most recent play, *El gran circo Eukraniano* (The Great USkrainian Circus, 1986), combines social criticism with a renewed interest in the question of identity. Casas avoids didacticism by using humor and metatheatrical techniques that involve the audience in the creative process.

Notes

1. Alvin Joaquín Figueroa calls this concern for national identity *"el unitemario puertorriqueño"* (Puerto Rico's only theme) (9).

2. *Cuarenta años después* (Forty Years Later, 1975) and *No todas lo tienen* (Not All of Them Have It, 1975) are two plays from this period.

The Great USkrainian Circus

BY MYRNA CASAS[1]

Translated from *El gran circo Eukraniano*
by Teresa Cajiao Salas and Margarita Vargas

Act I

Circus music.

GABRIELA JOSÉ:	(*Entering from the aisle.*) Hello! . . . Welcome to the Great . . . USkrainian Circus!
ALINA:	Ukrainian.
GABRIELA JOSÉ:	USkrainian.
ALINA:	It's Ukrainian, like Ukraine, Constitutional Republic of the Soviet Union, rich in agriculture . . .
GABRIELA JOSÉ:	Who are you, a geography teacher? Listen young lady, this circus has nothing to do with the Soviet Union.
ALINA:	Then, why did you call it that?
GABRIELA JOSÉ:	Because I felt like it. Since when do you need permission to give a circus a name? And what about you, what's yours?
ALINA:	Alina.
GABRIELA JOSÉ:	Who gave you that name?
ALINA:	I did.
GABRIELA JOSÉ:	Oh, you were born speaking, huh? Fantastic! Then you belong in the circus.
ALINA:	No, wait a minute! My mother named me Amaryllis after a character in a soap she was watching at the time. But kids in school would call me Amamelis, that's witch hazel in Spanish, you know. When I turned twenty-one I went to a lawyer and said, "I want to change my name to Alina, after a character in this great soap I'm watching."
GABRIELA JOSÉ:	How romantic!

ALINA:	Isn't it, though?
GABRIELA JOSÉ:	Wait, wait . . . you're interrupting the show which is about to begin. Now you know this circus is called USkrainian because I liked the name. Excuse me, the audience is waiting, so go back to your seat. Sandro, hurry up, it's getting late.
SANDRO:	(*Entering from the aisle carrying a suitcase and three stools.*) I'm coming, I'm coming. This is all very heavy. I need an assistant.
GABRIELA JOSÉ:	We don't have money for that. Let Igor help you.
SANDRO:	He's eating.
GABRIELA JOSÉ:	Again?
SANDRO:	He took off with Alejandra to a place called Don Goyo's little bar.
GABRIELA JOSÉ:	That's all we need. Now God only knows when we'll be able to start.
SANDRO:	Don't worry. Besides, Nené isn't here yet.
GABRIELA JOSÉ:	He should be here any minute. Takes time to do what he does.
SANDRO:	You always make excuses for him.
GABRIELA JOSÉ:	I'm not making excuses for him. He knows how to do his job.
SANDRO:	I used to know, too.
GABRIELA JOSÉ:	Please don't start.
SANDRO:	I'm not starting anything. I'm finishing it. Where were you last night?
GABRIELA JOSÉ:	In my room, sleeping.
SANDRO:	I knocked on your door. You didn't open.

GABRIELA JOSÉ: I was sound asleep with the air conditioner on; it's been years since I enjoyed that. This must be a very rich country. Every room is air-conditioned.

SANDRO: Couldn't get another hotel. But we'll have to move tomorrow. This one's too expensive.

GABRIELA JOSÉ: I refuse to move.

SANDRO: But we don't have enough money to pay for a second night. Besides, don't change the subject.

GABRIELA JOSÉ: What subject?

SANDRO: The only one that matters, you and I.

GABRIELA JOSÉ: That was over a long time ago.

SANDRO: Don't get me going. Since Nené came into this circus, you won't have anything to do with me.

GABRIELA JOSÉ: Don't be silly. He could be my son. Reminds me a lot of Ricardo. Wonder where he's now.

SANDRO: Where else? In that other circus, with his father. That's the way you wanted it.

GABRIELA JOSÉ: That was a grand circus, real modern, real sleek. Ricardo must be happy away from this rat hole, as he used to call it. I couldn't be selfish, I had to let him go.

SANDRO: He's the selfish one. He should have stopped to think of all you sacrificed for him.

GABRIELA JOSÉ: What else could I do? That's how we mothers are.

SANDRO: That sounds like a line in a soap or a play.

GABRIELA JOSÉ: Maybe I heard it on TV or at the theater. Wait, what was that play we got free tickets for? Had to do with marriage.

SANDRO:	Right, "Marriage Italian Style."
GABRIELA JOSÉ:	That's it. Beautiful play. Had a little of everything, laughter, tears, and more laughter. Wish I was an actress.
SANDRO:	If you hate the circus, why do you stay in it?
GABRIELA JOSÉ:	What else can I do? I was born in the circus, have worked my whole life in one and now I own one, a rickety one at that. But it's mine and I'm happy with it. And I wish everyone who sees our performances will enjoy them and will also be happy. Oh well, let's get to work. The rest of the company will be arriving soon and you know I like to start on time.
SANDRO:	(*Watching her leave.*) If only she knew how much I care for her. I couldn't be like that money-minded son of hers. I'd never leave her.
CÓSIMA:	(*Who has been listening sitting among the audience. Getting up.*) That's right. Exactly like a soap opera. I know the two of them quite well. Like her, I'd rather do something else.
SANDRO:	Yeah, but you don't know how to . . .
CÓSIMA:	Yes I do.
SANDRO:	Well . . .
CÓSIMA:	You don't believe me, do you? In my day I was a top executive. It's just that I got bored and . . .
SANDRO:	Yeah, yeah, I've heard that story before.
CÓSIMA:	Just like yours and Gabriela José's. No use whining.
SANDRO:	Who's whining?
CÓSIMA:	Oh, come on, Sandro. She doesn't love you anymore. Leave her alone.

SANDRO:	Yes, but only since Nené joined us.
CÓSIMA:	Come off it. She doesn't love you and that's that.
SANDRO:	I'll make her love me again. Some day she'll realize I've always been faithful to this circus. I used to be the one who talked to people when we came into town. Sometimes it took me two or three hours to find out what was going on. I'd talk to the guy at the drugstore, the butcher, and the shoe shine boys. I'd find everything out. I'd come back with the best description of whatever town we visited. Sometimes I'd sit in the town square and talk to the old people sitting in the benches. They know everything, you see. Other times, well, I'd go into an office with any old excuse. Then to the most popular restaurant. I'd even sneak into private clubs where everyone told stories that stayed here, inside this little head . . .
CÓSIMA:	You mean, fat head.
SANDRO:	Okay, I've got a big head. They say those of us with big heads have more brains. Yes siree, nothing escaped me. I listened to all the politicians, the evangelists, the . . .
CÓSIMA:	Hold it, hold it. You know Gabriela José wants none of that. No politics, no religion.
SANDRO:	All right, all right, you don't have to remind me. But you can't deny I was the best listener of all.
CÓSIMA:	You were the best but now Nené does that and you have to resign yourself with being circus manager. One must resign oneself with whatever life brings. Look at me, I was once a top executive and . . .
ALEJANDRA:	(*Entering.*) And you had an office with such an expensive rug . . . It was so plush it came up to one's knees. I can't imagine how everyone got around in that office. Jumping from one place to another, I guess.

CÓSIMA:	Jumping?
ALEJANDRA:	Sure, if the rug reached up to the knees, people had to get around like kangaroos, jumping.
CÓSIMA:	Aren't you funny!
IGOR:	Come on, girls, stop that.
SANDRO:	Right. Come on, let's get on with the show.
ALEJANDRA:	How can we start? Nené's not here yet.
SANDRO:	He left early. I would've finished by now.
CÓSIMA:	Maybe this is a complicated country.
ALEJANDRA:	Maybe he took a powder.
IGOR:	Took a powder? What powder?
ALINA:	I know what she means.
ALEJANDRA:	What was that?
ALINA:	That means escaping, it means . . .
IGOR:	I only asked . . .
ALINA:	And I . . .
CÓSIMA:	Listen, shut up and sit down. Take a powder, take a powder. He gets the best salary in this circus . . .
IGOR:	Well, I don't envy him his job. Running all over town to find out how things are. Remembering everything and then explaining it to us in detail. Don't envy him, I don't. It isn't easy, no . . .
SANDRO:	I did it better than he does.
ALEJANDRA:	What did you do better?

IGOR:	Alejandra!
ALEJANDRA:	I didn't say anything, I didn't say anything.
SANDRO:	Look, one of these days I'm going to . . .
IGOR:	You're going to what . . .
CÓSIMA:	Oh, come one, we just got here and . . . (*She separates them.*) Gabriela!
GABRIELA JOSÉ:	What is it? Oh, please, don't start fighting. Shame on you. We have a show to do.
SANDRO:	Nené's not here. We can't start without him.
CÓSIMA:	Of course we can. I can do the first number.
ALEJANDRA:	You don't know the city, the people. How can you start?
CÓSIMA:	I met this woman on the plane. She was sitting next to me and said . . . "Hey, I'm the one who calls out the numbers. Yes, honey, the numbers when we play Bingo. At the home, where I go . . . in Hartfor, Conerico. You know where Conerico is? A bit further up from New Yol. Amparo Mercado Torres is my name, your servant. They treat me real nice . . . What she say, what she say? The young lady? . . . English? No, not very good. Oh, she wants me to buckle up. Get all tied up. Okay. What a bother. Okay I'm all tied up. One's always tied to something, isn't one, honey? I'd forgotten about it. Haven't been to the island in so long. Since Santa, my sister, died. She's younger than I am. Was younger. Eighteen, there were eighteen of us. I was the oldest. I had to take care of them all. Well, not all, seven had already died. I raised all of them, yes sir. I was lucky to get work in one of the first factories. And Luis helped me, he was such a good boy. Was born right after Santa. And then my husband. In '51 we went to New Jersy . . . What's he saying, what's he saying? What's the matter

with that captain! We're all buckled up. No thanks, dear, that's not coffee. Honey, don't drink that, it'll kill you! Boy, do I make good coffee. My Vitín likes it hot and steamy, early in the morning, late at night. (*She laughs.*) Sorry, honey. My Quico also liked coffee. He died when he was seventeen. No one came to that funeral. But my Vitolo's was a big success, twenty-three cars. You know? My oldest son, forty-three he was. All his union pals came. Even the boss came. Everybody loved him. Cancer's what he had. Losing a son's the worst thing that can happen to you! You have any kids? No? I still have three. All girls. The youngest is gonna be a nurse. The other two are married. Hey, what's that light say? What's it say, what's it say? Look, up there. What! Fasten our seat belts? Again! But everybody's all buckled up. I'd like to see my old ladies sitting here. The ones I play bingo with. Not one of them would sit still. Can you imagine this plane full of old women playing Bingo. Twenty-two, buckle my shoe, Sweet sixteen, Shitty Fourteen . . . and I'd call out the numbers and they'd jump up and down yelling Bingo, Bingo, Bingo! Holy Mother of God, please forgive me. Well, when Vitín died I went to Hartfor with my daughter Carmela, the second one. I look after her little girl while she's at work. I take her to the kindergarten and I go fetch her. "Gramma, Gramma, I love you!" she says to me. I'd like for her to call me *Abuela*, but what can you do? And Saturdays I go play Bingo at the Home. I like it there. Maybe some day I'll stay. WHEN MY DAUGHTER DOESN'T NEED ME ANYMORE. My sister Guadalupe wants me to stay in Puerto Rico. She wants me to cook for her and those two lazy bums she's got for sons. BUMS! But that's not all, honey. She's a terrible cook! But that's her problem. When I get there, I'm gonna have to start cooking. Pasteles, rice, pigs' feet. She can't cook any of those things. What about you, where are you from? Where? Ohh, that's far away, isn't it? What you gonna do in Puerto Rico? Work! Holy Mother, I don't know anybody who goes to Puerto

Rico to work. Your first time there? Well, it's very pretty. Look, when we get there it's gonna look like heaven upside down. We're gonna get there at night, a little bit of heaven upside down . . .

NENÉ: (*Interrupting.*) I know, I know, I'm late. But, let me tell you, what a complicated country!

CÓSIMA: Don't interrupt me.

NENÉ: But . . .

ALEJANDRA: We were doing our first number.

NENÉ: The first? But I haven't given you the information yet.

SANDRO: You weren't here, so Cósima started to do . . .

GABRIELA JOSÉ: Well, now that Nené's here we can all start. Cósima, are you almost through?

CÓSIMA: I'm through.

IGOR: How can that be? You were right in the middle of your trip.

CÓSIMA: I hate being interrupted.

NENÉ: Sorry, I didn't . . .

IGOR: Come on, Cósima, finish your story.

ALINA: Yes, finish it. Let her finish it.

GABRIELA JOSÉ: We asked her, but she doesn't want to.

CÓSIMA: Why don't you finish it, sweetie, come on up here.

GABRIELA JOSÉ: Cósima!

ALEJANDRA: That's dangerous!

CÓSIMA: No it isn't. If she wants an end to the story, let her finish it.

ALINA: (*After she sits.*) What do I do?

SANDRO: Make something up.

ALINA: Make something up?

GABRIELA JOSÉ: That's what we do here. Everything's made up.

ALINA: That's easy.

IGOR: Well then, welcome to the Great USkrainian Circus, young lady.

ALINA: Well, ahhhhhh. What do I say?

CÓSIMA: Finish my story.

ALINA: Oh, yes, the lady on the airplane.

NENÉ: What lady?

ALEJANDRA: The one who sat next to Cósima.

ALINA: How did it go? Oh, yes, the seat belt, it bothered her.

NENÉ: Seat belt! What seat belt? I sat next to Cósima.

They all catch on and laugh.

ALINA: I don't see what's so funny.

CÓSIMA: Well, we had to start, didn't we? (*More laughter.*)

GABRIELA JOSÉ: Miss, everything here is made up, invented, an invention. Imagined. This is theater.

ALINA: I thought it was a circus.

IGOR: The circus is also theater.

GABRIELA JOSÉ:	This is a special kind of circus. We find out what's going on and then we act it out. In our special way, of course.
ALINA:	But the woman on the plane, she could've existed.
GABRIELA JOSÉ:	She could've. Everything can exist. Especially if we invent it like in the theater.
ALINA:	I don't understand.
SANDRO:	There's nothing to understand. Please go back to your seat.
NENÉ:	She could stay. Maybe later on she'll think of something. What do you say, Gabriela?
GABRIELA JOSÉ:	Maybe later. But now, we've got to get going. What did you find?
NENÉ:	I told you. A very complicated country. Crime, drugs, politics are driving them nuts . . .
GABRIELA JOSÉ:	No politics. We're just passing through.
NENÉ:	Okay. Well, everyone's kind of unhappy about things in general, unemployment . . . a lot of people get these checks . . .
ALEJANDRA:	Checks?
NENÉ:	They send you these checks and you go to the market or supermarket and you buy all you want.
CÓSIMA:	That I like.
GABRIELA JOSÉ:	What else?
NENÉ:	Cars. There are more cars than people because their transportation system doesn't work. The . . . wait a minute, let me look it up. The *guaguas* never arrive on time . . .
CÓSIMA:	The what don't arrive on time?

NENÉ:	The *guaguas*, that's what they call buses. They're never on time and when they do arrive they're packed. And there's no public transportation to visit the island.
ALEJANDRA:	Which island?
NENÉ:	Anything not in the metropolitan area they call "the island." Like it was another country.
IGOR:	Maybe it is.
GABRIELA JOSÉ:	I read in the paper this morning that they're going to do something about public transportation. It's called *aguaguagua*. I guess it's a bus that travels by water.[2]
NENÉ:	That's right. I went into a store to buy this T-shirt and they gave me a token for that *aguaguagua*.
GABRIELA JOSÉ:	Let's see. Nice, but it says here to be used in the year 2000.
NENÉ:	Well, at the store they said that at the rate the construction's going the *aguaguagua* won't be ready till then.
CÓSIMA:	Maybe we'll still be around.

They all laugh.

NENÉ:	Well, let me finish. There are a lot of schools. These people have an obsession about schools. There's one in every corner. Private, public, computer, modeling, beauty, polytechnic schools. An endless number of colleges and universities.
IGOR:	What do they do with so many degrees?
ALEJANDRA:	God only knows!
SANDRO:	Who cares about schools, cars, crime . . .

GABRIELA JOSÉ: These people do, and if they care, we'll improvise on it. Come on, let's get ready. (*To Nené.*) You keep on telling us more backstage.

NENÉ: Wait. There are also a lot of people roaming the streets. They beg, sleep on doorsteps, in the park . . .

CÓSIMA: There's a park?

NENÉ: There are two or three, I think. I'm not sure how many. Didn't have time to see them all.

GABRIELA JOSÉ: Who's roaming the streets?

NENÉ: Men, women, children, too, I think. It seemed to me they didn't have a home.

GABRIELA JOSÉ: That's sad. Well, come on . . . (*She exits.*)

IGOR: (*Staying behind.*) No home. Like us. But, I had one, once.

ALEJANDRA: Igor!

IGOR: Coming! I'm setting up some things on stage. I had a home. A long time ago, in a small town. Don't ask where or which country. It was so long ago I don't even remember the country. But it was a small town. Far from the big city or the big cities. There was one, no, three, no, I think there were five . . . Well, who cares? My mother worked hard, so did my father. There were eleven of us. One day my father disappeared. He couldn't face poverty. Little after that my mother died. Couldn't face poverty either. My two older sisters tried to help, but I knew it was impossible. One of them left with her husband. They went to another country. To look for a better life, ha! I waited till it got dark and I left, too. Sometimes I think I shouldn't have. I worked in the fields and I could buy a few things with what little I made. But I wanted to see what it was like outside that small town. What still hurts me is having left like I did, at night, like a thief in the dark. Maybe I should've gathered all of them and told them I was leaving . . . but it wasn't easy. It isn't easy to look hunger in the eye. My father couldn't, my mother couldn't, neither could I . . .

ALEJANDRA: Igor, what are you telling the audience?

IGOR: (*To the audience.*) Shhh! (*To Alejandra.*) I'm not speaking to them.

ALEJANDRA: As if I didn't know you! (*To the audience.*) Don't believe anything he said. His father was a millionaire. Yes, a millionaire. He kicked him out of the house because he didn't want to study. Didn't want to work in the family business. Wanted to be an opera singer. Ha! An opera singer. And the old man said one day, "Oh, yeah, well get going, go make a living on the road." And on the road he met me.

IGOR: Shut up!

ALEJANDRA: Doesn't like the truth. Nobody does. Come on, Nené's filling us in on everything. We'll be right back.

IGOR: (*To the audience.*) That's a lie. He wasn't a millionaire. He abandoned us.

ALEJANDRA: (*Outside.*) Igor!

IGOR: (*Exiting.*) Coming!

ALINA: (*Getting on stage.*) Hey! (*To the audience.*) What is this? What a strange play. I thought it was supposed to be a circus. You, too, huh? Am I right? Did any of you think it was a play? Well, they're actors and actresses. I'm going to find out what they're doing back there.

Alina goes back stage. Suddenly circus music is heard and she goes back to her seat screaming. They all enter dressed as several different characters. Sandro as a lion and Igor as a gorilla doing pirouettes.

GABRIELA JOSÉ: Ladies and gentlemen, boys and girls, welcome to the great USkrainian circus. House of illusion and truth, invention and certainty. Yes, ladies and gentlemen, going back to a small town tradition, please understand, SMALL town not LITTLE, I quote an adorable old man by the name of Emilio Pasarell who wrote in minute detail the history of our theatrical tastes in a book called Development of Theatrical Taste in Puerto Rico.[3] Well, Don Emilio said that in this Small country, not Little, there is an age old circus tradition which dates back to the last century. So today we visit this beautiful island, bringing you the great USkrainian Circus and its international stars. The unmatched, the incomparable Cósima and Alejandra! (*Both enter.*) Shining stars of the trapeze because once they dazzled audiences with their graceful and nimble movements. They were also dancers (*Cósima dances.*) And singers (*Alejandra sings and walks the tightrope.*) Let's give them a big hand! Thank you, thank you, thank you. Girls, a big smile for this nice audience. And nowww, our beloved animals. Sandro Roskoff, the lion-man or the man-lion, as you wish. (*Sandro gives her flowers.*) Thank you Sandro. And Igor Iconenko, our sweet and melodious orangutan, I mean, gorilla, which is not the same. And last, but not least, our Nené, quick messenger, gatherer of information and illusion. These five artists and I, Gabriela José, make up the great circus family which today brings you this Small town Kaleidoscope or Amber Prism, of tropical shortsightedness of an Island-Metropolis or a Metropolis-Island called the Great USkrainian Circus.

ALINA: (*Coughs.*)

GABRIELA JOSÉ: Oh no! Now she's coughing. Why don't you do that at intermission? Igor, did you bring the cough drops? Give her one. Thank you, Igor. And don't make any noise with the wrapper, that's also distracting.

ALINA: I'm sorry, I was just a little nervous. I wanted to
                     clear my throat.

GABRIELA JOSÉ: So you could interrupt us again, huh? In that case
                     it's better you have a sore throat.

ALINA: No, look, I . . .

GABRIELA JOSÉ: If you keep interrupting, this is going to become a
                     dialogue between us two.

ALINA: I have so many doubts.

GABRIELA JOSÉ: So does everyone on this island. And we have to go
                     on with our show.

*Music. Nené, Cósima, Alejandra go down to the audience. Sandro and
Igor do pirouettes.*

NENÉ: (*Shows a mirror.*) Look, look here and there. You'll
                     see your portrait, maybe you'll see a friend or
                     someone you know, a relative, perhaps.

ALEJANDRA: Recognize yourself. Take a good look at yourself.
                     Look deep into your eyes, your soul, and then
                     maybe you'll see yourself in me, there on the stage.

CÓSIMA: I tell fortunes or perhaps misfortunes. Maybe. Who
                     knows?

GABRIELA JOSÉ: Enough, enough. Let's start the show. Let's see,
                     what will be our first number?

CÓSIMA: I did the first one.

GABRIELA JOSÉ: Fine, the second one, then.

*Igor, without the others seeing him, signals that he already performed
his.*

GABRIELA JOSÉ: Alright, the second.

NENÉ: A test, a test. Just to see if I really understood
                     something about the country.

IGOR:	Something easy.
ALEJANDRA:	Something they might know.
CÓSIMA:	No, that's not fair.
GABRIELA JOSÉ:	Fine, fine, I'll explain. The first, I mean, the second number, illustrates a situation that takes place in many countries. We've done it before. Let's see if it applies here. And now, the second number of the Great USkrainian Circus.

Everyone exits except Cósima, Nené, and Sandro who act the different roles into the following short play.

CÓSIMA:	Hey, listen! Are you going to wait on me? Are you going to? I said, are you going to wait on me or not? I've been here since six A.M.!
SANDRO:	No need to shout! I'm not deaf.
CÓSIMA:	Well, if you paid attention to me, I wouldn't have to shout.
SANDRO:	You're disturbing the peace.
CÓSIMA:	The peace?
SANDRO:	Aha! You know what I'm talking about. All you people pretend you don't understand.
CÓSIMA:	Look, no preaching, please. All I want is for you to wait on me.
SANDRO:	Do you have a number?
CÓSIMA:	What number?
SANDRO:	You have to take a number and wait your turn.
CÓSIMA:	What do you mean?
SANDRO:	I told you not to play dumb. If you don't have a number, no one will wait on you.

CÓSIMA:	Well, if no one tells me . . .
SANDRO:	If no one tells you its' because you're supposed to know.
NENÉ:	I tell you, here you gotta know it all, or else . . .
SANDRO:	Who asked you?
NENÉ:	Me? Nobody, and stop being so rude or I'll report you.
SANDRO:	You don't say? To whom?
NENÉ:	I got connections and some pull.
SANDRO:	If you've got so much pull, why are you waiting here?
NENÉ:	I'm not waiting.
SANDRO:	Well, then, why don't you leave? This is for those who are waiting.
NENÉ:	I don't feel like leaving and I don't feel like waiting. So what are you going to do about it?
SANDRO:	I'm going to call the authorities.
NENÉ:	What the hell, what authorities?
SANDRO:	Watch it!
CÓSIMA:	Ah, for God's sake, just explain this thing about the number.
SANDRO:	What number?
NENÉ:	Yeah, what number?
CÓSIMA:	The number you gotta have.
NENÉ:	Say, you don't know nothing. If you don't know nothing, what are you doing here?

CÓSIMA:	I . . . well . . . I . . .
SANDRO:	Precisely. She's come to disturb the peace. That's it, disturbing the peace.
CÓSIMA:	Ah . . .
NENÉ:	If you're going to disturb the peace, then there's no hope for you, and without a number, you've had it!
CÓSIMA:	But all I want is service!
SANDRO:	Well, well, all she wants is service! Look you, who do you think you are? A congresswoman, the president or what?
CÓSIMA:	I don't think I'm anything like that.
NENÉ:	Ha! Not only does she disturb the peace, she's also ignorant.
SANDRO:	Pull won't do you any good here. If you don't have a number you won't get your turn.
CÓSIMA:	I don't have pull, he's the one with pull.
NENÉ:	Who said? Liar. I don't even know her. You see, you try to help someone and that's what you get. Ungrateful!
CÓSIMA:	Don't call me that. I didn't ask for your help. The only thing I asked for was service.
SANDRO:	Service! This is an office, not a hospital. Have you ever seen anything like this? Some nerve! I don't know how this will end.
NENÉ:	Neither do I.
SANDRO:	Can't do anything with anybody anymore.
NENÉ:	We'll have to kill some people.
CÓSIMA:	Kill! But I . . .

SANDRO:	That's it. Kill a few. Not having a number deserves the death penalty.
CÓSIMA:	We don't have that here.
SANDRO:	Says who?
CÓSIMA:	The law.
SANDRO:	Screw the law.
NENÉ:	What good is the law? Everyone does whatever they want and to hell with the law.
CÓSIMA:	What about the number for your turn?
NENÉ:	What numbers, what turns?
SANDRO:	Yeah, what turns?
CÓSIMA:	You have to wait your turn for this too.
SANDRO:	For what?
CÓSIMA:	For this, to kill off a few, to kill . . .
NENÉ:	You don't need a number to do that.
SANDRO:	Well, maybe you do.
NENÉ:	You think so?
SANDRO:	This will require a consultation.
NENÉ:	Who with?
SANDRO:	With the authorities.
NENÉ:	Alright, then, we'll have to consult them. Let's go.
SANDRO:	What?
NENÉ:	Let's go consult the authorities.

SANDRO: Yes, let's go, but . . .

NENÉ: But what?

SANDRO: We'll have to have a number to wait our turn.

   Music. They change roles.

SANDRO: Hey, look . . .

NENÉ: Wait your turn.

SANDRO: But I . . .

NENÉ: Wait your turn!

SANDRO: But it hurts.

NENÉ: That's not my problem. Everyone suffers.

SANDRO: Maybe so, but it hurts me more than anyone else.

NENÉ: That's what they all say. Did you fill out the form?

SANDRO: No.

NENÉ: What's your name?

SANDRO: Mmmm . . .

NENÉ: If you don't know your name, how are you going to fill out the form?

SANDRO: It's that I'm confused.

NENÉ: With whom are you confused?

SANDRO: Well, look, I . . .

NENÉ: Hey, listen, if you don't know who you are, how do you know it hurts?

SANDRO: Oh, that I do know.

NENÉ:	For all you know, maybe the other one is suffering.
SANDRO:	What other one?
NENÉ:	The one you're confusing yourself with.
SANDRO:	I'm not confusing myself with anyone.
NENÉ:	Well, that's what you said, and furthermore, if you haven't even filled out the form and if you don't have a number for your turn, there's nothing anyone can do. Who is your next of kin?
SANDRO:	My wife.
NENÉ:	Your wife is not a relative.
SANDRO:	Why not?
NENÉ:	Because. That's the law. Don't you have another relative?
SANDRO:	I only got one wife.
CÓSIMA:	Well, let me tell you. I got three husbands and I'm looking for someone to dump them on.
NENÉ:	And who asked you?
CÓSIMA:	Nobody asked me, okay? And don't act so smart. I'm only giving away one or two husbands.
SANDRO:	I don't need a husband.
CÓSIMA:	Well, say, you'd never know it!
NENÉ:	You're out of line.
CÓSIMA:	No I'm not. I'm only trying to help my friend.
SANDRO:	I'm not your friend.
NENÉ:	Of course not! What do you think? Some friend!

Giving away husbands! God only knows what
kinda husbands she's giving away.

CÓSIMA: Looky here, Baby, not even God knows that!

SANDRO: Please, this is very painful, please help me.

NENÉ: You'll have to wait your turn and that takes time.

SANDRO: But I . . .

NENÉ: Enough. I've already wasted enough of my time on
             this. Furthermore, this isn't even my job. If you
             don't have a number for your turn and if you
             haven't even filled out the application, you're
             missing the main thing.

CÓSIMA: You can see that this is the main thing. Nothing
             works without a number and without an
             application. Of course, if you had the pull I have,
             then they'd at least wait on you. If you had at least
             three husbands . . .

SANDRO: I think I'm going to be sick.

NENÉ: Well, go get sick someplace else. Not here. Go on, get
             out. The supervisor will be here any minute and
             then it'll be my fault, I'm the one who'll pay . . .

CÓSIMA: He's dead.

NENÉ: Well, tough, he died in the wrong place. Taking
             CARE of the dead is not my job.

CÓSIMA: He didn't even have a number or an application.

NENÉ: Tough shit! But that's his problem. Not yours, not
             mine. I do my job and you do yours.

CÓSIMA: I don't have a job.

NENÉ: Well then, this is not the place for lazy bums. So,
             get outta here.

CÓSIMA:	You wouldn't be interested in a husband, by any chance?
NENÉ:	No thanks!
CÓSIMA:	How about two?
NENÉ:	No.
CÓSIMA:	Or three!
NENÉ:	No!

Music. They change roles.

NENÉ:	Mmmm . . .
CÓSIMA:	I'm leaving.
NENÉ:	But, I, err . . .
CÓSIMA:	What?
NENÉ:	It's just that . . .
CÓSIMA:	Look, make up your mind. I'm not here to waste my time, and I'm leaving now, anyway.
NENÉ:	It's just that I wanted . . .
CÓSIMA:	Everyone wants something. Ask, ask, ask. Gimme, gimme, gimme. But never, take, take, take.
NENÉ:	I only want some information.
CÓSIMA:	For that you need a number for your turn.
NENÉ:	What for?
CÓSIMA:	To get some information. Everyone around here wants, wants . . .
SANDRO:	That's for sure. Ask, ask, ask.

CÓSIMA:	And who the hell asked you?
SANDRO:	Stop being such a smart mouth or I'll report you right now.
CÓSIMA:	Oh, yeah? Where? Where are you gonna report me?
SANDRO:	Upstairs.
CÓSIMA:	Upstairs! Ha! Nobody can go there. They're packed like sardines up there already.
NENÉ:	Hey, that's true. I was just up there.
SANDRO:	Ha! With that face, you ain't been no place!
CÓSIMA:	I don't know who'll receive you anyway, without a number. Forget it!
SANDRO:	Wow! Without a number? And I bet you haven't filled out the application either?
NENÉ:	Application?
SANDRO:	What? Don't you even know about that?
NENÉ:	Well, if someone would give me the information.
CÓSIMA:	But, who does he think he is?
SANDRO:	Let me tell you. You can't get anywhere without any of this.
CÓSIMA:	Where are you from?
NENÉ:	Well, not from around here.
SANDRO:	You're not from around here? Oh, well, don't worry, you'll get by without a number or a form.
CÓSIMA:	Listen, let me ask the questions. Just remember that my time is up and I've already given you more attention than you deserve!

SANDRO:	I'm here to see you do your job right and also to help this gentleman.
NENÉ:	I don't need help.
CÓSIMA:	Don't be ungrateful. This man is your friend and . . .
NENÉ:	I don't have any friends.
CÓSIMA:	This is why you're looking for information. Well, you're not going to get it here.
NENÉ:	Well, where then?
CÓSIMA:	How should I know? That's not my job. I'm leaving.
NENÉ:	But I just arrived.
CÓSIMA:	So why should I care if you got here late! And on top of it, you're putting pressure on me.
SANDRO:	Look here. You can't put on the pressure. That's the worst thing you can do.
NENÉ:	All I want is some information. That's all!
CÓSIMA:	Be quiet! Shut up! Who do you think you are? Don't get hysterical!
SANDRO:	Oh, oh, hysterics. That's bad news!
NENÉ:	Woe!
CÓSIMA:	He's dangerous! I'm going to call upstairs and they'll really let him have it.
SANDRO:	Shut up! They're going to let you have it!
NENÉ:	But, I just want . . .
CÓSIMA:	Another one that wants!

NENÉ:	I just want you to explain . . .

SANDRO: We can't.

NENÉ: Why not?

SANDRO: Because you need a number.

NENÉ: What?

SANDRO and CÓSIMA: Number, number, number!

Music. They sing "ERAN TRES" accompanied by salsa music by Ismael Mario. Once they finish, Alina gets up.[4]

ALINA: That's easy. This is what they do, improvise on themes? I can do that.

ALEJANDRA: Don't worry, you'll have time to show off. And get out of here because it's my turn. I'm the third number.
       They shot Alejandra Sital's son right through the forehead. The bullet went out through here and his head exploded, just like President Kennedy's. I ran over and saw him lying there in the small hallway between his mother's apartment and mine in the housing project. I bent down and put this finger (*she wiggles her little finger*) in the bullet hole in his forehead. You do the weirdest things! Blood was all around his head like a halo, like those they paint on saints, but not golden, no, red. Papoooo! The scream was deafening. Alejandra threw herself on the body and started calling him, "Papo, Papito, my dear son, Papo, Papito." She repeated, and repeated, and repeated. I tried to hold her by the shoulders, to get her away from the body, but there was no way. In a second, the neighbors were all over the place. I think Luisito, Alejandra's oldest son was finally able to get her off the body. Someone yelled, "Police, police, somebody call the police." And someone else said, "What for? What the hell can the police do now? He's dead."

Papo was around seventeen. A good kid.
Minded his own business. Average grades. He
would've graduated from high school this
month. He wanted to be an auto mechanic. He
hung out at Luisito's shop and was always
covered with grease. He had a steady girlfriend.
They were planning to get married. Nothing
special. Just your normal kid.

Alejandra had worked as a maid in some
people's house in Condado, Ocean Park, or
Miramar, I don't know, I never asked her where
she worked. She had some money saved.
Luisito, who was single, helped her out, and
Papo was the apple of his mother's and
brother's eyes. I don't know anything about his
father, he cleared out when Papo was three
years old. Luisito's father also disappeared. I
think he went to Chicago and good riddance.
Nothing, the usual story. We all came out in the
Vocero. I didn't look so good because that bitch
Scarface Moncha, stood right in front of me. But
you can see part of my right ear and a bit of my
arm.

Poor Luisito. I feel sorry for him because
Alejandra never loved him. It was always Papo.
And Luisito just accepted it and all that was his
was also Papo's. And so, they both were alone
now with nobody to care for. I just got outta
there and who knows what happened to them.
Who knows? Maybe Luisito took off for
Chicago, too.

We never found out anything about Papo.
Why he was killed? Who did it? Nothing, the
usual story. They even wrote it up in the
newspaper and did a story on TV, but nothing.
Moncha said the kid was mixed up in drugs. But
that's a dirty lie, he was a good kid. I knew him
well. Just lousy gossip from that Moncha. As
soon as there's a problem here, everyone says
it's got to do with drugs. Well, who knows? Poor
Alejandra. Maybe she's all alone. Maybe she
went back to work . . .

ALINA: Hey!

ALEJANDRA: What?

ALINA: Isn't your name Alejandra?

ALEJANDRA: Yes, so what?

ALINA: Aren't you talking about someone called Alejandra Sital?

ALEJANDRA: Alejandra Sital? No miss, that's my name.

ALINA: You said the boy was the son of someone called Alejandra Sital.

ALEJANDRA: I said that?

ALINA: Yes ma'am. You sure did. (*To the audience.*) Right?

ALEJANDRA: You heard wrong. I'm Alejandra Sital. And what boy is this?

ALINA: Papo, the one they killed.

The others have come on stage.

ALEJANDRA: (*To the others.*) Now she's saying they killed a boy by the name of Papo.

IGOR: Alejandra, let's go inside.

SANDRO: Yes, yes, Alejandra. Let's go.

ALEJANDRA: I haven't finished.

NENÉ: But we've to get on with the other numbers.

ALEJANDRA: Well, I've done mine.

NENÉ: You haven't done anything.

CÓSIMA: I'm the one who did mine.

SANDRO:	You always want to do what you damn well please.
IGOR:	OK, OK, let's go.
GABRIELA JOSÉ:	Leave her alone. It's OK, Alejandra. Thank you, it'll do. We've got to prepare something else. Come on.
ALEJANDRA:	No.
GABRIELA JOSÉ:	(*She signals the others to leave.*) Okay . . .
ALEJANDRA:	I'm sorry, Gabriela, it's just that the interruption shook me up.
GABRIELA JOSÉ:	I understand.
ALEJANDRA:	You always say you understand everything. Sometimes I wonder if it's true or if you're just saying it to make us feel better.
GABRIELA JOSÉ:	No, I'm not just saying it. I do understand you. I don't like interruptions either, especially when I'm talking seriously.
ALEJANDRA:	I was talking seriously. She was my neighbor. It wasn't me. I was just going through my act, doing my duty. Gabriela, why are we doing this?
GABRIELA JOSÉ:	Because it's what we do.
ALEJANDRA:	No, this is not normal. Roaming around the world pretending we're other people.
CÓSIMA:	(*Who has heard part of the conversation.*) So, what is normal?
ALEJANDRA:	Well, I don't know. A house, a shack, a family . . .
CÓSIMA:	You had that.
ALEJANDRA:	No, not a family. Igor didn't want one. He always said we couldn't bring up a child the way it should be. Circus people shouldn't have children.

CÓSIMA: Why not?

ALEJANDRA: We belonged to a very poor circus. Igor played the part of the strong man in his gorilla suit and would stand up to anybody. And me, I had my dancing dogs. I was very good at training them. But they started dying one by one. And little by little, Igor started losing his strength. One day we ended up in the same village. Remember, Gabriela? That's when we got together.

GABRIELA JOSÉ: Of course I remember. We were doing a show during a tremendous downpour and the roof was leaking. Cósima was already one of us then.

ALEJANDRA: Our circus tent also used to leak.

All of them giggle.

GABRIELA JOSÉ: And they gave us cocoa. Hot cocoa with delicious cookies, which you ate three at a time, Cósima.

CÓSIMA: And you, you ate two at a time. And they also gave us some white cheese that Sandro gobbled up like magic.

GABRIELA JOSÉ: We hadn't eaten for days. We had just arrived from the last country with only the clothes on our backs. Well, Sandro and I with a suitcase and you with a large tote bag where you kept all your belongings.

CÓSIMA: It was pink, blue, and black. I remember it. Pink, blue, and black. Woven. I bought it in a country that had a market full of beautiful things.

GABRIELA JOSÉ: Do you remember the people, Cósima?

CÓSIMA: What people?

GABRIELA JOSÉ: The people in the town that had the social club.

CÓSIMA: What town? We went to so many towns that had a social club.

GABRIELA JOSÉ: The ones who gave us hot cocoa. What lovely people. That night one of the women took us to her house, I mean, her mansion. Oh! That's where we met, Alejandra.

ALEJANDRA: That lady's brother had gone to the circus. We hadn't had anything to eat either and he invited us to his house.

CÓSIMA: They cooked a terrific meal for us. That lady went straight to the kitchen at two in the morning and the next day they gave us a lot of bread and coffee. I'll never forget the coffee.

ALEJANDRA: I still remember the coffee.

GABRIELA JOSÉ: And I remember the people. They were wonderful. You just don't run into that kind of people too often.

ALEJANDRA: Which country was it?

GABRIELA JOSÉ: Would you believe I can't remember. But I do know that this particular town was near the sea.

CÓSIMA: No, no, it was inland.

GABRIELA JOSÉ: Are you sure?

CÓSIMA: Okay, it was inland, but the sea was there, too. Yes, it was inland, but the sea wasn't very far. Like in my hometown.

ALEJANDRA: Your hometown? I thought you came from a big city where you were an executive.

CÓSIMA: Executive?

ALEJANDRA: You have always claimed that before joining Sandro and Gabriela you were an executive.

CÓSIMA: Oh, well, that was a long time ago. How long have we been roaming the world?

GABRIELA JOSÉ: Too long, Cósima. And it's true. You did live in a big city. Sandro and I were working at the Municipal Theater for a while and you came backstage to see us after the show. We started talking, we became friends, and you decided to join the company. You were tired of the business world. It was a long time ago, but there are things in life one never forgets, chance meetings one never forget.

ALEJANDRA: Cósima, do you ever miss the big business life?

CÓSIMA: No, never.

ALEJANDRA: And your family?

CÓSIMA: You are all my family.

NENÉ: (*Entering with three small cups of coffee.*) Coffee, girls?

GABRIELA JOSÉ: Huh?

ALEJANDRA: Oh, yes.

CÓSIMA: That's just what we needed.

ALEJANDRA: This coffee is great.

CÓSIMA: Hmmmm!

GABRIELA JOSÉ: Yesss.

Suddenly the three of them look at each other.

NENÉ: Hey, what's going on?

GABRIELA JOSÉ: Nothing really. It's just that the coffee reminded us of something we were talking about.

NENÉ: A girl brought it, in a thermos. She said it was for the actors, but . . . how strange! You know something? Come to think of it, she said her aunt had made it because Alejandra liked it so much. Now, how does this woman know you like coffee so much?

ALEJANDRA: What woman?

NENÉ: The one who sent the coffee.

ALEJANDRA: I don't know. I don't know anyone here. I've never even been here before.

GABRIELA JOSÉ: Just what did she say, Nené?

NENÉ: She said, "I brought coffee for the actors. My aunt made it because Miss Alejandra likes it so much."

CÓSIMA: Maybe it's someone who knows you and who moved to this town.

ALEJANDRA: Could be.

GABRIELA JOSÉ: Well, we'll find out when she comes back for the thermos.

NENÉ: No, the girl said we could keep it, that her aunt said we needed it more than she does.

GABRIELA JOSÉ: How nice of her. Maybe she'll come to see the show and then we'll find out who she is.

ALEJANDRA: Yeah, maybe . . .

NENÉ: What's going on? Aren't we going to do another number?

CÓSIMA: I'm not. I've already done mine. (*She exits.*)

ALEJANDRA: Me too. I'm going to have more coffee. (*She exits.*)

NENÉ: But we've got to do more numbers. That's why we're here. What did I bring so much information for?

GABRIELA JOSÉ:	Be patient. There's still time. I also want more coffee. Why don't you make something up?
NENÉ:	Me? Alone?
GABRIELA JOSÉ:	It's about time you did.
NENÉ:	But, I've never done it.
GABRIELA JOSÉ:	There's always a first time. It'll be easy. You'll see. (*She exits.*)
NENÉ:	(*He looks at the audience and addresses Alina.*) Hey, you! Yeah, you, get up here. (*She does. They move center stage and Nené whispers something in her ear. After a couple of beats, she violently kicks one of the chairs on the stage.*) Hey, hey, now listen, hold on a second. (*She pushes him.*) Look, I don't know nothing about this! Listen to me, please, I didn't say nothing. (*She punches him and once he is on the floor begins to kick him.*) DON'T KILL ME! DON'T KILL ME . . . I SWEAR TO GOD I DIDN'T DO IT!!! I don't know . . . I don't know . . . (*Pause.*) Okay, okay, it was . . . ah . . . it was Papo, yeah, that's it, it was Papo, Luisito's brother. Yeah, he snitched . . . Luisito told him everything . . . (*Pause.*) Oh God, not my face. IT WAS PAPO! Luisito asked him to make a drop and Papo said no . . . I was at the shop that day and I heard everything. (*Collecting his thoughts.*) Look, ah, Papo told Luisito that if he didn't get out of the business he was gonna tell their old lady. Luisito begged him not to do it and to drop the rock for him 'cause he was in trouble and somebody was after him. Then, ah, Papo told him, ah, that if he was in trouble then he, that's Papo, was probably in trouble too and they'd be after him 'cause he was Luisito's brother and that besides, he didn't want to get his hands dirty. AND THEN, LUIS ASKS ME TO MAKE THE DROP FOR HIM!, and I told him "No way, man . . . uh, uh, no go bro' . . . they're keeping an eye on me, if they nail me, they're gonna bust my ass . . . ah, ah, . . . DAMN IT LUIS, I'M ON PROBATION. And

I got the hell outta there . . . Next thing I knew was that the boss had been busted . . . and then I skipped town for a while, till things settled down, you know, just to play it cool . . . But I'm no snitch . . . uh, uh, tell me . . . which one of you has ever known me for a snitch? (*Turning away from "them."*) Uh, uh . . . not me . . . (*Turning back.*) As a matter of fact . . . (*The "men" are gone.*) I . . . I've never . . . I better get outta here. (*He starts to leave the stage.*)

ALINA: Look!

NENÉ: What?

ALINA: It was you, wasn't it?

NENÉ: It wasn't me, it was Papo.

ALINA: Liar. Papo was a good kid. The lady said so.

NENÉ: What lady?

ALINA: Alejandra. (*To the audience.*) Don't you remember? See, they remember.

NENÉ: I didn't hear anything. I don't know what you're talking about.

SANDRO: (*Entering.*) What is it, Nené?

NENÉ: This young lady says Alejandra was talking about some guy called Papo.

SANDRO: Papo? Who's Papo?

NENÉ: I don't know.

ALINA: You're all too much. You, listen. (*To Nené who is exiting.*)

SANDRO: Take it easy, Miss. We have an intermission now. Listen, come back stage with me, maybe you can learn to improvise with us. Come on. (*To the audience.*) See you soon.

End of Act I

During intermission Nené comes on stage and tells the audience to get up, smoke, go to the john, whatever . . .

Act II

The Great USkrainian Circus

Circus music. Everyone on stage except Gabriela.

ALINA:	Ladies and gentlemen. Good evening again. We continue with The Great USkrainian Circus. (*To Nené.*) Was I okay?
NENÉ:	Fine, just fine.
CÓSIMA:	Gabriela is just going to love her.
ALEJANDRA:	She sure is.
IGOR:	Girls, girls!
NENÉ:	She's back stage, counting the ticket return. She said we could start.
CÓSIMA:	Okay, then, let's start.
NENÉ:	(*To Alina.*) You come with me.
ALEJANDRA:	This one's going to act?
NENÉ:	I explained everything to her. She'll do alright.
SANDRO:	On with the show, then. (*To the audience.*) Our next number is called, "Miracle on Providencia Street, a Metropolitan Morality Play between Carolina and Cangrejos."[5]

They sit together in couples.

CÓSIMA:	It's three in the morning and I am Carmen.
IGOR:	It's three in the morning and I am José.
ALEJANDRA:	It's raining cats and dogs and I am Cuca.
SANDRO:	It's raining cats and dogs and I am Pancho.
NENÉ:	I'm Bobby and you're Baby. (*He takes Alina by the hand and sits down.*)

Salsa music. The Miracle play begins.

CUCA:	What happened to us, Pancho?
PANCHO:	What?
CUCA:	What happened to us?
PANCHO:	When?
CUCA:	To us?
PANCHO:	When?
CUCA:	What do you mean when?
PANCHO:	Didn't you ask what happened to us?
CUCA:	Yeah, that's right.
PANCHO:	Well, when?
CUCA:	Not when . . .
PANCHO:	Hey, are you nuts?
CUCA:	No, I'm thinking.
PANCHO:	Nuts, then.
CUCA:	I'm serious.
PANCHO:	Nuts, nuttier than ever.

CUCA: I'm not kidding. I've been wondering about it for days and it dawned on me again.

PANCHO: At three in the morning and in the middle of this downpour?

CUCA: Watch it! You ran the red light.

PANCHO: Nobody's on the road at this hour. If I stop here, we'll get mugged.

CUCA: Mugged! You just said there was nobody on the road.

PANCHO: Anybody can show up in this neighborhood.

CUCA: I don't know why you always take this shortcut.

PANCHO: Because I'm dead tired and if I don't get home soon, I'll fall asleep at the wheel. What happened to us about what?

CUCA: If you keep running the red lights, I'll jump out of the car.

PANCHO: You're going to look great! A wet hen in the middle of the road. Then, you'll really get mugged. And look, at this hour of the morning one can run the lights.

CUCA: Oh sure, I'm getting out! Why did you stop?

PANCHO: I don't know. Oh, yeah, you were getting out.

CUCA: Don't try to be funny and keep driving. Whenever I want to talk serious you play dumb.

PANCHO: You're the dumb one.

BABY: Betty looks awful.

Bobby doesn't answer.

BABY: I said Betty looks awful.

BOBBY:	I heard you.
BABY:	So?
BOBBY:	So what?
BABY:	Well, what do you think?
BOBBY:	She looks awful.
BABY:	You're lying. I saw you flirting with her.
BOBBY:	Look here, don't you start.
BABY:	You see. You always get angry when I tell you the truth.
BOBBY:	Baby, don't be stupid. I danced with her for a while. She was the hostess, wasn't she?
BABY:	A while? A real long while. You looked like you were glued together.
BOBBY:	If we'd been glued together, we'd still be dancing.
BABY:	Aren't you funny!
BOBBY:	You're the funny one.
BABY:	That's it, change the subject. I should be used to all this by now.
BOBBY:	That's right.
BABY:	Watch out! You're going to get us killed.
BOBBY:	It's starting to rain and I want to get home. It's almost three.
BABY:	So, drive slowly.
BOBBY:	Don't tell me how to drive! Goddam rain!
BABY:	(*Shouting.*) Watch out!

BOBBY:	You idiot! He almost killed us. Stupid! With that piece of crap for a car. No wonder he drives like a madman.
BABY:	You're the one driving like a madman.
BOBBY:	Fuck it, shut up!
CUCA:	Pancho . . .
PANCHO:	Hmmm?
CUCA:	Pancho . . .
PANCHO:	What is it?
CUCA:	What do you think happened?
PANCHO:	Here we go again.
CUCA:	No, it's important. We can never talk.
PANCHO:	Come off it. Talk, at this hour, inside the car and in this rain.
CUCA:	So when are we going to talk?
PANCHO:	Tomorrow.
CUCA:	Always tomorrow.
PANCHO:	Well, tomorrow's Sunday.
CUCA:	Today is Sunday.
PANCHO:	Stop that nonsense. We'll talk later.
CUCA:	Susana says the same thing is happening to her. She says she doesn't know what's wrong. She says she can't stand Jorge, she can't stand people.
PANCHO:	Maybe she's going through menopause.

CUCA:	I'm the one going through menopause. I've got these hot flashes.
PANCHO:	Happens to every woman. Don't worry about it.
CUCA:	I don't. It's us I'm worried about.
PANCHO:	Us? What's wrong with us?
CUCA:	Not you and me. Our group. All of us. People on this island. I think it's money.
PANCHO:	Money?
CUCA:	Yes, when we had less, we had fewer problems.
PANCHO:	Don't be silly. When we had less we wanted more, like everybody else.
CUCA:	Well, we don't have more now. We have more loans to pay.
PANCHO:	Everybody does.
CUCA:	That doesn't help.
PANCHO:	I pay mine on time. And listen, quit gabbing, we'll talk tomorrow.
CUCA:	Susana says she's going to get a divorce. It's all over between Jorge and that young thing. Now he's got one that works in Las Americas Mall.
PANCHO:	What does she do?
CUCA:	I don't know.
PANCHO:	How did Susana find out?
CUCA:	Her cousin María Luisa told her.
PANCHO:	That blabber mouth.

CUCA:	I think María Luisa likes Jorge and told Susana about that girl in the mall to cover it all up.
PANCHO:	That's between Jorge and María Luisa.
CUCA:	Aha! You see. You know something. You see, I was right. It is María Luisa.
PANCHO:	What about María Luisa?
CUCA:	You just said so yourself.
PANCHO:	I didn't say anything. You said it. If you don't shut up . . . Goddam it! Did you see that? Those two jerks! That piece of crap almost hit the Mercedes. Wow! What a car!
CUCA:	You jerk! You big bully!
PANCHO:	Shut up.
CUCA:	Bully! Son of a bitch!
PANCHO:	Shut up, or I'm going to get it!
CUCA:	Son of a bitch! What the hell, he can't hear me, with this rain and all our windows up.
CARMEN:	I think that priest is going to marry her.
JOSÉ:	Who?
CARMEN:	The priest.
JOSÉ:	What priest?
CARMEN:	Sandra Rivera's brother.
JOSÉ:	Who?
CARMEN:	They should give him dispensation.
JOSÉ:	What dispensation are you talking about? Priests can't get married.

CARMEN: But on TV it's different. On TV you can do
               anything, since everything is made up.

JOSÉ: Television, is that what you're talking about?
               Television? That's a lot of crap.

CARMEN: Just because you don't like it you don't have to call
               it crap.

JOSÉ: Same old crap. A lot of problems and then
               everything turns out okay. Soap crap.

CARMEN: How do you know everything turns out okay? HA!
               You watch it too. I've seen you. And that Alba
               Nydia isn't even in this one. You like watching her,
               I bet.

JOSÉ: She's got some shape.

CARMEN: Bah, shape!

JOSÉ: Jealous, you're jealous.

CARMEN: Oh, stop it and look where you're going.

JOSÉ: Let's go to Piñones Beach?

CARMEN: Where? At this hour? Are you nuts?

JOSÉ: You used to like it.

CARMEN: That was a long time ago.

JOSÉ: Yeah, sure, a long time. And now, nothing.

CARMEN: What do you mean, nothing? I work like a dog all
               day in that office building. You know that people in
               this island are slobs. They throw everything on the
               floor. Dirt all over the place. And then, home to
               cook and clean and you want me to feel like a
               beauty queen . . . One of these days I'm going to
               get the hell out.

JOSÉ: Ah, knock it off. I've heard this before.

CARMEN:	You ran a red light.
JOSÉ:	So what! It's late, if I stop here, I'll get mugged.
CARMEN:	We can't go on like this. It's impossible to live in this island anymore.
JOSÉ:	So we leave.
CARMEN:	Where to?
JOSÉ:	Well, Luis is doing very well in Connecticut.
CARMEN:	I'm not going to live with that bunch of bums.
JOSÉ:	Don't call my brothers and my people bums.
CARMEN:	Bums! Living off welfare. I'd rather rot in that office building.
JOSÉ:	And you don't think I'm rotting in that damn garage? Dealing with beat up cars all day long.
CARMEN:	The more beat up they are, the better for you. And talking about beat up cars, look at this one, full of those awful spots.
JOSÉ:	I told you I'll paint it when I have time. Inside it's like a beautiful babe.
CARMEN:	Beautiful babe . . . Bah! Sell that garage to your nephew and let's get out of here. Hey, you ran another red light.
JOSÉ:	You want me to get shot? Last Saturday they asked a man for a ride right here and the idiot stopped. They beat the hell out of him.
CARMEN:	Stupid ass.
JOSÉ:	It's impossible to live here anymore. Seriously, honey, let's go to Connecticut.
CARMEN:	I hate cold weather.

JOSÉ:	Well, Miami, then.
CARMEN:	There are no more Puerto Ricans there. Are you kidding? Hey, take it easy!
JOSÉ:	He thinks this is a racetrack. I hope he kills himself.
CARMEN:	Shitpot! Who the hell does he think he is? He's got a Mercedes! I told you to take it easy!
JOSÉ:	Goddam rain.
CARMEN:	It's pouring! Now we won't find a parking space.
JOSÉ:JOSÉ:	So we sleep in here.
CARMEN:	You don't say.
JOSÉ:	Once you used to liked it.
CARMEN:	Keep driving and don't bug me.
BABY:	Those parties bore me.
BOBBY:	Where's the thing?
BABY:	What?
BOBBY:	The thing, the garage door opener?
BABY:	In the glove compartment. Well, it was here . . .
BOBBY:	Damn it, don't tell me it's in your car. I tell you . . .
BABY:	Shut up, here it is.
BOBBY:	If I have to ruin this suit . . .
BABY:	You're not. Here it is, I told you.
BOBBY:	Don't shout.
BABY:	I'm not shouting. The door's open. Go on in. Fuck you!

ALINA:	(*She looks around at the others.*) Wait a minute . . . Wait a minute . . . This is supposed to be a morality play. A morality play or a miracle play is of religious nature. In Spain, in the Sixteenth Century, . . .
CÓSIMA:	Ohhhh, listen to Miss Higher Education.
ALEJANDRA:	Attention! Attention! The young lady will now give us lessons in Theater History.
IGOR:	I'm too old to go to school.
SANDRO:	It's a morality play about three different couples inside three different cars . . .
ALINA:	I know that. Nené had explained it to me. But I don't think you should swear in a morality play.
NENÉ:	We should what?
ALINA:	Swear.
SANDRO:	Swear?
ALEJANDRA:	What's that?
ALINA:	Swear. Use bad words. You're all swearing right and left.
CÓSIMA:	We're swearing? We? Who swore?
ALINA:	Now, don't you start playing games with me. I'm one of you . . .
IGOR:	One of who?
CÓSIMA:	Who do you think you are? One of us . . . (*Bronx cheer.*)
ALINA:	But I improvised with you.
ALEJANDRA:	And you're pretty lousy at it too.

NENÉ:	I wouldn't say that. She lacks experience, but . . .
SANDRO:	That comes with time, doesn't it? Is that what you were going to say?
NENÉ:	Well . . .
SANDRO:	(*To Alina.*) With time, miss, takes time. (*To Nené.*) And you, someday you may be even better than I am, takes time.
IGOR:	Let's go.

They all exit except for Nené and Alina.

ALINA:	Why are they leaving?
NENÉ:	It's that . . . well . . . They don't like to perform with new actors.
ALINA:	But at first they accepted me. Well, I mean, not at first, but afterwards . . .

Nené shakes his head.

ALINA:	No?
NENÉ:	No.
ALINA:	How do you know?
NENÉ:	Because I do. I know them.
ALINA:	Why are they like that?
NENÉ:	Look, they're . . . I mean, we're like a family.
ALINA:	New people come into families all the time.
NENÉ:	This one is different. I should know. Anyhow, why do you want to belong to this one?
ALINA:	What you do seems fascinating. You travel, meet

people from different countries. (*Nené laughs.*) Why are you laughing?

NENÉ: You sound so romantic.

ALINA: I think it is romantic. I think you are all wonderful, what you do, live other lives . . .

NENÉ: That's neither romantic nor wonderful. It's a lot of hard work.

ALINA: You haven't been with them long, have you?

NENÉ: Hmmm . . .

ALINA: Then, why do they accept you?

NENÉ: They don't accept me. They put up with me.

ALINA: You're not really one of them, are you?

NENÉ: You ask too many questions. That's not going to get you nowhere.

ALINA: Anywhere.

NENÉ: What?

ALINA: Anywhere, not nowhere. Double negative.

NENÉ: Oh, come on now, cut it out, Miss Know It All. Listen, I'm paying attention to you because I like you, but I can damn well leave you here all by yourself and see how you handle all those people in the audience, huh? All alone with them. Come on, why don't you stay with them. Go ahead, talk to them, go on.

ALINA: No, not me.

NENÉ: Come on, say something. Confront them. Face them like we do. I haven't been with this circus for long but I do what I can. And you know why?

Because I haven't got anything else. Because they picked me up. Gabriela José saw me one day standing in front of a cafe where they were eating, I was starving. She came out, gave me a couple of bucks and said. "Here, put that in your belly, don't smoke it," and I laughed and followed her in and I quit because . . . (*He sees Sandro approaching and tries to change the topic of conversation.*) I learned to do what Sandro did because he, because he . . .

SANDRO: Because he what?

NENÉ: Well, because you were tired.

SANDRO: Who told you I was tired?

NENÉ: Gabriela José.

SANDRO: That's a lie. She didn't tell you that. You talked her into giving you the job.

NENÉ: No, I didn't.

SANDRO: Liar, you big liar. Always standing around with that sweet baby face, that cemetery angel face.

NENÉ: Sandro, I never meant to hurt you, believe me.

SANDRO: Believe you! I wouldn't believe you if my life depended on it, even if you said a Hail Mary, an Our Father, or the Holy Rosary, all of it. Believe you!

NENÉ: What took you so long to say this?

SANDRO: Better late than never, Nené. And it's very late, because now I'm up to here (*pointing to his neck*) with you. You think you own this circus.

NENÉ: No I don't . . .

SANDRO: Shut up! I'm talking to you. You think you own it because Gabriela José gave you a hand. She

should've let you die in that gutter, that gutter
where Igor and I got you from. (*To Alina.*) He
wasn't standing in front of a cafe, he was lying in
the gutter. Do you know what kind of people end
up in gutters? Bums like him. And no matter how
hard he tries to get out of it, he can't. Because his
head stays there, in the gutter. (*To Nené.*) You may
act real smart, you may even get more information
than I ever got; a real good boy, the baby, Nené, like
Gabriela called him because he didn't have a name,
because nobody knows what his name is, so young
lady, have no illusions. No name. Nené, baby face,
cemetery angel face but with his mind in the gutter,
always plotting to take away what belongs to
others. Isn't that true? Always scheming with your
gutter mind, you bum. If you think you're going to
take over this circus . . .

As he grabs him by the lapels, Gabriela enters.

GABRIELA JOSÉ:	Sandro! Let go of him, Sandro! Go backstage, Nené. (*To Alina.*) Go back to your seat.
ALINA:	Who, me?
GABRIELA JOSÉ:	Go on, back to your seat. Enough.
ALINA:	No, I want to stay with you.
GABRIELA JOSÉ:	With us? And what are you going to do with us?
ALINA:	Act. I can learn . . . I already did a number . . .
GABRIELA JOSÉ:	What number?
ALINA:	The miracle play. (*To Sandro.*) I didn't do so bad, did I?
SANDRO:	What miracle play?
ALINA:	I acted right along with them. He's denying it because they all swore right and left.

GABRIELA JOSÉ: My actors don't swear. We do nothing that may offend our audience.

ALINA: What? You're always criticizing . . .

SANDRO: Criticizing, yes.

ALINA: Well, then, don't tell me you don't offend anyone.

GABRIELA JOSÉ: It's one thing to criticize and another to offend.

SANDRO: They're two very different things.

ALINA: Listen, Sandro, you were also swearing and now you're denying it.

GABRIELA JOSÉ: Wait a minute. He's Mr. Roskoff to you. What do you mean calling him Sandro!

ALINA: Mr. Roskoff. My, my aren't you dramatic!

GABRIELA JOSÉ: You don't know what dramatic means.

ALINA: Look, I'm sorry. I just want to stay and act. I was telling Nené that what you do seems so romantic, wonderful, fascinating.

GABRIELA JOSÉ: Listen to me. This takes blood, sweat and tears and guts, you hear me, GUTS. And you spill them all over, spill them all over the road but not laughing, sweetie, not laughing.

ALINA: Don't get so angry.

GABRIELA JOSÉ: And why not? Why shouldn't I get angry? What do you know about this life? About having or not having guts. You know what it's like? It's like having to eat powdered glass and getting your gut packed with it.

SANDRO: And then you throw up all that powdered glass along with you bloody guts, and your bloody sweat and your bloody tears, and that's what all this is made up of, that's what you call romantic, fascinating.

GABRIELA JOSÉ: Wonderful.

ALINA: You don't frighten me. You don't frighten me with this bloody guts stuff. If it were so difficult, you'd do something else.

SANDRO: We don't know how to do anything else.

ALINA: That's all you have to say, isn't it? You don't fool me. It's not that you don't know, it's that you don't want to do anything else. Okay, I'll leave, but I warn you, I'm going to show up in the next town or in the next country. You wait and see. One day you'll have to accept me. (*She exits.*)

SANDRO: (*Looking toward the exit.*) Is she gone?

GABRIELA JOSÉ: Looks like it.

SANDRO: Thank God we're rid of her.

GABRIELA JOSÉ: I don't think we're rid of her.

SANDRO: Why?

GABRIELA JOSÉ: I don't know. Something tells me she'll be back.

SANDRO: Nah, she won't.

GABRIELA JOSÉ: She said so.

SANDRO: She was bluffing.

GABRIELA JOSÉ: Maybe she wasn't.

SANDRO: We can't feed another mouth.

GABRIELA JOSÉ: How was she?

SANDRO: What?

GABRIELA JOSÉ:	How did she do?
SANDRO:	When?
GABRIELA JOSÉ:	At the beginning of this act when I was backstage? Don't look so innocent. I know that once in a while . . .
SANDRO:	We had to do something. We didn't swear much and the scene was important.
GABRIELA JOSÉ:	Alright, alright, but you haven't answered my question.
SANDRO:	What question?
GABRIELA JOSÉ:	About the girl.
SANDRO:	She wasn't bad. But, Nené's enough for now.
GABRIELA JOSÉ:	Here we go again! Don't you realize I gave him the job so you wouldn't have to go all over town like you used to?
SANDRO:	I liked it.
GABRIELA JOSÉ:	You want to go back to that?
SANDRO:	Who'll manage the circus?
GABRIELA JOSÉ:	I can do it again.
SANDRO:	No, it's alright. You deserve a rest. I'm going for some more coffee. Want some?
GABRIELA JOSÉ:	No, thanks. I already had some.

Sandro exits.

GABRIELA JOSÉ:	It's not that I don't love him, like Cósima told you. I'm fond of him, sure I am. Sometimes I even feel sorry for him. He looks strong, but I feel he's insecure, defenseless, lost inside himself,

maybe . . . And it reminds me of the times I spent at
my grandmother's. I used to look out the window
through the rain and run out to save the little birds
that hid from the wind, near our doorsteps. I
brought them inside, the ones I could catch; I dried
them, put them in an old bird cage, gave them
some sugar, and if the sun was out, let them go the
next day. Just like a little bird, sure in flight but
frightened in a windstorm, some men are like that.
In this circus Sandro has a bird cage. We are all nice
to him. I think he finally feels at home, as if we
were his family, sometimes friends are closer than
family. And Nené, he shouldn't be so jealous of
him. He's also insecure. I found him in one of those
towns we performed in. He was a hungry little
animal, looking for his daily bread, he wanted so
much to please. His big grey eyes reminded me of
my son, my Ricardo. I talked to him about our
company and I said there was room for one and he
joined us. Oh, how did we start this circus? If only
you knew. It was so simple. Sandro and I were in a
professional theater company. He played a number
of roles. When somebody was sick he'd fill in; he
would even substitute for the guy who always
said, "Madam, dinner's served." I was always the
good friend who ended up losing the leading man.
One day Sandro and I were having a drink in a cafe
by the sea. Suddenly we looked out to the sea and a
thought came into our heads. We looked at each
other and said, "Why don't we do something
else?" And just at that moment an organ grinder
went by, playing an organ as old as he was, like in
the movies. He was playing circus music. Sandro
and I sang it along with him. We looked at each
other again and said, "A circus, that's it, let's get a
circus together." And we made up this rather
peculiar circus. Igor and Alejandra joined us in
some little town. Cósima was already with us and
Nené was last. Sandro used to do what Nené does
now. He'd go out and gather the information on
whatever was happening and then, like you've
already seen, we'd act it out. I think that after so
many years of holding a mirror up to the audience,

perhaps it hasn't been worth it. I'm not sure, I really don't know if it has . . . Well, if it hasn't, it's sad. I think back, I remember and my son's face is quite clear to me, his big green eyes with tiny yellow lights looking up at me, trying to keep them open, trying not to fall asleep while I sang his favorite cradle song . . . (*Sings song.*)

A young man enters from the aisle and sings along with Gabriela.

GABRIELA JOSÉ:	Ricardo!
YOUNG MAN:	Pardon me?
GABRIELA JOSÉ:	Ricardo? Is your name Ricardo?
YOUNG MAN:	No ma'am, my name's not Ricardo.
GABRIELA JOSÉ:	Sorry. What do you want?
YOUNG MAN:	I'm looking for my sister. Every time a circus comes to town, she wants to join it.
GABRIELA JOSÉ:	She was here.
YOUNG MAN:	Oh really? Did you invite her to join?
GABRIELA JOSÉ:	No.
YOUNG MAN:	I knew it. I told her she couldn't join a circus. If it had been a theater company, maybe . . .
GABRIELA JOSÉ:	Right, if it had been a theater company . . . But this is a circus.
YOUNG MAN:	Ukrainian.
GABRIELA JOSÉ:	USkrainian.
YOUNG MAN:	Ukraine, associated Republic.
GABRIELA JOSÉ:	Ah, ah, ah . . . I've been through that with your sister.

YOUNG MAN:	I just wanted to know . . .
GABRIELA JOSÉ:	Do you have a ticket?
YOUNG MAN:	No ma'am, I only came to see if my sister was here. Sorry. (*He's about to leave.*)
GABRIELA JOSÉ:	Listen!
YOUNG MAN:	Yes?
GABRIELA JOSÉ:	The song, where did you learn it?
YOUNG MAN:	My father taught it to me. My mother used to sing it when I was a baby.
GABRIELA JOSÉ:	Is your mother from here?
YOUNG MAN:	No, she wasn't. She died a long time ago. Good night. (*He exits.*)

Gabriela is going to go after him. Sandro stops her.

SANDRO:	Gabriela, Gabriela . . .
GABRIELA JOSÉ:	Leave me alone. It could be, it could be . . .
SANDRO:	Your son's in the big top.
GABRIELA JOSÉ:	That song, how does he know it? He says his mother used to sing it to him when he was a baby.
SANDRO:	He's not your son, Gabriela. He's working in a big circus. Don't you remember?
GABRIELA JOSÉ:	I don't know where he is.
SANDRO:	What do you mean you don't know?
GABRIELA JOSÉ:	I don't know, I don't know.
SANDRO:	What's the matter Gabriela?
GABRIELA JOSÉ:	He's not working in a circus.

SANDRO:	Sure he is. With his father, the Great Lion Tamer.
GABRIELA JOSÉ:	There's no such tamer.
SANDRO:	What are you talking about?
GABRIELA JOSÉ:	He wasn't in the circus.
SANDRO:	But . . .
GABRIELA JOSÉ:	I told you that to convince myself. Then I told the others. His father didn't belong to the circus.
SANDRO:	Who was he, then?
GABRIELA JOSÉ:	He came from a good family, rich. I met him somewhere, some town where we performed for a couple of weeks. He made me leave the circus, we got married, I had Ricardo. And soon I found out what he was like. A despot, mean to everyone. I couldn't take it and I ran away with my son. He soon found me and took Ricardo away. He disappeared.
SANDRO:	People don't disappear so easily.
GABRIELA JOSÉ:	You'd be surprised.
SANDRO:	You didn't go to the police?
GABRIELA JOSÉ:	I was in a foreign country. It wasn't mine. Nobody wanted to help me. Nobody knew anything.
SANDRO:	What about your family?
GABRIELA JOSÉ:	What family, Sandro? You are my family, all of you.
SANDRO:	I know. We are now. But, then?
GABRIELA JOSÉ:	My parents were dead. I left the circus and then I joined the company where you worked and the rest you know . . . (*The Young Man enters again.*) The others have entered one by one.

YOUNG MAN: Ma'am? Excuse me . . .

GABRIELA JOSÉ: Yes . . .

SANDRO: Gabriela . . .

YOUNG MAN: Pardon me, but just for a moment I thought . . .
Well, I wonder . . . How do you know that song?
It's not very common.

GABRIELA JOSÉ: I must have heard it somewhere. I don't really
remember. It's a song just like any other.

The young man exits. The others approach Gabriela as circus music is heard. Gabriela smiles and they exit through the aisles.

End of *The Great USkrainian Circus*

Notes

1. For permission to stage the play, the author must be contacted directly: Calle España 1951, Santurce, Puerto Rico 00911.

2. *Guagua* is the common word for bus in some of the Caribbean countries. *Agua* is the word for water, therefore, the combination *aguaguagua* is a water bus.

3. *Desarrollo de la afición teatral* is the original title of this study.

4. The translation of *"ERAN TRES"* is "They Were Three."

5. Carolina and Cangrejos are two neighborhoods in San Juan, Puerto Rico.

Teresa Marichal (Puerto Rico, 1956)—actress, director, costume and stage designer, and producer—is an active member of the Puerto Rican theatrical movement the *Nueva Dramaturgia Puertorriqueña*. Her creative production ranges from plays for popular, guerrilla, and puppet theater to children's theater.

While in her first play, *Las horas de los dioses nocturnos* (The Time of the Nocturnal Gods, 1978), she explores the intricacies of human psychology, in the ensuing dramas she resorts to satire and humor to expose the inadequacies of society. She structures her criticism by setting up binary oppositions such as the older generation versus the younger one, the establishment versus marginal groups, and the oppressor versus the oppressed.[1]

During the early 1980s she experimented with popular and revolutionary theater and headed one of the guerrilla theater groups at the University of Puerto Rico.[2] In the mid eighties she turned to a highly symbolic theater that stresses ritualism and is structured around both universal and personal myths. Two representative plays of this trend are *Jong Song Do: la tierra donde los esclavos son vendidos* (Jong Song Do: The Land Where Slaves Are Sold, 1984) and *Vlad* (1985). The former is a parable that thematizes slavery, racial discrimination, and freedom. The latter is based on the Icarus myth and is dedicated to all those who have experienced persecution. Moreover, the protagonist's quest for his own identity reflects the contemporary concern of many Puerto Rican dramatists with national identity.

In *Paseo al atardecer* (Evening Walk, 1984) Marichal no longer expresses her concern for society's problems through dichotomies, but exercises a post-structuralist approach intent on dismantling traditional patterns, specifically the rewriting of canonical texts, the destruction of masculine hierarchies, and the dissolution of social stereotypes.

More recently Marichal has framed her plays utilizing modern technology and means of mass communication such as the telephone, the radio, and television to reflect on the impact that they have had on human alienation and freedom.

Notes

1. These problems are dramatized in the trilogy entitled *El parque más grande de la ciudad* (The Largest Park in the City, 1979), which contains *Divertimento liviano* (Light Divertimento), *Parque para dos* (Park for Two), and *A Capella*.

2. *Amor de medianoche* (Midnight Love, 1984) stands out among her "popular theater" plays. Some of the revolutionary pieces include

El que no sabe quien es, está loco (Crazy Is He Who Doesn't Know Who He Is); *Prohibido hablar* (No Talking); *Caos* (Chaos); and *Yo, una prisionera de guerra* (I, Prisoner of War).

Evening Walk

BY TERESA MARICHAL LUGO[1]

Translated from *Paseo al atardecer*
by Teresa Cajiao Salas and Margarita Vargas

On stage, two women. One of them is rocking a baby carriage, the other one standing on a wooden box. In the background, a gigantic photo of a woman in a bathtub full of bubbles: one of her arms is hanging out and her wrist is slit.

GERTRUDIS: At a distance
You could see
The sun setting.
Dusk was falling.
The sea reddened with death
Before the skittish gazes
Of the fishermen who could still see,
Far away, the bodies of the shipwrecked
Floating on the waters already calmed of their fury.
And those who survived the terrible disaster
Recalled the last words that were screamed:
Hang the windows!
Raise the flags and sails!
Chop off their heads once and for all,
Everyone must be decapitated.
Slavery was reaching earth.
Spit on each other, yes, spit on each other.

THE MOTHER: (*She moves the carriage and looks in front of her.*)
Excuse me, would you please speak softer? The baby's sleeping.

GERTRUDIS: And there, stepping on the sand,
lowering their dogs rabid with history,
clawed dogs
teeth dogs
biting dogs

THE MOTHER: Please, the baby's sleeping!

GERTRUDIS: Sh, sh.
The baby's sleeping! (*She gradually raises the tone of her voice.*)
The baby's sleeping!
The baby's sleeping!

THE MOTHER: The baby's sleeping! (*Crying.*)
Please, the baby's sleeping,

> sleeping,
> my baby's sleeping,
> my angel's sleeping . . .

GERTRUDIS: (*She goes over to the mother.*)
              Please, sing softer.
              My spirit is sleeping (*She laughs boisterously and
                   then begins humming a popular tune.*)
              Hmmm, Hmmm, Hmmm, Hmmm, Hmmm,
                   Hmmm

She returns to the box. She begins rummaging through her purse. She takes out papers, books, librettos.

GERTRUDIS: Why is it that they still haven't invented lit
              cigarettes? What's the use of so much progress!
              One still has to waste valuable time looking for a
              stupid book of matches . . . here it is . . . Everything
              takes time, even finding matches, lighting them
              and waiting for death while rotting with cancer!

She lights the cigarette.

THE MOTHER: Evening's falling.

GERTRUDIS: Uh hum.

THE MOTHER: I always take him out for a walk in the evening,
              sometimes in the morning. In the afternoon it's
              usually too windy.

GERTRUDIS: The afternoon, the evening . . . How sweet,
              "Evening Walk!"

THE MOTHER: What?

GERTRUDIS: A commercial title for a novel . . .

THE MOTHER: For a novel?

GERTRUDIS: I'm a writer.

THE MOTHER: A writer! No wonder.

GERTRUDIS:	What?
THE MOTHER:	Nothing, just no wonder . . .
GERTRUDIS:	You also think I'm crazy.
THE MOTHER:	No, I don't. That's not what I meant.
GERTRUDIS:	But you said it.
THE MOTHER:	No, I haven't said anything. I only . . .
GERTRUDIS:	Shut up!
THE MOTHER:	I didn't mean to . . .
GERTRUDIS:	You meant it, you said it, I heard you . . . Well, it doesn't matter, it goes with the territory.
THE MOTHER:	It's that I thought . . .
GERTRUDIS:	What a crazy, eccentric woman; she must be mad!
THE MOTHER:	Who do you work for?
GERTRUDIS:	For myself.
THE MOTHER:	No, I mean, for what publishing house.
GERTRUDIS:	For none, I'm unemployed.
THE MOTHER:	I'm . . .
GERTRUDIS:	No, don't be sorry. I work, I have fun, I smoke, copulate, eat, laugh, sing, cry, sleep, dream . . .
THE MOTHER:	Forgive me.
GERTRUDIS:	No, I can't forgive you, I don't feel like it,

I've been forgiving all my life.
Do you think I look like God?
No. God's a man.
I'm a woman,
God is old.
I'm young.
God forced Mary to be unfaithful to Joseph.
Not me, I don't get involved with married men.
I'm somewhat wild, but I would never
ask the clouds to cry
in order to drown humanity.
I would've never allowed Abraham
to be unfaithful to Sarah.
What do you expect?
What does everyone expect?
That I would be born to forgive?
No. I was born to sin and never be forgiven.
Perfect! "Evening Walk";
I'll start right now.

THE MOTHER: I don't know what to say . . .

GERTRUDIS: You better not say anything. Sh!, sh!, sh!, sh! Shut
                up, I think you're a woman like all the rest.

THE MOTHER: I'm a mother . . .

GERTRUDIS: I know, I can see. Your little one sleeps and sleeps
                and sleeps.

THE MOTHER: He cries a lot, he's still very young. Sometimes he
                exasperates me.

GERTRUDIS: You were the one who wanted him, but now . . .

THE MOTHER: No, it wasn't me. My husband begged me, cried, he
                even threatened me with divorce.

GERTRUDIS: I can imagine. Then you let yourself be
                blackmailed by that stupid husband of yours
                and . . .

THE MOTHER: And nine months later I gave birth to a little
                boy . . .

GERTRUDIS:	And he's the family's pride and joy?
THE MOTHER:	Yes, the family's pride and joy.
GERTRUDIS:	I don't know why you succumbed?
THE MOTHER:	It goes with the territory.
GERTRUDIS:	Yes.
THE MOTHER:	What are you going to do with the novel?
GERTRUDIS:	Finish it.
THE MOTHER:	It must be hard to write.
GERTRUDIS:	Oh no, you only have to know how to listen carefully.
THE MOTHER:	It's that easy . . .
GERTRUDIS:	Yes, as easy as giving birth.
THE MOTHER:	That's not easy.
GERTRUDIS:	I know . . . it's awful.
THE MOTHER:	What?
GERTRUDIS:	To have children.
THE MOTHER:	Yes, people think that this business of raising a family . . .
GERTRUDIS:	They should give a medal to everybody.
THE MOTHER:	War heroes.
GERTRUDIS:	No, all those who raise families are courageous, national heroes, those are the true heroes. Those who go to war, those wounded, mutilated,

deaf, crazy heroes, they're all a bunch of cowards
who never dared to say NO,
who rigidly march to courageously fulfill
their mission to kill others . . .
Forward, march

THE MOTHER: Hut, two, three, four

BOTH: Hut, two, three, four

GERTRUDIS: Hut, two, three, four
You march very well.

THE MOTHER: I was a girl scout.

GERTRUDIS: I thought so.
All girl scouts
know how to march,
sew, cook,
then they become the Future Homemakers of
America.

THE MOTHER: Then we marry
a boy scout . . .

GERTRUDIS: And you have many French poodles.

THE MOTHER: That go bow wow.

GERTRUDIS: Blip, blop.
Hut, two,
Blip, blop.
two, one.

THE MOTHER: Three

GERTRUDIS: Mrs. Rodríguez, it's been so long.

THE MOTHER: Glad to see you again, Mrs. Rodríguez.

GERTRUDIS: Oh, Mrs. Rodríguez
if I could only tell you how Mr. Rodríguez
took off his underwear last night.

THE MOTHER: Oh, Mrs. Rodríguez, if only I told you
how Mrs. Rodríguez
was dressed last night for the cocktail party.

GERTRUDIS: Mrs. Rodríguez is a . . .

They both laugh.

THE MOTHER: Everyone says it . . .

GERTRUDIS: Gossip,
gossip,
history is a piece of gossip,
and the human being a gossiper,
per,
per,
per,
per

THE MOTHER: per,
per,
per,
per

GERTRUDIS: And all of a sudden Goldilocks arrived
and said to her grandmother,
"Grandmother,
grandmother, what big eyes you have."

THE MOTHER: "The better to see you with, my dear . . ."

GERTRUDIS: "What a big nose you have."

THE MOTHER: "The better to smell you with, my dear . . ."

GERTRUDIS: "What big ears you have."

THE MOTHER: "The better to hear you with, my dear . . ."

GERTRUDIS: "What a big mouth you have."

THE MOTHER: "The better to eat you with, my dear . . ."
Fraud . . . killer, where's Little Red Riding Hood?

Where did you hide her?

GERTRUDIS:	My mother made her into a strawberry shortcake

and she's here in my little basket,
but suddenly,
wham! . . .
Goldilocks turned into a
handsome prince
and the grandmother wolf
into a huge pumpkin.
The prince took out his golden sword
and split the pumpkin in two
and out came thousands of bugs
cockroaches, mice . . . the plague . . .
HORROR! The prince had opened
Pandora's box
and it became dark
forever.

THE MOTHER: Oh, I didn't know Pandora was a prince.

GERTRUDIS: No, he was actually a degenerate transvestite
who loved to disguise himself as
Little Red Riding Hood
little basket, little ball . . . all, all, all

THE MOTHER: How funny! And what became of the
grandmother?

GERTRUDIS: She was poisoned to death
after having eaten her granddaughter turned into a
strawberry
shortcake.

THE MOTHER: Oh, be quiet!

GERTRUDIS: And Goldilocks ended up as one of those
homosexuals who parade up and down the bus
stop . . .

THE MOTHER: Shut up!

GERTRUDIS: What's wrong with you, huh?

Getting a little too bold?
The girl scouts are going to punish you for . . .

THE MOTHER: Shut up, please!

GERTRUDIS: I didn't know you were so sensitive.

THE MOTHER: The granny . . .

GERTRUDIS: She was poisoned to death.

THE MOTHER: Yes.

GERTRUDIS: Does it make you sad?

THE MOTHER: It scares me.

GERTRUDIS: Don't worry,
I'll write the story for you,
okay?

THE MOTHER: Yes.

GERTRUDIS: Fine, sit down. (*Clearing her throat.*) Humph,
humph . . .
the grandmother lived happily ever after
along with her little granddaughter,
the little basket,
Goldilocks, and the wolf,
and she will never get sick again.
There it is. You like
happy endings, don't you?

THE MOTHER: Yes, when I was a little girl they were always
happy.

GERTRUDIS: Mine, too . . . it wasn't till later that
I discovered the world
and my entire vision changed,
they were all sad endings.
When one grows up everything's different . . .
Hey, what about the baby?

THE MOTHER: He's asleep!

GERTRUDIS: Fine, fine, calm down, don't get so worked up.
                I'm not going to start screaming,
                I'm not that inconsiderate.

THE MOTHER: It's just that I got scared.

GERTRUDIS: You got scared?
                Hey, what's wrong with you?
                What did that stupid husband of yours do to you?

THE MOTHER: Don't call him stupid!
                He's like all the others,
                with his rules, outdated ideas,
                emotional blackmail.

GERTRUDIS: He's hateful!
                I would've left him a long time ago.

THE MOTHER: Are you married?

GERTRUDIS: I was . . . four different times.

THE MOTHER: Four?! . . .

GERTRUDIS: Yes, nowadays that's common . . .
                just read the Bible . . . it's common
                for people to marry and unmarry a couple of times.
                What do you think, that Cinderella didn't
                get a divorce?
                Yes, after several years, she did.

THE MOTHER: What was your husband like?

GERTRUDIS: Which one?

THE MOTHER: Well, tell me about all of them.

GERTRUDIS: They were all the same, the only
                thing that was different was . . . sex . . .
                some were better, others okay . . .
                others . . . same as the movies

do you understand? PG, R, X, Y, Z, triple X,
exactly the same . . .

THE MOTHER: Did you become sad when . . .

GERTRUDIS: Every time I separated I knew
exactly what I had to do . . .
call the lawyer . . .
papers . . . signatures . . .
the judge who looked like a beefsteak . . .
exactly like it happens in cheap movies.

THE MOTHER: You've experienced a lot . . .

GERTRUDIS: Gosh, no, nobody ever experiences
too much.
That only happened during the Renaissance . . .
Oh, and in the Bible,
of course.

THE MOTHER: I see you read the Bible a lot . . .

GERTRUDIS: You can't see anything . . . you only hear . . .
Yes, I read it once in a while,
it's so morbid and so angelical, the
eunuchs, the annunciation, Noah, Moses,
Abraham, Christ himself . . .
It's a fun book.

THE MOTHER: In school we had to . . .

GERTRUDIS: Go to church, . . .
and to think that women
didn't smoke and that it was a sin
to take the pill.
Bah! They should plant bombs in all
the schools . . . all they do is
mess up people's heads.

THE MOTHER: I graduated with honors.

GERTRUDIS: What for? So that your stupid
husband would get you pregnant.

THE MOTHER: I worked for a while . . .
              I'm a dietician.

GERTRUDIS: You went to college?
              But how could you possibly
              waste so much time?
              I don't understand it, you seem intelligent . . .

THE MOTHER: Why do you say that?
              Everyone goes to college.

GERTRUDIS: Why do I say it?
              I say it because soldiers march,
              because women clean all day long,
              because bishops drink wine,
              because teachers are allergic to chalk,
              because children die of hunger,
              because men use prophylactics
              because young people can dance to rock music,
              because grannies can make onion soup . . .
              I say it because what good is it to go to
              college if, anyway, a stupid man
              is going to come along and get you pregnant . . .

THE MOTHER: It was a little boy!

GERTRUDIS: Eve gave birth to two of them and look where that
              got us . . .
              What do I care if it was a little boy
              or a little girl?
              Anyway, you're there
              and I'm here.

THE MOTHER: Do you have any children?

GERTRUDIS: No. I was never interested in
              becoming a slave.

THE MOTHER: Being a mother isn't the same as being a slave.

GERTRUDIS: Come, come.
              What happened to your people?
              To your bastard children?

Being a mother isn't the same as being a slave!
How sweet! How dedicated!
So what does it mean to be a mother?

THE MOTHER: It means . . .

GERTRUDIS: To forget oneself
in order to give oneself to others.
To be a mother is nothing important . . .
If you were a philosopher . . . a scientist
at least you could be proud
of having a profession.

THE MOTHER: I do have one! I'm a dietician, I already told you.

GERTRUDIS: And what do I care if you're a dietician?
You haven't contributed anything to history . . .
the lives of others don't depend on you
nor will you be missed
in the writing of one more chapter
of this pigsty called history . . .

THE MOTHER: My son depends on me,
I'm indispensable to him.

GERTRUDIS: That's a lie!
If you die, your mother or your mother-in-law will
    take care of him,
he'll grow up like the rest.
Those who plan to be parents . . .
should be examined first.

THE MOTHER: What for?

GERTRUDIS: Not everyone was born
to do this.
Sometimes it becomes an obligation.
If you don't do it, they think you're sterile.
Eve? Eve, what did you do?
They should prosecute her.

THE MOTHER: Who?

GERTRUDIS:	Eve, for being so stupid.
THE MOTHER:	I, I mean, my husband . . .
GERTRUDIS:	It's the same, the two of you are a couple of stupid people.
THE MOTHER:	How dare you?
GERTRUDIS:	Dare what? That's what bothers you. That I dared and you didn't, you let him blackmail you.
THE MOTHER:	You're a . . .
GERTRUDIS:	Oh no, please don't say it, I could get frantic, I become furious, I could yank your head off.
THE MOTHER:	You're so insensitive!
GERTRUDIS:	Or perhaps I could become depressed for a couple of months, I would have to take tranquilizers, go to the psychiatrist . . .
THE MOTHER:	You should go . . .
GERTRUDIS:	Where?
THE MOTHER:	To a psychiatrist.
GERTRUDIS:	They don't know anything, they're a bunch of busy bodies, all they like to do is listen to someone else's problems and reach absurd conclusions. I'd rather go to a priest and confess, it's the same. In the end they're the same . . . a bunch of busy bodies.

Hey, your baby sleeps a lot.
Can I see him?

THE MOTHER: No!

The mother chases Gertrudis throughout the stage either on all fours or curling her fingers like the claws of a lioness.

GERTRUDIS: The lioness . . .
Once upon a time
There was a tiny baby boy
Who lived in a baby carriage . . .
His mother was a lioness
And the sad part of the story
Is that one day
While the baby was sleeping
His mother ate him,
She couldn't resist the tender and delicious smell
Of young flesh.

THE MOTHER: Shut up!
You don't know anything.
He's my son.
You'll see,
I'll call my husband.
Cruel!
You're very cruel.
Do you think you know everything?
Be quiet! Be quiet!
I'll kill you!

GERTRUDIS: You'll kill me?
You wouldn't dare.
You didn't even dare
to say no to that stupid
husband of yours . . .

THE MOTHER: You don't know anything!

GERTRUDIS: I know. I don't know anything.
I'm lost, lost in this chaotic world . . .

Gertrudis cries.

THE MOTHER: Forgive me, don't cry,
                   please,
                   forgive me . . .

Gertrudis gets up furious.

GERTRUDIS: I already told you I'm not God,
                   that I can't forgive,
                   that I hate nylons,
                   beauty shops,
                   social gatherings,
                   stinky grannies,
                   beer bellies,
                   punch cards,
                   people who refuse to think,
                   who imprison themselves.

THE MOTHER: Stop crying, please.

GERTRUDIS: You're right, I'm not going to lose
                   my mind simply because
                   I'm depressed,
                   because I've been depressed
                   for thirty years,
                   no, that's no reason.

THE MOTHER: I'm telling you
                   you should see a psychiatrist.

GERTRUDIS: What for?
                   So that he can start a medical record for me
                   where it says that I'm an incurable schizophrenic?

THE MOTHER: Maybe he could help you . . .

GERTRUDIS: I know what's wrong with me,
                   that's the problem, I know myself,
                   I'll have to put up with myself . . .
                   until I die.

THE MOTHER: You have to finish the novel.

GERTRUDIS: That's true.
                   Can I hold your baby for a little bit?

THE MOTHER:	No!
GERTRUDIS:	What's the matter?
THE MOTHER:	He's very little.
GERTRUDIS:	I've held babies before . . . I know how to do it.
THE MOTHER:	He might wake up, he's very little.
GERTRUDIS:	I think he has slept too much.
THE MOTHER:	He always sleeps a lot.
GERTRUDIS:	Let me see him, they look so cute.
THE MOTHER:	No! I don't want anybody to see him, he's mine.
GERTRUDIS:	I know he's yours, I'm not going to take him away from you, I won't hurt him.
THE MOTHER:	No. I prefer you didn't see him.
GERTRUDIS:	You're selfish.
THE MOTHER:	No, don't·say that.

She starts crying.

GERTRUDIS:	What's the matter with you?
THE MOTHER:	Nothing . . . the baby's sleeping . . .
GERTRUDIS:	When he's older he'll be able to enjoy the evening walks . . .
THE MOTHER:	No, I want him to stay this small.

GERTRUDIS: Don't be ridiculous!
                  Everyone grows up,
                  it's logical for us to grow, natural . . .

THE MOTHER: He'll stay this small . . .

GERTRUDIS: Come on, let me see him.

THE MOTHER: No, please . . .
                  he cried so much . . . so much . . .
                  it exasperated me to hear him cry . . .
                  I didn't want to have him,
                  I knew I couldn't,
                  but . . . so many pressures . . .
                  He told me he was going to look for another
                      woman,
                  that I was good for nothing,
                  that a child would bring us happiness,
                  he cried so much . . .

Gertrudis goes over to the carriage, she lifts the blanket, she sticks her head inside, she's horrified . . .

                  I didn't know what to do,
                  he's so little,
                  so defenseless,
                  he's a little boy, you know,
                  the first grandson . . .
                  They're all very happy,
                  but he cries so much . . .

Gertrudis begins to cry.

GERTRUDIS: I told you that soldiers march
                  hut two, three, four
                  that grandmothers make onion soup
                  hut two, three, four
                  that mothers clean
                  hut two, three, four
                  that Mrs. Rodríguez laughs without a care
                  hut two, three, four
                  that girl scouts

have lots of French poodles
hut two, three, four

THE MOTHER: It scares you, huh?
It horrifies you?
Now it's you who fears,
you're the stupid one,
the one who doesn't know what to do
You think it was easy?
Well, it was,
it was as simple
as crushing him . . .
as simple as being a girl scout,
as simple as laughing or crying . . .
You can't accept it . . .
a simple woman like me,
just an ordinary dietician,
with an ordinary husband,
and an ordinary house . . .
what do you have to say now?
Will you be able to finish your novel?
Will you be able to continue lighting cigarettes?
Will you be able to continue having four
    husbands?
Do you think that nothing is worthwhile?
Do you think that you'll continue being a shitty
    writer?
Perhaps no one will forgive me,
perhaps no one will ever understand me . . .
just an ordinary dietician . . .
Perhaps this is the last evening,
the last evening walk . . .
We don't know anything,
we don't even know ourselves,
there's no happy ending
in this story . . .
Here the grandmother was poisoned to death,
and so was Little Red Riding Hood,
also Goldilocks,
and the prince . . .
In this story the little boy also died
and the sweet little mother
became a ferocious wolf . . .

GERTRUDIS: You had no right,
                    I was here peacefully . . . alone . . .

THE MOTHER: What are you going to do?
                    You give it an ending.
                    It can be happy;
                    it can be sad.
                    It all depends on how you end the novel . . .
                    On paper everything is much easier . . .
                    simpler . . .
                    you just put down whatever comes to your head.
                    It could be that the little mother never
                    went out for a walk
                    or that the little boy grew strong and healthy . . .

GERTRUDIS: It could be that the writer never met
                    the little mother
                    nor her grandmother,
                    that she never knew anything,
                    that everything was just one more page
                    in her novel . . .

THE MOTHER: It could be,
                    it could be,
                    it could be . . .
                    Shshshsh, the baby's sleeping,
                    he could wake up . . .

GERTRUDIS: There could be two endings . . .
                    the little mother could escape
                    and the writer could take care
                    of the little boy,
                    She herself could call the police
                    and say that she kidnapped him
                    and then . . . this could be the ending . . .

THE MOTHER: Or the little mother could sit down,
                    rock her baby,
                    while the writer
                    calls for help
                    and the little mother insistently says . . .
                    the baby's sleeping, the baby's sleeping . . .

The two endings are staged in slow motion and in silence.

> Which ending will you give it, writer?
> Which one of them will be the real one?
> With which one will you end your novel?
> You're the only one who knows,
> you're the only one who can create it . . .

The mother is rocking the baby carriage.

> Simple, easy . . .
> You decide . . . you shitty writer!
> Only you will decide

The mother rocks the carriage vigorously as she stares in front of her.

The writer picks up her purse, begins looking for the matches, lights a cigarette; she stands on the wooden box and begins to scream.

GERTRUDIS: Hang the windows,
                Raise the flags and sails . . .

The writer looks at herself, gets off the box, looks at the woman, turns around, looks at the audience.

THE MOTHER: You're the only one
                who can give it an ending . . .

GERTRUDIS: HELP, help, . . . police, police, police,

The lights dim gradually, the windows are lowered.

Spotlight on the mother's face.

THE MOTHER: Shshshshsh,
                the baby's sleeping . . .

She looks toward Gertrudis.

THE MOTHER: Shitty writer!

The lights go off.

End of Evening Walk

Note

1. For permission to stage the play, the author must be contacted directly: c/o Flavia de Marichal, Apdo. 21894 U.P.R. San Juan, PR 00931-1894

Diana Raznovich (Buenos Aires, Argentina, 1945)—dramatist, poet, cartoonist, novelist, essayist—has been involved in the arts, particularly in theater, since childhood. Her literary career began with the publication of a book of poems entitled *Tiempo de amar* (Time to Love, 1963). Simultaneously, she wrote *Buscapiés* (A Squib, 1968), which marked an important milestone in her career, for it not only premiered in the renowned San Martín theater of Buenos Aires but also received that year's Municipal Prize. Since then she has been writing steadily for the theater, having created sixteen plays, including a children's musical comedy. Her plays have been staged not only in her native country but also throughout Europe, South America, the United States, and Australia.

Although Raznovich's work deals with political issues, the emphasis on aesthetics and the use of highly stylized characters and dramatic situations veil the political content. Another issue prevalent in her plays is the question of identity, which she addresses by pitting the public persona against the private individual. This allows her to examine professional integrity, the tension between social constructs and authenticity, and the importance of role playing in the search for a "true" identity. Through the effective use of metatheatrical devices, Raznovich constructs the framework that this search requires to undergo the inevitable process of self-reflexivity.

Dial-a-Mom[1]

BY DIANA RAZNOVICH[2]

Translated from *Casa matriz*
by Teresa Cajiao Salas and Margarita Vargas

Stage

A room appropriate for a thirty-year-old woman who is a poet and a professor of literature. More than a room, however, the scenery should reproduce the untidiness of a bedroom in which things have been strategically disarranged.

The salmon-color linen on the bed is in total disarray.

Books are piled up on the corners. Stockings and nightgowns carefully hang from the open drawers of a chest. The dominant colors are different shades of pink and red. The main character is also wearing the same colors as if she were a part of a space, her space, theatrically created to receive the substitute mother.

There is an empty clothes rack full of hangers. Everything seems to he on hold, awaiting nothing. The scene creates the sensation that the room is floating.

Characters

GLORIA:	Thirty years old. A very sensuous and attractive, but moody and grouchy woman. (Translators' Note: In the original, this character's name is Barbara. We changed the name to be able to carry out a play with words that occur in the text.)
SUBSTITUTE MOTHER:	About fifty years old. A woman of meticulously beautiful features. Trained in histrionics, she is able to perform radical changes. She moves naturally from one role to the next. She is an employee at the Mother Center.

AUTHOR'S EXPLANATORY NOTE

The Mother Center is a business that rents out substitute mothers. Whoever requests this service has the right to select, among the highly qualified staff, a woman who will perform a series of mother roles agreed upon in advance by the Mother Center and the customer.

The performance will take place either in the customer's home or in a place deemed suitable by the customer for the unfolding of the sequence of multiple mother roles requested. The cost of the service and the number of mother roles will be stipulated in advance.

> *When the play begins, Gloria is wearing a tight salmon-color silk slip. Standing on a flimsy box, she is directing Bach's "Magnificat" with a baton and is possessed by the music which drowns the stage with its high volume.*
> *The doorbell rings: she doesn't seem to hear it.*
> *She continues "directing" Bach. The doorbell then rings repeatedly.*

> *Gloria, in a sudden fit of rage, motivated by the repeated ringing of the doorbell, breaks her baton: the music stops as if by magic:*

GLORIA: It was a very important moment! I had achieved a decisive encounter with what I would undoubtedly one day call "my happiness" (*Upset, she opens the door.*)

> *The woman at the door, dressed in a modern tailored suit and carrying a suitcase, examines her with a blank face.*

SUBSTITUTE MOTHER: (*With a neutral, efficient, controlled voice.*) Am I late?

GLORIA: (*Playing the role of "daughter."*) Come in mother, come in . . . You look great in that suit! You always look so elegant! Is it a Chanel?

SUBSTITUTE MOTHER: Oui, ma cherie . . .

GLORIA: How was your trip?

SUBSTITUTE MOTHER: (*Even though she still doesn't know what trip her "substitute daughter" is talking about she must adapt quickly.*) Wonderful! (*Acting out of character, she speaks quickly to get some information.*) Excuse me miss, where was I supposed to have gone?

GLORIA: (*Puzzled.*) Didn't they tell you at the Mother Center? When I hired you, I specified everything . . .

SUBSTITUTE MOTHER:	They told me I was supposed to return from a trip . . . That . . . (*She tries to remember.*) Are you the customer who requested a mother who recently returned from India?
GLORIA:	No.
SUBSTITUTE MOTHER:	(*Insisting.*) But, aren't you the woman who needed a mother who is fond of riding elephants with a Hindu lover whose ancestor was Ghandi?
GLORIA:	You're mistaking me for another customer. I never requested such a mother. (*She paces furiously up and down the stage.*) Someone else must have requested that option!
SUBSTITUTE MOTHER:	(*She opens a folder where she has notes about her customers. She checks.*) You're right. I got you mixed up with another customer. I apologize, I'm very busy. It doesn't happen to me often. But sometimes I confuse one customer with another, and I act out the substitute mother someone else requested . . . Forgive me . . . That mother was requested by Mr. . . . well we don't give out names . . . but it's a gentleman I have to visit tomorrow. He's addicted to suffering from nostalgia. (*She checks her notes.*) Oh, yes . . . you contracted Plan G. I've got it written down here. Do you want me to start from the beginning?
GLORIA:	No. Let's continue. (*She yells.*) Incompetent!
SUBSTITUTE MOTHER:	I? I've been working as a substitute mother for years.
GLORIA:	How can you mix up your customers! I scrimped and saved to afford to hire a substitute mother. And in your first scene you confuse me with another customer!
SUBSTITUTE MOTHER:	(*Self-assured.*) Well . . . my job is to cause

passions to run wild. And I just accomplished
it with you. You're extremely jealous of my
other customer.

*Gloria, touched and offended, slaps the woman. It's an unexpected
punishment which creates a tense moment.*

SUBSTITUTE MOTHER: You hit me before you were supposed to.

GLORIA: And you acted out the entrance scene paid for
by somebody else.

SUBSTITUTE MOTHER: I liked the idea of coming from India. They
rarely ever ask for women who ride on
elephants . . . The entrance you requested,
however, is a sad cliché.

GLORIA: I requested you make me wait a long time. I
asked to be given time to build up an illusory
feeling of anxiety. You didn't give me time to
doubt! I wanted to be afraid you wouldn't
show up! I paid for the uncertainty of not
knowing whether my mother was coming or
not, but you ruined everything by arriving so
damned early. Do you have any more
customers later on?

SUBSTITUTE MOTHER: Before and after. I always have a lot of
customers.

GLORIA: But what does the mother who rides elephants
have to do with that cold and heartless mother
who used to make me wait trembling?

SUBSTITUTE MOTHER: You didn't tremble before I arrived?

GLORIA: I was beginning to tremble. If you had delayed
five more minutes, and hadn't gotten your
customers mixed up, your entrance would've
been a success. (*She suddenly changes her tone.*)
You've made this same mistake all your life.
You've always given me what belonged to my

brother John, and to John what belonged to Paula.

SUBSTITUTE MOTHER: (*She plays the role of the mother again.*) Your house looks great, Maria.

GLORIA: Gloria.

SUBSTITUTE MOTHER: (*She corrects herself.*) Your house looks glorious, Maria.

GLORIA: No, I was telling you my name is Gloria and not Maria.

SUBSTITUTE MOTHER: I know. But you want me to mix you up with someone else, Maria. You paid so I wouldn't remember your name.

GLORIA: But, how can my own mother not know my name? It was you who gave it to me. When you saw me coming out of your own body, a few minutes after the delivery, you whispered, glorious! (*Her eyes fill with tears.*) You didn't give me a name, you gave me an adjective!

SUBSTITUTE MOTHER: Are you reproaching me?

GLORIA: You have to reproach me for not being sufficiently glorious. For that I suppose you must have the appropriate costume.

SUBSTITUTE MOTHER: (*She nods.*) Of course, I'm a professional. I have anticipated everything.

She opens her bag and begins to take out the appropriate clothes to act out the different mother roles: she hangs them on the clothes rack Gloria had prepared for her. She undresses quickly; she puts on a flower-print robe, a cap with hair curlers, and worn-out shoes with low heels. She changes her posture: she becomes a reproachful mother.

SUBSTITUTE MOTHER: I curse the moment I baptized you! Whatever gave me the idea of calling you Gloria?

GLORIA: I also curse it, mother. With such a name you doomed me to failure.

SUBSTITUTE MOTHER: If you had listened to me, you would've married the diplomat you met at your friend's house. Now you would really be living in Glory. But you married Joe . . .

GLORIA: Joe isn't such a bad guy, mother . . .

SUBSTITUTE MOTHER: He's never worked in his entire life . . . And he's given you all these kids . . . whom I support.

GLORIA: My salary barely pays the rent . . .

SUBSTITUTE MOTHER: Joe, hmmf! Where in hell did you find him? Did you win him in the Lotto or on the "Price is Right?" You're such an idiot, Gloria! You're nothing like me.

GLORIA: Why? Was dad any better than Joe?

SUBSTITUTE MOTHER: At least he worked. He would spend it on wine. But, he got drunk with his own money and never asked me for anything.

GLORIA: Joe doesn't drink. He takes care of the kids. He's honest.

SUBSTITUTE MOTHER: He's another idiot. You're a pair of idiots, and I have to support you. You and your descendants.

GLORIA: They're your grandchildren, mother!

SUBSTITUTE MOTHER: My grandchildren! They're my burden. You leave them with me all day long while Joe sleeps. You work. And I take care of the children, and spend my savings trying to feed you . . . Some deal! And to top it all off, I named you Gloria. You of all people, to be named Gloria!

Gloria starts crying all of a sudden.

SUBSTITUTE MOTHER: An idiot like you . . . poor little Gloria!

Gloria cries bitterly.

SUBSTITUTE MOTHER: (*Merciless.*) I should've called you Punishment, Desolation, Boredom, Putrefaction, Shit. Those names fit you.

GLORIA: (*Gloria smiles satisfied.*) That's it! It's exactly the type of mother role I requested. You're really very good!

SUBSTITUTE MOTHER: (*Excited.*) I'm very good and you are a scourge. You're worse than Satan. It's killing me to spend all my money on Joe and those kids who eat like horses.

GLORIA: (*She screams all of a sudden.*) That's enough. Today is my birthday, mother. How can you say those things?

SUBSTITUTE MOTHER: (*Out of character.*) At the Mother Center they told me you specifically requested this type of overbearing mother.

GLORIA: I know, I know. But I've had enough masochistic satisfaction for one day. I'm telling you, though, today is really my birthday.

SUBSTITUTE MOTHER: Are you thirty?

GLORIA: Yes.

SUBSTITUTE MOTHER: That's common, we're used to being hired for special occasions. Not only birthdays, but during other holidays as well. During Christmas we have a lot of work. And on wedding anniversaries! Sometimes they hire two substitute mothers, one for each person in a couple.

GLORIA:	So you're telling me I'm not an exception.
SUBSTITUTE MOTHER:	I'm telling you that situation is common place.
GLORIA:	But I was asking you to wish me a happy birthday, and to act like the charming mother I also requested.
SUBSTITUTE MOTHER:	Okay, okay . . . Of course. (*She goes to the clothes rack. She takes off her clothes and puts on a very funny dress from the sixties: platinum wig, bright lipstick. She smiles. She puts on a pair of tap dance shoes. She unpacks a huge present, very prettily wrapped, and she gives it to Gloria.*) Oh my darling Gloria . . . I wish you all the happiness in the world. Happy birthday to you!

Gloria, thrilled, takes the present. It's a beautiful dress: somewhat childish. Gloria puts it on. Happy music, which evokes the traditional "Happy Birthday" tune, is heard.

SUBSTITUTE MOTHER:	(*Singing.*) Happy birthday to you . . . (etc.).

Gloria thanks her: she kisses her warmly. They hug.

GLORIA:	How nice! . . . I'm so glad to see you! You're so thoughtful.
SUBSTITUTE MOTHER:	The dress looks great on you. You're so pretty . . . I'm very proud of you, my dear Gloria . . .
GLORIA:	Every day I thank God for the blessing of having such a special mother . . . so understanding . . .
SUBSTITUTE MOTHER:	There's nothing to be understanding about. You've never caused me any problems. You're a fabulous daughter. I was right in naming you Gloria. That name fits you perfectly. There are few people who deserve the name they have, and who carry it as well as you do.

They hug tenderly.

SUBSTITUTE MOTHER: I love you . . . I love you so much . . .

GLORIA: And I love you, mother . . .

SUBSTITUTE MOTHER: You're the best thing that ever happened to me. My great act of inspiration.

GLORIA: Well . . . (*Modestly.*) I'm like you . . .

SUBSTITUTE MOTHER: You're much better than I . . .

GLORIA: It does me good to hear you say those things . . .

SUBSTITUTE MOTHER: I can imagine. I say them very well.

GLORIA: (*Out of sorts.*) What are you saying?

SUBSTITUTE MOTHER: I mean . . . just look at how well I perform the different personalities requested by the customer.

GLORIA: Wait a minute. I didn't pay for you to come here and brag about your talent! . . .

SUBSTITUTE MOTHER: I realize that.

GLORIA: I'm getting tired of you. This charming mother you were acting out never says "I realize that." She says: You're marvelous, Gloria.

SUBSTITUTE MOTHER: You're marvelous, Gloria.

GLORIA: Say something that's your own. Something that I haven't suggested.

SUBSTITUTE MOTHER: You're a joy. (*She hugs her.*)

GLORIA: I feel like celebrating, what about you?

SUBSTITUTE MOTHER: (*She dances an American tap dance. Gloria puts on an appropriate record. She claps. She brings in a bottle of champagne and opens it.*) Great! Let's toast!

Gloria pours the champagne.

GLORIA: Here's to the best mother in the world.

SUBSTITUTE MOTHER: To your happiness! Because you deserve the best! To the privilege of being your mother!

They toast and drink: then they kiss.

SUBSTITUTE MOTHER: And Peter? When's he coming?

GLORIA: Peter . . .

SUBSTITUTE MOTHER: (*She gets close to her and takes her hand.*) Is something wrong with Peter, my love?

GLORIA: No . . . there's nothing wrong . . .

SUBSTITUTE MOTHER: We were always confidants. Don't hide anything from me . . .

GLORIA: There's nothing to hide.

SUBSTITUTE MOTHER: But a few months ago you told me Peter had proposed.

GLORIA: Yes. It's true.

SUBSTITUTE MOTHER: You seemed to be in love . . .

GLORIA: Oh . . . love . . . it doesn't last long . . . what a pity, huh? How have you and Dad managed to be in love for so long?

SUBSTITUTE MOTHER: It's a miracle that still endures.

GLORIA: Well, then let's say that with Peter there was neither a miracle nor endurance.

SUBSTITUTE MOTHER: I must admit; I could see it coming . . .

GLORIA: You seemed to like Peter.

SUBSTITUTE MOTHER: Oh, yes! He's a nice guy. Besides, I know his parents very well. I had nothing against him, and if you loved him, there was nothing left to say. But . . .

GLORIA: But . . .

SUBSTITUTE MOTHER: You're better than he is in every way, Gloria. You're more brilliant, more intelligent, more capable, more seductive, and to top it off, you make almost twice as much. That's very hard for a man to take . . . A competition is established which isn't good. He needs a bimbo. You're special.

GLORIA: We're still good friends.

SUBSTITUTE MOTHER: He must be devastated . . .

GLORIA: No, just a little depressed.

SUBSTITUTE MOTHER: It's not easy losing someone like Gloria.

Gloria laughs.

GLORIA: (*She steps out of the daughter role for a moment.*) Say it as though you really mean it. I paid a lot of money to hear this.

SUBSTITUTE MOTHER: I said it's not easy losing someone like my dear daughter Gloria. You're absolutely irreplaceable.

GLORIA: (*Enjoying it. Demanding.*) Make the sentence better. Be more explicit.

SUBSTITUTE MOTHER: (*Compliant.*) You're unique, dear. No man could resign himself to losing you. You're wonderful. (*She kisses her.*)

GLORIA: Irreplaceable . . . I like being irreplaceable.

SUBSTITUTE MOTHER:	You are. (*She steps out of her role and shouts.*) I, on the other hand, am totally replaceable. I'm a substitute mother . . .
GLORIA:	(*Persistent.*) Don't remind me now just when we had achieved this unforgettable scene. Talk about me.
SUBSTITUTE MOTHER:	Yes, forgive me. (*She resumes her role of a charming mother.*) My dear Gloria: you're irreplaceable, you're unique even in your ordinariness, you're original even when you're obvious and above all, you're a great person.
GLORIA:	Repeat that. It was very expensive. This mother is one of the most expensive ones.
SUBSTITUTE MOTHER:	Gloria, you're the best person I know.
GLORIA:	You can't say that. You're my mother.
SUBSTITUTE MOTHER:	I'm not the only one who says it. It's an opinion held by many. Everyone who meets you is fascinated.
GLORIA:	Say that more slowly.
SUBSTITUTE MOTHER:	(*Slowly.*) Everyone who meets you is dazzled.
GLORIA:	Louder.
SUBSTITUTE MOTHER:	Every person who meets you feels the impact of your radiant personality.
GLORIA:	Enough. You've gone too far. Your flattery is smothering. You always overdo everything a little.
SUBSTITUTE MOTHER:	We're instructed to do that. Our training demands it. Otherwise, no one would hire a substitute mother. We would all be out of work. Every customer has or has had a real mother. We can't be realistic in our acting, since

our job is to impersonate other imaginary
mothers.

GLORIA: It's a fascinating experience.

SUBSTITUTE MOTHER: That's what the Mother Center sells.
Fascinating experiences.

GLORIA: (*Enthusiastically.*) You're not limited to the one
mother who brought you into the world. You
can experience other models . . .

SUBSTITUTE MOTHER: You've understood the value of our service.

GLORIA: Put this house in order. Now you have to play
the submissive mother!

SUBSTITUTE MOTHER: (*She protests.*) Everybody, absolutely everybody
needs to see me in the saddest bondage. I can
never get away without cleaning the house.
Not even for the more progressive ones. We've
turned in complaints to the Labor
Commission. This job has denigrating effects.
We're substitute mothers and we're taken for
maids!

The substitute mother puts on a disheveled wig, a MAID's *uniform, and
then takes cleaning equipment out of the suitcase. She takes off her
shoes and puts on a pair of huge wool slippers. She starts cleaning
frantically. Gloria watches her pleased.*

SUBSTITUTE MOTHER: Do you prefer her nagging or archetypal?

GLORIA: Quiet. Suffering. Silent. Make me feel she
really suffers.

*Substitute mother cleans and sighs; she complains of a back ache. She
continues cleaning. She squats to clean the floor. Gloria dresses
seductively. She wants to irritate the archetypal mother; she puts on a
pair of tight jeans and a very tight T-shirt. She puts on make-up. She
fixes her hair.*

SUBSTITUTE MOTHER: (*While cleaning.*) Are you going out with that
junkie?

GLORIA:	It's none of your business.
SUBSTITUTE MOTHER:	(*Pleading.*) Have pity on me. You're all I have left in this shitty life. Your father took off with my own sister . . .

Gloria laughs.

SUBSTITUTE MOTHER:	And to top it off, you laugh. What do you have for a heart? A rock? I'm dressed in mourning as if he had died.
GLORIA:	You bore me, mother. Always the same old story. Did you iron my green jacket?
SUBSTITUTE MOTHER:	That jacket is too . . . too provocative . . .
GLORIA:	But, have you ironed it for me?
SUBSTITUTE MOTHER:	Of course. Have I ever denied you anything?
GLORIA:	Where in hell did you put it?
SUBSTITUTE MOTHER:	(*She brings her the jacket.*) Here it is.
GLORIA:	You've ironed it too well. It's not supposed to be worn like that. (*Brashly, she wrinkles the recently ironed jacket.*)
SUBSTITUTE MOTHER:	Gloria, what are you doing? I spent almost an hour ironing that jacket . . .
GLORIA:	I'm fed up with you, mother. You do everything too well. (*She messes up the bed.*) Luis likes to fuck in a very messy bed.

She opens the dresser: she scatters all over the room the clothes that had been neatly put away.

SUBSTITUTE MOTHER:	Gloria, I beg you. This can't go on any longer. I don't know what to do with you.
GLORIA:	With me? And what do you want to do? It's too late to do anything. My father ran off with

your sister. I've got to lead my own life. Or do
you want me to be a maid like you?

SUBSTITUTE MOTHER: You're right . . . you're right . . .

Gloria pours herself some whiskey.

SUBSTITUTE MOTHER: Are you drinking again? You told me you had
quit!

GLORIA: I lied to you. I enjoy lying to you. Since you
believe everything . . . I'm pregnant, mother.

SUBSTITUTE MOTHER: Oh, darling! (*She gets close to her; Gloria pushes
her away.*)

GLORIA: Keep on cleaning. I don't like for you to touch
me.

The substitute mother moves away, suffering. She continues cleaning.

SUBSTITUTE MOTHER: How far along are you, darling?

GLORIA: Three months.

SUBSTITUTE MOTHER: But that man is married. How could he have
done this to you?

GLORIA: I don't know if he did it. I don't know who the
father is.

The substitute mother doesn't answer. She sweeps in silence.

SUBSTITUTE MOTHER: Then, you sleep around with more than one
man?

GLORIA: (*She stops the game.*) It's obvious that if I say I
don't know who the father is, it's because I fool
around with more than one man. Besides, you
promised to suffer.

SUBSTITUTE MOTHER: (*Professionally.*) I'm suffering terribly, miss. Do
you want me to externalize it?

GLORIA: Of course, it's my birthday. What better gift
                           than a submissive mother externalizing her
                           suffering?

SUBSTITUTE MOTHER: (*She resumes her role. She cries loudly.*)

Gloria puts on some rock music to muffle the crying.

GLORIA: I can't stand your crying, mother. Why are you
                           crying? I'm the one who's pregnant. Why don't
                           you find me a solution instead of spilling your
                           tears on my sheets? You've made me like this,
                           mother. Now you'll have to put up with this
                           thirty-year-old daughter who refuses to give
                           up adolescence and continues tied to your
                           apron strings.

The subtitute mother cries profusely. Then she stops.

SUBSTITUTE MOTHER: Here, touch these. Real tears. You can't
                           demand a more tragic effect. The Mother
                           Center has a first rate staff.

GLORIA: You seem to be very familiar with this type of
                           mother.

SUBSTITUTE MOTHER: It's frequently requested. They all want to be
                           rebellious children, and they like to humiliate
                           submissive mothers, it's a very simple task. On
                           the other hand, it's very difficult to rebel
                           against a liberated, emancipated mother. Or
                           against an international diva. They rarely
                           request that type of mother! They all enjoy trite
                           situations; they pay for shy, typical, denigrated
                           mothers. They like to see me cry. But no one
                           hires an amusing mother, one who has fun.
                           One who laughs. One who fucks.

*She changes her clothes: she puts on the latest fashion clothing and a
huge, elegant picture hat. She looks like a model. She puts a beautiful
fox stole around her neck. She walks around with papers in her hand.
She becomes a successful, international person. She completely changes*

her social status and the way she walks and talks. Gloria is flabbergasted.

SUBSTITUTE MOTHER: (*From this new perspective, she observes Gloria who is still wearing the same shirt and tight pants which irritated the previous mother.*) That informal look becomes you. Are you going to have an abortion or have the kid?

GLORIA: (*She adapts immediately.*) I lost it. You're not going to be a grandmother! Relax! You just had a face lift and I wouldn't want to spoil your new image with a grandchild.

SUBSTITUTE MOTHER: You must admit that giving me a grandchild was a dirty trick. You have talent and beauty like I do. And like me, you hate to conform to the general norm.

GLORIA: Don't psychoanalyze me.

SUBSTITUTE MOTHER: Do you have any whiskey? (*Gloria gives her some.*) It's the fourth one I've had today. We might as well forget about the rest of the day. Aren't you going to get drunk with me, love?

Gloria pours herself some and they drink happily.

SUBSTITUTE MOTHER: Did you finish your play?

GLORIA: Which one?

SUBSTITUTE MOTHER: The one in which I was the protagonist. You portrayed me so well! The scenes you mailed me to New York were astounding. I saw myself exactly as I am. Despotic, evil, divine. You even had me wearing this picture hat and this fox stole. Nevertheless, something worried me: in the play you doubt I'm really your mother. (*She laughs.*) Darling: I've been able to confuse you!

GLORIA: Yes, I finished it. They're rehearsing it now.

SUBSTITUTE MOTHER: And who's playing the protagonist? I mean: who plays me?

GLORIA: Joan Collins.

SUBSTITUTE MOTHER: A wonderful actress. But my advice to her would be to free herself from the real model; to reinvent me.

GLORIA: But of course . . . she's a pro! She knows how to create a character.

SUBSTITUTE MOTHER: But, does the character know how it wants to be created? (*She spoils the magic: she stops playing her role.*) You lack rebelliousness, miss. Didn't we agree you were going to . . . ?

GLORIA: (*Fed up.*) I'm the one who makes demands. You're mine. I hired you for a lot of money. I paid quite a sum for all this "splendor you exhibit." But we've got a long way to go yet.

SUBSTITUTE MOTHER: You're fascinated with me, darling.

GLORIA: (*She resumes her role as the daughter of this type of mother.*) You never told me I was adopted.

SUBSTITUTE MOTHER: That's your father's obsession. Tell my ex-husband to stop chasing after those fifteen-year-olds with whom he runs around in my favorite places in New York. And make him admit we conceived you with great love, Gloria! Isn't today your birthday, my love?

GLORIA: I turn thirty today, mother.

SUBSTITUTE MOTHER: So many years! (*She stretches her face and lifts her breasts.*) I don't know what else to have lifted! Do your thirty years show on me? Have you had any lifts done?

GLORIA: Do you think I need to? Do you see some wrinkles on me? (*Very worried.*)

SUBSTITUTE MOTHER:	It's time for you to start taking care of your wrinkles. Thirty is a dangerous age. Everything begins to sag. Besides you're a fabulous playwright, always being followed by the paparazzi. You must think of your image, darling!
GLORIA:	You think so? (*Worried, she looks at herself in the mirror.*)
SUBSTITUTE MOTHER:	(*She stops the game.*) What about the rebellion? You're about to decide to have plastic surgery when you have perfect skin.
GLORIA:	(*She screams.*) I can't rebel against you. I can do nothing more than see you come and go, fascinated by you! Is that why I like women? (*The mother is shocked and Gloria notices.*)
SUBSTITUTE MOTHER:	(*Immediately she resumes the role of a splendid mother.*) What! You like women?
GLORIA:	I sleep with men, but I fall in love with women.
SUBSTITUTE MOTHER:	Any time now, you're going to be curious about caressing a female body, I see you're very tempted.
GLORIA:	I've already tried it. I'm involved in an intense affair, mother.
SUBSTITUTE MOTHER:	(*She recovers.*) Fabulous! I think it's good for you to take action. I've had enough of this hypocrisy! And with whom are you having this intense affair?
GLORIA:	With your friend Lulu.
SUBSTITUTE MOTHER:	Lulu! Oh my stars! How could Lulu, who's such a moralist, have done . . . this to us?
GLORIA:	We both needed to rebel against you, mother. (*She laughs boisterously. She stops the game.*) See

	how I was able to rebel? Did you see how I screwed you, my lady?
SUBSTITUTE MOTHER:	I'll admit that was ingenious on your part to invent the affair with Lulu.
GLORIA:	(*She resumes the role she had been acting out.*) Should I pour you some whiskey, mother?
SUBSTITUTE MOTHER:	Do you always have such bad whiskey?
GLORIA:	Lulu gives it to me.
SUBSTITUTE MOTHER:	She lacks originality even in that.
GLORIA:	She also gives you the same whiskey?
SUBSTITUTE MOTHER:	The same whiskey under the same circumstances; she was the first woman in my life. Lulu is spellbinding. Or at least she knows our weak spots.
GLORIA:	(*She stops the game.*) You're going too far. I didn't pay for you to have the same type of affair with Lulu.
SUBSTITUTE MOTHER:	Rebel! I'm not a submissive little mother who keeps everything in order for you. I don't suffer, darling. How does one rebel against a mother who doesn't suffer?
GLORIA:	(*Negotiating the deal.*) You came here to please me.
SUBSTITUTE MOTHER:	This is the way the mother you requested in your program pleases her clients. You're not going to disgrace me by sleeping with my best friend!
GLORIA:	And you, you're not going to come here and tell me, precisely on my birthday, that my greatest love was also your lover. That's overdoing it.

SUBSTITUTE MOTHER:	I've already told you we're trained to outdo ourselves.
GLORIA:	I'm going to kill Lulu, mother.
SUBSTITUTE MOTHER:	Oh, no. Write. You overcome a lot of things by writing! Besides, you have more than enough material. You've got everything on a silver platter. A *ménage à trois*. If you kill Lulu in fiction, you'll be tremendously relieved. One question: Did Lulu give you that shirt?
GLORIA:	The shirt, the pants, the color of this room, and Bach's Magnificat. (*The Magnificat can be heard as it was at the beginning of the play.*)
SUBSTITUTE MOTHER:	The Magnificat, too! Turn it off!

Gloria raises the volume and picks up a baton. She stands on the box and "directs" the imaginary orchestra.

GLORIA:	We've already experienced jealousy. And now you're the one who's jealous, mother. (*She laughs.*)

The substitute mother grabs her baton and breaks it. The Magnificat stops.

Pause.

GLORIA:	I enjoyed winning this game.
SUBSTITUTE MOTHER:	That's why you paid hundreds of dollars to the Mother Center. And those dollars allow you to be the winner of some of the games. I didn't cause you to feel guilty. You could take revenge . . . oh, well . . . Those are the pleasures the Mother Center offers to its distinguished customers.
GLORIA:	Are you going to breast feed me?
SUBSTITUTE MOTHER:	Not with these clothes on, I'm not!

She removes her hat and puts on a white slip and a huge round rubber breast. She sits down. Gloria happily gets on her lap. The substitute mother takes out the breast full of cream. Gloria grabs the nipple.

GLORIA: Mmmmmm, Mmmmmm . . .

The substitute mother squeezes the breast and white foam comes out of it which covers Gloria completely. Gloria, soaked in the white cream, clings to the mother's neck.

GLORIA: It's a grand finale, like in the opera. I'm going to hire you for next week.

The substitute mother stands up: she takes off the enormous false breast and puts it away. She tidies herself and then puts on the clothes she was wearing at the beginning. She puts away everything she used in the previous scene. Gloria continues eating cream with her finger. The substitute mother carefully puts away all her props.

GLORIA: This is what you call a premature weaning.

SUBSTITUTE MOTHER: I have another customer waiting, Miss. A banker.

GLORIA: Don't give me details. I hate to hear the details when people abandon me. Take everything with you. Leave me devastated. You may now play the cruel mother you should've impersonated at the beginning.

SUBSTITUTE MOTHER: The one who called you Maria?

GLORIA: Aren't you going to give me a kiss, mother?

SUBSTITUTE MOTHER: You're full of . . . You're all dirty . . . I'm wearing a Christian Dior outfit, for Christ's sake.

GLORIA: I thought it was a Chanel.

SUBSTITUTE MOTHER: I'm fed up with your mistakes.

GLORIA: And what else?

SUBSTITUTE MOTHER:	And also with your success.
GLORIA:	Why did you come, mother?
SUBSTITUTE MOTHER:	I came for the thousand dollars you owe me.
GLORIA:	(*She stops the game.*) I owe you $700. Check the bill from the Mother Center, lady!
SUBSTITUTE MOTHER:	The breast feeding service is extra. And also the cleaning of the room. Read the fine print!

She shows her the contract. Gloria looks at it. She takes a thousand dollars out of a drawer and gives them to her.

GLORIA:	We're even, mother.
SUBSTITUTE MOTHER:	Gloria, I would rather . . . not see you for a while . . . you're a very . . . demanding daughter . . . Is demanding the right word?
GLORIA:	(*She stops the game.*) If I choose you next week and I pay . . . you'll have to come back.
SUBSTITUTE MOTHER:	Where are you going to get the money?
GLORIA:	I'll get a loan. There's a series of mothers I need you to play for me.
SUBSTITUTE MOTHER:	My vacation starts next week. Another staff member will come. I recommend you ask for Shirley Markowitz. She's very pliable. Guilt is her thing. And besides, she's fat. That adds certain maternal qualities. You'll love her.
GLORIA:	I . . . want you. That is to say . . . I don't need . . .
SUBSTITUTE MOTHER:	I don't need you either. We put our feelings aside. That's why you have your real mother. (*Out of character.*) You do have a mother, don't you? Is your mother alive?
GLORIA:	Yes, of course.

SUBSTITUTE MOTHER:	And who, of all the women I played today, is she like?
GLORIA:	It's none of your business!
SUBSTITUTE MOTHER:	I felt a rush of true jealousy. That shouldn't happen to me. Good-bye, Gloria. (*She shakes her hand.*)
GLORIA:	Do you . . . have . . . any children?
SUBSTITUTE MOTHER:	We substitute mothers never answer realistic questions. Go to the Mother Center every time you need to.
GLORIA:	(*Gloria takes out money and gives it to her.*) Wait a minute! You deserve a tip.
SUBSTITUTE MOTHER:	Just what we agreed on. We don't accept tips.

She throws the money. She picks up her bags and leaves.

Gloria is left all alone. She screams.

GLORIA:	(*Forsaken.*) Mother!

Notes

1. The present translation is one of the 1980 versions of *Casa matriz*. Later on, Raznovich extended the play and included more mother roles for the Substitute Mother.

2. For permission to stage the play, the author must be contacted directly: República de la India 2739 Piso 12A, Buenos Aires, Argentina.

Mariela Romero (Caracas, Venezuela, 1949) has experienced the theater in different capacities: as an actress, director, producer, and stage designer. She started writing brief literary pieces when she was fourteen years old and, during her acting studies at the *Ateneo* of Caracas, discovered that those early pieces could be turned into plays. Thus, in 1966 she produced *Este mundo circo* (This Circus World), *El baile de los vampiros* (The Vampires' Dance), *El cáncer es incurable: no lo malgaste* (Cancer is Incurable: Don't Waste It), and *Algo alrededor del espejo* (Something Around the Mirror). The latter was awarded first prize for best play by the Fundación Neuman and premiered the following year at the Universidad Central de Caracas.

Romero's best-known play is *El juego* (The game), which was staged by director Armando Gota and received the 1976 Ministry of Justice Prize for best play. It is considered the first play of a trilogy formed by *Rosa de la noche* (Night Rose, 1980) and *El vendedor* (The Salesman, 1984). In all three pieces, the characters find themselves in sado-masochistic relationships marked by dominance and dependence as well as by a lack of communication.

Esperando al italiano (Waiting for the Italian, 1988), was staged in 1988 by the New Theater Group of Caracas under the direction of Armando Gota and received the Critics Award in 1989. Romero incorporates different elements from other genres such as music, soap operas, and movies to re-create the climate of the 1940s. The play depicts four middle-aged women who have pooled their financial resources to form a cooperative. The idea is to hire an ideal macho lover who will fulfill their sexual needs and make them feel attractive, alive. Even though their enterprise fails, the play's open ending suggests—in contrast with the hopeless awaiting of *Waiting for Godot*—the possibility of renewed hope. Once they finally admit that their lover is not coming, they find a new prospect in the personal section of a magazine.

Waiting for the Italian

BY MARIELA ROMERO[1]

Translated from *Esperando al italiano*
by Teresa Cajiao Salas and Margarita Vargas

Characters

JACINTA	early 60s
MARIA ANTONIA	mid 50s
JUAN JOSÉ	mid 50s
ROSALBA	early 50s
TERESA	early 50s

Act I

María Antonia's apartment. Jacinta—a sixty-year-old, strong and energetic mulatto woman—is mopping the floor. All the dining-room chairs are on top of the table. The rugs and the rest of the furniture are placed against the wall.

JACINTA: (*Singing.*) María Antonia's as crazy as a loon,
she writes with a broom
and sweeps with a Papermate.

Jacinta keeps singing until the door opens and María Antonia, a woman in her mid fifties, appears at the door. She's carrying a bunch of flowers in her arms and is pushing a heavy box with her feet.

MARIA ANTONIA: Jacinta! Jacinta! Stop what you're doing and come help me. Anybody called?

JACINTA: No. Watch out! The floor's wet. (*She tries to take the flowers from her.*)

MARIA ANTONIA: Not the flowers, you idiot! The box!

JACINTA: (*Lifting the box.*) Humm . . . hard liquor! And what about the vegetables you were gonna buy?

MARIA ANTONIA: I didn't get around to it. (*She sets the flowers on the table.*) It was so crowded at the Commissary! It was like Christmas Eve before Black Friday[2] . . . and everybody was buying liquor. I'll bet they're gonna raise the prices again. No doubt about it!

JACINTA: Poor lushes! I myself don't care since I don't

drink . . . (*She goes to the kitchen singing.*) María
Antonia's as crazy as a loon . . .

MARIA ANTONIA: Very funny!

JACINTA: (*From the kitchen.*) It's a song Gualberto Ibarreto
made famous, don't you remember? I mean, the
song made him famous.

MARIA ANTONIA: (*Kicking her shoes off.*) Oh, what a relief! These shoes
were killing me. Did you make the chicken soup?

JACINTA: (*From the kitchen.*) And the tossed salad and the
baked plantains, and I got the ice and put it in the
ice bucket. (*She enters.*) I've been doing the same
thing every Saturday for years . . . how could I
forget?

MARIA ANTONIA: I'm gonna take a shower. If Juan José arrives . . .

JACINTA: I'll let him in and serve him a whiskey. (*María
Antonia nods in agreement and goes to her room.
Jacinta continues singing.*) María Antonia's as crazy
as a loon . . . What should I do with these flowers?

MARIA ANTONIA: Put them in a vase! (*She goes into her room.*)

JACINTA: Every single Saturday the same old thing! She
comes in, kicks her shoes off, leaves them lying
around because . . . she's got a maid. She wouldn't
even bend down for a hundred dollar bill. (*She
picks up the shoes.*) Why is she surprised her feet
hurt? She bought these shoes when she weighed
thirty pounds less. Now her feet look like over-
sized yams. Oh, yes . . . and that habit of hers of
buying flowers you take to funerals. (*Imitating her.*)
"These flowers last longer!" But who cares . . .
what really matters is that they bring bad luck.
Even the General used to tell her . . . "these flowers
smell of death, María Antonia" . . . but she
wouldn't listen to him. I'm not surprised he left
and has never come back . . . who can live with the
smell of a wake forever . . . the scent of the flowers

sticks to everything and the ... *(The doorbell rings
and she opens the door.)*

*Juan José enters. He is approximately fifty-five years old, but tries to
appear younger. He is wearing an old corduroy jacket and carrying a
book under his arm.*

JUAN JOSÉ: Hi, Jacinta!

JACINTA: Come in. I'll get you a whiskey right away. María
                 Antonia's in the shower.

JUAN JOSÉ: And the others?

JACINTA: They're not here yet. You're the first to arrive, as
                 usual.

*Juan José, as always, makes himself comfortable by moving things aside
while Jacinta goes to the kitchen with the flowers.*

JACINTA: *(Singing.)* Here comes Juan José, here comes Juan
                 José, he's coming from the big city ... *(She keeps
                 singing.)*

JUAN JOSÉ: *(Sitting down.)* I wish you would change your
                 repertoire, Jacinta. *(He opens the book and leafs
                 through it.)*

MARIA ANTONIA: *(From her room.)* Jacinta, Jacinta ... bring me the
                 mop!

JUAN JOSÉ: Wait a minute. She's getting me a whiskey.

MARIA ANTONIA: *(From her room.)* Oh ... you're here? I'll be there in a
                 minute.

*Jacinta comes back with a tray with glasses, whiskey, and a bucket of
ice.*

JUAN JOSÉ: María Antonia wants you to get her the mop.

JACINTA: I heard her. *(She goes to get the mop.)*

Juan José pours himself his first whiskey. María Antonia enters, looking cool and refreshed after her shower.

MARIA ANTONIA: Hi! (*She kisses him.*)

JUAN JOSÉ: (*Inhaling.*) Jean Naté.[3]

MARIA ANTONIA: (*Nods in agreement.*) As always! Is that the book you promised me?

JUAN JOSÉ: *Lola Dark Mirror.* I had a hard time finding it.

MARIA ANTONIA: I'll start reading it tomorrow. (*She serves herself a whiskey.*) Oh, that Jacinta! She's slowing down!

JUAN JOSÉ: She's getting old.

JACINTA: (*She comes in with the mop.*) Oh, Juan José, I feel so sorry for you! Look at what's left of you . . . now you can't even hurt a fly. (*She goes toward the bedroom, singing.*)

JUAN JOSÉ: And finally, what about Margarita?

MARIA ANTONIA: She called Teresa, last night. She's supposed to arrive on the noon flight.

JUAN JOSÉ: With the Italian?

MARIA ANTONIA: Jacinta . . . don't leave those slippers behind the door! Pick them up and put'em away. Put out clean towels and another roll of toilet paper . . . the one with the flower pattern . . . the U.S. brand.

JUAN JOSÉ: Imported toilet paper! Well, the Venezuelan economy's not so bad after all.

MARIA ANTONIA: When has the economic situation been bad for the Army? It's bad beyond their doorstep, darling . . . but for them! . . . They're (*She points to her temple to indicate shrewdness.*)

JUAN JOSÉ: Look who's complaining! You wipe your behind with imported toilet paper.

MARIA ANTONIA:	Fortunately, I still have the card that gives me access to the Commissary, darling.
JUAN JOSÉ:	And a nice behind . . . you're still in luck. (*She smiles mischievously.*)
MARIA ANTONIA:	The Commissary was fully stocked with Gouda cheese, prosciutto, cans of paté . . .
JUAN JOSÉ:	And thousands and thousands of boxes of rum!
MARIA ANTONIA:	And the women shopping there! All the same! The same hairdo, the same frosted hair, all loaded with cheap costume jewelry . . . as if they were in a window display. But me, darling, if it weren't for that card . . .
JUAN JOSÉ:	The only souvenir from the General.
MARIA ANTONIA:	(*Looking at him reproachfully, she decides to ignore his remark.*) Did you bet on the numbers I gave you?
JUAN JOSÉ:	No, María Antonia.
MARIA ANTONIA:	But I told you the pot's really big right now . . .
JUAN JOSÉ:	I belong to the Bingo generation, María Antonia. I'm not sold on that Lotto invention. It'll never convince me. (*Pause.*) Is Margarita coming with the Italian?
MARIA ANTONIA:	Of course! That's why we paid for her trip. (*Juan José laughs.*) Did I show you his picture? (*He shakes his head.*) I'll show it to you now. (*She looks for it.*) Look! What do you think?
JUAN JOSÉ:	At least he looks Italian; you can't deny that: the gold chain around his neck . . . the linen shirt unbuttoned to the waist to show his hairy chest . . . oh, look at him . . . his pointed shoes . . . everything!
MARIA ANTONIA:	A hunk!

JUAN JOSÉ: But you should've asked him to send a photo in the
                     nude, too. That bulge looks more like a sanitary
                     napkin to me.

María Antonia snatches the photo from him.

MARIA ANTONIA: You're jealous! (*Jacinta returns to the room.*) Jacinta,
                     are you sure no one called me while I was out?
                     Please, try to remember because you never bother
                     to write down messages . . .

JACINTA: Huh! If you don't believe me you better get an
                     answering machine. (*She goes to the kitchen.*) I may
                     be old, but my head works very well . . . unlike
                     others'.

MARIA ANTONIA: That woman's getting more and more insolent!
                     One of these days I'll get up on the wrong side of
                     the bed and I'll send her right back to her village.
                     How are your boys?

JUAN JOSÉ: Fine. Just this morning I stopped by to see them.
                     They're doing fine.

*The doorbell rings in a special way to announce another member of the
group.*

MARIA ANTONIA: That's Rosalba.

*María Antonia opens the door. Rosalba enters and kisses her. She's an
elegant and languorous woman, about fifty years old, who looks much
younger. Her hair is done up professionally. She is carrying a box of
pastries.*

MARIA ANTONIA: I knew it was you.

ROSALBA: (*Kissing her.*) Oh, darling! Check to make sure I'm
                     not blocking anybody. It's impossible to find a
                     parking space. Hi!, Juan José.

JUAN JOSÉ: (*Kissing her hand.*) How are you, Rosalba?

ROSALBA: Marvelously well! Excited! Happy!

MARIA ANTONIA: You parked behind me, didn't you? (*Rosalba nods.*) Then, you're not in anybody's way. That parking space belongs to the Portuguese who owns the grocery store. They towed his car away last night.

ROSALBA: I bought a jelly roll, darling, because all the other cakes looked awful, stale, old . . . and we already have plenty of that around here. (*She laughs.*)

JUAN JOSÉ: You're not referring to yourself, Rosalba. You're like the portrait of Dorian Gray: the personification of eternal youth.

MARIA ANTONIA: Doesn't she look gorgeous!

ROSALBA: Honey, I looked gorgeous at the end of Pérez Jiménez's dictatorship. Unfortunately, thirty years have gone by . . . thirty years of an unbearable and eternal democracy.

JUAN JOSÉ: Thirty years! That's nothing, Rosalba. Don't you remember that tango?

ROSALBA: Yes. But, that's exactly why Carlos Gardel died.[4] He was the only one who dared to say "twenty years are nothing for the gentle gaze." If he were still alive and could see himself in the mirror, I'm sure he'd sing a different song. Where's Teresa?

MARIA ANTONIA: She'll be here shortly.

ROSALBA: I'm dying to see her.

JUAN JOSÉ: What are you gonna drink, Rosalba?

ROSALBA: You mean to say you didn't wait for me? Me, the VIP? (*María Antonia laughs.*) Well, then whiskey, as usual, darling, I don't want to change my habits. Oh, María Antonia, look . . . I brought you a relic. Do you remember the Agustín Lara record I mentioned?[5] (*She takes out a cassette.*) My daughter recorded it for me. Put it on.

MARIA ANTONIA:	In a moment, in a moment.
JUAN JOSÉ:	I was telling María Antonia that the Italian you're waiting for . . .
ROSALBA:	He is arriving today, right? (*María Antonia nods.*)
JUAN JOSÉ:	I think you'll be disappointed.
ROSALBA:	Honey, if you think that . . . it must be because you haven't seen his picture.
JUAN JOSÉ:	Precisely.
ROSALBA:	Then keep your comments to yourself because you don't know a thing about men.
JUAN JOSÉ:	And you do, don't you? They're your specialty.
ROSALBA:	I've never lacked good taste, dear. (*To María Antonia.*) By now Margarita must be embarked.
JUAN JOSÉ:	That's exactly what I was telling María Antonia.
ROSALBA:	I mean boarding the plane. You'd better keep your opinions to yourself, okay? María Antonia, can you imagine Margarita? Knowing her, she'll come back with Gucci luggage like a queen. She's probably walking through the Fiumiccino concourses . . . with the Italian two steps behind her.
JUAN JOSÉ:	What's the name?
ROSALBA:	Fiumiccino, darling. Are you deaf?
JUAN JOSÉ:	I'm referring to the guy . . . What's his name?
MARIA ANTONIA:	Gian Piero. I don't remember his last name.
ROSALBA:	We don't have to know it. All we need is the first name.
JUAN JOSÉ:	That means you don't know a thing about him. Nothing about his past, about his family, about . . .

ROSALBA:	Look, J.J., we don't exactly want to start a dynasty with him.
JUAN JOSÉ:	But when one buys an animal . . . let's say, a breeding animal, you're always concerned with its pedigree.
ROSALBA:	(*Pointing at Juan José.*) What's wrong with him, honey?
MARIA ANTONIA:	(*Raising her glass.*) To Gian Piero!
JUAN JOSÉ:	To the Italian. (*He takes a sip.*)
ROSALBA:	What makes you think, J.J., the Italian's gonna disappoint us?
JUAN JOSÉ:	You're asking me?
ROSALBA:	Yes . . . you! Jealous, J.J.?
MARIA ANTONIA:	(*Laughing.*) Oh, honey, you call him J.J. and it sounds as if he were wealthy.
ROSALBA:	Him, wealthy? Since I first met him, and that was many, many moons ago, he's always lived in the same boarding house, bought used books, used public transportation, and worn the same old jacket, which has become part of his identity. What he is . . . is poor, poorer than a church mouse.
JUAN JOSÉ:	But proud of it.
ROSALBA:	And he hasn't died from hunger because he gets free meals here . . . (*Emphasizing.*) and booze, too.
MARIA ANTONIA:	Oh, but he doesn't believe in the Lotto . . . how's he ever gonna get ahead? On the other hand, look at me . . . I won eight thousand six hundred *bolívares* the first time I played.
JUAN JOSÉ:	And what did you do with the money? (*They look at each other.*)

ROSALBA:	(*Defiant.*) She invested them in the Co-op. (*Juan José laughs.*) Do you think it was a bad investment?
JUAN JOSÉ:	Everything you do seems wonderful to me. (*He pours himself another drink.*)
ROSALBA:	By the way . . . you haven't finished telling me why, according to you, the Italian's gonna disappoint us.
MARIA ANTONIA:	Jealousy, honey, what's wrong with him is that he's jealous. (*The doorbell rings.*) That must be Teresa!
ROSALBA:	Me, me, me! Let me open the door. (*She opens the door and in fact it is Teresa. She is approximately the same age as Rosalba, but her clothes make her look sexier, more aggressive.*) Surprise! (*But the one who is surprised is Rosalba when she sees Teresa leaning against the door in a Gilda pose.*)[6]
ROSALBA:	(*Amazed.*) Oh, Teresa, you look wonderful! (*She lets her in. Teresa enters modeling her recently reshaped bust.*) I hadn't seen you since the operation, girl! They look perfect . . . beautiful . . . even better than those of the Venus de Milo, darling . . . even better than those of the statue of María Lionza!
TERESA:	(*Proudly.*) And without a bra!
MARIA ANTONIA:	(*Reproachfully.*) She spent all of her retirement fund on this!
TERESA:	(*Paying no attention to her remark.*) Touch 'em, darling . . . touch 'em so you can appreciate them. (*Juan José takes a peek.*) Not you, rascal!
JUAN JOSÉ:	I liked the old ones better. (*To María Antonia.*) They were heavier.
ROSALBA:	Not even in your prime, did you look so good, Teresa.
TERESA:	Later on I'll get a tummy tuck.

MARIA ANTONIA:	I don't know how you'll manage.
TERESA:	Oh, María Antonia . . . don't be pessimistic. You know one can always manage . . . (*She kisses her and goes to pour a whiskey for herself.*) And how are you?
JUAN JOSÉ:	Fine . . . here, waiting for the Italian.
TERESA:	(*Ill-intentioned.*) You, too? (*They laugh.*)
ROSALBA:	Him, too. He's waiting for the Italian to find out why we didn't choose him instead.
TERESA:	(*Sneering.*) Oh, but that's obvious, darling.
JUAN JOSÉ:	It might've been cheaper and maybe then, Teresa, you would've had enough money for a rear tuck.
MARIA ANTONIA:	That's rude, darling, much too rude.
TERESA:	Ignore him, María Antonia. Sticks and stones . . .
JUAN JOSÉ:	Sticks and stones, what?
ROSALBA:	Tell me, what did Margarita have to say? You're the only one who's talked to her.
TERESA:	The connection was awful . . . you couldn't hear a thing.
ROSALBA:	But what did she tell you? Did you talk to him?
TERESA:	I'm gonna tell you everything in a minute . . . but first let me sip this slowly. Antonia, isn't there any music?
ROSALBA:	We have Agustín Lara, darling.
TERESA:	At this time of the day? No, honey. María Antonia, put on the cassette I like, Gatica's.[7] (*To Rosalba.*) Do you remember the day we met him? It was in front of the radio station where you'd gone to apply for a job. (*To all of them.*) When she found out who he was, she wet her pants.

ROSALBA:	(*Embarrassed.*) You're exaggerating!
TERESA:	It ran down your nylons. How embarrassing . . . in front of that man! (*To the others.*) She was so refined, so exquisite, as pure as a virgin. And I can attest to that; back then she was still a virgin. She crossed her legs to hide the accident while he walked by, barely noticing us. He was my idol, my star. Suddenly I turned around and saw the little puddle on the ground and Rosalba was as pale as a ghost!
ROSALBA:	(*To change the subject.*) Jacinta should bring us some snacks.
TERESA:	Yes, get with it Antonia . . . there's no food, no music . . .
MARIA ANTONIA:	There's plenty of food, music, and Lucho Gatica. What no longer exists is your savings account.
TERESA:	So what! It was my money, wasn't it?
MARIA ANTONIA:	It's up to you if your boobs are more important than saving for your old age!
TERESA:	Oh, no, María Antonia, don't give me that again. No, not today.
JUAN JOSÉ:	María Antonia has always planned ahead. (*He laughs.*) That's why she gambles to increase her retirement fund. When she's not playing the lottery, she's playing Lotto or betting at the races, and when . . .
ROSALBA:	I didn't come here to talk about money . . . and much less about money that doesn't exist in bank accounts, in annuities, or anywhere else.
JUAN JOSÉ:	It certainly exists in the Italian's pocket!
TERESA:	(*To María Antonia.*) You make it sound as though I'd broken the law or committed a mortal sin!

MARIA ANTONIA:	No, not a sin, but a real stupidity!
TERESA:	But they look like a fifteen year old's, don't they?
MARIA ANTONIA:	Yes . . . I see that. The only problem is they don't match your fifty-year-old body.
ROSALBA:	Oh, please . . . if we're gonna start talking about age . . .
TERESA:	(*Uneasy.*) Look, honey, it's really none of your business. I felt like doing it. I wanted to treat myself. It was my money and they were my tits. Period!
ROSALBA:	That's true. Are you gonna argue about such nonsense?
MARIA ANTONIA:	Just don't come and ask me for a loan later on.
TERESA:	When have I ever borrowed money from you?
MARIA ANTONIA:	Oh darling, should I add up what you owe me? The problem is you don't have a good memory for certain things.
ROSALBA:	(*Trying to appease her.*) Enough, enough, María Antonia! Let's listen to Lucho Gatica, darling. Let's get romantic, in the mood for love. Another drink, Antonia? Where's your glass? (*She finds it and pours another drink.*)
JACINTA:	(*Entering to water the plants.*) That man really knew how to sing! Remember the song . . . (*She sings.*) "Clock, don't strike that hour . . ."
JUAN JOSÉ:	(*Completing the line.*) "Because the love of my life is dying . . . she's the la la la la . . ."
TERESA:	(*To Rosalba.*) And how are the girls?
ROSALBA:	Fine. Well, I guess they're fine. It's been a while since I last talked to them . . . I rarely see them.

Well, I saw Beba yesterday, but only for a moment.
She passed by the house like lightning to drop off
the children and a cassette by Agustín Lara. (*As if
apologizing for her daughters.*) The poor girls are so
busy . . . you know . . . they don't even have time to
take a breath. I don't understand how they can live
like that, Teresa, as if the world were gonna end
tomorrow . . . as if each moment marked the end of
something extremely important. Even though I'm
always telling them "Take it easy, girls, otherwise
you're gonna get old before your time." (*Brief
pause.*) Oh, but my grandchildren are real darlings.
It's a miracle they didn't destroy my apartment
yesterday!

TERESA: Mine are exactly the same when they come over. I
can't believe my furniture's still in one piece.

MARIA ANTONIA: When they repossess it, you won't have to worry
about it anymore.

TERESA: (*Angrily.*) Listen, María Antonia, if this is gonna
continue all evening, let me know so I can leave.

ROSALBA: Oh no, how can you leave? What about the Italian?

TERESA: I won't let anyone make me miserable for a pair of
boobs. I came here in a very good mood to wait for
Margarita . . . to visit with you . . . to wait for the
Italian.

JUAN JOSÉ: (*Changing the conversation.*) By the way, does he
speak Spanish?

MARIA ANTONIA: I assume Margarita taught him a few words.

ROSALBA: And if she didn't, it's okay. We don't want him here
to talk, but for something else. The less he
understands, the better!

JACINTA: Will he like chicken soup Venezuelan style? Do
they eat chicken soup in Italy?

JUAN JOSÉ:	We'll have to ask him if he likes it . . . (*Ill-intentioned.*) though he may prefer raw flesh.

Jacinta laughs heartily.

ROSALBA:	Oh, no. What's happening here? Today's a very special day . . . the day we've been waiting for so long and you're gonna spoil it with such bitterness and terrible moods?
TERESA:	She's right. What's wrong with you, María Antonia? What's bugging you? Because it's obvious you're upset, you really are . . . and I can't believe it's only because of my boobs.
MARIA ANTONIA:	(*Ignoring her.*) How strange . . . Auristela isn't here yet.
TERESA:	Why should she? She's not a member of the Co-op.
MARIA ANTONIA:	But I invited her. She also wants to meet the Italian.
JUAN JOSÉ:	Oh . . . that man doesn't know the mess he's gotten into.
ROSALBA:	J.J.!
JUAN JOSÉ:	I didn't say anything. I'm getting another drink, do you want one? (*Rosalba nods.*) What about you, Teresa?
TERESA:	Yes . . . please.
ROSALBA:	He'll be so excited when he meets us. Besides, everything's ready . . . we're here to welcome him . . . the atmosphere . . . the music . . . the flowers . . . everything is ready.
JUAN JOSÉ:	Even the roll of toilet paper, which is imported, and if you haven't noticed, Rosalba, it, too, has flowers.
TERESA:	(*Realizing what's wrong with María Antonia.*) Oh! You went to the Commissary? Now I understand why you're in such a bad mood!

MARIA ANTONIA: Shut up and let me listen to the tape! (*She sings along with the music.*)

TERESA: What happened? (*María Antonia continues singing.*) Did you finally run into him and that's why you're like this?

MARIA ANTONIA: I've been going to the Commissary for ten years. Everything there is cheaper and I've never seen him there . . . so what makes you assume I ran into him today?

Pause. They all look at each other.

TERESA: You saw him, right?

MARIA ANTONIA: I don't go there to see him, but to save money. Because unlike you, darling, I have common sense, . . . I live in accordance with the country's situation . . . I get up every day, and after reading the news I can tell the economic situation is getting worse every day, and I look at the calendar and at myself in the mirror and realize that it won't be long before I'm worthless . . . that it's better to have a savings account instead of a pair of boobs stuffed with polyethylene just to go around making a fool out of myself. Who's gonna admire them, who's gonna caress them?

María Antonia angrily finishes her drink. There's a moment of heavy silence with Gatica's voice in the background.

JACINTA: The Italian, of course! She's gonna model her new boobs for the Italian . . . isn't that why you're bringing him here? Besides, they look really good, Teresa.

MARIA ANTONIA: You shut up, stupid old woman . . . and go to the kitchen, where you belong. (*Jacinta exits singing.*)

JACINTA: (*Singing.*) When a parakeet wants her mate to go to church . . . she gets up early and irons his shirt, his shirt . . . (*She continues singing.*)

JUAN JOSÉ:	*(To break the tension.)* Is it really true you wet your pants when you met Gatica, Rosalba?
ROSALBA:	That's her story. I don't remember that. Let's dance. *(She sings along with Gatica.)* "Oh, uncertainty is so cruel . . . does she deserve my suffering or should I forget her . . ."
JUAN JOSÉ:	*(Getting up to dance with her.)* "Oh!, this bitter sorrow . . . la la la la . . ."
ROSALBA:	You've never learned a whole song. *(She finishes it.)* "If you're gonna judge her, don't ever say she was evil!"
TERESA:	*(Now near María Antonia.)* You saw him, didn't you? *(María Antonia nods.)* And did you talk?
MARIA ANTONIA:	What could we say?
TERESA:	You ought to know if you have something to say to him. *(María Antonia shakes her head.)* And, how is he?
MARIA ANTONIA:	Fat . . . old as I am . . .

Juan José and Rosalba continue dancing without singing. They're more interested in what the others are saying.

TERESA:	You aren't old, darling. None of us is old. Look at you! Look at us! *(She models her new figure.)* I'll bet many women younger than we would like to look as good as we do. María Antonia, we're in what people call "our prime" . . . we're alive . . . clinging to life . . . and full of dreams . . . because . . . what else is the Italian but a dream we wanted to turn into reality . . . We've had many wonderful experiences and have just as many beautiful memories.
MARIA ANTONIA:	And bitterness, grudges, and a loneliness we can barely hide every Saturday night. We're also full of that.

ROSALBA:	(*Still dancing.*) We're not alone. We have one another and our friendship . . . and soon we'll have the Italian to share, as we've shared so many things in life.
MARIA ANTONIA:	And full of frustration . . . I had left that one out!
TERESA:	Then you did talk to each other.
MARIA ANTONIA:	"How are you? Fine. How's everything with you? As usual. What's new? Nothing."
ROSALBA:	Oh! What a trivial conversation!
MARIA ANTONIA:	We don't have anything else to talk about.
ROSALBA:	Well, that's also true.
JUAN JOSÉ:	But, you mean to say you weren't even curious enough to ask him . . .
MARIA ANTONIA:	(*Curtly.*) Ask him what?
JUAN JOSÉ:	Why he left you without any explanation.
MARIA ANTONIA:	But I don't want one. Why should we talk about that after so many years?
ROSALBA:	That's what I say. The past should be understood but not constantly remembered. So, let's not talk about it anymore.
TERESA:	María Antonia, we're among friends . . . tell us what you talked about.
MARIA ANTONIA:	(*Singing.*) "It's not worth suffering . . . if everything's gonna end . . . if everything's gone . . ."
ROSALBA:	(*Continuing.*) "After all the illusions I created during my sleepless nights, after I set all my hopes on your love . . ."

MARIA ANTONIA:	Jacinta, Jacinta. Bring in more ice, there's nothing but water now. I'm gonna change the cassette. Teresa, excuse me, but it would be better to listen to something else. (*To Rosalba*.) Unless you want to continue dancing *boleros* with J. J.
TERESA:	Why not? When they dance, they look exactly like Marga López and Roberto Cañedo in "Salón México."[8]
ROSALBA:	Well, when you don't have the real thing . . .
MARIA ANTONIA:	Are you sure it was Roberto Cañedo?
JACINTA:	(*Entering with the ice.*) Oh! Why did you stop playing Lucho Gatica?
TERESA:	Because we're not in the mood for memories, Jacinta. That's why.
JACINTA:	Oh, well, I remember the first time Lucho Gatica came to sing in Caracas.
JUAN JOSÉ:	And our aspiring radio announcer peed all over her hose!
ROSALBA:	Which were made of silk, not nylon!
JACINTA:	He appeared on Víctor Saume's show. Do you remember, María Antonia? And what about poor Pájaro Chogui who was very popular back then, do you remember? He suffered the same fate as the bird in the song: it fell from the tree and died. Don't you remember, María Antonia?
MARIA ANTONIA:	I was very young, then.
JACINTA:	Sure you were! By then, you had already gone through one divorce . . . and then there was that damned islander who put you through all that legal mess to marry him only to find out he was still married to a woman from the Canary Islands and in addition was involved here with a Black girl

from Mamporal called Crucita who was
pregnant . . .

MARIA ANTONIA: Damn it!, Jacinta . . . You've got such a good
memory for certain things!

JACINTA: I've always had a good memory. Should I serve the
chicken soup?

ROSALBA: Oh no, Jacinta! What about the Italian? We gotta
wait for him. When he comes through that door,
the first thing I'll do is . . .

JUAN JOSÉ: Give him his check, I suppose . . .

ROSALBA: Don't be silly! The first thing I'll do is introduce
ourselves formally, because Europeans love
protocol.

TERESA: And you'll clarify the by-laws of our Co-op, just in
case Margarita didn't explain them fully.

ROSALBA: Caro, Gian Piero, benvenuto! Io sono la dolce
Rosalba . . .

TERESA: The merry widow!—grandmother of three
unbearable little rascals with angel faces, former
employee of a very important public relations firm,
former Mardi Gras queen (when we used to have
Mardi Gras parades with floats and everything) at
present, a part-time saleswoman who sells costume
jewelry and lingerie on credit. Owner of a warm
and inviting *garçonnière*, overlooking the *Avila*,[9] all
paid for and filled with *Lladró* figurines, Bohemian
crystal goblets, Dutch lace cushions, and *papier
mâché* miniature houses. In addition to the match
boxes and souvenir teaspoons which she collected
during her trips abroad when the dollar was four
bolívares and thirty cents and for which dear, old
Dr. Serrano—always incognito—paid. She has a
Siamese kitten, Tiffany lamps, moth balls
strategically placed between the linen sheets, and
everything outdated, like herself. She's willing to

share all this with the Italian the weekend he gets to spend with her.

MARIA ANTONIA: You forgot to mention that, as president of the Co-op and originator of the idea, she'll reserve for herself certain benefits related to her sexual fantasies, which according to gossip, were the cause of the late, always incognito, Dr. Serrano's death.

JUAN JOSÉ: Really, Rosalba, what fantasies?

ROSALBA: Oh, darling . . . you don't expect me to share my secrets with you.

JUAN JOSÉ: Oh, well! . . . And what in the hell does the Italian have that I don't?

ROSALBA: And then I'll introduce the rest of you. You, Teresa . . .

MARIA ANTONIA: Five times divorced from the same type of scoundrel— one of them now in jail for pushing drugs . . . or narcotics, as the new law calls them; another fleeing from justice for repeated embezzlement; another working the piece of land in Barinas which she foolishly allowed him to take away from her . . . because, when it comes to men, Teresa has always followed the same pattern . . . and what about the others, Teresa?

TERESA: Buried in oblivion.

JUAN JOSÉ: Then, you can tell him you're a widow, too.

MARIA ANTONIA: Former swimming champion, better known as the Venezuelan Esther Williams; a former stunning brunette, who changed into a dangerous blonde in order to hide her gray hair; a tenant . . . is that the right word? . . . in a modest apartment, from which she'll probably be evicted for not paying her rent, unless she decides to move out in the middle of the night with everything she owns; former holder of

savings accounts in a bank and in the Savings and
Loan Association of the Government office where
she currently works as a secretary when she's not
on sick leave. As you can see, *caro mio*, she doesn't
own anything, except those fabulous, recently
acquired boobs, which we assume are guaranteed
for at least five years.

JUAN JOSÉ: A reasonable period! After that, God will provide!

TERESA: And here we have our dear and charming hostess!
A professionally bitter woman; a former member
of one of our nation's foremost oligarchic families,
from which she was exiled with nothing but the
clothes on her back because they didn't give her
time to take anything else; a former secretary of the
Secretary of Defense, who decided to make her his
mistress, and now all she has left are a few bitter
memories and a Commissary card . . . *that* she does
have . . . so she may continue to drown her sorrows
in rum, while at the same time saving for a place
for herself in an old-folks' home, where her life can
end with her room and board paid on time, unless
she dies earlier than planned, in which case, the
money saved can be used for her tombstone. She
doesn't have children nor illusions and, apparently,
the only thing she has is a long-standing and
boring bitterness because one day, a long time ago,
the Secretary told her, "I'm going out to buy pizza,
darling. What kind do you want?" And she's still
waiting for her pan pizza and making everyone
else pay for her frustration![10] (*She picks up her glass
and takes a long drink.*)

JUAN JOSÉ: (*After a brief pause.*) Geez! Are you friends?

TERESA: We're all introduced now: three ridiculous,
outdated, tired, and stubborn old ladies, who one
day decided to search for a macho—excuse me,
Juan José—who can once in a while make them feel
they're still alive . . . that they still have something
to look forward to and that's why they put on
make-up and that's why they hide their

wrinkles . . . and that's why they dye their hair and hide their gray hairs and have their boobs lifted and hang on to a youth they no longer have.

ROSALBA: (*On the verge of crying.*) Oh! Enough Teresa . . . enough!

TERESA: Is that enough, María Antonia? Or should I add something else?

JUAN JOSÉ: All this hullabaloo for a pair of boobs!

Pause.

Teresa looks exhausted.

JACINTA: (*Breaking the tension.*) And are they really made of plastic, Teresa?

ROSALBA: They're made of whatever material they have to be made out of, Jacinta. And though Teresa may not have a single cent to her name, she looks lovely, stunning, and we're neither old, ridiculous, bitter, lonely, nor boring. And María Antonia's gonna have a whiskey right now and tell us what she talked to the general about and afterwards, she's gonna have another one and we'll never bring up the matter again. It'll be erased, forgotten, eliminated. (*She feels dizzy.*)

JUAN JOSÉ: And meanwhile we'll rehearse another introduction. What's wrong, Rosalba?

TERESA: Come on! Don't throw up on the carpet, please . . .

ROSALBA: Oh! I don't like to see you, girls, like this . . . so aggressive, remember that violence is the instrument of those who are wrong. We're friends . . . we're like sisters and we're happy, aren't we? . . . the Italian's coming . . . we're waiting for him, right? Serve the drinks, J.J., what are you waiting for? (*She goes to the bathroom.*)

MARIA ANTONIA: (*After a long pause.*) He played dumb.

JUAN JOSÉ: (*Reacting.*) No, I'm gonna serve them, right now.

MARIA ANTONIA: The general . . . he played dumb . . . when he saw me.

JUAN JOSÉ: Oh! (*He serves the drinks.*)

MARIA ANTONIA: Perhaps he felt embarrassed to see me so old, so ugly . . . or maybe he didn't recognize me, or if he recognized me, perhaps he thought, "what's the point of talking to her? What are we gonna talk about?"

TERESA: Was he alone?

MARIA ANTONIA: (*She nods.*) He was loading his cart with vegetables . . . bald . . . he's lost a lot of hair, you know.

JACINTA: He always had a receding hair line.

MARIA ANTONIA: He looked at me for a few seconds and I thought he was gonna say hello. I think he was afraid.

JUAN JOSÉ: I would've felt the same way. (*He hands her the drink.*)

MARIA ANTONIA: How ridiculous, huh? Because, at that moment, I thought . . . if he greets me, what should I do? Should I answer him? Should I ask him how he's doing? What's new? How are things going for you?

JACINTA: As if you didn't know. In these last few years, you've followed step by step every event in his life and you even have all the clippings from the society columns in which his picture appears. When he retired . . .

MARIA ANTONIA: But he turned around and kept going, no greeting, not even a gesture . . . as if I were not there . . . as if I had never meant anything to him . . . He kept going along the aisle, pushing the cart full of vegetables, hurrying . . . tapping his heels very hard . . . without turning around. Then I thought, "I'm gonna follow him . . . I'm gonna catch up with him and shout his name to make him turn around and face me. And when he turns around . . . right there, in front of everybody, I'm gonna spit in his face for his cowardice . . . because you can't deal such a low blow to a woman . . . I'm gonna denounce his behavior next to the cans of tomato sauce and the butter containers so he'll feel even more ridiculous." (*Brief pause.*) But I didn't do a thing . . . I didn't do or say a thing. I stared at him for a while, and I watched him get lost among the jars of jelly, the tapping of heels, and the women with frosted hair and beauty-parlor hairdos.

JUAN JOSÉ: Overloaded with cheap costume jewelry . . .

MARIA ANTONIA: Then I turned around . . . and ducked behind the people, just in case he might've turned around feeling remorseful.

JACINTA: Men like him don't ever feel remorse for anything!

MARIA ANTONIA: Ten years . . . ten years tormented by rancor, nurturing it uselessly . . .

JACINTA: Okay, honey, that's enough . . .

MARIA ANTONIA: Ten years ago I would've confronted him . . . ten years ago I wouldn't have remained silent. How pathetic! . . . today, I appeared to be the traitor . . . the guilty one . . . the coward . . . You were right, Teresa . . . I'm bitter by nature.

TERESA: (*Hugging her.*) I didn't mean that, María Antonia . . . Really, I didn't.

MARIA ANTONIA: But I am bitter . . . I've been bitter for so many years, uselessly. And what makes me madder is that now I feel stupid!

TERESA: And how do you think he's feeling now?

JACINTA: He? Hmm . . . . He probably doesn't even care!

TERESA: You gotta know you're much better than that
                    scoundrel . . . that's what you've got to believe, my
                    girl . . .

*Rosalba, wearing a Manila shawl around her shoulders and a Spanish
comb in her hair, enters the living room. She's carrying an open fan,
which she snaps shut to announce her presence.*

ROSALBA: (*Singing.*) "Little dove . . . Little dove . . . be careful
                    with your young ones because the hawk's
                    watching your nest . . ."

JUAN JOSÉ: (*Applauding.*) Bravo! . . . *Bravissimo!* . . . ladies,
                    young women, girls, everybody . . . I have the great
                    honor of introducing to you, in an exclusive
                    performance, the most admired, the most
                    marvelous, the unrivalled Rosalba, the queen of
                    zarzuela and *chotís*.[11]

Rosalba begins to sing "Lola."

Lights dim gradually.

End of Act I

Act II

*The same stage setting. Some time has gone by. Jacinta, Teresa, and
María Antonia are playing cards at the dining-room table. Rosalba
enters from the kitchen, carrying more ice, accompanied by Juan José,
who is bringing in more whiskey.*

ROSALBA: Come on J.J. . . . tell me the truth . . . aren't you in
                    love with María Antonia?

JUAN JOSÉ: My goodness, girl!

JACINTA: (*Laying down her cards.*) Rummy!

TERESA:	Again?
JACINTA:	It's not my fault. (*To María Antonia.*) Shuffle the cards.
ROSALBA:	I'm under the impression . . . I mean: I'm almost completely convinced you've been secretly in love with María Antonia all your life and you haven't shown your real feelings for some strange reason or fear.
JUAN JOSÉ:	Should I add water to your drink?
ROSALBA:	Only a little. Don't make it too weak.
MARIA ANTONIA:	(*To Jacinta.*) Cut the deck!
ROSALBA:	And I wonder J.J. . . . . What do you do with your feelings if you can't express them freely . . . liberate them . . . extemporize them? . . . Did you like that word? Pretty, isn't it? Ex-tem-po-ri-ze!
TERESA:	What's next?
JACINTA:	Two flushes and three of a kind.
TERESA:	But I can't do a thing with this hand, María Antonia!
ROSALBA:	Because the only real thing, the only unique and important thing . . . What is it? Feelings! Don't they say that love moves mountains. Well, make up your mind, my friend, make a decision and move something even though it may only be a small dune . . . a little portion of your being (*Juan José laughs.*) Oh!, you feel like laughing. It makes you laugh, doesn't it ? But, listen! It's a nervous laugh. Could it be that I'm putting my finger on the sore spot?
MARIA ANTONIA:	I'll buy that two.
JUAN JOSÉ:	Why don't we play your Agustín Lara cassette?

ROSALBA:	There's a perfect example! Agustín Lara was never afraid of feelings . . . even though during his lifetime the audience considered him a sentimental fool . . . because people continue to fall in love during a night of serenading in spite of the many years that have gone by since he wrote the song . . . *Noche de Ronda.*[12]
JUAN JOSÉ:	You're beginning to talk nonsense, Rosalba, honestly.
TERESA:	Listen, Rosalba, why don't you play cards with us?
ROSALBA:	Play, what?
MARIA ANTONIA:	Rummy.
ROSALBA:	I'm sorry, darling, but that's a teenagers' game . . . I think it's a stupid game! I'd rather waste my time in a different way.
TERESA:	Oh! Listen to her! I bet when she's with her high-class friends at the club, she doesn't say that.
MARIA ANTONIA:	They don't play rummy there . . . they play bridge.
ROSALBA:	Don't make fun of me! Don't make fun of me! Sometimes you're so superficial, so trivial . . .
JACINTA:	What are we? I don't understand! . . .
MARIA ANTONIA:	Stupid, Jacinta . . . in short, she's saying we're stupid.
ROSALBA:	Superficial! Unlike you, I am talking to J.J. about transcendental matters, about things that are vital, essential to human beings. I'm talking about feelings. That is, about love. I assume you all remember what love is, right?
JACINTA:	(*Singing.*) Love is a many splendor thing . . .
JUAN JOSÉ:	(*Addressing the others.*) What did you do with the Agustín Lara cassette?

ROSALBA: (*Concentrating.*) I do remember. I always have the image of true love fresh in my mind because unlike you, who only have bitter memories of the men in your lives, my memories are full of tenderness, of pleasant nostalgia, of loving warmth . . . of . . .

TERESA: Oh, my! As soon as Rosalba has a few drinks, she becomes nostalgic.

JUAN JOSÉ: She'll get over it as soon as the Italian comes through that door and says "Vini, Vidi, Vinci!"[13]

ROSALBA: That's not true. What time is it? Don't you think the plane should've arrived by now? Teresa, didn't she say they'd arrive at noon?

TERESA: (*To María Antonia.*) I'm sorry, but that two is mine. Change your three-of-a-kind.

MARIA ANTONIA: It wasn't for you, darling.

ROSALBA: Don't you think we should call the airport to find out if the plane has arrived?

TERESA: If it had arrived, we'd know by now. Margarita agreed to call us as soon as she set foot in the country.

ROSALBA: But look at the time . . .

MARIA ANTONIA: Rummy!

TERESA: That's not possible. So quickly? Let me see . . .

MARIA ANTONIA: My two flushes . . . my three twos and the game's over!

JACINTA: (*Getting up.*) When she deals, she's really dangerous!

TERESA: Aren't you gonna play any more?

JACINTA: No. I've got a lot to do in the kitchen. (*She exits.*)

TERESA: And you, Juan José?

JUAN JOSÉ: I want to know what you did with the Agustín
                        Lara cassette Rosalba brought.

ROSALBA: Oh, darling! Forget about Agustín Lara. Right now,
                        our song is *Torna a Sorrento* . . . or *Arrivederci Roma*.
                        What's the number, Teresa? I'm gonna call.

TERESA: Sometimes flights are delayed. A whiskey, please,
                        Juan José.

MARIA ANTONIA: Like us late bloomers . . . who created this absurd
                        Co-op . . .

ROSALBA: Ah! Now, it seems absurd to you. But when I
                        mentioned my idea to all of you for the first time,
                        your eyes popped out, María Antonia . . . you
                        congratulated me and praised my ingenuity
                        and . . .

JUAN JOSÉ: You're right. It was really a brilliant idea, Rosalba.
                        When I remember how you all started the whole
                        thing— . . . it was like a game . . . like an
                        imaginative exercise now on the verge of
                        materializing—I realize you're not late bloomers at
                        all.

ROSALBA: The idea was mine, darling. It stemmed from here.
                        (*She points to her head.*)

TERESA: And from here.

She puts her hands between her legs. Juan José laughs.

ROSALBA: You're so vulgar.

JUAN JOSÉ: (*Mocking Rosalba.*) "Don't you think that what we
                        need is a man?"

TERESA: And you're offended!

ROSALBA: I don't understand why. To be honest with you
                        Juan José, sometimes I think it's a pity you're not

	gay . . . if you were, you could share the Italian with us!
TERESA:	Don't get carried away by your erotic fantasies, Rosalba! One dead lover to your credit is enough!
JUAN JOSÉ:	And how did you manage to kill him, Rosalba. What did you do to poor Dr. Serrano?
MARIA ANTONIA:	Poor? The incognito Dr. Serrano was filthy rich, honey. Where do you think the *garçonnière* overlooking the *Avila* came from? At the beginning that place was their love nest . . . their rendezvous . . . because appearance, etiquette, and discretion are essential to Rosalba. She was always the perfect mistress: discreet, silent, reserved; even among us she'd refer to him as "My friend Dr. Serrano." We got to the point where we wondered if the man really existed or was just a figment of her imagination and she had created him to make us jealous.
JUAN JOSÉ:	The fact that he died proves he existed. (*To Rosalba.*) Is it true the fire of your passion killed him?
ROSALBA:	Those are Teresa's stories. She's green with envy because she has never found anyone to support her. She always had to support them. A bunch of rascals!
MARIA ANTONIA:	He died, vulgarly speaking, like Saint Lawrence. It's too bad we never got to see him, not even in a photo.
ROSALBA:	He was a very refined man . . . a man out of this world . . . a gentleman! Which is more than you can say about your soldier!
JUAN JOSÉ:	Damn it! Don't start that again! Let's talk about the Co-op!
MARIA ANTONIA:	But, Rosalba, with an imagination that has always characterized her, one day said: "A man!" Of

course, a man we can share . . . you may wonder, Juan José : Why not a Portuguese . . . or a Dutchman . . . or a Creole?

TERESA: Because we checked all the available men in Caracas and, excuse me, Juan José, we reached the conclusion that there was no one here who met our expectations.

MARIA ANTONIA: (*Amused.*) It wasn't exactly like that. She just (*pointing at Rosalba*) convinced us that the best lovers in the world are the Italians. Thus, we decided to lease one legally. But the problem was . . . where were we gonna find him? "In the Piazza Navona in Rome," Margarita said, "where else?"

JACINTA: (*Entering.*) I suggested Miranda Square, but they didn't mind me.

ROSALBA: Because he couldn't be from here, Jacinta. Don't you see it would've been too risky! It had to be a man who didn't have anything to do with us . . . A man who wouldn't cause us any trouble or change our lifestyles. Young, single . . . and with enough physical prowess to satisfy our needs on weekends.

JUAN JOSÉ: One weekend for each one of you.

ROSALBA: For sixty days . . . because, of course, we gotta pay all the expenses . . . imagine . . . the plane tickets and Margarita's stay in Rome while searching for him . . . and we didn't have enough money to keep him for a year.

JUAN JOSÉ: And since it was your idea, why didn't they send you to get him?

MARIA ANTONIA: Her! Are you crazy? First of all, she would've probably stayed there with the Italian . . . and second, she doesn't speak Italian . . . only cutí,[14] and just barely . . .

TERESA:	Then, by default, Margarita, the only polyglot, was chosen. She's also trustworthy.
MARIA ANTONIA:	Yes, because if we had given you the money . . .
JUAN JOSÉ:	You know what I don't understand, María Antonia, is how they got you involved in this adventure . . . you're so stingy.
MARIA ANTONIA:	Well . . . the truth is . . . at the very beginning, it seemed crazy to me . . . just as you said . . . a senseless adventure . . . but, all of a sudden, the game began to take shape and every time we discussed it, the plans became more and more serious . . . and . . .
ROSALBA:	And we convinced her. And not only that . . . she even invested the money she won in the Lotto.
JUAN JOSÉ:	And where did you get your part, Rosalba?
TERESA:	She sold a diamond . . . a memento from the late Dr. Serrano.
MARIA ANTONIA:	And Margarita didn't have any problems because she's on sabbatical.
TERESA:	I sacrificed the most; I sold my VCR, my stereo, and on top of it, I owe a month's rent.
JUAN JOSÉ:	Well . . . and the first weekend . . . that is to say, this one . . . which one of you will be spending it with the Italian?

All of them look at each another and realize they hadn't thought of that.

JACINTA:	Oh boy, talk about opening a can of worms.
ROSALBA:	That's right, María Antonia . . . who's first?
JACINTA:	If you are gonna consider seniority . . .
MARIA ANTONIA:	Shut up! Seniority doesn't count here.

JUAN JOSÉ:	You'll have to reach an agreement. I can't believe you didn't think of it beforehand!
TERESA:	Well, when the Italian comes . . . we'll let him decide.
MARIA ANTONIA:	He has no say in the matter. We'll decide.
TERESA:	(*Distrustful.*) Oh, yes. How?
JUAN JOSÉ:	I would think that María Antonia, as the hostess . . .
MARIA ANTONIA:	No, sir. It's easy. There are four of us, right? We'll cast lots. I suggest we have a raffle.
ROSALBA:	Pardon me, but I don't agree. With the raffle, yes . . . but not among four . . . No, honey. Margarita has already spent more than a week with the Italian.
JUAN JOSÉ:	(*Egging her on.*) Rosalba's right, María Antonia . . . it wouldn't be fair.
TERESA:	I could go first, to try out my new look.
MARIA ANTONIA:	But you won't. We'll have the raffle, period! Jacinta . . . bring me a piece of paper and a pencil.

Jacinta obeys.

ROSALBA:	Oh! How exciting . . . a raffle!
JUAN JOSÉ:	It'll be better if you're the last one, Rosalba . . . otherwise we may have a death, but not exactly the "small death" you'd like to experience.
ROSALBA:	You're a boor!
JACINTA:	(*With paper and pencil in hand.*) Here it is!
MARIA ANTONIA:	Write our names, Juan José . . . legibly, please. (*Juan José does it.*) And you, Jacinta, come here! We need an innocent hand. (*María Antonia takes a big goblet.*)

TERESA: This seems so ridiculous to me . . . why don't we
                    allow him to choose?

JUAN JOSÉ: Ready! Watch carefully so later on you don't think
                    there was any cheating . . . all three names are here,
                    right? Now, I fold the little pieces of paper, place
                    them here, and turn and turn the drum! Who will
                    the winner be? (*He shakes the papers in the goblet.*)
                    Jacinta . . . pick one.

Jacinta obeys. She opens the piece of paper. She looks at them, baffled.

ROSALBA: Read it, once and for all!

JACINTA: I have the luck of the Irish! I drew María Antonia's
                    name. (*She hugs her.*) Congratulations, dear!

MARIA ANTONIA: Oh! I . . . I . . . Let me see the paper (*She looks at it.*)
                    Yes . . . I won . . . See . . . Here's my name!

TERESA: Well, fine . . . fine . . . It's not such a big deal. Pick
                    another. (*Jacinta does so.*)

JUAN JOSÉ: (*To María Antonia.*) You should thank me, I did it
                    for you!

María Antonia smiles.

JACINTA: Here it says . . . Rosalba!

Rosalba screams.

ROSALBA: Really? Swear to it, Jacinta! . . . let me see! (*Jacinta
                    shows her the piece of paper.*) Oh! I can't believe it . . .
                    I'm gonna faint . . . disappear . . . I feel like I'm in
                    seventh Heaven!

JUAN JOSÉ: Teresa, there's a proverb that says: "He who laughs
                    last, laughs the best."

Teresa is not amused.

ROSALBA: Well. María Antonia, you gotta train the Italian
                    very well.

María Antonia smiles, flattered.

MARIA ANTONIA: Now that the matter is settled . . . let's celebrate!

JACINTA: See, María Antonia, and you were reluctant at first.

MARIA ANTONIA: (*Euphoric.*) Ladies and gentleman . . . this round is on the house. (*She pours drinks for everybody.*)

TERESA: (*Sluggishly.*) Girls . . . look at the hostess, all of a sudden she's so generous!

MARIA ANTONIA: Stop being so sarcastic, Teresa . . . the raffle was as fair as the lottery, and it took place in the presence of witnesses. It's not my fault I won.

JUAN JOSÉ: Well . . . What are you gonna do with him on weekdays?

MARIA ANTONIA: Feed him.

TERESA: And let him rest, of course.

ROSALBA: He has from Monday through Friday to rest and recuperate.

MARIA ANTONIA: Besides, we gotta work . . . we have families . . . and responsibilities . . .

JACINTA: And years, Juan José, we're old!

ROSALBA: We? You're not included in the Co-op!

JACINTA: And I don't care. I've never liked monsieurs . . .

JUAN JOSÉ: Your salary doesn't allow that, right, Jacinta?

The phone rings.

ROSALBA: Oh! It's her! It must be Margarita . . . (*She runs to pick up the phone.*) Let me answer. (*She picks up the phone.*) Hello? (*She covers the speaker.*) Jacinta . . . Jacinta . . . please, answer it . . . I'm not here. (*To the others.*) It's Beba.

JACINTA: And what should I tell her?

ROSALBA: Make up something.

JACINTA: (*She picks up the phone.*) Hello? No, honey . . . Your
                mother isn't here. (*Brief pause.*) What voice? (*Brief
                pause.*) No, that was not her but . . . (*They get cut off.*)
                Okay . . . ? I'll tell her if she comes. (*Brief pause.*)
                You're welcome! (*She hangs up. To Rosalba.*) Your
                daughter . . . she says she knows very well you're
                here . . . that you should remember she has to go
                out . . . she wants to know when you'll be home so
                she can bring the children over. (*Rosalba seems
                upset.*)

TERESA: Why don't you tell your daughter the truth? I'm
                sure she would be amused to discover her
                mother's secret adventures.

JUAN JOSÉ: Here it is! I finally found it! (*He holds up the Agustín
                Lara cassette.*) Should we play it, Antonia?

María Antonia goes to put it on.

ROSALBA: (*To Teresa.*) I don't like your remarks, Teresa. I don't
                like them.

TERESA: Come on, honey. Don't frown!

ROSALBA: I don't like them. You know I want my daughters
                to think highly of me . . . I don't fool around with
                those things.

TERESA: Oh, Rosalba . . . Don't take things so seriously,
                please. We all know you're a better mother than
                Libertad Lamarque[15] in *The Lady with the Veil*.

JUAN JOSÉ: (*Imitating Montero, the protagonist in the movie.*)
                "You, did it to yourself, you asked to be deported.
                See how I kept you away from Raúl. The only thing
                I can't do is stop you from seeing him for the last
                time. Make sure the meeting is as short and
                pleasant as possible."

ROSALBA: (*Taking up the role of Libertad Lamarque.*) "You're so
                cruel!"

JUAN JOSÉ: "It's your fault! I wanted to avoid the scandal but
                you made sure everyone found out about your
                sins. You've ruined my career. I can't face anyone.
                You've left me no choice but to remain here all
                alone."

ROSALBA: "Then, only your pride is hurt."

JUAN JOSÉ: "Have you forgotten my love for you?"

ROSALBA: "Don't talk of love when you're proving you never
                loved me."

JUAN JOSÉ: "Or that I loved you too much and finally realized
                you married me for my money."

ROSALBA: "It's not true! But even if I'd been wrong a hundred
                times you had no right to take such a revenge. No
                one's entitled to separate a son from his mother."

JUAN JOSÉ: "That's the punishment you deserve. Your lover
                was lucky to die, but you, you're condemned to
                live year after year in loneliness, yearning for your
                son till you die!"

MARIA ANTONIA: At that moment the little boy comes down the stairs!

TERESA: Mommy! Mommy! . . .

ROSALBA: "Sweetheart!"

TERESA: "Mommy . . . where were you?"

ROSALBA: "Traveling, darling . . . but very close to you. You
                were always on my mind. (*She hugs Teresa.*) Let me
                look at you! You're so handsome!"

TERESA: "Are you gonna stay?"

ROSALBA: "I can't, my dear. I gotta take a very long trip, but

	I'll come back and bring you many toys . . . and a little train . . . Would you like a train?"
TERESA:	"Yes!"
ROSALBA:	"You won't forget me, will you? You can't forget me. No one can love you as much as mommy does . . . no one!"

He hugs her again.

JUAN JOSÉ:	"Lupe, take the boy away!"

Jacinta runs and separates Teresa from Rosalba.

ROSALBA:	"One more minute . . . I've barely seen him! Bring him back to me!"
TERESA:	"Mom . . . Mom . . . take me with you!"
ROSALBA:	(*Falling on her knees.*) "Bring him back! Bring him back! Raúl, darling . . . remember me forever." (*Jacinta takes Teresa away. Rosalba turns dramatically to Juan José.*) "You're gonna die before I do. You're ill. You're gonna die before I do and then I'll return and he'll be mine again!"
MARIA ANTONIA:	In the next scene she was leaning against a lamp-post at the night club where she used to work looking like a tart, and singing.
ROSALBA:	(*Singing.*) "I'd like to cut my veins very slowly And spill my blood at your feet To prove I can't love anyone The way I love you, And then die afterwards. But your blue eyes, As blue as the sky and the sea, Are unaware of me, They don't realize I'm here Lost in my loneliness. Shadows, only shadows

Caressing my hands.
Shadows, only shadows
In my trembling voice.
I could've been happy
But here I am
Suffering,
Living, amidst tears,
The most horrendous moments
Of this drama without end.
Shadows, only shadows
Between your life and mine.
Shadows, only shadows
Between your love and mine."[16]

Everyone applauds.

MARIA ANTONIA: Oh, no, but you're forgetting the part when they're inside the car and the son doesn't know she's his mother and he's ready to go down the abyss and she screams: "No! You can't . . . You don't have the right to take the life I once gave you." (*Everyone remains in suspense looking at María Antonia. María Antonia looks at Teresa who has turned pale.*) Forgive me.

TERESA: It doesn't matter.

ROSALBA: Enough talk about films. The plane should've arrived by now. To make sure, I'm gonna call the airport. (*She goes to the phone and dials.*)

MARIA ANTONIA: (*To Teresa.*) Forgive me, darling, forgive me.

JUAN JOSÉ: I'm gonna pour more drinks. (*He gets the glasses.*)

MARIA ANTONIA: Sometimes one forgets . . .

TERESA: I told you it doesn't matter. And please, don't keep talking to me so sheepishly because I can't tolerate it. I know one forgets. I forgot.

JACINTA: (*To break the tension.*) Let me know if Margarita got so excited with the Italian she decided to keep him all for herself.

ROSALBA:	She'll have to request asylum in an embassy for life. I get no response, there seems no way to put the call through.
JUAN JOSÉ:	So much urgency on Rosalba's part makes me imagine a long and passionate summer. (*Rosalba shrugs and goes to the bedroom. To María Antonia.*) Your drink.
TERESA:	I'll pour mine, if you don't mind.
JUAN JOSÉ:	What about Lara, María Antonia? Weren't you gonna put on the cassette?
MARIA ANTONIA:	Oh yes! . . . (*She puts it on.*)
JUAN JOSÉ:	See . . . that guy, he was really lucky! Despite his ugly face, his crooked mouth—ruined by a nightclub dancer with a knife—he had the most beautiful women in the world.
JACINTA:	How ironic . . . to think that you, who looks like a leading actor from the forties can't succeed in attracting them.
JUAN JOSÉ:	I can't complain, Jacinta. I haven't done so badly either.
TERESA:	That's true, Juan José . . . Why didn't you marry? Can it be, as Rosalba says, that you've always been secretly in love with María Antonia.
MARIA ANTONIA:	Don't talk such nonsense.
JUAN JOSÉ:	I didn't marry, my dear friend, because I don't believe human beings were made to live as couples. There's nothing worse than waking up every day and finding beside you the same face growing old, fat, and wrinkled.
TERESA:	Oh yes, you say that because your face is so smooth.

JUAN JOSÉ:	No, because I never get tired of myself.
JACINTA:	I think women are the ones who get tired of you.
JUAN JOSÉ:	It's very possible . . . and since, unfortunately, I can't afford to hire an Italian woman . . . I'm satisfied with whatever I can find . . . and you might not believe it, but I always find something.
TERESA:	I think you haven't married because there hasn't been a woman who wanted to marry you . . . you must be very lazy and boring in bed.
MARIA ANTONIA:	Don't start picking on him.
JACINTA:	But once he was very close to marrying. Oh, I still remember . . . He showed up here, many years ago with his children's mother . . . she was extremely thin . . . shy, with her straight hair down to her waist and that enormous belly which almost tilted her forward. (*She imitates Juan José.*) "María Antonia, I want you . . . you who are my best friend, a sister to me . . . to be my first child's godmother, and I want this woman, with whom I've decided to share the rest of my life, . . ."
TERESA:	Three years and two children!
JACINTA:	" . . . to be your friend, like I've been." And that poor girl looked at María Antonia as if she were seeing the Virgin herself.
JUAN JOSÉ:	We all make mistakes, Jacinta.
JACINTA:	(*Laughing.*) She made the mistake of getting pregnant twice.
JUAN JOSÉ:	I never promised to marry her. As far as that goes, I've been faithful to my principles.
TERESA:	And that faithfulness to your principles allowed you to abandon her in that cheap boarding house, with half a can of instant dry milk and a two-

burner kerosene stove? Because that's the situation she was in when we rescued her, right, María Antonia?, after the poor woman called here . . . saying "Juan José hasn't shown up . . . he told me he was going to Puerto Cabello to collect some money to pay for my room and board . . . the landlord's about to throw me out of the house and I don't have any place to go . . ."

MARIA ANTONIA: (*Reproachfully.*) Teresa . . . Teresa . . .

JUAN JOSÉ: They put me in jail. María Antonia knows I was sent to jail. I was working a deal with that navy captain . . . How was I supposed to know he was involved in a conspiracy against Betancourt?[17]

TERESA: Oh sure, all we need now is for you to try to convince us you were a political prisoner. You've got to be kidding, darling! You were put in jail because you were a bum, and you were put in a cell full of faggots who used to pick up young sailors in the harbor.

JUAN JOSÉ: That's not true!

TERESA: And when we went to get you . . . there you were, in heaven . . . reading Shakespeare . . . but in French (*ironically*) which, incidentally, is the best way to read him.

JACINTA: Do you speak French, Juan José?

TERESA: I'm not surprised that woman doesn't allow you to set foot in her house nor that your children, who accept you out of pity, feel ashamed of being your offspring.

JUAN JOSÉ: But none of them committed suicide!

MARIA ANTONIA: (*Upset.*) Oh, shut up . . . let me listen to Agustín Lara. What's going on? Rosalba . . . Rosalba . . . where in the hell's Rosalba? (*Teresa freezes. Juan José goes to pour himself another drink.*) Rosalba!

Rosalba comes back dressed as a "rumba" dancer.

ROSALBA:	(*Singing.*) Mambo . . . it's an exciting mambo . . . mambo how exciting it is . . . is . . . is . . .[18]
MARIA ANTONIA:	She's so crazy. (*To Rosalba.*) Where did you get that, honey?
ROSALBA:	It was in your closet. I bet you didn't recognize me!
MARIA ANTONIA:	(*Nervous on Teresa's account.*) It must be full of moths. Take it off!
JACINTA:	Oh no, María Antonia . . . she looks exactly like Ninón Sevilla!
ROSALBA:	(*Singing and dancing.*) "Just look at how well and sensuously Mexicans dance the mambo . . . they sway their hips and shoulders exactly like the Cubans!" (*To Teresa.*) What happened? That was your hit at "Avila's" . . . (*To Juan José.*) Get rid of that silly old guy and put on Toña la Negra's cassette![19]
JACINTA:	Oh, Rosalba . . . that's how you should be dressed for the Italian . . . that way he'll get a taste of real Latin flavor.
ROSALBA:	(*Insisting.*) What's wrong, Teresa? Aren't you gonna say anything?
MARIA ANTONIA:	You're gonna get a skin rash . . . that dress is ancient!
ROSALBA:	(*Singing.*) "Let's enjoy Bartolo's carnival . . . Let's enjoy Bartolo's carnival." (*She tries to force Teresa to dance.*)
TERESA:	Stop this nonsense. You're nuts!
ROSALBA:	(*To María Antonia.*) I went to your closet to look for some cologne and discovered this great costume! I'm not crazy, Teresa. And look! It really fits snugly . . . isn't it fabulous?

JUAN JOSÉ:	The costume or the body?
ROSALBA:	Both, J. J. . . . because the last time I wore this costume I was thirty-four years old . . . and, look . . . it still looks great!
MARIA ANTONIA:	I've always said that of all of us, you're the one who looks the youngest.
JACINTA:	How can she not look young when she gets up at ten, goes to the gym . . . from there to the beauty parlor . . . from there to the club . . . from the club she goes home and watches a soap opera . . . with such pampering, who wouldn't look young?
JUAN JOSÉ:	The proletariat has spoken. Complete with its typical resentment.
JACINTA:	You're telling me! I've been breaking my back ever since I was thirteen. That's when I started working as a maid at María Antonia's house.
MARIA ANTONIA:	You should be thankful I continue to be nice to you and still support you. It's not Rosalba's fault she's had such an easy life.
JACINTA:	(*Ironically.*) No, I don't blame her, I envy her.
ROSALBA:	Teresa, do you remember when you used to go into "Avila's" in your cat costume? The orchestra would stop . . . it caused a big commotion and even the musicians would stand up and play a fanfare . . . (*to the others*) and she would parade all over the club and climb on the tables . . . and on the bar counter. Once everyone had admired her all wrapped up in that black outfit, she would grab her tail and would . . . (*María Antonia meows like a cat.*) And then the orchestra would start playing again! (*She sings and dances.*) "Mambo . . . it's an exciting mambo . . ." And Teresa would make a feline jump and would fall on the dance floor and would be the queen . . . the great diva . . . everyone would move back to admire her and all the men

would fight to dance with her. Once we even raffled her ... do you remember, María Antonia?

MARIA ANTONIA: (*Smiling.*) Those were crazy days!

ROSALBA: We raffled her complete with the tail and all! That was a sensational night!

JUAN JOSÉ: Your flash-type appearances were sensational! (*Rosalba laughs.*) I imagine even now people still wonder who that mysterious woman was who appeared in the middle of the dance with her black mask and her black leather coat.

ROSALBA: Oh, yes, I still have it!

JUAN JOSÉ: Her act was like a gunpowder flash, Jacinta ... black hose the kind you wore with a garter belt ... black high heels ... a black mask and a black leather coat ... she used to walk around the tables greeting everybody with a nod like a queen and once all eyes were on her, zoom! ... she would open her coat and show herself stark naked ... five seconds ... ten seconds ... then she would disappear leaving everybody with their mouths open.

MARIA ANTONIA: And then she would go to the bathroom to change her costume. Oh, if the late Dr. Serrano had seen her!

ROSALBA: (*Laughing.*) He wouldn't have recognized me with the black mask.

JACINTA: Your easy life would've ended right there and then.

ROSALBA: Dr. Serrano would've never found out because he was a very serious man who never set foot in a carnival dance.

JUAN JOSÉ: I suggest we all dress in costumes and give Margarita and the Italian a big surprise ... let's welcome them with a great carnival dance.

ROSALBA:	Oh, yes María Antonia! . . . look for Teresa's black outfit.
JACINTA:	Now they've all gone crazy!
ROSALBA:	I'll dress like a rumba dancer . . . Jacinta, like a freed slave which is the costume that best suits her . . . you, Juan José . . . you've been dressed as the poor intellectual ever since we met you, and you, María Antonia, like a general with a military cap and everything . . . come here, Teresa . . . (*She takes her by the hand.*) We'll rehearse the introduction and when I name you, you . . . What did she sound like, María Antonia ?

María Antonia meows again.

JUAN JOSÉ:	(*Taking Jacinta by the hand.*) Come on, Teresa . . . perk up!
TERESA:	(*She jerks herself away.*) He did not commit suicide!
JUAN JOSÉ:	(*Surprised.*) What?
TERESA:	It was an accident. He never intended to take his life.
ROSALBA:	(*Astonished.*) What are you talking about, darling?
TERESA:	My son did not commit suicide! I loved him . . . I gave him everything a mother can give her son . . . he didn't have any reason to do that, none whatsoever, (*to Juan José*) do you understand me, you bastard? None whatsoever!
MARIA ANTONIA:	What's wrong, Teresa? It's all right . . . it's all right!
TERESA:	No it's not! And no one has the right to blame me for that accident . . . no one!
MARIA ANTONIA:	No one's talking about that, Teresa.
TERESA:	He is. But listen, you know how it is. I don't feel guilty, you hear? I live with my sorrow, but I don't feel guilty.

MARIA ANTONIA: (*Trying to calm her down.*) Let's not talk about that, Teresa, we all know it was an accident and . . .

TERESA: He doesn't! (*To Juan José.*) And you, bastard, I won't let you rake me over the coals!

ROSALBA: No, darling! No insults, please! If you do that again I'll be sick . . .

TERESA: Then, vomit on the carpet . . . it won't be the first time! Listen! He wasn't well! He was sick . . . sick from depression . . . he was depressed. But he didn't want to kill himself . . . if I had been there I could've talked to him . . . I could've advised him . . . all he wanted was . . . to sleep . . . and he took too many . . . those damned pills . . . (*She begins to cry.*)

ROSALBA: (*Moved.*) Don't cry, Teresa . . . look . . . your make-up will run and Margarita and the Italian, who are about to arrive, will find you're a mess . . . and we don't want that . . . do we, María Antonia? We want them to find us happy, festive . . . amusing . . . with the costumes, Teresa, with the cat's tail . . .

TERESA: Shit! Don't talk about costumes! . . .

JUAN JOSÉ: Teresa, I didn't mean that . . .

TERESA: You're a pathetic faggot . . . you're a jerk and you shouldn't judge me or accuse me of anything.

MARIA ANTONIA: I'm sure he . . .

TERESA: I was a good mother, wasn't I, María Antonia? But I also had the right to live my life . . . How could I know he felt so lonely . . . so awful . . . I couldn't imagine that he would dare do something like that . . . What for? To punish me? But what did he lack, María Antonia? Tell me, what was missing in his life? . . . What did I fail to give him? Nothing! But I was also alone . . . It was also very difficult for me to be alone, wasn't it, María Antonia? You know me, darling . . . That letter wasn't true . . . he was always so difficult . . . since he was little . . . so reserved . . . introverted . . . but what he wrote wasn't true. We didn't understand each other but I loved him . . . in spite of his silence . . . despite his accusatory stares . . . he was always criticizing me . . . he was always judging me . . . despite his defiant stance . . . his ironic comments . . . his rejections . . . I loved him. What he wrote in that letter wasn't true . . . He didn't believe what he said. He was confused . . . That was all. I never failed him. You can say I was reckless, but I never failed him, did I, María Antonia?

MARIA ANTONIA: Look . . . I don't know why you gotta torture yourself with those memories. Come here, wash your face . . . refresh yourself with cologne . . . (*María Antonia guides her away.*) Comb your hair a little and I'll help you put on your make-up again.

TERESA: I was a good mother . . . I shouldn't be blamed or judged . . . Okay, I admit I had many lovers . . . perhaps too many, but I never abandoned my children, did I, María Antonia?

MARIA ANTONIA: Nobody's judging you . . . no one's throwing anything at you . . . come on.

They exit. A heavy silence fills the room.

JACINTA: There must be something wrong with the rum. (*She goes to the kitchen.*)

ROSALBA: (*After a brief pause. To Juan José.*) You shouldn't have said anything. That was cruel!

JUAN JOSÉ: Shit, I don't even know how it started . . . I swear . . . I don't know!

ROSALBA: We were gonna put on costumes . . . we were gonna wait happily for the Italian and you spoiled everything.

JUAN JOSÉ:	I swear it wasn't my intention. (*They look at each other.*)
ROSALBA:	Turn off the cassette player, please.
JUAN JOSÉ:	Shit, now I feel terrible. Now all I want to do is leave.
ROSALBA:	Go, then . . . I'll explain everything to them. Besides, you're not interested in meeting the Italian, are you?
JUAN JOSÉ:	No . . . of course, not. Tell María Antonia that . . .
ROSALBA:	Don't worry, J. J. Go. (*Juan José exits. She sings softly.*) Little dove . . . little dove . . . be careful with your young ones because the hawk's watching your nest . . .
JACINTA:	(*Entering with cups of chicken broth.*) Where's J. J.?
ROSALBA:	He left.
JACINTA:	I brought you this cup of chicken broth to make you feel better.
ROSALBA:	Thank you, Jacinta.
JACINTA:	I don't know if I should set the table . . . because look at the time and no one's had lunch yet.
ROSALBA:	Don't you think the Italian would be surprised to find me like this?
JACINTA:	If he comes at all . . .
ROSALBA:	He'll come, Jacinta . . . We're waiting for him. He's gotta come. Margarita went to pick him up at the Piazza Navona . . . Rome . . . Italy.

María Antonia returns.

MARIA ANTONIA:	Where's Juan José?

ROSALBA: He left. He wasn't interested in meeting the Italian. Is Teresa feeling better?

MARIA ANTONIA: Yes.

JACINTA: María Antonia, I was wandering if I should set the table or . . .

MARIA ANTONIA: Of course, you should set the table, dummy . . . You're not planning to starve us to death, are you? (*The doorbell rings.*)

ROSALBA: Oh, now . . . it's Margarita! Oh, my God . . . and here I am such a mess . . . Don't open the door, yet, Jacinta . . . Don't open it . . . Teresa . . . Teresa . . . The Italian's here . . .

MARIA ANTONIA: I'll get it . . . I'll open the door and introduce everybody . . .

TERESA: (*Coming into the room.*) What's up?

ROSALBA: The Italian, darling . . . he just arrived . . . he's here!

María Antonia opens the door. It's Juan José. María Antonia's disappointed. The others are too.

JUAN JOSÉ: I found this in your mailbox, María Antonia.

María Antonia takes the postcard Juan José hands her. She starts reading. Juan José comes in and closes the door behind him. The others surround María Antonia.

ROSALBA: What is it, María Antonia?

María Antonia looks up and stares at them.

TERESA: Who sent you that postcard?

JUAN JOSÉ: It came from Vienna . . . it's from Margarita.

TERESA: (*Grabbing the postcard.*) What's the problem? (*She reads.*) Romantic Vienna . . . Vienna is a waltz . . .

Gian Piero and I happy . . . I hope you'll
understand. Kisses. Your friend. Margarita. (*Pause.*)
But I don't understand . . .

ROSALBA: What do you mean, a waltz? What do you mean
Vienna? What does all of this mean, darling?

JACINTA: Oh boy . . . what a fiasco!

TERESA: I don't understand a thing, darling, I don't
understand a thing.

MARIA ANTONIA: (*In an outburst.*) Then it means you're stupid! Or a
moron because it's as plain as the nose on your
face . . . Margarita deceived us . . . she made fools
of us . . . she took us for a ride . . . she betrayed us
and she kept the Italian. She took off with him
alone . . . do you understand now?

ROSALBA: (*On the verge of crying.*) It can't be . . . It can't be . . .

JUAN JOSÉ: She not only kept the Italian, but also your
money . . . the money you had put into the Co-op.

MARIA ANTONIA: (*Accusing Teresa.*) You told me you talked to her on
the phone last night.

TERESA: Yes, I swear . . . I did talk to her!

MARIA ANTONIA: And where did she call you from, moron? This
postcard was sent last week!

TERESA: But darling . . . how in the world was I supposed to
know where she was calling from?

JACINTA: I suppose Margarita's asking for asylum at some
embassy.

MARIA ANTONIA: Eight thousand six hundred *bolívares* . . . the eight
thousand six hundred *bolívares* I won in the Lotto,
lost . . . I was taken like an idiot.

TERESA: But María Antonia . . . it's not my fault . . .

MARIA ANTONIA: Yes, it is! Because you should've realized she wasn't in Rome . . . that all that baloney about the plane was a lie . . . that she didn't have the slightest intention of coming back!

JUAN JOSÉ: From the very beginning I said that . . .

MARIA ANTONIA: You shut up! Eight thousand six hundred *bolívares,* Teresa . . . eight thousand six hundred *bolívares!*

ROSALBA: María Antonia . . . calm down . . . it must be a mistake . . . it must be one of Margarita's bad jokes . . . it has to be that.

MARIA ANTONIA: (*Waving the postcard in front of Rosalba's face.*) A joke? Look at the date, stupid . . . what does it say here? (*Rosalba is shaking.*) Do you think she's gonna go all the way to Vienna to play a joke on us? She deceived us, which is a different story . . . and I lost eight thousand six hundred *bolívares* and you, your diamond ring!

JUAN JOSÉ: (*To Jacinta.*) I think we'll need more ice.

MARIA ANTONIA: We don't need any ice. How stupid of us . . . (*Mocking Teresa.*) Let Margarita go . . . she's the most trustworthy . . . (*To Teresa.*) This is all your fault!

TERESA: She deceived us all, María Antonia . . . all of us!

MARIA ANTONIA: And me more than anybody else! Because from the very beginning I said this was a crazy thing . . . that it wouldn't work . . . and you insisted . . . you convinced me . . . and I warned you . . . how in the world can we rent an Italian? And you, in a real frenzy over the idea because all your life you've been absolutely crazy . . . and I, instead of sticking to my guns, as I should've, fell for it . . . I let myself be talked into it like an idiot!

ROSALBA: It's not fair . . . It's not. Margarita didn't have any right to spoil my plan . . .

TERESA:	*(To get on María Antonia's good side.)* María Antonia . . . I lost even more!
MARIA ANTONIA:	But you're used to being exploited . . . I'm not. And what's worse, I was deceived by a friend . . . that makes me even angrier! *(Brief pause.)* I'm sorry about your new figure, Teresa . . . you won't get to show it off!

Teresa shrugs her shoulders as if it didn't matter.

JUAN JOSÉ:	Your weekend went down the drain, María Antonia.
MARIA ANTONIA:	I deserve it for being so stupid . . .
JUAN JOSÉ:	Well, don't take it so badly . . . who knows, maybe after Vienna . . .
TERESA:	Oh, get out of here, you brought us bad luck!
JUAN JOSÉ:	*(Laughing as he leaves.)* And how am I to blame?
MARIA ANTONIA:	My god, how could I not see it coming? How could we be so stupid . . . so naive!
ROSALBA:	Look María Antonia . . . I . . .
MARIA ANTONIA:	You had the brilliant idea of looking for an Italian . . . you should've known this could happen. But you couldn't anticipate this, could you?
JACINTA:	And to think the first weekend was yours. *(María Antonia gives her a dirty look.)* I better go set the table . . . *(She exits.)*
MARIA ANTONIA:	Eight thousand six hundred *bolívares* . . . eight thousand six hundred *bolívares*!
TERESA:	But darling . . . money's the last thing we should think of now.

María Antonia also gives her a dirty look.

ROSALBA: (*Reminiscing.*) Romantic Vienna . . . Vienna . . . How does it go? (*She picks up the postcard and reads.*) Vienna is a waltz . . .

María Antonia takes the postcard away from her and tears it to pieces. The phone rings. No one moves.

MARIA ANTONIA: (*To Teresa.*) Answer. It might be Margarita, home already.

TERESA: (*She picks up the phone.*) Hello. (*She covers the mouth piece.*) It's your daughter again! (*Rosalba signals to her to say she is not there.*) Hello . . . yes, Beba honey, this is Teresa. (*Pause.*) Just fine, thank you, darling . . . and you and the little ones? (*Pause.*) Who? No darling . . . she left a while ago. (*Pause.*) Oh, but why should I lie to you? (*Pause.*) But how can I tell her if she's not here? (*Teresa hangs up.*) What a brat . . . she hung up!

ROSALBA: What did she say?

TERESA: I quote: "I know my mother is there, Teresa . . . please tell her not to get so foolishly drunk again . . . that she should remember I've gotta go out and she has to take care of my children" . . . and she hung up!

ROSALBA: Without even saying good-bye . . . or good evening . . . nothing?

TERESA: That's it.

ROSALBA: She doesn't take after me. I would never behave like that. (*María Antonia begins to laugh.*) What's so funny?

MARIA ANTONIA: We . . . our situation. So much preparation . . . so much emotion . . . so much time waiting for the Italian, for nothing! But how could we imagine some Italian would be interested in three ridiculous old ladies?

ROSALBA: Well . . . apparently he got interested in Margarita. And I don't like you calling us old ladies, María Antonia . . . Look at Teresa with her new boobs . . . look at me with the same dress I wore when I was thirty-four years old . . . look at yourself!

MARIA ANTONIA: Here, alone . . . like every Saturday . . . as Teresa said full of . . . memories . . . is that the word you used Teresa?

TERESA: Memories and experiences.

MARIA ANTONIA: That's it. Memories and experiences. Beautiful memories and marvelous experiences . . . that's all!

JACINTA: (*Entering to set the table.*) María Antonia's a woman who's as crazy as a loon . . .

TERESA: (*Just to say something.*) Shall we play another round of rummy? I can't drink any more!

JACINTA: What about after lunch? Excuse me. (*She removes everything from the table and puts on the tablecloth.*)

ROSALBA: Put on the Lucho Gatica cassette again, María Antonia . . . it brings back so many memories!

TERESA: Does it remind you of the day you wet your nylons?

ROSALBA: Wet my silk stockings, Teresa . . . I've never worn nylons.

MARIA ANTONIA: (*While putting on the cassette.*) She's always been so exquisite!

TERESA: And talking about silk . . . what about the lingerie you were gonna show us?

ROSALBA: I still haven't priced it . . . but I'll give you a special discount . . . a real bargain . . . because now bras will really look great on you . . .

MARIA ANTONIA:	If she has enough money left to pay for them!
JACINTA:	(*Setting down the plates and flatware.*) But I thought they were made of plastic? Then they should be able to support themselves, shouldn't they?
MARIA ANTONIA:	She's the one who won't be able to support herself . . . I can see her having to go out and ask for charity.
ROSALBA:	Oh, yes, like the heroine in the soap opera.
TERESA:	I didn't watch it last night. What happened?
ROSALBA:	Well . . . she got out of jail and went to visit the man, who, of course, didn't recognize her even though the only thing different about her is a few grey hairs here and there . . .
MARIA ANTONIA:	And has she seen her daughter yet?
ROSALBA:	No . . . last night it ended when she showed up at his house, just when they were in the middle of a coming-out party for the daughter. She entered and looked at everybody . . . with such indifference . . . as if they didn't have anything to do with her . . . and those jewels . . . I don't know where they came from, because after twenty years in jail, you wonder where she got all those jewels and beautiful clothes . . . but the fact is she gets to his house and no one recognizes her . . . except for his mother who looks at her like this . . . puzzled . . . and she asks the housekeeper . . . "Hortensia . . . who's that woman?"
TERESA:	Oh, but, of course . . . because Hortensia knows the secret . . .
JACINTA:	Of course, she does! She's the one who took the baby away from her and accused her of stealing.
ROSALBA:	"Hortensia . . . who's that woman?" And Hortensia . . . "I don't know, ma'am, but her face sure looks familiar."

MARIA ANTONIA:	It's obvious! Don't forget the same actress plays both roles!
ROSALBA:	"She seems a very rich woman who's just arrived in town." And the mother said . . . "find out Hortensia, because something tells me her presence in this house could bring us a lot of grief . . ." and she repeated with emphasis, "a lot of grief!" And that's how it ended!
JACINTA:	Okay, come and sit down before the chicken soup gets cold.
MARIA ANTONIA:	So tonight's episode should finally reveal the truth.
JACINTA:	Okay, come on and sit down . . .
ROSALBA:	Darling . . . I can't eat like this . . . with this costume on!
MARIA ANTONIA:	Leave it on!
JACINTA:	Oh, the more I see her, the more she reminds me of Ninón Sevilla!
ROSALBA:	No, no, no . . . you go ahead and eat . . . my stomach's upset. (*María Antonia and Teresa go to the table. Rosalba lies down on the couch.*) Look . . . Juan José forgot this. (*She shows them the book.*)
MARIA ANTONIA:	He didn't forget it. It's a gift for me.

Rosalba picks up a magazine and starts reading.

TERESA:	What a pity our plans fell through, huh? It would've been fun to share the Italian . . . (*She laughs.*) It would've been crazy, but fun!
MARIA ANTONIA:	Please, let's not talk about that again, Teresa. In any case, we've all gotten out of life what we've been able to . . . we've already loved as much as we could love . . . what's left?

ROSALBA:	(*Straightening up.*) Hey . . . hear this!
TERESA:	If it's the horoscope, I'm not interested.
MARIA ANTONIA:	No, it's an old issue.
ROSALBA:	No, girls . . . listen . . . (*The lights dim.*) Spaniard . . . businessman . . . mature, yet very young looking . . . affectionate . . . intelligent . . . reserved . . . looking for an elegant and well-educated woman—divorced or widowed who appreciates the arts—for friendship and possible marriage. She must be mature, affectionate, and sweet; children, okay. I am well-off and wish to share and enjoy the rest of my life with someone who is also tired of being alone.

The End

Notes

1. For permission to stage the play, the author must be contacted directly: Avenida Altamira, Edificio Doral Apto. 21-A, San Bernardino, Caracas, Venezuela.

2. Black Friday is the name Venezuelans give to the date when international oil prices were drastically reduced and a new era of economic hardship began for the country.

3. In the original, the fragrance is Heno de Pravia. We looked for its counterpart in cologne in order to elicit the same association from American audiences that Heno de Pravia does for Latin Americans.

4. Carlos Gardel, (1887–1935), famous singer of tangos, died in a plane crash in Medellín, Colombia. He was so popular throughout Latin America that the anniversary of his death is still commemorated in most countries every June 24.

5. Agustín Lara (1897–1970) was a Mexican musician. He composed many popular songs, such as "María Bonita," "Madrid," "Granada," "Noche de Ronda," etc.

6. Rita Hayworth, as Gilda, was the pin-up girl that World War II soldiers preferred.

7. Lucho Gatica, a Chilean singer, became famous for his interpretations of love songs, especially *boleros*.

8. Marga López and Roberto Cañedo, Mexican movie stars who had the leading roles in the movie "Salón México."

9. Avila is the name of a hill in the city of Caracas. It overlooks a neighborhood by the same name. In the play, it is also the name of a famous nightclub.

10. In order to adapt the text to American audiences, we substituted pizza for *arepas* which are a type of sandwich made out of corn bread. We used pan pizza in place of *reina pepeada* which is a fancy *arepa* filled with chicken and avocado.

11. *Zarzuela* is the Spanish light opera. The *chotís* is a type of popular song from Madrid, which is danced in couples.

12. "Noche de ronda" is one of Agustín Lara's most popular love songs. Its theme deals with the sufferings experienced by abandoned lovers.

13. The translation of *Vini, Vidi, Vinci* is I came, I saw, I conquered.

14. Cutí is an Indian language.

15. Libertad Lamarque is an Argentinean singer and actress who appeared in many Mexican films while in exile.

16. This translation is of the song "Sombras nada más" which was made popular by the Mexican mariachi singer Javier Solís.

17. Rómulo Betancourt (1908–1981) was Venezuela's president from 1945 to 1948 and from 1959 to 1964. He was the founder of the Democratic Action Party.

18. The *mambo* as well as the *rumba* are Cuban dances which were performed in nightclubs by people dressed in elaborate Carmen Miranda-type costumes. These rhythms are still popular and people dance to them in formal and informal social gatherings. Rosalba is singing a song popularized by Dámaso Pérez Prado, a Cuban exiled in Mexico City.

19. Toña la Negra, famous Cuban singer and dancer.

Beatriz Seibel (Argentina) has distinguished herself as a theater researcher, actress, director, producer, and playwright. She considers herself more a dramaturgist than a playwright,[1] since her plays are based on either literary works or materials taken from other genres in the world of entertainment.

Her first play, *El amor* (Love), was an experiment that integrated works by Argentinean poets and narrators on the theme of love, while her second piece, *Aquí Federico* (Here, Federico), dramatized poems by Federico García Lorca. With the first version of *7 veces Eva* (7 Times Eve), however, Seibel caught the public's and critics' attention during the 1980 Buenos Aires theater season. This play blends selections from the novels of four women writers and an anonymous legend from the Northern region of Argentina in order to profile seven moments in Argentina's history from the feminine perspective.

The second version, which is the one included in this anthology, was restructured by Seibel in 1987.[2] To add a greater dimension of humor to the play as well as greater dynamism, she deleted the sequences based on Silvina Ocampo's and Beatriz Guido's novels, and incorporated radio scripts by comedian Niní Marshall to ridicule the upper classes. She also adds a social dimension to her play by including a character from an unpublished short story by Norma Tow. This addition emphasizes the women's social struggles and the labor tensions in Argentinean society, due to the massive European immigration at the beginning of the century.

Seibel's contribution to the field of Argentinean theater encompasses more than her stage productions; it includes numerous articles and four important books that document Argentina's theatrical and cultural tradition.

Notes

1. Seibel, in interviews with Teresa Cajiao Salas in Puerto Rico (November, 1987) and with Salas and Margarita Vargas in Buenos Aires (May 1988) stressed that her main concern (as was Antonin Artaud's) in the preparation of theater texts is the creation of what she calls "un texto de espectáculo" (a theatrical text) rather than a "literary text."

2. *7 veces Eva*, in its second version, was performed at the Second Congress on Feminine Creativity in the Hispanic World that took place in November 1987 at the University of Puerto Rico in Mayagüez.

7 Times Eve

BY BEATRIZ SEIBEL[1]

Translated from *7 veces Eva*
by Teresa Cajiao Salas and Margarita Vargas

7 Times Eve
Staging and Adaptation
by Beatriz Seibel
with María Elina Ruas

Characters

MOSQUETERA AND VIOLANTE	from "La flor de hierro" (The Iron Flower) by Libertad Demitropulos
JUANA MANUELA	from "Juanamanuela mucha mujer" (Juanamanuela a Great Woman) by Martha Mercader
GLADYS AND MONICA	from radio scripts by Niní Marshall
THE TERESAS	from "Las que esperan" (Those Who Wait) by Norma Tow (unpublished)
TELESITA	from an anonymous legend
PALOMA	from "Solamente ella" (Only She) by Martha Mercader

Staging and Costume Design: Carlota Beitía
Costume Production: Lita Fuentes
Pianist: Eduardo Rivera López
Photography: Olkar Rámirez
Direction: Beatriz Seibel

Single Act

The lights go on. The stage is set with a table, two chairs, and a clothes rack with costumes. The actress enters dressed as the "Mosquetera."[2] *she is a young woman from a small town. The tune of Zamba Tucumana*[3] *is heard.*

MOSQUETERA: (*Addressing the audience.*) Good evening ladies and gentlemen! How are you ma'am? How are you, sir? How was the trip? Good? I'm glad. Welcome to Tucumán! Let me tell those of you who are outsiders. Here, in Medinas, there's only a few of us left. But in the past . . . (*Music begins:* "La tristecita"[4] *is heard.*)
    In the days when the Acapayanta or Acapianta land grant was active, there were a lot of people; there were so many people that it was a joy to live here. There was a factory that sold its carts all over

the country. My paternal grandfather was a cart driver, he learned the trade from his grandfather, and who knows how far back cart drivers go in his family! Trades are passed on from generation to generation, it's not just a matter of improvising.

I, for one, am a story teller, which is no easy job. My mother taught me the trade because she came from a family of story tellers. You have to learn to be discreet, acting as if nothing were going on; so they don't even notice you while you're observing it all. They don't even see you at the train station, and yet you notice every single detail: who arrives, who leaves, if someone bought a television set, if they ate chicken or lamb, and so many other things. When I get home I have to tell my mother everything in detail. Since she became crippled, poor thing, and a widow on top of that, I am her only source of information; I attend to her as she taught me. So when I ask her: "Should I buy the newspaper, mother?" She says: "What for, haven't I shown you how to be a good observer? What are you good for, anyway?"

My mother knows all the stories, those from Medinas and those from many other places. She knows the old stories that grandmothers used to tell, and the new ones that she heard while practicing her trade. She taught me everything I know. You know? See over there, that's the shell of the main house in the Acapayanta land grant, it is so big that it looks like a hotel. One room after another, a water well, corridors, and patios. Acapayanta bustled with the life of the masters and the comings and goings of the servants. Water flowed down the canals, there was a lot of activity. It was a pleasure to live here.

Spanish music from the 1600s is heard. The actress removes her "mosquetera" dress and puts on a seventeenth-century robe. Violante de Godoy is a young woman, the wife of a Spanish conqueror. She reclines in a chair and dictates her will to the notary, she is dying.

VIOLANTE: I, Violante de Godoy, legitimate daughter of the conqueror Pedro de Lorique, leave to my husband,

Diego de Medina y Castro, my only heir, the farm in Choromoros called Los Lules, the Aligilán land grant, and another one, between the Guaycombo and Acapianta rivers. I demand that my body be buried humbly, with no other adornment than the holy cross, not in a casket, but on a bier like the ones in which they bury the poor. I manifest that I am devoted to the Franciscan order and request that masses be sung on behalf of the Indians among whom eighty sheep should be distributed to show the great love I have for them. I request that when my husband Diego returns from the expedition against the Indians, he be told that I died in peace with God and how much I loved him and suffered for not having borne him children. Anything can happen when life cannot continue. Anything can happen. I wish that Diego, at this very moment, would come into our chamber, that, because his heart had skipped a beat, he galloped without stopping until he arrived in Acapayanta. I wish he would sit in the chair, where the notary's writing, and understand why he had felt his heart skip a beat. Then I wish he would take one of my hands and that his eyes would give me the glorious light flickering in them. Death can be stopped only when his lips come close to my ear and say: "Violante! Do you remember? You can't leave now because you know how to remember. Do you remember?"

("*Hoy comamos y bebamos,*"[5] *played on the flute, can be heard as background music while the actress speaks.*) There's my father embracing your father, they are deeply moved; my mother and your mother admiring the wedding apparel displayed on top of the oak chest. My trousseau . . . Your older brothers and their wives sitting in the parlor, and the guests, and you and I drinking to our happiness, to something that today, after six years, was more than we ever imagined.

My trousseau . . . I started embroidering it when I was a little girl, torn between laughter and fear. Needle pricks . . . sighs . . . smiles interrupted by the Angelus or the Hail Mary . . . Confessional secrets: Father, I accuse myself of thinking all the time of Diego de Medina y Castro; I accuse myself of desiring his lips and hands. Hail Mary, full of grace. I accuse myself of having lustful thoughts. I accuse myself of thinking of him while I embroidered my linen sheets.

My letters! Did you know that I learned how to write only to send you letters? You were away for so long! In San Miguel, the priest used to tell me that it's vain for a woman to learn to write, but I persisted. He told me it takes years to learn, and that it's unacceptable for a woman to even try. No one outdid me in stubbornness. I learned only to be able to write to you.

(*The actress takes out a letter from her pocket and reads.*) "It always seems that the happiness we most wish for is the one we are least likely to obtain. For loving you my heart became enslaved: my Diego, if I didn't know how to love, I wouldn't fear your absence.

Through ranges, hills, rivers, deserts, salt mines,
    brooks,
I would've walked anywhere to see you
to serve you, to please you,
because to my great desire,
mountains, hills, rivers, deserts, salt marshes, and
    swamps
would be a breeze."

(*She puts the letter away and shivers in her chair.*) In Acapayanta—lying on my double bed, where I slept alone most of the time, I longed for the child that never came—for me you were a restless anxiety. Every time you left, Teófila, the weaver, sang in the women's quarters amidst the laughter and teasing of her companions:

Oh my poor mistress
she has a double bed
but she sleeps alone.

I suffered because of your absences. I was distressed in Acapayanta, Diego. I felt that shameful fever that comes at dusk and invades the whole body after praying the rosary, when it's time for supper.

Then, alone in the bedroom, I prayed for you. I asked God for only one thing: to bring you back to me. I didn't care about conquests or foundings. And you were always coveting material things. What good are they? Why were you so intent on destroying Indian gods? Aguirre was right when he imposed respect for their beliefs. They're defending what is theirs, Diego. Leave them alone. Love me. Let's love each other, perhaps we still have time. *(She stands up stirred by the fever.)*

Do you understand that El Dorado doesn't exist?

You learned the natives' tongue to be able to read through the entanglement of fingers pointing at the road leading toward the fabulous El Dorado. There, it was all supposed to be singing, laughter, and enjoyment of wealth. Blonde hair would never turn gray and faces wouldn't grow old. The streets would be paved with gold . . . palaces made of marble . . . that city obsessed everyone; it was always just around the next bend. Day after day, mountain after mountain, shadow after shadow, searching. The horses fell from exhaustion. Farther on, farther away. Wasn't that a glow? A shining pink mirage? Those who are dying from thirst must stay. The sick must rot. Move on! With shining swords under the infernal sun. With Caesar's city within reach, who dares to think of love! You became obsessed with counting the iron flowers that grew on your sword. Flowers of coagulated blood formed on the sword's edge. Fever flowers, which seemed to be open and eager. Because of these flowers, no sadness or memory plagued you. No kiss surrounded your flesh. Move on, then, continue! They die for the Caesar . . . won't we die? *(The actress collapses. Music from the 1600s can be heard.)*

No anxiety in your memory. With a blood flower sighing on the blade of the sword, to think of the one who loves you would be like watching an entire river flow, and expecting that the river stop right there. I understand, Diego, I understand.

Violante dies. The actress remains still for a moment. The music becomes louder. Then she gets up and changes into Mosquetera's costume.

MOSQUETERA: Whew! I escaped by the skin of my teeth. (*She paces while she thinks.*) In the church, the tiles are engraved with the ranks and names of the acapayanos who are buried there. Some of the names are so old they're illegible. But I learned them all by heart, just in case some tourist or pilgrim insists on knowing what they say. You get tired of reading the inscriptions on the floor and the walls and you even feel weak in the knees when you walk around them.

Oh, there's a pink gravestone below doña Violante de Godoy's that says: "Doña Claudia Ramírez de Montalvo, second wife of Don Diego de Medina y Castro," from which I gather that this don Diego married twice, and death joined the two ladies who rest in eternal peace without bothering each other, and even without being jealous of one another, unlike many human beings I know.

Back then, water wasn't as scarce as it is now. To make matters worse, we are thirsty all the time. Now, even cart drivers have disappeared. For a long time, sitting on top of their carts, they brought big casks full of water from San Miguel. The cart-driver trade is very old and at one time they had plenty of customers to enjoy a decent life. They brought books for the teacher, medicines for the drugstore, cloth and magazines for women . . . anyway . . . too many things to mention. I still have a magazine called "The Album," which used to publish Juana Manuela's tales. Have you read "A Drama in Fifteen Minutes"? There you find out about everything that happens in the world.

Juana Manuela was a very famous lady, with medals and everything, and she was from Horcones, Salta, pretty much our neighbor. My mother knows absolutely everything about the

Gorritis, about Juana Manuela's father, who fought alongside Güemes;[6] about her uncle, who was a delegate to the Tucumán Congress;[7] and about Juana Manuela, who in spite of being a woman and having many children, had time to open a school, support her family, and write short stories. She was the very first writer in the country. My mother heard the stories . . .

Opera music from 1870 is heard. The actress takes off the "Mosquetera" dress and puts on Juana Manuela's, which has a bustle. She sits at the table and begins to go through the newspapers and her correspondence. She opens one of the newspapers. The music softens and then ceases.

JUANA MANUELA: They mention me in "Echo of Youth." Let's see what they say . . . "A George Sand from Salta, not as talented but more virtuous than the great French woman." I'll have to find out who's this J.M.R. who damns me with this faint praise. Perhaps, if it were reversed, it would offend me less: "A George Sand from Salta more talented but less virtuous than the great French woman." No, that doesn't work either. That would be fine in France but here, it doesn't work at all. So . . . let's drop it. (*She picks up a letter and reads.*)

On the other hand, there is this nice letter from the French consul in Lima, who compares me with Madame de Stael . . . now, that's encouraging.

(*She picks up another newspaper. She opens it and sees a note marked with a thick red pencil.*) But who sent me this? Who wrote this?

(*She reads.*) "On the occasion of Mr. Hilarión Funes y Funes's funeral—whose farms were acquired through royal grants—a boisterous female novelist was seen socializing with young men in a noisy and improper manner. But we're not surprised by the lack of propriety of the aforementioned lady. The lady in question was also dressed in unusual attire, obviously imitating French women. (*The actress looks at her bustle and shrugs her shoulders.*) It wasn't long ago that in a gathering someone heard her say: man's thought is a reproduction of the sort of thinking that surrounds him. How awful! Because morality is absolute and does not depend on the physical world like that newcomer pretends." (*She puts down the newspaper, gets up, and walks furiously.*) I, a newcomer? What is he talking about? About lineage? Well, I'll have you know that I don't envy anybody's genealogy! Don't talk to me about royal grants! Go and check the archives in Salta and Jujuy! You'll find out who my ancestors were! I, a newcomer? Are they perhaps referring to my profession? You fools should know that I practice it with much more zeal and sacrifice and with far more dedication than those who call themselves writers merely because they've written four miserable pages, between battles, than those who, tired of flattering everybody, and fixing elections and committing fraud left and right, sit down and compose a bunch of overloaded stanzas. And for that they think they have the right to belong to Parnassus! I, a newcomer? The gall of those people! With almost thirty books published! I don't have a doctorate because, in this America, universities aren't open to women, but I've read thoroughly every printed piece of paper that I can get my hands on, and if I haven't read more it's because there are no more books in this forsaken land where one hundred battles are fought for every school that is opened!

Let me tell you that in 1848 when all the men around me were only thinking about cavalry charges and coups d'état, I opened a school and directed it for thirty years. I, a newcomer? Ha! It makes me laugh! I've shown more loyalty to my literary principles than all of them to their political beliefs. And don't force me to name them. My list would be endless . . . And from where do they infer that morality isn't influenced by the environment? Fools! In the name of what scientific belief or religion are they talking? In the one that preaches striking one's chest in public and denying God in private? Now, that's a real sin, as are also slander and envy. Talk about absolute morality! If that is what it's all about, they're the ones who violate it! Oh, if I were to talk! . . .

And what's even worse is that there's no difference between the fanatic churchgoers and the priest haters; they'll be at each other's throats because of Voltaire and Garibaldi, but they'll gang up against any woman who distinguishes herself. As if I didn't know them! I will never allow another issue of "El Jején" in my home.[8] Anyway, I have too much reading to do. (*She stops.*) I'm going to have a cup of *boldo*[9] and peppermint, before this anger makes me ill.

(*She becomes infuriated again and talks with the newspaper in her hand.*) Up to now, up to now, not even don Bartolo's daily,[10] which is the one I distrusted most at the beginning, nor José C. Paz's,[11] nor Varela's,[12] have treated me badly. (*She picks up the newspaper and begins to tear it to pieces.*) The three most important newspapers acknowledged more or less, that "Mrs. Gorriti's books could serve for the instruction, enjoyment, and benefit of the innocent and modest young women as well as of the prudent and sensible housewife; of the studious youth as well as for the men in society and government; of the humble laborer or the great ruler."

(*She tosses the pieces of paper up in the air and tramples them.*) No. I can't complain. And everything will go well if I am cautious. Cautious, polite, until the day comes when I can start all over again.

Opera music is heard again and the actress takes off Juana Manuela's dress and becomes Mosquetera again. The folklore tune "La tristecita" is then heard.

MOSQUETERA: Oh, that Juana Manuela, she was daring! There was no man who could reach her level! Not only did she equal them, she surpassed them! She . . . be intimidated? Not even by journalists! I didn't let them intimidate me, either.

This morning, at the very moment a pickup truck from one of the Buenos Aires newspapers drove into town with a photographer, television cameramen, and a journalist; a long procession passed by on the way to church. (*Quena music is heard.*) Well organized with banners, standard bearers, a religious image, musicians, and pilgrims. People gathered, attracted by the drum beats. The moment the journalists from Buenos Aires saw them, they started hounding them as if they were from a different planet. Brazenly, they asked them to pose for photos. They told the pilgrims they were going to appear on TV and that they must answer a few questions on the microphone.

Finally, I got tired of their questions, so I stopped the journalist abruptly.

"Listen, how much are you going to pay for the photographs? And for the interviews, huh?"

"Pay?" he answered. "I'm working."

"And what do you think we're doing, twiddling our thumbs?"

"Get lost, I'm not talking to you."

And then and there, he shoved the microphone in one of the pilgrim's faces.

"Are you coming to pray to the Virgin for water, are you coming to pray for rain?"

"No," one of the pilgrims retorted, "to make it rain we lay a toad on its back, you see."

"So . . . what are you going to pray for, then?"

"Nothing. We want to give thanks."

"Thanks, for what?"

"Only for being alive."

So, the pickup truck left immediately with the people from Buenos Aires who had suddenly become furious with Medinas. That's because they don't really know them. That's the way Medinas is: poor, but proud. When thirsty, they don't ask for water. When in pain, they're grateful to be alive. They appear to be asleep, but they're alert.

Oh, and what if I now tell you Tere's story? My mother told it to me many times. A long time ago, around 1930, Tere left Medinas to conquer the big city. But when she arrived, she didn't do anything but scrub and scrub marble stairs. Until she fell in love with Juan. Then she had to go out and walk the streets to support her man, while he stayed happily at home. Many women did the same; others entertained men in luxurious houses . . . but they were white and blonde, brought from afar, from Europe, not from Tucumán. Poor Tere! She dreamed . . . "Buenos Aires, where the tango was born, my dear land . . ." She repeated what Azucena Maizani, the famous singer, used to sing.

The actress takes off the Mosquetera dress; she puts on a man's jacket and a "lengue" (a gangster's white scarf) and a "compadrito" hat imitating the Maizani style.[13] She leans against a chair. The pianist plays "La canción de Buenos Aires" by Maizani and Manuel Romero.[14]

AZUCENA: (*She talks over the sound of the music.*)
Buenos Aires, I miss you
under the sun of another sky
how my heart cries
listening to your nostalgic song.
Slum song, song of Buenos Aires,
there's something inside you that lives and lasts
        forever,
slum song, bitter lament,
smile of hope, sob of passion.
This is the tango, the song of Buenos Aires,
born in the slums, it now reigns
all over the world,
this is the tango that I carry deep inside me
stuck deep in my native heart.

The piano music continues, while the actress puts down her compadrito *costume and dresses as Tere, a prostitute of the 30s.*

TERESA: (*She looks tired, she takes off her shoes and complains.*)
The government should protect us! Wassamatter, ain't we workers? There's too many of us on the streets as it is! If a ship from Europe arrived full of doctors, they wouldn't let them come into the country, would they? Or full of English bobbies? Imagine a load of cops from Europe coming to work here!
    (*She looks at herself in a mirror, evaluating her anatomy.*) And just look at what does come! Ugh!

Blondes, pale skins, all of 'em Pollacks and Frogs!

(*She goes toward the table and starts peeling potatoes.*) But today I'll tell Juan: look, honey, it ain't gonna work.

You gotta go out on them streets and see for yourself what's happening. The competition's too stiff. And you better forget about the black patent leather shoes.

Gimme a break. The way them tarts dress! 'course, the Mafia guys give 'em everything! The best! Dressed like that, who wouldn't look great!

(*She cuts her finger with the knife.*) Fudge! . . . you can't do everything! They don't even cook! But today I'll tell Juan: look, honey, I'm not about to run all the errands, clean our place, wash everything, and then on top of that go out on the streets and hustle! Who d'you think you are? You've gotta help out, too!

(*She continues peeling.*) Poor baby, he wants them patent leather shoes so bad! Yeah, I want a lotta things myself . . .

And look, I could have 'em if I wanted to, ha!

(*She gestures with the point of the knife.*) Because the Italian with all the dough he's got . . . I can't even begin to tell you! I know he ain't as cute as you, that he gets himself a bit tongue-tied, I know . . . But when he sees me, he goes crazy! But then again, I'm not your run a' the mill broad either.

You, honey, don't know how to appreciate what you got. And I've had it up to here, you know, up to here! I'll tell you one thing, if I pay attention to the Italian he'll treat me like a queen! And the struggle will be over, right? I'll play the fine lady, whether you think I can or not! (*She stops suddenly.*)

Oh, I forgot to buy the wine! My God, I'm gonna get it! Oh, but I'll tell Juan today: look, honey, cut the crap, and if you're such a *macho*, make the courthouse your first stop, 'cause only a husband has rights! (*She laughs.*) Juan, a husband? I can't picture it!

Shit! We gotta do something about this profession . . . I know, I'll round up the girls and tell 'em . . . , what was it the doctor in that committee said? Comrade . . . comrades! No, I better start out by calling 'em fellow workers! No . . .

Ladies! That's it! (*She climbs on a chair and addresses the audience.*)

Ladies: listen to me! I, Teresa Guzmán, Tere, want to have a word with you. We can't allow frickin' foreigners, people from other lands, to come and crowd our streets, to come and take our jobs away from us, our profession, the one we've been practicing since the beginning of time, the work our mothers, our grandmothers did . . . I mean to say women from here, of our same skin. Don't we know how to speak out? Don't we know what's fair and unfair? Then we have to unite and clear out of our country all them women who come to rob our bread and butter.

These guys from the Mafia—the ones with the dough, the ones who talked 'em into coming here with lies—should take 'em back, poor things! They spend their frickin' time crying! That's it! The government should force 'em to get the hell out a' here!

Well, let's unite, let's talk to the bigwigs! Let's defend our rights. We women can do it. (*She repeats as if conducting a chorus.*) We can! We can! We can! (*She gradually loses her steam and sits down.*) Can we? Suuure we can, either the Mafia or the cops'll come and we're in for it! And afterwards, the doctors won't give us health permits to work.

(*She starts peeling the potatoes again.*) And the Italian, I wonder if he's still waiting for me? After all, who knows, I might even marry him!

(*She gestures negatively with her head.*) No, but today I'll tell Juan: look, honey, you should know I'm not taking off with the Italian, because I'm a decent whore. But you'd deserve it if I did! I can't take it any more, there's not enough godamn money for food! The trouble is I like you too much! You've got no idea how much I like you. No patent leather shoes and, on top of it, no wine . . . poor thing!

I'm gonna buy the wine, but today I'm telling Juan: look, honey, this is the last bottle I buy, the very last!

Another tango, "Pero yo sé," by Azucena Maizani is heard. The actress changes into Mosquetera's costume.

MOSQUETERA: (*She talks over the background music.*) But I know it was a lie . . . Poor Tere! It wasn't the last bottle . . .
    There are very lonely souls in the great city, among so many people . . . but there are lonely souls in the country, too, really lonely. Like Telésfora Castillo, an innocent soul who didn't even have a family. But, she really liked to dance! When a drum sounded in a peasant's hut, she would show up, as if fallen from the sky, and would dance till daybreak. They called her Telesita. And one day she caught on fire in the forest. Before dying, she asked the people not to cry for her, because she was going straight to heaven. She did ask that they take her flowers, and said if anyone wanted a favor, they should dance seven *chacareras* one after the other in her honor.[15] Telesita is a very kind soul. She died in a state of grace, and that is why she can intercede with God for any favor one requests. She burned to death dancing. Exactly the same as those actors who make you laugh, who make you cry, but out of pleasure . . . Like that famous actress who made people laugh on the radio, in the theater, at the movies, who travelled all over and who wrote her own scripts. She was a story teller like me. She observed everything as if nothing were going on; yet she noticed everything and would then tell the people. She would tell them all about Gladys, all about Monica . . .

"The Moonlight Sonata" or "For Elise" is heard on stage. The actress takes off the Mosquetera costume and puts on a girl's white apron, in the style of the 1940s. Gladys, the pedantic girl, enters.

GLADYS: (*She approaches the pianist and taps him on the shoulder.*) Excuse me, this is where the Contest for Precocious Children is being held, right? (*The pianist nods and Gladys faces the audience adopting classical ballet postures.*)

My name is Gladys Minerva Pedanticci, I'm very pleased to meet you. (*She greets the audience with a low bow.*)

Gladys with a "y" and an "s," Minerva with a labiodental "v" and Pedanticci just as it sounds. The three names begin with capital letters.

(*She changes her posture.*) My parents have educated me with great care, 'cause a poorly educated girl is not an unscented blossom, but a foul-smelling flower.

I attend a private school, and I also take piano, speech, and ballet lessons, as my mommy wishes, then I'll take philosophy, harp, and esperanto lessons, as my daddy wishes.

(*She adopts a different posture.*) My teacher loves me very much, because in addition to taking her flowers, I brush her dress, I fan the flies away, and I always give her the largest apple.

I'm a model student, and the teacher's favorite, because I'm also her confidant.

My wisdom causes envy and my secrets resentment, but I don't care, because my mother is my best friend.

(*She adopts a different posture.*) She dresses me like a doll: at the wedding we attended yesterday, I wore a brand-new dress, more elegant than the bride's. I looked gorgeous! And when the toasting began, my daddy placed me on a chair and I delivered a speech in honor of the newlyweds. They applauded me so much! I had to bow several times! A very distinguished gentleman, looking at me, said: "This is a forty-year-old woman." And my mommy felt proud, but a vulgar man exclaimed: "This girl gets on my nerves." And my daddy got offended. And very angrily he replied: "With girls who get on people's nerves, like this one, our country has become great, mister! At that moment, at my parents' request, I was about to recite a poem, when a jealous hand pushed the chair and my face got buried in the wedding cake! But I didn't cry! No, sir! I scorned that criminal

hand, with my chin held high, a defiant look in my
eyes, my nose full of whipped cream, and
removing meringue from my ear, I exclaimed:
"Ideas cannot be killed!"

(*Addressing the audience.*) If you'd like, I can
recite the poem now. Since you insist so much . . .
I'll go ahead and recite it. Maestro! (*She signals the
pianist to begin playing background music. "For Elise"
continues. The actress moves like a porcelain ballerina
on top of a music box.*)

"Modesty"
by Gladys Minerva Pedanticci

Though I shouldn't make this interjection
I am the very model of perfection,
Mommy's darling, polished pearl,
My daddy's pride and special girl!
At every party I'm the queen,
The best my school has ever seen
My teacher's favorite little lamb,
So hard working and demure I am!
Everyone is so admiring
That I am clean and not perspiring
I am sheer, unwrinkled charm
My lace will never come to harm,
It's not my style to bring disgrace
No single hair is out of place.
Take my example you naughty girls,
Let not the breeze disturb your curls.
Oh, I should not make this interjection
But why not? I am perfection![16]

*She curtseys and leaves. The pianist begins playing Mozart to
introduce Monica. The actress takes off Gladys' white apron and puts
on a long smock to impersonate Monica. She is a very snobbish woman.
She goes toward the piano and picks up the phone that is there. She
shouts at the pianist who doesn't stop playing.*

MONICA: Hello! Monica Vanderbuilt Rockfuller from the
house of Hugheston Melon Sunset Crouton![17] May
I use your telephone? Because the one at home is a
pain in the ass! It's simply a bloody nuisance! Do

you hear me, you fool? Stop! (*The pianist stops playing. Monica goes toward the table and sits on it.*)

(*To the pianist.*) Don't worry. I'll cut the damn thing short. (*She dials a number.*)

Oh shit! I'm a basket case! . . . Hello? Mimi? . . . Monica, Monica, Mimi! . . . Me? Fantastic! . . . Hmmm . . . Hmmm . . . Of cour . . . Look, listen, this is incredible! Biff Allbright McClog,[18] has a booth at the arts and crafts fair where you can buy birthday gifts. No, he doesn't hang out in his birthday suit! They're beautiful! Do you know that Biff used to be so lazy that he was on the verge of becoming a vagrant! He has changed completely, now he slaves so diligently it almost makes you dizzy! Apparently, yes, he has actually found something that motivates him, you know? . . . What? Did he study at the University? . . . Yes, he studied how to have a good time! Oh, no . . . never attended classes at all! . . . said his ambition was to become a river . . . in order to follow the course without leaving his bed! Isn't that clever? . . . And he's not getting any younger! . . . A career? . . . You gotta be kidding! . . . His only interest in medical school were the nurses . . . and in law school, divorced women. Hello? Oh, yes, of cour . . . His father got fed up and threw him out, you know? He went to live in a dump in San Telmo. It's so filthy it gives you the creeps.

(*The pianist interrupts the conversation with a few chords.*) (*To the pianist.*) Will you stop being such a nuisance? Oh, Mimi, what are you saying! How could Patty Patrick marry that guy![19] What a pair! Now I've heard it all! Do you know that they say that after the wedding, she told him: "I have something to confess that I've been keeping from you: I'm . . . color blind." And he said: "Don't worry I also have something to confess. I'm black!" Ha, ha! Isn't that funny? (*The pianist interrupts again with even longer chords.*)

(*To the pianist.*) You're unbearable! Do get lost, will you! . . . Hello! Oh, nothing, this idiot . . . He finally stopped playing . . . Tell me, Mimi, are you going to Nutsoletti's lecture tomorrow? . . . The famous psychopath! Join me . . . Put it on your calendar! . . . It's on "Psychoneurosis in the Abnormal Being." Terribly interesting! Incredibly scientific! Extremely erudite! I wouldn't miss it for the world! Come with me . . . What are you going to wear? Me, slacks and a tunic, I want to be comfortable! And sunglasses, to sleep through it, you know? But darling! With the active life I lead— meetings, bridge, volunteer work, golf, night clubs—I don't even have time to sleep! If I don't sleep at lectures and concerts, where do you expect me to get my rest? (*The pianist interrupts again with a very long sound.*)

(*To the pianist.*) You're such a pain in the ass! Okay! Okay! . . . Mimi, I'm going to hang up, because I'm being tortured here! Bye, dear, bye! (*She hangs up and goes toward the piano.*)

(*To the pianist.*) Look here, you have to be an imbecile not to feel honored whenever I use your tube, me, a Vanderbuilt Rockfuller from the house of Hugheston Melon Sunset Crouton! Tell me, do you have any blue blood whatsoever in your veins? No heroes or patricians? . . . Then you're just an ordinary person, a plebeian, riffraff, scum! . . . Bye, bye!

The pianist finishes with the Mozart theme he played at the beginning. The actress takes off Monica's costume and puts on Mosquetera's outfit.

MOSQUETERA: (*To the audience.*) Niní used to laugh about everything. She probably still laughs to herself about all the conceited people, because she, who is so famous and all, is as simple as any story teller, like me.

You know something? I would like to take up the trade of bird merchant, in addition to my own. Because amidst my little birds, I would end up being like a guitar, or better yet, like an organ, like those you find in the large city churches. And thus I would be able to go from town to town selling birds, selling songs, or what's the same, telling people stories set to music. But first, so that Telesita will help me . . . (*Chacarera music is heard. The actress*

*picks up a bundle, she opens it on the table. She unfolds
a white tablecloth and places a red paper doll which
represents Telesita on a silvery box. The lights dim. She
arranges some flowers, lights the candles, and starts the
ritual. She picks up a glass of wine and toasts.)*

Here's to your health, Telesita. And thanks, just
for being alive!

*(The actress dances a "chacarera" in honor of
Telesita. When she finishes, she burns the doll. The song
"La tristecita" accompanies the Mosquetera. She ties
her bundle together again.)* Yes, I've decided. I will be
a bird merchant. I'll start walking along the roads,
and wherever I go, so will the music of trills and
whistles, along with the old, the very old, and the
not so old stories. All of them savory because
they're full of life, and when one unravels them,
and learns the sweet trade of telling them, they
continue to live until the candles no longer burn,
and by themselves, they start rolling down the
edge of time.

Like this one, the last story I'll tell you: the one
about Paloma, Paloma Romero, the actress who
showed up here, in Medinas, for the Virgin's
celebration . . . You don't know that actress? I do; I
know her very well . . .

*Contemporary tango music by Astor Piazzolla is heard. The actress
takes off her Mosquetera costume and puts on a house dress to perform
the role of Paloma. She is an actress from Buenos Aires. She sits on the
chair and tells the audience her story.*

PALOMA: Let me tell you; it's a long and winding road. Years
as a sales clerk. Reading magazines in which I saw
fascinating photos of stars from other worlds . . .
Outside, it's dark and it's raining hard, as the
famous tango goes . . . Outside, it's daytime—a
quarter to seven already—and it's raining hard. So
you either get going to keep your job or else be
fired, which would mean being eaten by vultures,
not to mention lice.

But how to explain that one cannot take it any
more.

I could tell you, "I want to give a voice to all

those who don't have a voice." I could say: "I can no longer tolerate the clamor in my heart."

There, in the salesroom, it would sound just as ridiculous to say: I want to tell how we Argentinians live, to show the degree of craziness we've reached, or describe the total union we could achieve, which would be just as absurd.

I crossed the salesroom where I had spent about twenty-four hundred hours of my glorious youth, and I opened the door of the personnel office.

If, on the one hand, this interview defined my status as a worker, which went from suspension to dismissal, on the other, it pushed me toward other stumbling blocks. To try to make it in the artistic world using unconventional means was difficult, in spite of my perseverence, now that I had nothing else to do.

And thus, from television studios to theater offices, from paid publicity to unfair competition, I continued stumbling and being avoided, learning little by little how things worked, but refusing to accept reality.

This is the mess I was in when Alfredo came into my life and booked me to perform in his café-concert in San Telmo.[20]

(*The music is louder. The actress takes off her house dress and puts on the clothes appropriate for the next scene, a short evening gown.*) (*She goes up to the front of the stage with a carefree attitude.*) (*To the audience.*) Lies, lies. Time is never lost. I should've realized that when I went from office to office talking to negative impresarios; I would talk about a good performance and all they cared about were yields and profits. I haven't wasted a single moment of my life, that's what I learned from my debut.

It was as if I had been born on the stage. I made love to everyone. And no one, no one, could've imagined how scared shitless I was.

(*She curls up in a chair.*) The stage fright of opening night which had stifled me for weeks and made me feverish or depressed me with each new incident. Stage fright, which is not the same as terror or anxiety or fear or cowardice. It could push

me to reject, whimsically, a costume, or to shiver
before the criticism of anyone who gave a strong
opinion even though his understanding was weak.
A stage fright that became more and more
universal as the opening night got closer. I faced
the absurd desire of being liked by all. The stage
fright that makes you want to say: I rectify, I
repent, I withdraw my crazy ambitions, so as not to
see my inconsistencies stepped on by the lack of
perception in the audience and the critics.

Because I'm also vain. And I feel the immense
pleasure of being the way I am and that others
understand me and accept me.

Because being on stage means playing a game
with the other which is the audience, discovering
the secret control of each muscle, forcing me to
cross the barrier. But once you've done what causes
the greatest fear—to advance against the limelight
and toward the stares of the incorruptible
monster—it is easier to go forward. And you risk it
all; it isn't until you overcome all your fears that
you are then able to enjoy staring back at the
audience, to test them, and to relish the resonance
of your own voice.

And you grow stilts and wings and you allow
yourself to be loved during your fleeting
copulation with glory.

(*Music is heard.*) And the second show begins.
And the third. And the fourth. Every night a
premier. Every night you face the talkative monster
whispering when the lights go off; silent when the
spotlights go on; alert while I come out of the
darkness; I, attentive to the judge or adversary,
have to tame him until I make him my friend, and
create the magic which lasts only a moment, which
may linger forever like a memory, like a symbol of
union, like the proof that an angel has come down
and touched everyone, thanks to those who
summoned him like the witches in the forest.
While the voice which is growing crawls up my
thighs, and is reborn in my pelvis, my abdomen
and my back, changing my body into voice and my
breath into howls, complaints, folds and sadness

where it's easy to recognize ourselves as human beings here and now, because the transfiguration has occurred. So that everyone can travel in the wings of metamorphosis. (*The music changes.*) And afterwards, to bow, so that people know that the night has ended and it's time to leave. Then the audience disperses, and each one goes to a different home and a different night. (*The actress bows.*)

Blackout

Notes

1. For permission to stage the play, the author must be contacted directly: Beatriz Seibel, J. E. Uriburu 92 -2º C, 1027, Buenos Aires, Argentina.

2. In the northern Argentinian folklore, *Mosquetera* is the oral chronicler of a small town.

3. *Zamba Tucumana* is a samba from the province of Tucumán in Argentina.

4. The translation of *"La tristecita"* is "The Sad Tune."

5. The translation of *"Hoy comamos y bebamos"* is "Today Let's Eat and Drink."

6. Martín Miguel de Güemes (1785–1821) was an Argentinean general who, heading his Gaucho Army, defended the northern provinces against the Royalists. He died in a battle in Salta.

7. The Tucumán Congress was the gathering of patriots where the first Argentinean constitution was written.

8. "El Jején" was a fictitious name chosen by Martha Mercader to refer to a satirical newspaper of that epoch.

9. *Boldo* is a type of tea indigenous to southern Chile and Argentina.

10. Don Bartolo refers to Bartolomé Mitre (1821–1906), writer and military man who became president of Argentina in 1862. He was the founder of the powerful newspaper "La Nación" of Buenos Aires.

11. José Camilo Paz (1842–1912), diplomat and Argentinean journalist, founded "La Prensa" newspaper of Buenos Aires in 1869.

12. Héctor Florencio Varela (1832–1891), journalist and powerful Argentinean statesman.

13. The *compadrito* hat is a black gangster-style hat worn by the popular character known as the *compadrito*.

14. "La canción of Buenos Aires" (Song of Buenos Aires) is a classic tango that dates back to the first decade of the twentieth century.

15. The *chacarera* is a folkloric tune with a lively rhythm, from the countryside in Argentina.

16. We thank Kathleen Betsko for her accurate and splendid rendition in English of the original poem.

17. Monica's name is a satire of the high-class Hispanic families who use not only their aristocratic parents' surnames but also those of their grandparents to give an impression of grandeur. We have substituted her "Vedoya Hueyo de Picos Pardos Sunsuet Croston" with a sequence of some well-known aristocratic American surnames using similar orthographic changes. For example, the actual aristocratic name in Argentina for "Vedoya" is Bedoya.

18. We substituted this name for Maneco de Alzame Unzueco, which is a play on words that continues to satirize the aristocratic Argentineans' custom of using affected nicknames. Maneco could be a combination of the name Manuel and *muñeco* (doll). Alzame contains the imperative of the verb *alzar* which means to raise. Unzueco, appears to be a combination of the indefinite article *un* and *zueco*, which is the equivalent of clog. Alzame is reminiscent of the patrician family name Alzaga.

19. We substituted the cacophonic sequence in the Spanish nickname Pachacha Pacheco for a similar cacophonic English sequence, Patty Patrick.

20. San Telmo is one of the oldest sections in Buenos Aires and has become the most popular bohemian theater district of the city.

Maruxa Vilalta (1932)—dramatist—was born in Barcelona. As a result of the Spanish Civil War, she went into exile with her parents in 1936 and lived three years of her childhood in Brussels. She came to Mexico City in 1939 and completed there all her studies, from primary school until her Master's degree in Spanish literature.

Vilalta's theatrical works have been translated and published in various languages and produced in Mexico, as well as in other countries. The author has won the theatre critics' prize for the best play of the year ten times. In 1994 Maruxa Vilalta was designated *Artistic Creator* of the *National System of Creators of Art*.

The Fondo de Cultura Económica has published in Mexico the following collection of Vilalta's plays:

Teatro I. Colección Tezontle, 1972; 2nd ed., Colección Popular, no. 206, 1981; 3rd ed., 1992. It includes *Los desorientados* (The Disoriented), *Un país feliz* (A Happy Country), *Soliloquio del Tiempo* (Soliloquy of Time), *Un día loco* (A Mad Day), *La última letra* (The Last Letter), *El 9* (Number 9), and *Cuestión de narices* (A Question of Noses).

Teatro II. Colección Popular, no. 399, 1989; 2nd ed. 1992. It contains *Esta noche juntos, amándonos tanto* (Together Tonight, Loving Each Other So Much), *Nada como el piso 16* (Nothing Like the 16th Floor), *Historia de él* (The Story of Him), *Una mujer, dos hombres y un balazo* (A Woman, Two Men and a Gunshot), and *Pequeña historia de horror (y de amor desenfrenado)* (A Little Tale of Horror [and Unbridled Love]).

Teatro III. Colección Popular, no. 460, 1990; 2nd ed. 1991; 3rd ed. 1994. It contains *Una voz en el desierto. Vida de San Jerónimo* (A Voice in the Desert. The Life of Saint Jerome).

Francisco de Asís (Francis of Assisi). Colección Popular, no. 492, 1993.

Jesucristo entre nosotros (Jesus Christ Among Us). Colección Popular, no. 515, 1995.

En blanco y negro. Ignacio y los jesuitas (In Black and White. Ignatius and the Jesuits). 1997.

Maruxa Vilalta is also a stage director. She is the author of a book of short stories, *El otro día, la muerte* (The Other Day, Death), Joaquín Mortiz, Mexico, 1974, and of the novels *El castigo* (The Punishment), Editorial La Prensa, Mexico, August 1957; *Los Desorientados* (The Disoriented), Ediciones Selecta, Mexico, August 1958; 2nd ed. December 1958; 3rd ed. Libro-Mex, 1960; and *Dos colores para el paisaje* (Two Colours for the Landscape), Libro-Mex, 1961.

Vilalta's theatrical writings are as numerous as they are diverse; her plays have qualities of the epic theater, of existentialism, and of the absurd, as well as of metatheater. Nevertheless, a common factor unites all her plays: they all illustrate sociopolitical problems that affect individuals and reflect the flaws of Mexican and, by extension, modern society.

Her drama also denounces hypocritical countries that publicly present a democratic facade to hide their dictatorial governments and criticizes modern societies for dehumanizing their citizens, humanity's egoism and indifference toward disasters, corrupted political leaders who abuse their power, and the agression and violence in human relations.

The play we have included, *Una mujer, dos hombres y un balazo* (A Woman, Two men and a Gunshot, 1984), follows a Brechtian line and falls into the metatheatrical mode, thus giving Vilalta the opportunity to poke fun at others as well as herself. Both theatrical techniques prompt the spectator to detach her/himself from the plot and to become an accomplice to her criticism. She creates five characters who in turn stage four short plays that satirize melodrama as well as three different avant-garde theatrical movements: surrealism, the absurd, and the musical. In addition to these theatrical developments, she also criticizes social evils such as materialism, the abuse of power, the lack of ethical values, and the lack of communication in present-day society.

A Woman,
Two Men, and a Gunshot
A PLAY IN TEN SCENES
BY MARUXA VILALTA[1]

Translated from *Una mujer, dos hombres y un balazo*
by Kirsten F. Nigro

A Woman, Two Men and a Gunshot was first produced by the Universidad Nacional Autónoma of Mexico in the Teatro de la Universidad, Chapultepec Avenue #409, during the theater season beginning 3 July 1981. The dramatist directed the production. The cast included Enrique Castillo, Victoria Burgoa, Ana Silvia Garza, Adalberto Parra, and Luis Mercado. The sets were by Germán Castillo, with choreography by Joan Mondellini and Nicole Rovere. The original music was by Luis Rivero.

Characters

ACTOR NUMBER ONE:
Bobby, the Counsellor, Lecocq, the Gentleman Dressed in Black, the Narrator, Lenny, the Conscience

ACTRESS NUMBER ONE:
Louise, Elizabeth, the Nanny, Mrs. Mercier, the Alga, Mrs. Marshall

ACTRESS NUMBER TWO:
Cathy, Cynthia, The Maid, the Girlfriend, Bonnie

ACTOR NUMBER TWO:
Sophocles, Rodger, Mr. Bertrand, the Boyfriend, Morris

ACTOR NUMBER THREE:
Brijinski, Arthur, Mr. Mercier, the Lichen, Archie

Note

This work consists of four short plays: *In Long Island, That Night, The Merciers' Tea, The Drunken Boat,* and *Archie and Bonnie.* Each of these plays can be staged on its own, although in the present text they are related to each other.

The concept for the set design is by German Castillo.

The costumes should be as simple as possible in order to allow for rapid changes—sometimes in full view of the audience—so as to establish an informal tone and atmosphere. Each scene should follow the other—in an almost integrated fashion—with no interruption in the acting.

SCENE I: THE GROUP

An empty stage. Cyclorama. Enter Bobby (a homosexual, with an Afro wig). There is hardly any light. Bobby goes to put it on. He returns and looks at his watch. He waits. A spotlight is slowly turned on Bobby, who hears the sound of circus music.

BOBBY:
Ladies and Gentlemen . . . When I was little what I liked was the circus . . . I liked it a lot! . . . The clowns . . . the amazons . . . (*He opts for the clowns.*) the clowns . . .

My psychiatrist claims that what I really wanted was to be an opera singer (*He sings very badly.*) "Ridi pagliaccio . . ."

It all began when I was little, in the circus, that afternoon, when the lion tamer offered me a vanilla ice cream cone and then he turned out to be a . . . lady lion tamer. But according to my psychiatrist, the opera . . .

He's a real buddy. Sometimes he doesn't know what he's talking about, but he's a buddy. A bit crazy, but a buddy . . .

He should be around here somewhere. (*He looks in the house and spots an audience member.*) Doctor, how good of you to come, good evening, welcome, Doctor . . . Anyway, I've always been in sync with the theater. Isn't that right, Doctor? You know, don't you? (*To the audience*) I mean, like the theater is really something important to me . . . I mean, the theater and not cybergenics . . . Because if it weren't for the theater, you know . . . Because without the theater, because without the theater. I mean, the theater, for example . . .

Noise backstage of someone stumbling. Bobby returns to reality; his spot turned off.

LOUISE: (*Entering with Cathy.*) Shit!

CATHY: Did you hurt yourself?

LOUISE: Goddamned step. I almost broke my ass.

BOBBY: Watch out girls, don't go killing yourselves on me.

LOUISE: Hi, Bobby. What are you doing here?

BOBBY: The same thing as you, right? They called me.

CATHY: Who were you talking to?

BOBBY: Me? To nobody . . . Who do you talk to in front of an empty house? . . . I was talking to my psychiatrist.

LOUISE: Gosh Bobby, I really do like you.

CATHY:	I do, too. *(They kiss him.)*
BOBBY:	*(Pushing them away.)* Hey gals, let's have some respect.
LOUISE:	Robert, the great "Bobby" Dalton.
BOBBY:	*(Conceited.)* What do you want? That's my stage name.
LOUISE:	Let's see. Bobby, tell us all about this. What's up? When do we open?
BOBBY:	Oh, so you want to open already?
CATHY:	Sophocles called us. He says that he's already got us a backer.
BOBBY:	He'd better have. *(Noise at the back of the house.)* Who's there? *(He tries to see; the lights blind him and he shields his eyes with his hands.)* Goddamned lights. I can't see a thing . . .
SOPHOCLES:	*(From the back of the house.)* Did you turn them on, Bobby? I suggest you turn them off.
BOBBY:	And when did you get here?
SOPHOCLES:	*(He comes down to the stage, followed by Brijinski, who's carrying the scripts for the play.)* I've just arrived. Put on some work lights, we're going to read.
BOBBY:	Yes, sir. *(He goes out while Sophocles gives the scripts to Brijinski and gets up on the stage.)*
CATHY:	*(To Louise.)* It's Sophocles!
LOUISE:	You don't have to introduce him; we've lived together for two months. *(Some work lights are turned on.)*
SOPHOCLES:	Thanks, Bobby. . . . How are you, Cathy? . . . Louise? . . . I want you to meet Brijinski.

BRIJINSKI:	*(Nervous, he trips and tosses all the scripts on the floor. He hurries to pick them up.)* Good day . . . I mean, good evening . . .
LOUISE:	How are you?
CATHY:	Pleased to meet you.
BOBBY:	*(Entering.)* And who is this?
SOPHOCLES:	Don't try to remember; he's new.
BOBBY:	*(With a double meaning.)* New?
CATHY:	*(Charming, to Brijinski.)* What did you say your name was?
BRIJINSKI:	Wildemar Hieronymus Brijinski Jacovlovichovich . . . But you can just call me Brijinski . . . I am of Jewish origin.
BOBBY:	You don't say. And in addition to being Jewish, what else do you do?
BRIJINSKI:	Me? Well, I . . . ah . . . I study economics . . . I am an actor.
BOBBY:	*(Checking him out.)* An actor? . . . Where from?
BRIJINSKI:	Where from? . . . I don't understand . . . *(Stepping backwards, in an attempt to escape Bobby, Brijinski ends up bumping into him.)*
BOBBY:	Hey man, son of a bitch, don't step on me.
BRIJINSKI:	Son of a bitch? I mean, pardon? I mean, excuse me, sir.
LOUISE:	Don't pay any attention to him, that's the way Bobby is.
BRIJINSKI:	Thank you . . . Thank you, miss.
BOBBY:	What do you mean MISS! Do you think she's going to go around wasting her time? Don't be an ass.

BRIJINSKI:	*(Distressed.)* Ass? . . . did he say ASS?
LOUISE:	*(To Brijinski.)* Look, I'm liberated. Call me Louise.
BRIJINSKI:	Thank you, Louise . . . Hello, Cathy . . . You sure are pretty, Cathy . . . I mean, pardon, I mean, excuse me . . . *(He trips again and ends up in Bobby's arms.)*
BOBBY:	Watch it, my little virgin, don't you go getting hurt on me.
BRIJINSKI:	Little virgin?
SOPHOCLES:	Bobby, Brijinski is our producer.
BOBBY:	This little twerp?
BRIJINSKI:	*(About to cry.)* Little twerp?
SOPHOCLES:	Okay, Bobby, that's enough. *(To Brijinski.)* Don't let him get to you. He's really a good guy.
BOBBY:	I'm *aall* heart!
SOPHOCLES:	Brijinski is going to act in the play.
BRIJINSKI:	Let's see if I get it right . . .
BOBBY:	*(With a double meaning.)* Of course you'll get it right, my pet. Of course you'll get it right. *(Brijinski looks at him terrified; Bobby walks off cocksure.)* Don't worry, Hieronymus, you're not my type.
LOUISE:	You look real good, Sophocles . . . I'd heard that you've been insufferable since we broke up.
SOPHOCLES:	You're mistaken. I've been insufferable ever since I knew I was going to be a playwright. Ever since my parents named me Sophocles.
LOUISE:	As pedantic as ever.
SOPHOCLES:	Okay then, the producer will give us this theater and this billing. Brijinski will pay the actors' fee.

BOBBY:	And where does the little pet get his money from?
CATHY:	He's Jewish.
BRIJINSKI:	My parents loaned it to me.
BOBBY:	They're going to charge you interest.
SOPHOCLES:	Minimum wage, I already told you. About two months of rehearsals, maybe more.
BOBBY:	Son of a bitch!
SOPHOCLES:	Everybody take a script. *(They take one and sit down on the floor. Brijinski worries about getting himself dirty.)* Sit down.
BOBBY:	Make yourself at home. *(Brijinski finally sits down.)*
SOPHOCLES:	I am here with you in my triple role as author, director, and actor. My play consists of four stories or four different works on one theme, which is always the same. I set myself an exercise: to work, sometimes in parodic tome, with four different genres, chosen by chance. As regards the subject matter, in the first place I don't believe in it, but rather in how to develop it. Therefore I intentionally wanted it to be neutral, trivial, conventional. *(Happy.)* To make a long story short, the subject matter is really fucked up!
BRIJINSKI:	Fucked . . . up?
SOPHOCLES:	A wife, a husband, and a lover. A gunshot and the husband dies. I always kill off the husband: the conventional thing is for him to get in the way. And always from a gunshot. That's also more conventional than hanging him or drowning him in the bathtub, for example.
LOUISE:	*(Skeptical.)* So—a woman, two men and a gunshot. The same thing in all four plays.

SOPHOCLES: The same thing. And now, we're here for the first reading. Page number one: the title *(He reads.)* *Variations.* In parentheses: "Four Dramatic Works on the Same Theme." By Sophocles Smith.

LOUISE: It doesn't sound like much of a box-office hit to me.

SOPHOCLES: *(Very dignified.)* My theater does not aspire to commercial success. *(He turns the page.)* Page number two: settings. It's very simple. There are none. We'll make do with a cyclorama and other odds and ends.

BOBBY: *(To Brijinski.)* You had to be Jewish.

BRIJINSKI: But I didn't say anything.

SOPHOCLES: Page number three: cast of characters. Five actors for all the characters in four short pieces. They're numbered according to their order of appearance. Brijinski, you're Actor Number One and you take all of his roles.

BRIJINSKI: Me? Actor Number One?

SOPHOCLES: I'm Actor Number Two. Bobby, Actor Number Three. Louise, Actress Number One. Cathy, Actress Number Two.

BRIJINSKI: I'm Number One? What do you think, Bobby? I mean, Actor Number Three.

BOBBY: *(Real softly.)* If you call me Actor Number Three again I'll split your fucking brains open.

BRIJINSKI: My fucking brains . . .

SOPHOCLES: *(He turns the page, interrupting Brijinski.)* First play: Parody of a Melodrama. Its title: *(Melodramatic.)* In *Long Island, That Night.* On stage we have Actor Number One, Brijinski, and Actor Number Two, me. They're brothers. They haven't seen each other in twenty years. They meet again in the house of

Actor Number Two, who says, melodramatically, to Actor Number One: *(To Brijinski.)* Arthur! . . . And Actor Number One answers: *(A silence. Everyone waits for Brijinski to answer.)* Page four, line seven. Actor Number One answers. *(Silence again from Brijinski.)*

CATHY: Brijinski, line seven; you're Arthur.

BRIJINSKI: Oh, yes, yes . . . *(Clearing his throat.)* Arthur!

SOPHOCLES: No, I say Arthur. You say, melodramatically, Rodger!

BRIJINSKI: Oh, yes, yes! *(He finds his place and reads, hesitantly.)* Rodger?

SOPHOCLES: *(Patiently.)* Brijinski . . . two brothers . . . Twenty years. Melodrama. You should follow my lead. I'll give you the cue and you answer. *(Melodramatically.)* Arthur!

BRIJINSKI: *(Melodramatically.)* Rodger!

BOBBY: How cute! He can already say Rodger!

SOPHOCLES: Page four, from the beginning. *(Melodramatic, he reads.)* In Long Island, That Night. Arthur, badly dressed in a wrinkled suit, is standing next to the bar, like a man beaten down by life. *(They all turn to look at Brijinski, who shrinks up.)*

BRIJINSKI: Beaten down by life?

SOPHOCLES: *(He reads.)* Music for a melodrama.

The requested music is heard and a spotlight is turned on a disconcerted Brijinski. The other actors exit. Brijinski reacts and is going to leave too, when a beam of light for the next scene is lit in front of him, not letting him go. He goes to the other side of the stage and another beam of light stops him. He makes a last effort to leave, but Arthur's suit jacket is thrown at him from off stage, as if a command to stay. He puts it on and begins to turn into Arthur. He places a chair on stage.

BRIJINSKI: (*Melodramatic.*) Beaten down by life!

He collapses into the chair and is transformed into Arthur. At the same time, Beethoven's Fifth Symphony begins; all the lights are turned on at once, and a bar is suddenly lowered onto the stage, with bottles, glasses, and an expensive but tasteless chandelier.

SCENE II: *IN LONG ISLAND, THAT NIGHT* (A PARODY IN ONE ACT)

Arthur serves himself a drink. Rodger—a nouveau riche Texan— enters.

RODGER: (*Melodramatic.*) Arthur!

ARTHUR: (*Melodramatic.*) Rodger! . . . You, here!

RODGER: I'm in my own house.

ARTHUR: Yes . . . In your house!

RODGER: I was told that you insisted on seeing me . . . We're waiting for a guest to arrive.

ARTHUR: Does it bother you to see me in your house, (*With emphasis.*) brother?

RODGER: Shut up. The servants can hear you.

ARTHUR: You're ashamed of me? Or are you afraid of me, (*with emphasis, again.*) brother?

RODGER: Afraid? Don't make me laugh.

ARTHUR: So, you have this fancy pad for when you come to New York . . . Just for the weekends.

RODGER: Arthur, why have you come here?

ARTHUR: Maybe I shouldn't call you "brother." Perhaps . . . "Mr. Governor?" Or at least "Mr. Candidate?"

RODGER: I don't know what you're talking about.

ARTHUR:	That's because they haven't let the cat out of the bag yet.
RODGER:	I refuse to talk politics.
ARTHUR:	Why? Are you afraid of making a fool of yourself.
RODGER:	Arthur, this is not the right time.
ARTHUR:	This business about your candidacy is just a matter of days, isn't it?
RODGER:	I don't know.
ARTHUR:	You're right. In politics one never can be sure.
RODGER:	I'm sorry, but you've got to leave.
ARTHUR:	*(Sighing melodramatically.)* Twenty years of silence! . . . *(He fills his glass and drinks.)* And of booze.
RECORDING:	*(Tango "Volver," by Gardel-La Pera, originally sung by Carlos Gardel.)* Volver . . . con la frente marchita, las nieves del tiempo platearon mi sien . . .
ARTHUR:	But suddenly, I appear on the scene. Just at the opportune moment, with all of this business about your candidacy.
RODGER:	You're a failure. A loser. I feel sorry for you!
ARTHUR:	*(Melodramatic.)* You're right. I am a failure. But if my life has been destroyed, you're to blame!
RODGER:	I don't understand you. My guest is about to arrive. You must leave. *(He calls.)* Elizabeth! . . . Hasn't my wife come down yet?
ELIZABETH:	*(Wearing a ridiculous, nouveau-riche outfit.)* Here I am, darling.

RODGER:	The gentleman was just saying good-bye. Tell the chauffeur to see him to the door.
ARTHUR:	I'm sorry, little sister-in-law, but I'm staying.
RODGER:	What does this mean?
ELIZABETH:	I told you that Arthur didn't want to leave.
RODGER:	Arthur? . . . You call him Arthur?
ELIZABETH:	That's his name, isn't it?
RODGER:	How do you know his name? You shouldn't have let him in.
ELIZABETH:	I let him in because he is . . . your brother! I've known him for three months.
RODGER:	Three months!
ARTHUR:	*(Man of the world.)* We were introduced at a cocktail party.
ELIZABETH:	*(Melodramatic.)* Rodger, I know everything. I know all about your shameful behavior.
RODGER:	What behavior? Look Arthur, there were only . . . little disagreements . . . between us. That happens in all families.
ARTHUR:	You kept my part of the inheritance and you left me penniless. "That happens in all families." But I've decided to take advantage of what happens in ours.
RODGER:	And what advantage do you plan on taking? The whole matter is closed. My lawyers legalized everything. You have no proof.
ARTHUR:	What if I were to tell your friends my side of the story? . . . What position did you say your guest holds?

ELIZABETH: *(Who has taken advantage of the conversation to go to the bar and pour herself a drink.)* He's a friend of the president.

RODGER: You, shut up!

ARTHUR: I'm definitely staying for dinner. If you'll excuse me, I'll take the whiskey. *(He takes the glass and, triumphant, exits.)*

RODGER: I'll take the son of a . . . *(He grabs Elizabeth by the arm.)* This is for going to cocktail parties. *(He slaps her.)* And this is for letting people into the house without my permission. *(A second slap.)* And for talking too much. *(He throws her onto the floor.)*

ELIZABETH: You miserable beast!

RODGER: Don't you forget who's in charge here. Don't you forget that I bought you. I took you out of the . . . slums, where you mother was a junk peddler.

ELIZABETH: *(Challenging.)* But now I'm your lawful wife. *(He is about to strike her.)* No, not on the face, Rodger, not on the face.

RODGER: We'll settle this later. Right now I'm going to make sure that they throw my little brother out into the street. *(He's about to leave, but the doorbell rings.)* Too late! The Counsellor has arrived! I'll go out front and meet him. You'd better behave yourself. *(He leaves.)*

ELIZABETH: I hate you! I am going to kill you!

ARTHUR: *(Entering melodramatically.)* Elizabeth, my love! Did that monster hurt you?

ELIZABETH: It's nothing, I'm used to it.

ARTHUR: Poor little thing.

ELIZABETH: *(Melodramatic.)* Arthur . . . kiss me!

A la Rudolph Valentino, he draws her to him and kisses her.

RECORDING:	*(Tango "Besos Brujos," by Malerba-Sciamareli, original sung by Liberated Lamarque.)* Besos brujos . . . Besos brujos Que son una cadena . . .
ELIZABETH:	*(Melodramatic.)* Tonight, at your place!
ARTHUR:	And what if he doesn't let you out?
ELIZABETH:	We have separate bedrooms. As soon as he goes to his, I'll leave. Wait for me in the car. But don't let anybody see you. Remember that I am a virtuous woman, brought up according to the strictest norms of the Holy Church.
ARTHUR:	And I am your . . . lover!
ELIZABETH:	You don't have to announce it.
ARTHUR:	*(Melodramtic.)* Look at me, Elizabeth! Look at what Rodger has turned me into. Look at this threadbare suit, look at these worn out cuffs. I have to struggle to fit into a world where I don't belong any longer. To keep up appearances. Just to pass as a man of your same social class.
ELIZABETH:	Yes, I am a lady now. I play bridge with the governor's wife. With the wife of the . . . *retiring* governor, that is.
ARTHUR:	My brother stole my inheritance and now he takes my woman.
ELIZABETH:	It's more like you're taking *his* woman.
ARTHUR:	I hate him. I've always had to settle for his leftovers.
ELIZABETH:	Thanks a lot.

ARTHUR: But things are going to change. I'll be Number One. I'll have his woman! And he'll be . . . dead!

ELIZABETH: Arthur, you frighten me. *(Coquettish.)* Would you be capable of killing him for me?

ARTHUR: *(Melodramatic.)* For you ! *(Change.)* And for his millions. I'll get everything.

ELIZABETH: No. Let's not even talk about killing him until we know something about his candidacy. With a little bit of luck, I'll become First Lady.

ARTHUR: *(Melodramatic, he puts his hand on his waist.)* Elizabeth, I've come armed!

ELIZABETH: Arthur, for God's sake, Arthur!

ARTHUR: No more second place for me . . . No more worn out cuffs.

ELIZABETH: For God's sake, Arthur, calm down . . . Come, let's go to my bedroom.

They exit.

RODGER: *(Off stage.)* This way, please, come through here, Mr. Counsellor. *(The Counsellor enters, followed by Rodger: he is very proper, very well mannered.)* Come in, please, after you, sir.

COUNSELLOR: Very kind of you, thank you . . .

RODGER: Make yourself at home. Please allow me to introduce my wife, Eliz . . . *(He interrupts himself because she's not there.)* My wife Elizabeth should be around here. We are a very close couple. We very much appreciate your having accepted our invitation, sir.

COUNSELLOR: Please . . .

RODGER: *(To Elizabeth, who enters.)* Oh, darling, I was telling our guest that we are a very close couple.

ELIZABETH: Very close, yes.

COUNSELLOR: Ma'am, I'm your humble servant.

RODGER: *(He gets a second chair.)* But please sit down, sir, please sit down.

COUNSELLOR: Thank you. After you, ma'am. *(Courtesies; Elizabeth and the Counsellor sit down.)*

RODGER: May I offer you a drink before dinner? Whiskey? Vodka?

COUNSELLOR: Whatever you're having.

ELIZABETH: *(Very refined, very much a lady.)* For me, I'll just have a little bit of rum. *(Suddenly she screams, in a vulgar manner.)* Hee, ha, ha, haee! . . .

The Counsellor jumps to his feet.

Recording: "Oh, Susannah" or some similar kind of polka or country and western swing. Elizabeth dances like an Okie.

ELIZABETH: *(Vulgar.)* Hee, ha, ha, hee! . . .

RODGER: She's joking . . . My wife is abstemious.

ELIZABETH: Asstemious?

RODGER: Yes.

ELIZABETH: Yes, yes, asstemious. I'm joking.

RODGER: Please, sir . . . *(He points to the chair and the Counsellor sits down.)* If it's alright with you, I'll pour us two whiskeys. *(He pours them.)*

COUNSELLOR: Thank you very much.

RODGER: Well, yes sir, Mr. Counsellor, family life is always very important, isn't it? Especially back home in Texas. My wife and I just love it back in the Lone Star State.

ELIZABETH: We do? Yes, yes, we do.

RODGER: The truth is that we only come to this modest little
                  place on the Island every now and again.

ELIZABETH: In our jet; but it only takes a few hours.

COUNSELLOR: Your . . . jet?

RODGER: Well, yes, we do have a little jet. To get back to
                  work more quickly. To get back to our dear little
                  home town. (*Demagogic.*) My cup runneth over
                  with love for our little home town.

COUNSELLOR: Well, it seems that they love you a lot there as well,
                  Rodger.

RODGER: (*Happy.*) Really?

COUNSELLOR: That's what I hear

RODGER: (*Anxious.*) Do you know something?

COUNSELLOR: About what?

ELIZABETH: If you'll excuse me, I'll leave you alone. I'm going
                  with Arth . . . (*She corrects herself.*) I'm going to give
                  some instructions for dinner.

COUNSELLOR: (*Standing up again.*) Ma'am . . .

*Elizabeth exits and they sit down. Rodger drinks and the Counsellor is
about to do the same, but Rodger interrupts him.*

RODGER: I prefer to speak alone. These are delicate matters.

COUNSELLOR: These . . . matters?

RODGER: Perhaps you've brought me some news about . . .
                  Well, why not say it? About my candidacy.

COUNSELLOR: Oh yes, your candidacy . . . Well, I'm sorry, but I
                  don't have any news in particular.

RODGER:	Well, the truth is that I'm just dying to know. And because you are close to . . . *(He makes a sign with his head.)* . . . up there.
COUNSELLOR:	*(Looking up.)* Where?
RODGER:	Up there . . . You are very well connected . . . *(Same sign.)* up there.
COUNSELLOR:	*(Understanding.)* Oh, yes, yes . . . *(Same sign.)* Up there.
RODGER:	*(Standing up.)* With "him." With the president.
COUNSELLOR:	*(Standing up as well.)* With the president? Well, yes, he does honor me with his friendship, that's true. But there is nothing yet, Rodger, nothing yet. As you know the party has shuffled through a few names . . . To your health, Rodger! To your candidacy!
RODGER:	To you, sir. To you and to . . . *(Signals above.)* "him." *(They drink; rather, Rodger drinks and interrupts the Counsellor, who was about to drink.)* As I told you, sir, it will be an intimate dinner: just my wife and me.

From now on, the Counsellor will spend the rest of the play with his glass in his hand and without being able to drink, since every time that he is going to, something happens; just as every time that he sits down something forces him to stand up. Right now he sits down, but jumps up when he hears Arthur.

ARTHUR:	*(Entering.)* And me!
RODGER:	*(To himself.)* My candidacy!
ELIZABETH:	*(Entering.)* Arthur! For God's sake! *(But she is standing in front of the Counsellor.)* Oh, how are you, sir? . . .
COUNSELLOR:	Madam . . .
ARTHUR:	Thank you very much for inviting me. I accept *(With emphasis.)* brother.

RODGER:	*(To the Counsellor.)* My brother Arthur.
COUNSELLOR:	Pleased to meet you.
RODGER:	*(To Arthur.)* Counsellor Ainsworth, from the office of the president.
ARTHUR:	The pleasure is mine.
RODGER:	I'm afraid that you're not going to be able to stay. Something urgent has come up and some people are waiting for you.
ARTHUR:	For me? That's impossible.
RODGER:	If you'll allow me, I'll see you to the door.
ELIZABETH:	I'm going with you.
RODGER:	Just a few seconds, sir, please excuse us for a few seconds.
COUNSELLOR:	Of course.
RODGER:	After you, Elizabeth . . . *(Taking Arthur with him.)* And you get out of here, right away, you bastard.

They exit. The Counsellor sits down. But he stands up again immediately because Cynthia enters—dressed as a cabaret dancer.

CYNTHIA:	My god, my god, what am I going to do? . . . Where can Rodger be?

Recording: ("The Stripper.") Cynthia begins to dance a striptease. The music stops and she sees the Counsellor.

CYNTHIA:	And who are you?
COUNSELLOR:	Me? Well, I'm . . .
CYNTHIA:	*(Without letting him speak.)* Have you seen Rodger?
COUNSELLOR:	Yes, miss. He went out.

CYNTHIA:	So long. *(The Counsellor tries to explain to her that Rodger went out from the opposite direction, but she leaves.)*
COUNSELLOR:	So long. *(He sits down again, but jumps up like a spring, with his glass in his hand, when he hears Arthur scream.)*
ARTHUR:	*(Off stage)* Don't get near me! I'm armed!
RODGER:	*(Off stage.)* Have you gone mad? I'm going to call the aides.
ARTHUR:	*(Off stage.)* You're going to set your muscle on me? Ha, ha, ha, ha!
ELIZABETH:	*(Off stage.)* Wait, Rodger. I'll calm him down.
ARTHUR:	*(Off stage, melodramatic.)* Leave me alone! Leave me alone!
RODGER:	*(Entering.)* Sir, I think we'll be more comfortable in my study; it's more private.
COUNSELLOR:	Any . . . problems?
RODGER:	No, no, none at all . . . If you'd like to follow me . . .
COUNSELLOR:	Whatever you say, Rodger.
RODGER:	You're very kind, sir, please . . .

Rodger leaves in a great hurry, taking the Counsellor with him. Cynthia enters, impatient.

CYNTHIA:	He must be around here. *(She goes to the other end of the stage and calls.)* Rodger! . . . *(She goes towards the study.)* Rodg . . . !
RODGER:	*(Entering.)* Cynthia! *(He takes her far from the study.)* What the hell are you doing here? How dare you come to my house?
CYNTHIA:	I need your help. *(Melodramatic.)* Teddy is sick!

RODGER:	And what do you want me to do? Who let you in?
CYNTHIA:	I rang the bell and the chauffeur answered. I had to lie. I told him that you were expecting me. He turned out to be a fan . . . he's a patron at the Lido.
RODGER:	*(Ironic.)* Of course, the Lido. By the way *(Showing off his Cartier watch.)* isn't it time for you act?
CYNTHIA:	*(Melodramatic.)* You're making fun of me because I'm a . . . cabaret dancer!
RODGER:	Yeah . . . a dancer. A real artiste. Your little porno number is pure art.
CYNTHIA:	I came from a good family. But you took me away and made me your mistress. Only to later destroy me and throw me out on the street, when I couldn't go home anymore. Then you offered me to your friends. You passed me around . . . from bed to bed!
RODGER:	*(Melodramatic.)* Okay, I prostituted you. And so what?
CYNTHIA:	You're right. So what? Now I am "Sinful Cynthia."
RODGER:	And to think that your son believes that you make a living as a little seamstress.
CYNTHIA:	My son? Our son!
RODGER:	That's what you say.
CYNTHIA:	Scoundrel!
RODGER:	Go home. I have company.
CYNTHIA:	*(Melodramatic.)* Rodger, take pity on me! Teddy is sick! Get a good doctor. Call the best one you can find and ask him to see my son.
RODGER:	And who am I to call a doctor? What do I have to do with you and your son?

CYNTHIA:	You scoundrel! You beast!
COUNSELLOR:	*(Entering.)* Excuse me. Am I interrupting?
RODGER:	*(To himself.)* My candidacy! . . . *(To the Counsellor.)* Of course not, sir; you never interrupt.
COUNSELLOR:	I forgot my whiskey . . . Here it is . . . Excuse me, I'll leave now.
RODGER:	There's no need for you to go, sir. The lady was just about to leave.
CYNTHIA:	I am not leaving.
RODGER:	Sir, the lady is a . . . dancer.
COUNSELLOR:	*(He approaches her.)* I seem to know her . . . Miss, by any chance, you don't work at the . . . *(He remembers where he has seen her. He steps back.)* No, no, I'm mistaken. I haven't had the pleasure, miss. I don't know you.
CYNTHIA:	*(Like a prostitute.)* Aren't you a patron at the Lido, dollface?
COUNSELLOR:	The Lido . . . ? The Lido, miss? No, I don't seem to remember that place.
RODGER:	Of course not, sir. How could you frequent the Lido . . . that place.
CYNTHIA:	And why not?
RODGER:	The lady came to see my chauffeur.
CYNTHIA:	I despise you.
RODGER:	She's mistaken me for one of my friends. Excuse me for a few seconds, sir. I'll accompany the lady so that the chauffeur can take care of her.
CYNTHIA:	I'll kill you.

RODGER:	How funny! She's mistaken me! . . . (*Taking Cynthia with him.*) Please, miss, please, come this way . . . (*To himself.*) My candidacy!

They exit. Alone again, the Counsellor—progressively more nervous about what could happen next—looks for some secure place to put his chair. He thinks he's found it and sits down. But he jumps up again, with his glass in hand, when faced with the Nanny, an Okie with long braids, who enters screaming.

NANNY:	Ya' skunk. Ya' dirty bastard. (*Now she's in front of the Counsellor.*) You're gonna burn in Hell.
COUNSELLOR:	(*As always, very polite.*) Pardon me, ma'am?
NANNY:	No, no, I ain't talking to you. And just who are you?
COUNSELLOR:	Well, I'm . . .
NANNY:	(*Without letting him speak.*) I'm talking about the "boss," about Rodger, that low-down critter!
COUNSELLOR:	Apparently, ma'am, you are . . .
NANNY:	The old nanny, yes siree, the old nanny! . . . Me, who held that baby Lizzie in my arms ever since she was knee high to a grasshopper . . . Me, who took care of her, who fed her! . . . With these jugs, yes sir! With these old jugs! And now that cowboy, that Rodger, dares to offend me, to insult me . . . Stupid servant! . . . He called me a stupid servant! Me! A stupid servant! What do ya' think of that?
COUNSELLOR:	Very good, ma'am, very good. I mean,very bad, ma'am, very bad. Excuse me, ma'am. I think I'd better go back to the study.
NANNY:	(*Blocking his way.*) A maid, that's what he called me . . . But I ain't no maid. Do ya' know who I am?
COUNSELLOR:	Yes, ma'am. You're the old nanny.

NANNY:	*(Melodramatic.)* No! I'm not the nanny!
COUNSELLOR:	No?
NANNY:	*(Melodramatic; overcome with maternal feelings.)* My child.
COUNSELLOR:	Your child? Excuse me, but I'm not your child . . . You're not my mother.
NANNY:	Not yours, you jerk!
COUNSELLOR:	What?
NANNY:	*(Melodramatic.)* Lizzy's mother. I'm Lizzy's mother.
COUNSELLOR:	Lizzy's mother? You mean you're Rodger's mother-in-law?
NANNY:	The mother-in-law, yes, the mother-in-law. In other words, the old battle ax! They're ashamed of me. They hide me in the kitchen . . . Thats my place, peeling potatoes. They keep me hidden in the kitchen and don't introduce me to their friends. And that varmint Rodger, he's to blame for everything. He hoodwinked my baby Lizzy, he ruined her, talkin' about marriage, talkin' about money! The bastard! Ah, but I'll kill him! Rodger, I'll kill you. *(She ends this speech standing right in front of the Counsellor.)*
COUNSELLOR:	Yes ma'am. I mean, no ma'am, don't kill me! I mean, don't kill him. Excuse me, ma'am, I'll leave now.
NANNY:	*(Blocking his way.)* I'm not the maid! I'm the mother!
COUNSELLOR:	Yes, ma'am, you're the mother.
NANNY:	*(Leaving.)* I'll kill him, the miserable bastard! I'll kill him!

Rodger, who enters from the opposite direction, sees her leave.

RODGER: *(To himself.)* My candidacy! *(To the Counsellor, who jumps with fright.)* I hope that woman hasn't been bothering you.

COUNSELLOR: *(With the glass in his hand, trembling now.)* No, not at all.

RODGER: She's a bit cracked. She's Elizabeth's old nanny. We keep her out of pity. My wife and I always help the common folk. *(He begins a demagogic speech.)* Because, in the last instance, the common folk . . .

COUNSELLOR: *(Interrupting.)* Then that woman is not a member of your family?

RODGER: Of our family? Oh no, no way.

COUNSELLOR: Of you'd prefer it, Rodger, we can postpone dinner. I can come another day.

RODGER: I implore you to please honor us by staying for dinner this very evening.

COUNSELLOR: I said that just in case you have problems.

RODGER: Problems? Oh no, no problems at all.

COUNSELLOR: As you wish.

He sits down. But he gets up again immediately, at Rodger's invitation.

RODGER: If it's alright with you, we can go to the dining room. My wife should be waiting for us.

COUNSELLOR: Whatever you say. Could I . . . wash my hands?

RODGER: Yes, of course . . . This way, please, sir. After you, please.

They exit.

ELIZABETH: *(Coming in from the other side of the stage, behind Arthur.)* Arthur, for god's sake, Arthur!

ARTHUR:	I'm not leaving. Nor will I share anything with that bastard. I want all of his money. And his wife, to boot!
ELIZABETH:	*(Screaming.)* Don't talk so loud! *(Lowering her voice.)* I think they're in the study.
ARTHUR:	I'm fed up with speaking softly. *(In a lower voice.)* I'll shoot that son of a bitch of a brother!
ELIZABETH:	*(Melodramatic.)* Arthur! Kiss me!

A la Valentino, she now assumes the male role, draws Arthur to her and kisses him. But the Counsellor and Rodger enter from opposite directions, taking the couple by surprise.

RODGER:	*(To himself.)* My candidacy! *(In a loud voice.)* Elizabeth!
COUNSELLOR:	Excuse me. I fear I'm interrupting again.
ELIZABETH:	Sir. *(To Rodger.)* My dearest darling, Arthur and I were . . . rehearsing.
ARTHUR:	*(Macho.)* Rodger, I'll wait for you outside.

He leaves, assuming his usual triumphant attitude.

ELIZABETH:	We were rehearsing a play.
COUNSELLOR:	So you are also in . . . show business?
ELIZABETH:	Oh no, sir. How could you think such a thing? . . . We were rehearsing . . . for a charity benefit.
RODGER:	If you'll allow me, sir, I need to talk to my wife. *(Taking Eizabeth with him.)* You're going to explain this to me, you little bitch . . .

They leave. The Counsellor doesn't know how to react. He watches various entrances, as always, with his glass in his hand. Finally he dares to sit down but jumps up when he hears a gunshot. Rodger enters, wounded. Before the Counsellor's unbelieving eyes, Rodger falls to the floor. From now until the end of the scene all the characters assume the poses of high melodrama, except for the astonished Counsellor, who goes from surprising incident to surprising incident.

ELIZABETH: *(Entering.)* Rodger!

RODGER: My candidacy! *(He dies.)*

COUNSELLOR: *(Seeing Arthur enter with a gun in his trembling hand.)* His brother!

ELIZABETH: *(To Arthur.)* My lover!

Arthur struggles with the jammed pistol.

ARTHUR: I missed!

ELIZABETH: *(Heading off stage.)* My mother! It was my mother!

She runs quickly to put on the braided wig and is transformed into the Nanny.

COUNSELLOR: *(Seeing her.)* The mother-in-law!

CYNTHIA: *(Entering with a pistol in her hand.)* I killed him! I was his lover!

ELIZABETH: *(She quickly takes off the wig and faces Cynthia.)* His lover!

ARTHUR: My brother! I wanted to kill my brother!

CYNTHIA: My son! He was the father of my son!

ELIZABETH: A son!

COUNSELLOR: What a family!

They all freeze, except for the Counsellor, who is finally able to drink his whiskey and finishes it quickly while the lights are dimmed.

Lights out.

SCENE III: THE GROUP

Spot on Brijinski and the music from the beginning of the second scene, as the actors exit. Without knowing why, Brijinski finds himself with a pistol in his hand. He watches as the bar and chandelier disappear, while he steps out of the character of Arthur. He takes off his jacket and throws it off stage. He takes his script and joins the other actors, who enter again, as "the group," also with their scripts. A work light is turned on.

BOBBY: The cabaret dancer killed him!

CATHY: I killed him!

BRIJINSKI: And why did I miss?

BOBBY: *(With a double meaning.)* So you never miss, honey?

LOUISE: Hey Sophocles, we sure did real well, didn't we?

SOPHOCLES: All we need now is to act.

BRIJINSKI: What a pity. I don't have any scenes with Cathy.

LOUISE: No. You're my lover.

BRIJINSKI: What a pity. I mean, excuse me, Louise, I mean, it's great that I'm your lover! . . . Let me see if I get this right . . .

His eyes meet Bobby's, who blows him a kiss.

CATHY: That part as the cabaret dancer terrifies me. I really don't know what a cabaret dancer is like.

BOBBY: I'll tell you all about it, Cathy.

BRIJINSKI: *(Calculating his costs.)* A bar, a chandelier, the property man! . . .

LOUISE: The old nanny! Ah, but for Elizabeth, my black cocktail dress. Black suits me.

SOPHOCLES:	Louise, you will not wear black.
LOUISE:	Did the director say that? Or the ex-lover?
SOPHOCLES:	I called you because you are a good actress. Only because of that.
LOUISE:	Is that a compliment?
SOPHOCLES:	It is. But let that be clear once and for all.
LOUISE:	*(Angry.)* Yes, sir!
BRIJINSKI:	But it'll be a hit! I can already see the lines of people in the coat room.
BOBBY:	What coat room? There's no coat room in this place, you jerk.
BRIJINSKI:	Again?
BOBBY:	No offense meant, honey.
SOPHOCLES:	*(He turns the page.)* The second play: "The Merciers' Tea."
BRIJINSKI:	The . . . what?
SOPHOCLES:	Action in Paris. Theatre of the vanguard. Which of course no longer is in the vanguard. Page twenty. The Merciers welcome Mr. Phillipe Bertrand into their home. *(He reads.)* Petite-bourgeoisie interior. A checkered tablecloth.
BRIJINSKI:	*(Happy.)* The production doesn't sound expensive.
SOPHOCLES:	On stage Actor Number Two and Actress Number One.
LOUISE:	*(Sighing.)* You and me.
SOPHOCLES:	*(He reads.)* Mrs. Mercier, dressed extravagantly and out of fashion, sixty years old, flirting with . . .

LOUISE: *(Interrupting.)* Sixty years old! Impossible. The role isn't right for me.

SOPHOCLES: *(He reads.)* Flirting with Mr. Bertrand, forty years old, thin handlebar moustache. *(To Louise.)* Here I want a shrill, ridiculous little laugh from Mrs. Mercier.

LOUISE: A little laugh. Oh, hee, hee! Oh, hee, hee, hee, hee, hee! . . . Oh, hee, hee, hee, hee, hee!

Light and music for the change of scene. The actors bring on stage a table with a checkered tablecloth, a sofa, and a lamp.

SCENE IV: *THE MERCIERS' TEA* (A PLAY IN ONE ACT)

Enter Mr. Mercier—a timid, slight, insignificant man, wearing an old sweater, unbuttoned and hanging in front, granny glasses that he can peer over. He has several nervous mannerisms (for example, he constantly twists his neck). He goes on and off stage, bringing three chairs, which he puts around the table.

Although totally ignoring his presence, Mr. Bertrand and Mrs. Mercier enter at the same time as Mr. Mercier. They flirt with each other.

MRS. MERCIER: Oh, hee, hee, hee, hee, hee! . . . Don't say those things to me. Mr. Bertrand; don't say those things to me.

MR. BERTRAND: The rhododendrons are in bloom. How witty, my dear lady, how clever!

MRS. MERCIER: My dear Mr. Bertrand, you are very gallant. *(She offers him her hand and he kisses it.)* Oh, hee, hee, hee, hee, hee . . .

But suddenly she stops laughing. The three characters on stage freeze; a silence during which each of them express an inner anguish.

MRS. MERCIER: Tea will be served in a few moments.

MR. BERTRAND:	I have the feeling that you and I have met somewhere. Marseilles, perhaps? No, no, excuse me. It was Nice.
MRS. MERCIER:	Oh, no! I've never been to Istanbul.
MR. BERTRAND:	That's strange. And still, I could have sworn. Wasn't it during the Great War?
MRS. MERCIER:	*(Indignant.)* What?
MR. BERTRAND:	Oh, please forgive me. Of course, it couldn't have been during the Great War. You're so young. Perhaps then it was with Sherman in Atlanta.
MRS. MERCIER:	No, definitely not.
MR. BERTRAND:	Then you'll forgive me, my dear lady. Then it wasn't the two of us.

Mr. Mercier has finished his homework and is about to leave, but Mrs. Mercier calls him, authoritarian.

MRS. MERCIER:	Lisander!
MR. MERCIER:	*(As if caught red handed, he backtracks and answers, softly.)* Yes, dear?
MRS. MERCIER:	*(Severe.)* How are your English classes coming along?
MR. MERCIER:	Bad, I'm afraid, very bad.
MRS. MERCIER:	I guessed as much. I'm going to get you an instructress.
MR. MERCIER:	No, please, Matilde dear, not an instructress! Anything you want, except an instructress!
MR. BERTRAND:	Mr. Mercier, I have the feeling that you and I have met somewhere else.
MR. MERCIER:	Yes, I have the same feeling, Mr. Bertrand.

MR: BERTRAND:	With Teddy Roosevelt, on San Juan Hill?
MR. MERCIER:	No, I don't think so. I haven't ever been in San Juan.
MR. BERTRAND:	Then it wasn't the two of us.
MRS. MERCIER:	Mr. Bertrand will do us the honor of staying for tea. Everything is ready. *(To the maid, who enters lively, coquettish.)* N'est ce pas, Véronique?
MAID:	*(Curtsying.)* Oui, madame!
MR. BERTRAND:	*(Admiring the maid.)* Well, well. Véronique. French, of course.
MRS. MERCIER:	No. She's British.
MR. MERCIER:	*(Admiring the maid as well.)* I knew she was speaking English!
MR. BERTRAND:	British, huh?
MAID:	From the country of Wales. Celtic forefathers. But I came to Paris as a very young child.
MRS. MERCIER:	The world is a mess.
MR. BERTRAND:	You are right, my dear lady. You are absolutely right.
MAID:	Don't worry, Madame. I'll pop out of the cake at just the right moment.
MR. MERCIER:	*(Happy.)* Oh, goodie. There's a cake!
MRS. MERCIER:	*(Severe.)* It's a prop.
MR. MERCIER:	A prop?
MAID:	You can take it apart. I pop out of the cake and it's a big hit. You'll see. I don't pop out naked . . . My boyfriend is very jealous. He's a policeman and my

father's a gardener. We come from a very ancient
noble family. Although I don't believe all that stuff
about blue blood. I only come out of my cake, in
my itsy-bitsy bikini, and all the gentlemen
applaud. And the ladies, too . . . I used to come out
naked, with my whole body painted silver . . . But
the bikini is more practical: *(Quickly.)* you put it on
and you take it off and even if you don't take it off,
it doesn't matter, you still see everything . . . Well
then, I pop out of the cake and I kick a leg up in the
air. Like this! *(She does it and kicks off Mr. Mercier's
eyeglasses, which fall on the floor.)* Oh, excuse me, sir.

MR. MERCIER: *(Friendly.)* Don't worry. *(On his knees, he looks for the
glasses.)*

MAID: As I was saying, I kick my leg up in the air and you
can hear the "Hurrahs" and the "Bravos" . . . And I
smile, innocently . . . Do you remember Marilyn
Monroe? So young, poor little thing. Well, I smile a
la Monroe. Like this. *(She smiles a la Monroe.)* And
the act is a smashing success.

MR. MERCIER: *(Admiring the maid.)* Yes, it's very successful, I don't
doubt it. *(He shrinks when faced with Mrs. Mercier's
terrible look.)*

MR. BERTRAND: *(Admiring the maid.)* From the country of Wales . . .

MRS. MERCIER: Véronique, the cake act will come after tea. You can
go now.

MAID: *(Curtsying.)* Oui, madame. *(She leaves. Mr. Bertrand
follows her, but Mrs. Mercier calls him back.)*

MRS. MERCIER: Mr. Bertrand!

MR. BERTRAND: My dear lady, the black of your eyes has, as never
before, mysterious iridescent reflections.

MRS. MERCIER: Oh, hee, hee, hee, hee, hee! . . . But my eyes aren't
black.

MR. BERTRAND:	*(Stroking her brittle, straw-colored blond wig.)* The ebony of your curls leaves me senseless.
MRS. MERCIER:	Oh, hee, hee, hee, hee, hee! . . . My dear sir, don't say those things to me. Not in front of my husband.
MR. MERCIER:	*(All charm.)* Don't worry about me.
MRS. MERCIER:	*(Severe.)* Lisander, go and see if the rhododendrons have flowered already.
MR. MERCIER:	Yes, my dear. *(He takes a few steps and stops.)* But dear, we don't have any rhododendrons.
MRS. MERCIER:	It doesn't matter. Go and see anyway.
MR. BERTRAND:	Matilde, mon amour, tonight! . . .
MRS. MERCIER:	Phillipe, I'll leave the door to my room open tonight. But don't forget to come in through the balcony. It's more romantic.
MR. BERTRAND:	What a beautiful future we have in store for us! You, always young and beautiful and I, always romantic and in love . . . And your king-sized bed with its brass headboard.
MRS. MERCIER:	*(Embarassed.)* I must confess that making love with you, with Lisander there . . . *(She places an imaginary Mr. Mercier between them, stepping back to make room for him.)* asleep between us, bothers me a little.
MR. BERTRAND:	Bah, he hardly takes up any room!
MRS. MERCIER:	At any rate, it bothers me.
MR. BERTRAND:	Don't be old fashioned.
MRS. MERCIER:	I'm sure that he spies on us.
MR. BERTRAND:	Who? Lisander? He wouldn't dare.
MRS. MERCIER:	He pretends to be asleep, but he spies on us, I'm sure of it.

MR. BERTRAND: Well, that's his problem.

MRS. MERCIER: Besides, he coughs.

MR. BERTRAND: Now, *that* is annoying. When we're going to make love and he begins to cough, why that turns off my . . . inspiration.

MRS. MERCIER: Poor little darling! I'll tell Lisander to take some pills for his throat.

MR. BERTRAND: Matilde, you're an angel!

They're interrupted because Lecocq, who has crossed upstage from one end to the other, is observing them. Now he realizes they see him and disappears.

MR. BERTRAND: *(Starting again.)* Matilde, you're an angel!

Lecocq appears again. They see him and he disappears. But he appears again immediately and rings the doorbell. He disappears.

MR. MERCIER: *(Entering.)* Someone's at the door. *(He goes to open the door.)*

MAID: *(Entering.)* Don't bother yourself, sir.

MR. MERCIER: *(Surprised.)* Are you speaking to me?

MAID: *(Flirting.)* To you, of course. I'll get the door. That's what I'm the maid for. *(She goes to open the door, wiggling her fanny for Mr. Mercier.)*

LECOCQ: *(From off stage.)* Good evening. *(Referring to the maid.)* A beautiful creature. *(Already inside.)* May I come in? *(He introduces himself.)* Lecocq, Leopold. Of the Lecocqs of Ghent, but born in Paris. Unemployed. Anarquist. I was passing by. By any chance, ladies and gentlemen, by any chance, did you lose a little dog here?

MR. MERCIER: A little dog? Darling, did we lose a little dog?

MRS. MERCIER: Véronique, did we lose a dog?

MAID:	Probably, you never know.
MR. BERTRAND:	*(To Lecocq.)* Is it small, very small, with coffee-colored hair on its eyes?
LECOCQ:	*(Very dignified.)* Oh, no, no, no! The one I'm talking about is bigger, black and shaved.
MR. BERTRAND:	With a little rose-colored bow?
MAID:	Oh, how cute!
LECOCQ:	*(Drastic.)* No! With a leather collar.
MR. BERTRAND:	Then, my dear, man, it's not the same dog. This is not the place.
MRS. MERCIER:	*(Severe.)* This can't be the place because we don't have a dog.
LECOCQ:	You don't have a dog? *(Dejected, crushed.)* What a pity! This is a real pity!
MR. MERCIER:	Poor fellow.
LECOCQ:	*(Suddenly, with renewed spirits.)* Excuse me, sir, I'll leave now. Lecocq, Leopold. Of the Lecocqs of Ghent. Good night.
MRS. MERCIER:	Véronique, see the gentleman to the door.
MAID:	*(Curtsying.)* Oui, madame. *(To Lecocq.)* Come, it's quicker through the kitchen.

She takes him with her and he follows, happy. They exit, but Lecocq returns.

LECOCQ:	*(Dejected.)* What a pity! *(He leaves.)*
MR. MERCIER:	Poor fellow!
MRS. MERCIER:	Why poor fellow?
MR. MERCIER:	He seem so alone.

MRS. MERCIER:	So what's wrong with that? Anarchists are always alone. That's their duty.
MR. BERTRAND:	Their duty? How witty, my dear lady, how clever!
MRS. MERCIER:	Oh, hee, hee, hee, hee, hee! . . .

Suddenly she stops laughing. The three characters freeze. A silence.

MRS. MERCIER:	Hmm.
MR. BERTRAND:	Hmm, hmm.
MR. MERCIER:	The trains for London tonight will leave a little late. That's what it said on the news.
MRS. MERCIER:	My husband is a retired station master. That's why he always talks about trains.
MR. BERTRAND:	And which station did you retire from?
MR. MERCIER:	Well, I'm not really sure.
MR. BERTRAND:	What do you mean, you're not really sure?
MR. MERCIER:	There was an arrow, in the shape of a cross. One end pointed south, toward Lyon and the other pointed east, toward Strasbourg. I was only supposed to be in charge of the trains going to Strasbourg, but they forced me to watch those that were going to Lyon as well. It was an injustice.
MRS. MERCIER:	It doesn't seem so to me.
MR. MERCIER:	But dear, it was an injustice.
MRS. MERCIER:	*(Indignant.)* What? You contradict me?
MR. MERCIER:	No dear, I'm not contradicting you.
MRS. MERCIER:	You're calling me a liar.
MR. MERCIER:	No, dear.

MRS. MERCIER:	Oh, you've insulted me. *(She cries. She opens her hand bag and takes out a little handkerchief to dry her eyes.)*
MR. BERTRAND:	*(Indignant.)* Mr. Mercier, this is no way to treat a lady.
MRS. MERCIER:	*(Crying.)* He's a boor.
MR. BERTRAND:	Yes. He doesn't deserve our society.
MRS. MERCIER:	*(She suddenly stops crying.)* Lisander, go and feed the canaries.
MR. MERCIER:	Yes, dear. *(He's about to leave but he comes back.)* My dearest love, we don't have any canaries.
MRS. MERCIER:	Go and feed them!
MR. MERCIER:	Yes, dear. *(He leaves.)*
MRS. MERCIER:	What a jerk! *(She cries again.)*
MR. BERTRAND:	*(He dries her eyes with the handkerchief.)* Now, now, it's all over, my little dove, it's all over . . . Look at this pretty little handkerchief! . . . Let's put it away. *(He puts the handkerchief into Mrs. Mercier's handbag and finds something. He takes out a pistol.)* But what is this, my dear lady?
MRS. MERCIER:	This? . . . Why it's a . . . little pistol.
MR. BERTRAND:	A little pistol? I think we'd better put it away. *(He puts it back into the handbag.)* And what do you want it for, my dear lady? What do you want a little pistol for?
MRS. MERCIER:	*(In a low voice.)* You won't tell anyone, will you.
MR. BERTRAND:	No one.
MRS. MERCIER:	*(Very mysteriously.)* Well, you should know that there are . . . cockroaches in the kitchen.

MR. BERTRAND: No!

MRS. MERCIER: Yes!

MR. BERTRAND: My poor friend!

MRS. MERCIER: It's a dishonor to my marriage. I know it . . .

MR. BERTRAND: (*Serious.*) My dear friend, if you had married me . . .

MRS. MERCIER: You're right. You would have protected me from the cockroaches. Lisander, on the other had, only thinks about steam engines.

MR. BERTRAND: About what?

MRS. MERCIER: It's for his future. He's going to study the workings of steam engines in industry.

MR. BERTRAND: Steam engines! How modern!

MRS MERCIER: Yes, it's very advanced for our age.

MR. BERTRAND: But this is fantastic, my dear lady, this is fantastic. Now that the whole world is interested in electronics, steam engines will be a true discovery!

MAID: (*Off stage.*) Oh, Mr. Mercier, you have such an irresistible way of asking for things! . . . Oh, Mr. Mercier, take pity on an innocent girl . . . Mr. Mercier, please . . . (*Erotic sighs.*) Aah! Ooh! Mr. Mercier! . . .

MRS. MERCIER: (*Who has heard this, indignant.*) Lisander!

MR. MERCIER: (*Entering hurriedly.*) Yes, my dear.

MRS. MERCIER: What were you doing in the kitchen?

MR. MERCIER: Nothing, my dear, nothing.

MAID: (*Entering, straightening her clothes.*) Mr. Mercier was showing me how to . . . take care of the canaries.

MRS. MERCIER:	*(Indignant.)* I can't believe it!
MR. MERCIER:	Don't believe it, dear, don't believe it.

They interrupt themselves because they see Lecocq, who has crossed upstage again and has stopped to observe them.

MRS. MERCIER:	Again?

Lecocq dissapears. Mrs. Mercier goes to have a look. Lecocq appears suddenly and rings the bell. He disappears again.

MAID:	I'll go; don't bother yourselves. *(But Lecocq has already entered and is standing in front of her.)* Oh hi, Leopold!
LECOCQ:	Lecocq. Anarchist. I was passing by. By any chance this isn't number 273, apartment 7, is it?
MR. MERCIER:	Two hundred seventy and . . . No, it isn't.
LECOCQ:	*(Alarmed.)* No? Then it must be number 537, apartment 3.
MR. MERCIER:	Five hundred thirty . . .
MRS. MERCIER:	*(Interrupting.)* No, it isn't that either.
MR. MERCIER:	*(Friendly, to Lecocq.)* No, it isn't.
LECOCQ:	It isn't? *(Beaten, he crumples into the chair.)* It's a pity! A real pity! *(Suddenly he revives and gets up.)* However, excuse me, if you'll forgive me the question, I wouldn't want to be indiscrete . . . *(To Mr. Mercier.)* Your name isn't Jonathan by any chance, is it?
MR. MERCIER:	Jonathan? No, I'm sorry, that's not my name.
LECOCQ:	No? *(To Mrs. Mercier, distressed.)* And your name isn't Gertrude, is it?
MRS. MERCIER:	No!

LECOCQ:	*(To the maid.)* And you, miss, don't you have a boyfriend who's a fireman?
MAID:	*(Feeling insulted.)* No, sir! My boyfriend's a policeman.
LECOCQ:	*(At the height of desperation.)* And by any chance, have you seen a bald soprano around here?
MR. BERTRAND:	No. We haven't seen her.
LECOCQ:	*(Dejected, beaten.)* Then I have the wrong play. I mean, the wrong house. I have such bad luck!
MR. MERCIER:	Poor fellow!
MRS. MERCIER:	Véronique, see the gentleman to the door.
LECOCQ:	*(Suddenly revived.)* Excuse me, I'll leave now.
MAID:	*(Coquettish.)* So soon?
LECOCQ:	Lecocq, Leopold. I was passing by.
MAID:	Let's go, Leopold, through the kitchen.

They leave, the maid flirting and Lecocq happy. But suddenly he returns.

LECOCQ:	*(Overcome.)* Very bad luck!

He exits. Seated once again at the table, the characters on stage don't know what to talk about.

MR. MERCIER:	In London tonight, the trains . . .
MR. BERTRAND:	*(Interrupting.)* Well yes, the neuroses do dress up quite a bit.
MRS. MERCIER:	The neuroses?
MR. BERTRAND:	Especially for parties. When I invite my friends, I always ask them to bring their neuroses with them.

	That way the get-togethers are more fun. And everybody contributes . . . Who in our times doesn't have his little neuroses?
MRS. MERCIER:	Well, the poor don't have them.
MR. BERTRAND:	Don't you believe it, my dear lady. They also have them.
MRS. MERCIER:	You don't say.
MR. BERTRAND:	That's right. Today everybody has everything. The poor have their luxuries. They have TVs and neuroses.
MRS. MERCIER:	Incredible! And all that because of the French Revolution! . . . Fortunately, Lisander and I are very busy and we are not aware of these things. Isn't that right, Lisander?
MR. MERCIER:	That's right, my dear.
MRS. MERCIER:	During the French Revolution I told my husband: You'll start your English classes right now. And when all that business about the atom, Hiroshima, and Nagasaki started, I sat down to embroider. I hate oriental things! It's cross stitching for me. Like the French do it!

Optimistically, like someone who arrives at home happily, with a loaf of bread under his arm, Lecocq crosses upstage, whistling "Qui a peur du méchant loup." He stops behind them and observes them. They see him.

MRS. MERCIER:	No!

Lecocq disappears. Mr. Mercier goes to see. Lecocq appears and disappears right under Mr. Mercier's nose. Finally, he rings the bell, and as always, disappears again.

MAID:	(Entering.) I'm coming, my darling, I'm coming. (But Lecocq is already inside.)
LECOCQ:	Lecocq, Leopold. From Ghent. You didn't order a loaf of bread by any chance, did you?

MR. MERCIER:	A loaf of bread? Let me find out. Darling, did we order a . . .
MRS. MERCIER:	*(Interrupting.)* No, we didn't!
LECOCQ:	No? What a pity! *(Overcome, he throws himself onto the sofa.)*
MAID:	Don't worry, Leopold. Don't worry, darling.
LECOCQ:	*(Suddenly optimistic, he takes out some yarn and needles and begins to knit.)* I was passing by and thought . . . If one day people decided to stop at a house like this one and offer their neighbors a loaf of bread, the world would be a different place, don't you think?
MR. MERCIER:	Yes, it would be a different place.
LECOCQ:	*(Becoming despondent.)* It's always good to have a house where one can take a loaf of bread.
MR. MERCIER:	*(In Lecocq's tone.)* Yes, it's always good.
LECOCQ:	*(He cries.)* Every night I buy a loaf of bread, but I live alone. It's not the same to take a loaf of bread home when you live alone as when someone is waiting there for the loaf of bread.
MR. MERCIER:	*(He cries.)* It's not the same.
LECOCQ:	*(Desperate.)* I always wanted to have someone to take a loaf of bread home to.
MR. MERCIER:	*(Same tone as Lecocq.)* Poor fellow! . . .
LECOCQ:	*(Suddenly more sure of himself, aggressive.)* Of course, I take the loaf of bread home, for myself. But it's not the same. Besides, I don't like bread.
MR. BERTRAND:	If you don't like it then why do you buy it?
LECOCQ:	*(Very dignified.)* One has to do something to occupy one's time, doesn't one?

MR. MERCIER:	You're right about that.
MRS. MERCIER:	Lisander!
MR. MERCIER:	Yes, dear?
LECOCQ:	I'll leave now. I already know the way. Through the kitchen.
MRS. MERCIER:	Véronique, see him to the door.
MAID:	Let's go chéri. *(They leave. As always, Lecocq returns, but this time he remains optimistic.)*
LECOCQ:	Excuse me, if I don't come back again today. It's late. But tomorrow, without fail, I can come again . . .
MRS. MERCIER:	*(Interrupting.)* Goodbye!
LECOCQ:	Goddbye. *(He leaves, but comes back and corrects Mrs. Mericer.)* Until tomorrow! *(He exits.)*
MR. MERCIER:	He's probably thinking about moving in to live here with us.
MRS. MERCIER:	The instructress, tomorrow, right away.
MR. MERCIER:	But I was only saying . . .
MRS. MERCIER:	We will not let that anarchist in again.
MR. BERTRAND:	Mrs. Mercier, Mr. Mercier, now that we're talking about anarchism, as a friend of the family I feel it my duty to let you know that the rise in gold prices has posed a danger to the smooth flow of traffic in Paris.
MR. MERCIER:	But gold is falling.
MR. BERTRAND:	It's also going up. The rise in gold has caused unrest among the lower classes.
MRS. MERCIER:	How awful, the lower classes.

MR. MERCIER:	I didn't realize that the lower classes were worried about gold.
MR. BERTRAND:	The farmworkers think that the rise in gold could have repercussions on the sesame crop. And they've become truly insufferable. On the other hand, the nobility and the Third Estate . . .
MR. MERCIER:	You mean the Third World.
MRS. MERCIER:	*(To Mr. Mercier.)* He means the politicians and us.
MR. BERTRAND:	On the other hand the nobility has joined forces with the clergy. And with all this, the stock market might crash.
MRS. MERCIER:	Wouldn't you know it!
MAID:	*(Enters, crying.)* I'm pregnant! I'm pregnant! *(Coquettish.)* And I don't know by which of these three gentlemen.
MRS. MERCIER:	What?
MAID:	I don't know if the child is Mr. Bertrand's.
MRS. MERCIER:	What are you saying? *(To Mr. Bertrand, who is sneaking away.)* Phillipe!
MR. BERTRAND:	Ah . . . I . . . well, I'm afraid that while we were talking about forestry in the country of Wales . . . Well, it was merely a fling.
MAID:	*(Coquettish.)* Or Mr. Mercier's.

Mr. Mercier hides behind the couch.

MRS. MERCIER:	Whose?
MAID:	The child is probably Mr. Mercier's.
MRS. MERCIER:	Lisander!
MR. MERCIER:	*(He peeps over the couch.)* You see my dear, it turns

out that while I was teaching Véronique how to feed the canaries . . .

MRS. MERCIER:	That's enough!
MAID:	*(Coquettish.)* Or Leopold's.
MRS. MERCIER:	*(Who sees Lecocq crossing upstage.)* The anarchist!
MAID:	The child could also be Leopold's.

Lecocq, who was about to ring the doorbell, changes his mind and disappears.

MRS. MERCIER:	*(Referring the Lecocq.)* Oh! . . . *(To the maid.)* But how is this possible? Why, you only saw him to the door.
MAID:	*(Very dignified.)* I saw him to the door three times, ma'am. There are those who get pregnant the first time.
MR. MERCIER:	That's true, my dear, that's true.
MRS. MERCIER:	Shut up!
MAID:	Madam, I'm leaving. You'll have to find someone else to pop out of the cake.
MRS. MERCIER:	What? You're leaving?
MAID:	My boyfriend is very jealous. If he finds out about what goes on in this house . . . I'm leaving right now! *(She leaves.)*
MRS. MERCIER:	It can't be! Who will serve us tea? *(She throws herself onto the sofa.)*
MR. BERTRAND:	Don't worry; I'll try to convince her to stay.
MRS. MERCIER:	Thank you, Mr. Bertrand, thank you . . .
MR. BERTRAND:	At least until she pops out of the cake. *(Leaving.)* Véronique! Miss! . . .

MR. MERCIER: What can we do? Don't be upset. Today everybody gets pregnant. Women, men—with all this surgery business. Don't be upset. What can we do? *(Mrs. Mercier takes the pistol from her handbag.)* What is that, my dear? Oh, what a cute little pistol, so feminine! . . .

MRS. MERCIER: Very feminine. *(Suddenly she pokes him with the pistol.)* Does it seem soon to you?

MR. MERCIER: I thought that we might share one more night, a few more classes, a few more canaries.

MRS. MERCIER: Are you going to go romantic on me?

MR. MERCIER: At the moment of death one does so many things . . .

MRS. MERCIER: Lisander, all day I've wanted to be alone with you.

MR. MERCIER: But dear, we don't make love anymore.

MRS. MERCIER: Don't be conventional. I wanted to be alone with you for this! Clic! *(She shoots him. The gun's a toy; a little toy chick pops out of it.)*

MR. MERCIER: Oh, I'm dying unjustly. I'm dying for the lower classes. *(He falls, in a seated position, like a little bird, still saying)* Chirp, chirp, chirp, chirp. *(He dies.)*

MRS. MERCIER: *(Disdainful.)* I always did think that you were a supporter of the French Revolution.

MR. BERTRAND: *(Entering.)* I was able to convince her. She's staying!

MRS. MERCIER: My dear Mr. Bertrand, I'm willing to forget this little incident with the maid.

MR. BERTRAND: *(Passionate, he goes to her.)* Matilde, mon amour! . . . *(The corpse of Mr. Mercier—the little bird falls over.)* Oh, but what is this?

MRS. MERCIER: This? It's Mr. Mercier.

MR. BERTRAND: He's dead.

MRS. MERCIER: *(She cleans the pistol with her hankie.)* My dear friend, will you keep a secret for me?

MR. BERTRAND: A secret?

MRS. MERCIER: I've obviously just murdered my husband . . . *(Coquettish.)* But that can be a little secret between you and me. *(She puts the pistol in her handbag.)*

MR. BERTRAND: Oh, I understand . . . I understand, my dear friend . . . You did this for me, for our love.

MRS. MERCIER: Don't be conventional! Mr. Mercier wasn't getting in the way of our love. I did it to save having to pay for the instructress.

MR. BERTRAND: The instructress! How witty, my dear lady, how clever!

MRS. MERCIER: My dear Mr. Bertrand, you are very gallant. *(She offeres him her hand, which he kisses.)* Oh, hee, hee, hee, hee, hee! . . .

She stops laughing and they freeze. Silence.

MRS. MERCIER: Tea will be served in a few moments.

They freeze again, looking at Mr. Mercier's corpse. The same music that started this scene is heard again, while Lecocq enters upstage, happily whistling his song. He stops and sees the dead man. He's frightened and disappears. The lights are dimmed. Lecocq reappears, smiling, once again sure of himself. He takes out a pistol and shoots it at the house. A little flag pops out, which Lecocq shows the audience. The flag says:

INTERMISSION

SCENE V: THE GROUP

Empty stage. Work lights. The group with scripts in hand. Louise rehearses, with an imaginary pistol.

LOUISE: . . . Alone, with you, for this. *(She shoots an imaginary pistol.)* For this . . . *(She shoots again and realizes the others are watching.)* What do you think about that? I killed poor Lisander.

BRIJINSKI: You had to kill him. He was the husband.

CATHY: The rehearsals aren't going to be easy.

SOPHOCLES: Certain gestures, even nervous mannerisms, could help Mr. Mercier convey his insignificance. *(A thought occurs to him.)* Brijinski, you'll twist your neck every now and again. *(He does it, imitating Mr. Mercier's tic.)* It's an escape mechanism.

BRIJINSKI: I'll twist my neck? *(He tries to do it, but it doesn't work.)* Let's see if I get it right . . .

BOBBY: You were saying . . .

SOPHOCLES: *(To Brijinski.)* You'll also need a pair of glasses, for moral support. They'll underscore your character's moods. He's insecure; he needs to hold on to something, even if it's only his glasses.

BRIJINSKI: I'm going to hold on to a pair of glasses?

SOPHOCLES: *(Without answering him, inventing.)* Very small, like granny glasses.

BRIJINSKI: They're going to fall off.

BOBBY: What's falling off?

SOPHOCLES: Let us continue: *(He turns the page.)* Third play.

BRIJINSKI: Excuse me, I want to go wee wee.

CATHY: I'm hungry . . . I brought a cake.

SOPHOCLES: All right. Ten minutes for wee wee and cake.

BRIJINSKI: *(To Cathy.)* Come on, let's go. Well, let's move it. You take the cake and I'll . . .

They exit.

BOBBY:	*(Going after them.)* You're inviting, right? Even if it's just for the cake . . . *(He exits.)*
LOUISE:	What does this mean? We're going to break now, in the middle of the reading, just when we were getting hot?
SOPHOCLES:	This way we'll cool down.
LOUISE:	Pig!
SOPHOCLES:	And I'm going to take a nap. *(He lies down on the floor.)*
LOUISE:	A nap? At night?
SOPHOCLES:	Don't get bourgeois. Any time is a good time for taking a nap.
LOUISE:	Sophocles, get up from there. I want to talk to you.
SOPHOCLES:	What's up? Don't you like your roles?
LOUISE:	It doesn't have anything to do with the play, but with us.
SOPHOCLES:	*(He sits down.)* You're wrong, Louise. While we're on this stage it does have to do with the play.
LOUISE:	Okay, okay, but we're not going to be on this stage the rest of our lives. *(Softly.)* Not even the rest of the night . . . What'll you do when we leave?
SOPHOCLES:	When we leave?
LOUISE:	I invite you to come over to my place. We can start by having tea. I'll bet you were inspired by us. We always started by having tea. Do you remember?
SOPHOCLES:	Yes, I remember.
LOUISE:	First tea and then . . . whatever's your pleasure.

SOPHOCLES:	I'm sorry Louise. Not today. *(He lies down again.)*
LOUISE:	*(Furious.)* You insolent! . . . You think you're real clever. You vain . . . you . . . you . . . *(She can't find the right word.)* you egotistical son of a bitch!
SOPHOCLES:	Louise, the melodrama is over . . .
CATHY:	*(Entering, sharing the remains of an imaginary cake with Brijinski.)* Look Brijinski, my boyfriend is very jealous.
BRIJINSKI:	The policeman?
CATHY:	What policeman? No, I mean my fellow, the real one . . . I'm going to invite him to the opening of the play!
BRIJINSKI:	Of course.
CATHY:	And to think that he's going to see me as a cabaret dancer.
BRIJINSKI:	And as a pregnant maid!
LOUISE:	*(To Sophocles.)* And pedantic, too! *(She leaves.)*
CATHY:	What's wrong with her?
SOPHOCLES:	Nothing. She's a good actress.
CATHY:	I'll go with her.
BRIJINSKI:	And what are you doing on the floor?
SOPHOCLES:	I'm taking a nap.
BRIJINSKI:	You're sleeping?
SOPHOCLES:	Soundly.
BRIJINSKI:	That's a strange way of sleeping.
BOBBY:	*(Entering.)* Why strange? Nothing in the theater is

strange. Of course, it's more delicious to be an audience member asleep in the stalls. *(To spectator.)* Isn't that so, Doctor? How good of you to come. You've changed seats.

BRIJINSKI: Who are you talking to?

BOBBY: *(To Brijinski.)* Alone at last. Let's see, my little virgin, come here.

BRIJINSKI: I'm not your little virgin, you goddamned fag.

BOBBY: What did you say?

BRIJINSKI: I'm sorry, I didn't mean to offend you. Excuse me.

BOBBY: It's alright. I'm gay.

BRIJINSKI: You are?

BOBBY: Don't tell me you're surprised.

BRIJINSKI: I thought you were play acting . . . that you were just pretending to be queer.

BOBBY: Well, when it's in my better interests I also act. The truth is that I'm going through an ambidextrous phase.

BRIJINSKI: Ambidextrous?

BOBBY: And then one day you realize that your life has come and gone in the theater. *(He becomes Louis XIV.)* "Your Majesty" . . . *(An aside, as Bobby.)* . . . the king said to his court playwright . . . *(He becomes Louis XIV again.)* "Your Majesty had other things on his mind and wasn't paying attention to your play the first time that he saw it." *(As Bobby, he explains.)* Louis XIV to Moliére.*

---

*Approximate quote, according to a contemporary chronicle by Grimarest, reprinted in Les chefs d'oeuvre de Moliēre, Rio de Janeiro: Edit. Americ; 50 copies published.

BRIJINSKI:	I don't understand.
BOBBY:	*(Serious, to himself.)* What can help you is believing in God. I talk to Him sometimes.
BRIJINSKI:	I don't understand.
BOBBY:	*(Nervous, he sings.)* "Ridi pagliaccio . . ."
BRIJINSKI:	Bobby, you're shaking.
BOBBY:	Look, my little vir . . . young man. Do you really think it's possible to work all at the same time on a goddamned television program, on a series of dubbings, to be an extra in a film in the morning, the M.C. for a cabaret show in the early morning, and the medicine man in a children's show in the afternoon, an actor at night . . . and then not shake!
BRIJINSKI:	Well yes, that is a lot . . . Too much.
BOBBY:	Why too much? It leaves you a little shakey, that's all.
BRIJINSKI:	Bobby, I like you!
BOBBY:	*(Sexy.)* That sounds exciting.

But Brijinski slips by him, towards Cathy, who is entering.

BRIJINSKI:	Cathy dear, so long without seeing you.
CATHY:	*(Amused.)* Did you miss me a lot?
BRIJINSKI:	You have no idea how much!
SOPHOCLES:	*(Standing up.)* Nine and a half minutes. To work. Take your scripts. Where's Louise?
LOUISE:	*(Entering.)* There are rats in the dressing rooms!
SOPHOCLES:	Did you actually see one?
LOUISE:	No, but the dressing rooms have been turned into a storage area and I'm sure that . . .

SOPHOCLES:	*(He interrupts her.)* Louise, you didn't see any rats, right?
LOUISE:	Right.
SOPHOCLES:	Third play. In honor of Rimbaud, it's entitled "The Drunken Boat."
BRIJINSKI:	*(Dreamily.)* "The Drunken Boat" . . .
SOPHOCLES:	Of course, there is no boat.
BRIJINSKI:	No?
SOPHOCLES:	It's lost at sea. *(Pedantic.)* Although Rimbaud's poem can be considered the point of departure for Symbolism, my play, which has a little bit of Symbolism and also of Romanticism and even some Impressionism, is perhaps basically Surrealism.
BOBBY:	Surrealism? Son of a whore!
CATHY:	Surrealism, what a bitch!
BRIJINSKI:	Well, is it a whore or a bitch? Make up your minds.
LOUISE:	*(Turning the pages of the script.)* Yes, it's true. I got the part of a seaweed.
BRIJINSKI:	And I got the one of a . . . what does it say here? . . . a lichen! What's that?
CATHY:	It's a plant.
SOPHOCLES:	Page forty-five. Let's read. *(He reads.)* The sea. A beach. The Boyfriend and the Girlfriend seated on a bench. They're dressed in blue. *(Already seeing his imaginary characters.)* In the blues of Chagall.
LOUISE:	Why Chagall?
SOPHOCLES:	Because I like his blues. *(He reads.)* Two sea lichens, Chondron Crispus, that is to say, two red marine

algae who, to differentiate them, will be called Alga and Lichen, on a rock which every now and again is enveloped by the waves . . .

BRIJINSKI: I'm an alga!

SOPHOCLES: The ones of this species come from deep waters and the sea casts them on the shore. I wanted them to be rooted on a rock.

LOUISE: Well, you're the author, after all.

SOPHOCLES: *(He reads.)* A gentleman dressed in black enters and crosses the stage. *(He turns around to look at Bobby.)*

BOBBY: Yes, me.

SOPHOCLES: *(He reads.)* He has a net for hunting gayly colored butterflies.

BOBBY: *Gayly colored* butterflies.

A loud, intensely colored screen casts a violent hue on the stage. The actors exit, except Bobby, who jumps around with an imaginary net pretending to catch butterflies. He exits at the same time that the two seaweeds enter, inside a "rock costume" which they share and through which their faces, head-dresses and hands show. They drag their feet in a zigzag motion until they reach their place on the beach. They kneel, sink their heads into the rock, leaving only their hands out. A bench is brought on stage, on which the Boyfriend and Girlfriend are seated motionless. The colored screen disappears and the lights for the next scene are turned on.

SCENE VI: *THE DRUNKEN BOAT* (A PLAY IN ONE ACT)

The sea. Enter the gentleman dressed in black, with the net for catching butterflies. He wears a suit from the 1920s and a bowler hat. He crosses the stage, as if he didn't belong to this time, to this story, without seeing the other characters, who also didn't notice him. He catches a butterfly but then lets it go. Dragging the net, he exits. The only light now is a spot on the Boyfriend and Girlfriend. They speak in a neutral, distant tone.

GIRLFRIEND: The sea seems bluer today.

BOYFRIEND: There is something strange in the air.

GIRLFRIEND: There is no way out through the sea.

BOYFRIEND: Or through the land, either:

GIRLFRIEND: Our dead parents, and our grandparents, and our great-grandparents have the beach surrounded.

BOYFRIEND: They're always watching over it. I know that they even use radar.

GIRLFRIEND: And the guards won't let us escape through the sea.

BOYFRIEND: Rocks, seaweed, sea urchins, parasites . . .

GIRLFRIEND: A hundred years on this beach.

BOYFRIEND: A hundred years.

GIRLFRIEND: Watching the sea . . . But the drunken boat will come to get us. And we'll go away from here. *(They lose their neutral attitude.)*

BOYFRIEND: I think of you every afternoon, when the clock chimes six.

GIRLFRIEND: Me. too! At six o'clock on the dot the canary on my wristwatch chirps and I see you in your workroom . . . I see you, so young and strong, building your dodecahedrons, gluing the sides with Elmer's.

BOYFRIEND: Geraldine!

GIRLFRIEND: Gerald!

BOYFRIEND: I'll build my castle of dodecahedrons and we'll escape through it. To the region of uncorrupted air, where the lazer beams intersect with drive-in

theaters. Where Superman flies by and
earthquakes open up fissures in the sky, farther
away than the atomic bomb. That's where we'll
have our home and teach our children to build
little dodecahedrons.

GIRLFRIEND: Oh Gerald, it's a dream! . . .

The gentleman enters. Lights on all the stage.

BOYFRIEND: Silence! Here he comes!

GIRLFRIEND: He's early today.

BOYFRIEND: Pretend that you don't see him.

*The gentleman ignores the couple. He drags the net, no longer tryong
to catch butterflies. He walks up and stops in front of the sea. He looks
out at the sea.*

GIRLFRIEND: He always looks off into the distance.

BOYFRIEND: There's a whole life contained in that look . . .

GIRLFRIEND: We could make friends with him.

BOYFRIEND: Don't trust him. He's dangerous.

GIRLFRIEND: He doesn't seem dangerous.

*Suddenly the gentlman turns around. He walks away and exits. The
general lighting is turned off as he exits and the only light left is the
spot on the Boyfriend and the Girlfriend.*

BOYFRIEND: (*As the gentlman turns around.*) Maybe he's not a
                 butterfly collector, but something even worse.

GIRLFRIEND: What could be worse? . . . Oh Gerald, I'm afraid!

The Alga and the Lichen, in the rock, move their heads.

BOYFRIEND: Silence!

GIRLFRIEND: What was that?

BOYFRIEND:	I don't know. The sea . . .
GIRLFRIEND:	The guards.
BOYFRIEND:	*(Quickly.)* The sea.
GIRLFRIEND:	*(Quickly.)* I don't want to see them.
BOYFRIEND:	Come on, let's walk further down on the beach.
GIRLFRIEND:	I don't want to see them.
BOYFRIEND:	Come on, let them have the sea . . .

They freeze on their bench and will not get up from it throughout the play. Their spot is turned off at the same time that another is lit on the rock.

LICHEN:	. . . To go away from here.
ALGA:	You don't know what you're saying.
LICHEN:	Yes I do. I want to go away from here.
ALGA:	*(She lifts her head out of the rock.)* But little Lichen . . .
LICHEN:	*(He peeps out of the rock also.)* Don't call me little Lichen! *(Amused.)* I'm your husband.
ALGA:	And my son, as well.
LICHEN:	I guess so.
ALGA:	What do you mean you guess so?
LICHEN:	*(Amused.)* Human beings would call it incest.
ALGA:	Anyway, I'm your mother and your father at the same time, in the same way that you'll be the father and mother of your children. Among us there are no problems . . . That's what my first husband, the Lichen, always said. *(She sighs.)* He abandoned me and I was left all alone, in the immensity of the blue sea . . . A sad story like so many others.

LICHEN:	*(Serious.)* I want to go away from here.

ALGA:	Macbeth never understood Shakespeare, but he was very much like my first husband.

LICHEN:	I want to go away.

ALGA:	You, however, resemble Hamlet. *(Quickly, with no transition.)* But little Lichen, how can you leave?

LICHEN:	I want to become a human being.

ALGA:	What are you saying?

LICHEN:	I want to be a man. And you, Alga, a woman.

ALGA:	That's impossible.

LICHEN:	Why impossible? I want to make love to you the way that men and women make love.

ALGA:	*(Pleased.)* Little Lichen! . . .

LICHEN:	I want your laugh, like a sea shell, when factory chimneys begin to belch smoke.

ALGA:	*(Pleased.)* Oh! . . .

LICHEN:	I want your skin, at the time when stores caress the cellophane on gifts. And your teeth, when cars with loud speakers drive through dowtown Manhattan.

ALGA:	Oh! . . .

LICHEN:	I want to kindnap you on horseback in a film about galaxies and I want to have breakfast with you every morning on a terrace in the Trocadero, when factories begin to turn their electric bulbs. I want to wake up at your side every morning, lying down on a blade of a steel sword, listening only to NPR, at eight-sixty on the radio dial. I want to make love to you under the light of a golden and fiery moon,

on the grass where the scarabs copulate, while the room next door to Einstein is busy resolving his theory of relativity. I want Newton and his apple and Washington's Federalist Constitution and the Thirty Years War to place at your feet. For you I want to be the microbe that will kill penicillin, the bacillus that will poison the entire Milky Way, the traffic cop who interrupts the movie show when He is about to plunge the knife into Her, who is naked in the shower. I want to eat a piece of black bread with cream cheese with you for dinner tonight. And this is your husband's declaration of love, he who is the most in love of all.

ALGA: My son!

LICHEN: Mother!

They kiss on the mouth. Noise of a jet flying overhead. The spot on the Boyfriend and the Girlfriend lights up.

GIRLFRIEND: Did you hear that? Is it the siren's song?

BOYFRIEND: No, it's the six-thirty jet.

GIRLFRIEND: How romantic! *(They freeze.)*

ALGA: It's the prisoners. We have to keep watch over them.

LICHEN: Why watch over them? Let them escape.

ALGA: Have you gone mad? Our ancestors left us in charge of them, Since our family has been in charge, not one couple has escaped alive from us.

LICHEN: Why not let them go free?

ALGA: There is an order of things. We must defend order.

LICHEN: I don't agree! I don't agree! *(He's "cooled down" by a wave that bathes him.)* Shit! *(The Alga laughs.)*

ALGA AND LICHEN: *(As they sink into the rock.)*
Gluglugluglugluglugluglug . . .

Their spot is turned off.

BOYFRIEND: Miss, since I met you I've realized that I can stop taking Excedrin.

GIRLFRIEND: *(Flattered.)* Sir!

BOYFRIEND: Since I met you I've known that the iridescent flowers on the hem of your dress were going to invade my existence and that there would be no response for me, either in building dodecahedrons or in listening to the chord of the "allegro enérgico ed appasionato" of Brahms' *Fourth Symphony*. I have known that there no longer will be any calm or tranquility for me until a sigh from your sky-blue mouth tells me that when your trachea swallows a sip of French cognac it feels compulsions only for me.

GIRLFRIEND: Oh! . . .

BOYFRIEND: For you I will industrialize my dodecahedrons and we will spend our honeymoon in the castles of Loire. We will be Medieval. I can no longer stand the age of the Ultrasonic.

GIRLFRIEND: Oh, how brave!

BOYFRIEND: Miss, I love you the way one loves a borrowed hankie, a stolen moment . . . The way that the madrepore love each other during the mating season.

GIRLFRIEND: *(Scandalized.)* Sir!

BOYFRIEND: Pardon me. I meant to say that I love you the way one loves a sunrise in Hyde Park; like a tree's first encounter with light, like the roar of a subway that passes, beckoning the suicide victim with its song.

GIRLFRIEND: *(Romantic.)* I believe that you truly love me . . .

BOYFRIEND: I love you like the man who at dusk awaits the
                   footsteps of a woman on the street. I love you like a
                   debaucher loves minors; like an addict loves drugs
                   when he doesn't get a fix on time.

GIRLFRIEND: Oh, how romantic! . . .

*They freeze. Their spot is turned off and the one for the seaweeds, who
remain in their rock, is turned on. The sound of the sea . . .*

LICHEN: Alga?

ALGA: Lichen?

LICHEN: (He sticks out a hand.) Come, sit here with me, in
                   front of the fireplace.

ALGA: (She sticks out a hand.) Is it lit?

LICHEN: Tell me about my grandparents, the Sea Lichen.
                   About my great-great-aunts, the Claudea Algae.
                   I've heard that they were very elegant.

ALGA: They were, my son—tall and elegant. You've
                   descended of noble blood, of this you can be sure.
                   We, the red seaweed, come from cleaner waters,
                   from the deepest part of the sea, there, where light
                   can't even reach.

LICHEN: Tell me about when I was little . . .

ALGA: Metallic stars were sparkling on the beach. The
                   silver sea reverberated . . . All the other seaweeds
                   were asleep. And I sang a siren's song for you. I
                   sang to you in my most tender voice. (The Alga
                   and the Lichen lift their heads out of the rock and,
                   instead of a "tender song," she sings.)
                   Pralalalalalalalalalalalalala! . . . At first I sang it to
                   you every night and then, because you liked it so
                   much, I recorded it on a cassette and put the tape
                   recorder next to your cradle . . . You were so clever!

All on your own, with your tiny lichen hands, you
turned the tape recorder on, at the right speed.

LICHEN: Mother!

ALGA: Son! *(They kiss on the mouth.)*

*The gentleman enters: lights on all the stage. The Boyfriend and the
Girlfriend remain frozen. The Alga and the Lichen draw apart.*

ALGA: Watch out! It's him!

LICHEN: He's coming here.

ALGA: *(Quickly.)* Hide!

LICHEN: *(Quickly.)* I don't want to.

ALGA: *(Quickly.)* Hide!

*She takes him by the hand and forces him to sink down into the rock
with her. The gentleman come forward. He stops. He's obviously in
conflict with himself. He makes a decision now: it's a renunciation. He
throws the butterfly net far away. He takes a few steps, moving away.
But, fatally, the rock attracts him. Little by little, he faces the rock and
slowly goes towards it. He observes the still hands of the Alga and the
Lichen. clasped together over the rock. A tear falls from his eyes. He
turns around and goes away hastily. He exits. Under the spot, which is
now the only light on stage, the Alga and the Lichen lift their heads up
out of the rock.*

LICHEN: He was crying . . .

ALGA: Don't trust him. He's dangerous.

LICHEN: He doesn't seem dangerous.

ALGA: He's capable of stretching out his hand and tearing
              us off the rock . . .

LICHEN: *(Ironic.)* Is that how he seduced you?

ALGA: I don't understand . . .

LICHEN:	Did he stretch out his hand and caress you? *(Without letting her answer.)* Or did you caress him? Tell me, Mother dear, did you caress him, did you seduce him?
ALGA:	Son, please . . .
LICHEN:	Yes, Mother dearest, you seduced him . . . You thought that I was asleep, but I saw you. He approached you, little by little . . . He seemed fascinated . . . He approached you on this very rock, here, in our bed . . .
ALGA:	So you weren't asleep! . . .
LICHEN:	He knelt down and brought his face down close, attracted by you. And you clung to him and kissed him. You kissed him, sticking to him and you covered his whole face. You were under him, spread all over his face; all of you was open to him. The sea was tranquil and every now and then the beam from the lighthouse flashed on the rock and lit you up. Lit us up . . . You stuck to his face and he was breathing, taking all of you in.
ALGA:	Well . . .
LICHEN:	*(He is not speaking to her anymore.)* He didn't want to hurt you. He waited until a wave covered you and he freed himself gently, little by little, just as he had approached you. One more wave and he took your tentacles off his face, carefully, until you were separated.
ALGA:	It's all over, forget it.
LICHEN:	He has not forgotten.
ALGA:	Nonsense. Human beings always forget.
LICHEN:	He was crying.
ALGA:	He'll get over it. Humans always do get over it.

LICHEN:	Not always.
ALGA:	How do you know that? He's a scientist. He's not interested just in me, but in all seaweeds. And in butterflies, too.
LICHEN:	He's not a scientist. He's a poet.
ALGA:	It's all the same. Let's not worry about minor details.
LICHEN:	You could have drowned him.
ALGA:	Maybe. If the embrace had lasted too long.
LICHEN:	When he approached you, Alga, how he looked at you! A drunken, absent look, but also a pleading look . . .
ALGA:	Forget it.
LICHEN:	Just for that I would like to be human. To get near a rock one night and look at an alga the way that he looked at you.
ALGA:	Well, I don't even remember now how he looked at me.
LICHEN:	Be quiet, listen . . . *(A silence. The sea can't be heard.)* Do you hear it, Alga? . . . It's the sea . . . That's how humans hear it. That's how humans breathe it . . .
ALGA:	Little Lichen, you scare me . . .

The spot on the Boyfriend and the Girlfriend lights up. The four charactrs on stage now speak in blank, neutral tones.

LICHEN:	Alga, let's go away from here.
GIRLFRIEND:	Let's go away from here.
BOYFRIEND:	We can't.
ALGA:	We can't.

GIRLFRIEND: The drunken boat will not come.

LICHEN: The drunken boat of freedom.

There is a change of tone; the characters lose their blank, neutral attitudes.

ALGA: Lichen, what are you saying?

BOYFRIEND: *(Amused.)* To escape through the wing of a palm tree. To escape through a fountain pen until becoming a fountain head.

GIRLFRIEND: Gerald, what are you saying?

BOYFRIEND: *(Amused.)* To escape through the keys of a typewriter until becoming the blue juice of a dead letter. To escape through the business world. To jump over Wall Street, to laugh at the stock market and be integrated into the world of Coleoptera and tadpoles. To raise the perfume of roses to the third power and spend an orgiastic night with the birch trees.

GIRLFRIEND: Gerald, you scare me.

LICHEN: *(Amused.)* To balance on the tightrope of a third-grade equation.

ALGA: Lichen, you scare me.

LICHEN: To escape through the letter *e* until becoming an *l*. To escape through all the Company & Companies, through the Ltds., through the Sons & Sons, and through the Smithsons & Brothers. To escape through all the dollar bills used to light up cigars, to reach the slippers of beautiful women teeming with whiskey. To escape through the multiplication table until being lost in calculators, through hyphens and diereses until following unknown arrows and sinking into taboos; to disappear among the zeroes minus zero, minus zero to the infinity of real numbers. To escape through the

>   lineal to the circular, through the immovable to the
>   terrestrial.

ALGA: Little Lichen!

LICHEN: Don't you ever call me little Lichen again, you old
                 whore.

The gentleman enters again. Lights on all the stage.

ALGA: Watch out! He's there again.

GIRLFRIEND: He's coming towards us.

ALGA: He's coming toward us.

GIRLFRIEND: What a different look . . .

*The gentleman approaches, in a decided manner. He stops in the middle
of the stage.*

ALGA: *(To the Lichen.)* Hide.

LICHEN: *(Quickly.)* I don't want to.

ALGA: *(Quickly.)* Hide.

LICHEN: *(Quickly.)* No!

*As before, she forces him to hide and they sink into the rock, but their
clasped hands remain outside. The gentleman takes out a pistol and
stretches his arm and fires in the opposite direction of the rock. The
Alga and Lichen's hand tremble along with the gunshot and they fall,
wounded. The Alga dies. The Lichen still has time to take her hand.*

LICHEN: Tell me about when I was little. *(He drops her hand
                 and dies as well.)*

GIRLFRIEND: He shot into the water. He's gone mad.

*The gentleman puts the pistol away, turns around and speaks to the
audience.*

GENTLEMAN: "Beauty will be convulsive. Or it will not be."

Carefree, he now walks in the direction of the couple, as if they were old friends.

GENTLEMAN: *(Taking off his hat.)* Good afternoon.

BOYFRIEND: Good afternoon.

GIRLFRIEND: Good afternoon.

The gentleman puts his hat on again. Carefree, he walks off and exits. On stage and under their respective spots, the Boyfriend and the Girlfriend are seated on the bench and the seaweeds' hands are over the rock. The sound of the sea is heard.

GIRLFRIEND: There is something strange in the air.

BOYFRIEND: It looks to me as if there are two red seaweeds floating on that rock.

They freeze. Their spot dims and is turned off. The spot on the seaweed dims as well. Lights out.

SCENE VII: THE GROUP

The violent color lights up all the stage. The bench with the motionless Boyfriend and Girlfriend is removed, while the seaweeds stand up, take off their "rock suit," and remain as Louise and Brijinski, wearing ridiculous underwear.

BRIJINSKI: What heat!

LOUISE: My knees are killing me!

Suddenly they realize that they're standing in front of the audience. They get embarrassed and leave. All the cast come back on stage, as "the group," with their scripts. The work light is turned on.

SOPHOCLES: And that's how the play ends. This one's very short.

BRIJINSKI: But there's a double murder.

CATHY:	(Sighing.) They were married!
LOUISE:	(To Sophocles.) You mean we were married by the Church and all?
BRIJINSKI:	That poor gentleman, the Alga's lover.
BOBBY:	(Knitting.) Don't worry about me: men, women, monkeys, lettuces . . . I'm not particular.
SOPHOCLES:	Bobby, what are you doing?
BOBBY:	(Angry.) I'm rehearsing for Lecocq. For the seaweed, I've already learned "all" my lines.
CATHY:	What I liked most was the line by the gentleman.
BOBBY:	"Beauty will be convulsive. Or it will not be."
CATHY:	What a great line! That's the best part of your play, Sophocles.
SOPHOCLES:	Thank you very much. But it's not original.
CATHY:	It's not?
SOPHOCLES:	No, it's in quotes in the text. It's André Breton's.
CATHY:	I blew it.
SOPHOCLES:	(He turns the page.) Fourth scene, last play. A parody of a musical comedy.
BOBBY:	This is where we'll really knock 'em dead.
SOPHOCLES:	Do you really think so?
BOBBY:	Well, the truth is, who knows.
BRIJINSKI:	(Alarmed.) A musical? We're going to need a revolving stage.
SOPHOCLES:	(Very dignified.) What do you take me for?

BOBBY:	When one is an actor, one does not need revolving stages. One makes them revolve!
BRIJINSKI:	And the orchestra?
SOPHOCLES:	We'll make do with recordings.
LOUISE:	*(Ironic.)* Because you're a real artist.
SOPHOCLES:	No. Because it's cheaper. *(Transition.)* The play is called *(With a Chicago accent.)* "Archie and Bonnie."
BRIJINSKI:	*(Happy to understand.)* It's English!
SOPHOCLES:	American. It's not only a musical, but a real U.S. of A. "meeusical." "Archie and Bonnie." Everything's upbeat, do you see? The American Way of Life. "My unforgettable character." Everything is edifying. Everyone is wholesome, like apple pie. Okay?
ALL THE CAST:	Okay!
BOBBY:	Sugar . . .
SOPHOCLES:	We'll look more at this later. For now it's enough to know that it's a melodramatic musical, that its realism is stupid, and that the music is *ad hoc.*

The music for the opening is played. A spot moves up through the house. The actors exit, dancing. On its own, the spot dances about as well, on the stage, the seats, the floor . . .

SCENE VIII: *ARCHIE AND BONNIE* (A PARODY IN ONE ACT)

SONGS (WORDS BY MARUXA VILALTA AND ORIGINAL MUSIC BY LUIS RIVERO)

The Poor People of the Future	Archie and Lenny
It's the Dollar!	Bonnie, Mrs. Marshall, and Morris
Will He Be Able To?	Morris, Archie, and Mrs. Marshall
His Conscience Has Spoken to Him	Morris and the Conscience
We'll Be Happy	Archie, Bonnie and Mrs. Marshall

The dancing spot comes to a stop. The Narrator enters, all smiles and optimism, and puts his face under the spot.

NARRATOR: *(Euphoric.)* Honored public. We are in the United States of America. The U.S.A.! Chicago! *(A placard saying "Chicago" is lowered.)* A city of pigs, gangsters, and big bucks. The action takes place in the house of Mrs. Marshall, a lady who suffers from a compulsive neurosis, for which she compensates by doing charitable deeds.

The lights change and he exits, at the same time that Mrs. Marshall and Morris enter.

MRS. MARSHALL: Please, my dear Morris, try to understand my situation. My charitable deeds are everything to me. If it weren't for my poor people I never would have sent my little daughter Bonnie away to boarding school because I didn't have time to take care of her.

MORRIS: Mrs. Marshall, you are very dangerous.

MRS. MARSHALL: And you, my dear Morris, are such a Junior Exec, so spiffy, so Junior, so filthy rich.

MORRIS: Filthy rich, yes. But not a Junior. My father died at the peak of his career *(An inside to the public.)*—this implacable Chicago—of a heart attack, leaving me as the sole heir to his marmalade factories. Since then, madam, I am not a Junior, but a Senior.

MRS. MARSHALL: Anyway, my dear Morris, you certainly look like a Junior, so spiffy, so full of marmalade, so filthy rich. I, on the other hand—widowed and alone—with my poor little helpless Bonnie. And with my poor people's shelter to maintain. If it weren't for my poor people I never would have sold you my daughter!

MORRIS: Please, don't speak of "selling" . . . Our agreement was that the day I married Bonnie, your many debts to me would be cancelled, debts that you

	never would be able to pay anyway. And as regards Bonnie, I don't want to be put off any longer.
MRS. MARSHALL:	Put off?
MORRIS:	Mrs. Marshall, please let me point out that among my finer qualities is that I'm a good American. And a good American should have, above all else, a sense of what is practical. I was taught to be practical ever since I was a little boy, since kindergarden. For that reason I won't mince words with you: I've paid your debts, I saved you from foreclosure on your house, I financed a new place for your poor people's shelter. Now I want to marry Bonnie.
MRS. MARSHALL:	Of course . . . What happened was that Bonnie didn't know about all the money I owed you. But she does now. I told her yesterday. So now she is madly in love and ready to get married.
MORRIS:	I hope so.
MRS. MARSHALL:	About my poor people . . . perhaps we could expand our horizons . . . Open another shelter, not just for young people, but for the elderly, the infirm—those who can't get away so easily— battered and abandoned wives, perhaps the war mutilated . . . When there is another war, which won't be long now.
MORRIS:	Mrs. Marshall, where is Bonnie?
MRS. MARSHALL:	She'll be here right away, Morris. In the meantime allow me to introduce you to my poor people . . . two young men from the shelter. They're in the next room . . . They have a surprise for you. (*Calling them.*) This way, boys, come in! . . .

Archie and Lenny enter, smiling, optimistic, wearing their little robes from the shelter.

MRS. MARSHALL: Morris, I want you to meet Archie and Lenny. Boys,
                  Mr. Morris William Jackson is your benefactor.

MORRIS: (*Flattered.*) Well . . . there is some truth to that.

MRS. MARSHALL: We've prepared a musical number in your honor,
                  Morris. It's called the "Asylum Song," I mean, the
                  "Shelter Home Sweet Shelter Song." Ready boys?

ARCHIE: We're ready Mrs. Marshall.

LENNY: Ready teddy!

Song: The Poor People of the Future (*Archie and Lenny*)

ARCHIE   We are . . .
AND LENNY: The poor people . . .
                  We are the happy poor people . . .

ARCHIE: He who doesn't hear never misses a beat

ARCHIE   We are the happy poor people . . .
AND LENNY: Perfectly, oh perfectly hygienic
                  Very aseptic
                  Full of pills, educated, manipulated, politicized . . .
                  Oh yea! Yea!
                  ....

ARCHIE: We're always fasting . . .

LENNY: Never, oh never annoying . . .

ARCHIE:·   We're always smiling . . .

LENNY: And never obstructing . . .

ARCHIE   We are the happy poor people . . .
AND LENNY: Among the truly, really saved
                  We're redeemed
                  Always beaming
                  Always pleasing, so well behaved
                  Oh yea! Yea!
                  ....

ARCHIE:	I don't cross the Iron Curtain, I'm not a communist.
LENNY:	I don't cross the Iron Curtain, I'm a capitalist.
ARCHIE AND LENNY:	Bones to the air, just like in Cambodia.
ARCHIE:	Day and night, we only have bread and water.
ARCHIE AND LENNY:	Oh yea! Oh Yea!

....

ARCHIE AND LENNY:	We are . . . we are the poor people We are . . . we are the poor people We are the poor people of the future! Oh yea! Yea . . . Yea!

They exit and come back on stage. Reprise, sung at a faster rhythm.

ARCHIE AND LENNY:	We are . . . we are the poor people We are . . . we are the poor people

Slowly

We are . . .
The poor people of the fu . . . ture!
Oh yea! Yea . . . Yea!

The song ends. Mrs. Marshall and Morris applaud.

MRS. MARSHALL:	Very good, very good! You can go now.
ARCHIE:	Good day.
LENNY:	Good day. *(Very polite and proper, they exit.)*
MRS. MARSHALL:	Charming, aren't they?
MORRIS:	Mrs. Marshall, would you please call your daughter?
BONNIE:	*(Entering.)* Here I am.

MORRIS: Oh, Bonnie, darling!

BONNIE: Morris, I've come to tell you *(Singing in a high-pitched voice.)* that I will not marry youuuuuu!

MORRIS: *(Singing.)* Bon.. . . . nie!

BONNIE: *(Singing in a low voice.)* I love someone el . . . . . . se!

MRS. MARSHALL: *(Singing.)* Someone else? . . . *(Speaking.)* Then what you want is to see your mother in jail? Ah! Oh! *(She faints.)*

BONNIE: *(Impatient.)* No, Mother, I don't want to see you in jail. Mother, what is wrong with you?

MRS. MARSHALL: *(Reviving.)* Well, if you don't want to see me in jail, you have to marry Morris. I already explained this to you.

BONNIE: I can't. I have a lover.

MRS. MARSHALL: A lover? Ah! Oh! *(She is about to faint but comes to immediately.)* You're too young. You don't know what a lover is. You'll marry Morris. Isn't that right, Morris?

MORRIS: Well . . . yes, I think you're right, Mrs. Marshall. I suppose that we could get married anyway. I'm a good American. I'm practical. I don't demand virginity.

MRS. MARSHALL: Ah, well then, everything is settled!

BONNIE: Thank you very much, Morris, but I'm not going to marry you.

MORRIS: Think about it, Bonnie. I'll give you some more time. *(He goes to exit.)*

MRS. MARSHALL: You're leaving!

MORRIS: If you don't mind, I'll excuse myself for the rest of the day. *(He exits.)*

MRS. MARSHALL: So this is the way you pay me back for everything that I've done for you since you were little. That boarding school cost me a fortune. What you want is for me to end up in jail!

BONNIE: No, Mother.

MRS. MARSHALL: Wait, Morris, I'll go with you! . . .

She goes after him. Archie enters cautiously from the other side of the stage. The lovers meet: if there were music it would surely be violin music.

BONNIE: Archie!

ARCHIE: Bonnie!

BONNIE: What are you doing here?

ARCHIE: Your mother wanted to hear the "Asylum Song," and I volunteered so that I could see you . . . I overheard everything.

BONNIE: I will not marry Morris. I love you, Archie.

ARCHIE: If you love me, I am more of a millionaire than him! Stronger than him! *(He flexes his puny biceps.)* In the shelter they teach us to be optimistic.

BONNIE: Let's be optimistic. Archie!

ARCHIE: Let's be optimistic, Bonnie!

They assume an optimistic pose, which will be the same one throughout the play.

BONNIE: We'll get married. I'll be . . . one of the poor people of the future!

ARCHIE: Bonnie, there's something I have to tell you. I'm not well.

BONNIE: What's the matter?

ARCHIE: A lump in this finger . . . Do you see it? They're going to have to operate on me.

BONNIE: Oh, Archie!

ARCHIE: Tomorrow. The doctors say that they might have to cut my finger off.

BONNIE: Oh, Archie! . . . Well, what's a finger?

ARCHIE: Maybe . . . maybe the whole hand.

BONNIE: The whole hand? . . . So, what's a hand? We'll get married even if you are missing a hand.

ARCHIE: *(Happy.)* Really, Bonnie?

BONNIE: Of course, Archie!

ARCHIE: That's my girl! . . .

They exit happily, while the Narrator enters from the opposite direction. Always euphoric, he announces:

NARRATOR: Two months later, in Morris's house. *(He waits, but nothing happens. Again, as an order.)* In Morris's house!

The lights change and a dollar sign is lowered onto the stage. Satisfied, the Narrator exits, at the same time that Morris, followed by Mrs. Marshall and Bonnie, enters from the other side of the stage.

MORRIS: Don't insist on it, ma'am, please. I cannot wipe off your debts. My lawyers already have taken action.

MRS. MARSHALL: To jail! Ah! Oh! *(She is about to faint.)*

MORRIS: *(Impatient.)* Mrs. Marshall!

MRS. MARSHALL: My God, what a house, what a palace! . . . Have you seen what a palace this is, Bonnie? Bonnie? Bonnie, where are you? *(She's right in front of her.)* Have you seen what a palace this is?

BONNIE: Yes, Mother, I have.

MRS. MARSHALL: This could be yours, my daughter. It could be ours.
                     Oh, my war—mutilated would be so comfortable
                     here!

BONNIE: Please, Mother.

MRS. MARSHALL: Morris, I must tell you that the poor crippled
                     Archie is still in the . . .

BONNIE: *(Interrupting.)* Don't call him a cripple.

MRS. MARSHALL: Is still in the hospital. And don't you worry about
                     him; he's out of the running now.

BONNIE: That's not true!

MORRIS: Mrs. Marshall, your time for paying up runs out
                     today and there's still been no wedding. My
                     lawyers have orders to proceed.

MRS. MARSHALL: To proceed? To proceed with what? . . . Oh, my
                     daughter, my daughter, help me!

BONNIE: Please, Morris . . . *(Melodramatic.)* Have Mercy!

Song: Its the Dollar! *(Bonnie, Mrs. Marshall and Morris.)*

BONNIE: Have mercy!

MRS. MARSHALL: Have mercy!

BONNIE: Have merrrcy!

TOGETHER: Mercy!

MORRIS: I am a good American . . . logical, practical, and
                     healthy.

BONNIE: Have mercy!

MRS. MARSHALL: Have mercy!

BONNIE: Have merrrcy!

TOGETHER: Mercy!

MORRIS: The dollar, the dollar is worth more.
                   And excuse me if I upset you a little . . .
                   But you Mother's directly off to jail.

BONNIE: No!

MORRIS: Yes!

MRS. MARSHALL: Oh!

MORRIS: Only a while her debts to liquidate! . . . Yes!

BONNIE AND
MRS. MARSHALL: He's white . . . Anglo-Saxon . . . He's Protestant . . .

MORRIS: I'm a racist! . . . I'm a fascist! . . . I'm a racist!

BONNIE: Logical . . . practical . . . and healthy . . .

MORRIS: Like every, every good American.

BONNIE: Have mercy!

MRS. MARSHALL: Have mercy!

BONNIE: Have merrrcy!

TOGETHER: Mercy!

MORRIS: The dollar, the dollar is worth more.

BONNIE: Do reconsiiiiiiider.

MRS. MARSHALL: Morris, Morris, please . . .

MORRIS: Nothing, nothing's worth more than the dollar . . .

From now until the song is over, Morris gets turned on by (read, mentally masturbates with), the idea of making money. At the same time, Bonnie and Mrs. Marshall begin a very sexual dance, which they occasionally interrupt to hold hands and pray. This same routine is repeated various times.

MORRIS: Up and down . . . down and up . . . up and down . . . down and up . . .

BONNIE AND
MRS. MARSHALL: *(Praying.)* He's white . . . Anglo-Saxon . . .

MORRIS: Up and down . . . it's the . . .

BONNIE AND
MRS. MARSHALL: *(Praying.)* He's Protestant . . . *(Sexual dance)*

MORRIS: Up and down . . . down and up . . . up and down . . . down and up

BONNIE AND
MRS. MARSHALL: *(Praying.)* Logical . . . practical . . .

MORRIS: Up and down . . . it's the . . .

BONNIE AND
MRS. MARSHALL: *(Praying.)* and healthy . . . *(Sexual dance)*

MORRIS: Up and down . . . down and up . . . up and down . . . down and up . . .

BONNIE AND
MRS. MARSHALL: *(Praying.)* A racist . . . a fascist . . .

MORRIS: Up and down . . . it's the . . .

BONNIE AND
MRS. MARSHALL: *(Praying.)* He's a racist . . . *(Sexual dance)*

MORRIS: Up and down . . . down and up . . . up and down . . . down and up . . . it's the . . . dollar!

MRS. MARSHALL: . . . Morris, please!

She faints and the song ends.

BONNIE:	*(Melodramatic.)* Morris, do it for me!
MORRIS:	Okay, I'll give you more time. *(Mrs. Marshall come to.)* But on one condition. Bonnie, the 26th of August is my birthday.
MRS. MARSHALL:	Oh, you're a Virgo!
MORRIS:	So it seems, ma'am. Bonnie, on the 26th of August the debts will be cancelled. But it's also the day that we'll be married.
BONNIE:	The 26th of August . . .
MRS. MARSHALL:	Ah, that's a long way away!
MORRIS:	*(To Bonnie.)* I'll give you time. I want you to be convinced of my love.
BONNIE:	But I love Archie.
MRS. MARSHALL:	Don't you mention that cripple again. *(Taking Bonnie with her.)* Let's go, before Morris regrets this.
BONNIE:	I love Arch . . .
MRS. MARSHALL:	Shut up! I forbid you to speak.
BONNIE:	I love Archie!
MRS. MARSHALL:	Poor little thing, she's not able to say anything else. Don't you worry Morris, I'll convince her.
MORRIS:	I warn you that there won't be another delay. My lawyers know what to do.
MRS. MARSHALL:	Know what to do, yes. *(To Bonnie, who wasn't going to say anything.)* Shut up!
BONNIE:	Shit!
MORRIS:	Quite a romantic farewell.

MRS. MARSHALL: Forgive her Morris, forgive her . . .

She goes out after Bonnie, followed by Morris. With his usual enthusiasm, the Narrator enters and announces:

NARRATOR: On the following day, at the hospital!

The dollar sign disappears and the lights change. A Red Cross logo is lowered onto the stage. The Narrator exits and Archie enters, wearing pajamas. He's missing an arm.

BONNIE: *(Entering.)* Archie, your arm! . . .

ARCHIE: Yes, Bonnie, they had to cut it off.

BONNIE: So, what's an arm? . . . Let's be optimistic, Archie!

ARCHIE: Let's be optimistic, Bonnie!

They assume their optimistic pose and Bonnie leaves, at the same time the Narrator enters, enthusiastically, from the opposite direction

NARRATOR: Time flies by!

He waits. Archie mutilates one of his legs, as the Narrator exits, satisfied.

BONNIE: Oh, Archie! Your leg!

ARCHIE: Yes, Bonnie . . . It couldn't be helped.

BONNIE: So, what's a leg? Let's be optimistic, Archie!

ARCHIE: Let's be optimistic, Bonnie!

He manages to assume an optimistic posture without falling down. She leaves, while the Narrator enters, from the opposite direction, pushing a wheelchair.

NARRATOR: Flies by.

He waits for Archie to sit down, with his one arm and now without any legs. Happy, the Narrator exits.

BONNIE:	(*Entering.*) Archie! . . . Your other leg!
ARCHIE:	Yes, Bonnie . . .
BONNIE:	Well, you still have one arm . . .
ARCHIE:	Bonnie, we can't let Mrs. Marshall go to jail. You'll have to marry Morris to save your mother.
BONNIE:	I'll marry him, but I'll never be his. I'll die first!
ARCHIE:	Let's not talk about dying.
BONNIE:	You're right! Let's be optimistic, Archie!
ARCHIE:	Let's be optimistic, Bonnie!

She adopts the optimistic pose and so does Archie, although he topples over. Bonnie leaves, at the same time that the Narrator enters from the opposite direction, taking Archie away in his wheelchair.

NARRATOR:	(*Happy.*) Flies by so quickly (*With one push, he shoves Archie's wheelchair off stage. Loud noises.*) that August 26th arrives. (*The sound of wedding bells. the Narrator pauses, moved by the occasion. Beaming, he immediately announces.*) The house of Mrs. Marshall!

The lights change and the Red Cross logo disappears. The Narrator exits and Mrs. Marshall enters, all dressed up for the wedding.

MRS. MARSHALL:	As for me, I'm ready. We can get married when you want. (*She waits for someone. She begins again.*) As for me, I'm ready. We can get married when you want. (*Bonnie enters, wearing her wedding dress.*) Bonnie, you look divine!
BONNIE:	(*Lost in thought.*) What day is today?
MRS. MARSHALL:	(*Solemn.*) My dear daughter, it's August 26th. Your wedding day, the happiest day of your life.
BONNIE:	The happiest . . . (*She exits.*)
MRS. MARSHALL:	These young people today . . . (*Morris enters from*

the opposite side, all dressed for the wedding.) Oh
Morris, how spiffy you look, how Junior, how
filthy rich! . . .

MORRIS: Thank you, ma'am, thank you. I'm a bit early
because I need to talk to you.

MRS. MARSHALL: Don't worry, Morris. We won't let you down. She's
already in her wedding dress. Bonnie and I will
marry you in an hour.

MORRIS: I need to ask you to talk to Bonnie so that she
won't . . . reject me.

MRS. MARSHALL: Oh, but she hasn't rejected you! We're just about to
go to the church.

MORRIS: I mean so that she won't reject me . . . tonight!

MRS. MARSHALL: Oh, well! That's your problem. That didn't enter
into our agreement, you know, that didn't enter
into the agreement.

MORRIS: Mrs. Marshall, the truth is that I have a problem.
It's something psychological . . . It seems that it's a
product of my childhood. A combination of an
Oedipus complex with retroactive inhibi . . . Oh
well, it's too long a story. In a nutshell, when I feel
rejected by a woman, I become impotent.

MRS. MARSHALL: Impoten . . . ! Who would have thought it of you!
So Junior, so filthy rich!

MORRIS: But only when I'm rejected!

MRS. MARSHALL: Oh well, then.

MORRIS: Mrs. Marshall, you're about to become my mother.
Make Bonnie see how much I love her. If she rejects
me tonight I won't be able to perform.

MRS. MARSHALL: Yes you will, my son!

MORRIS: No, I won't, Mommy! I won't! *(They continue talking.)*

NARRATOR: *(Entering, dynamic.)* Meanwhile, back at the hospital . . .

A little hospital area is lit up at one end of the stage, where the Red Cross logo is lowered again. The Narrator exits and immediately returns, pushing Archie in his wheelchair. He places it in the hospital area.

NARRATOR: Archie seems to have renounced the optimism of every good American. *(Disdainfully.)* Now he behaves just like an ordinary Latin lover: he's jealous. *(He exits.)*

Song: Will He Be Able To? *(Morris, Archie, and Mrs. Marshall)*

MORRIS: I could never make her mine . . . oh, not against her will.

ARCHIE: He could never make her his . . . oh, not against her will.

MRS. MARSHALL: Yes you will.

ARCHIE: Yes he will.

MORRIS: I will?

MRS. MARSHALL: You will!

ARCHIE: He will . . .

MORRIS: No!
                   ....

ARCHIE: He loves her, loves her too much.

MORRIS: I love her, love her too much.

ARCHIE: He loves her, loves her too much.

MORRIS: I love her, love her too much.

ARCHIE: He loves her, loves her too much.

MORRIS: I love her, love her too much.

MRS. MARSHALL: One can never love a woman
                   too much, too much!
                   ....

MORRIS: I have always been . . . very macho.

ARCHIE: He has always been very macho.

MRS. MARSHALL: You're a very macho . . . macho.

ARCHIE: I'm a very macho . . . macho.

MORRIS: But . . .

ARCHIE: But . . .

MRS. MARSHALL: But . . .

MORRIS: But I could never rape her.

MRS. MARSHALL: Rape her!

ARCHIE: Rape her?

MORRIS: Rape her!
                   ....

MRS. MARSHALL: On a wedding, wedding night
                   A little, little rape's not such a bad thing . . .

ARCHIE: On a wedding, wedding night . . .

ARCHIE and
MRS. MARSHALL: A little, little rape's not such a bad thing . . .
                   ....

MORRIS: I could never make her mine . . . oh, not against her
                   will.

ARCHIE: He could never make her his . . . oh, not against her
                     will.

MRS. MARSHALL: Yes you will.

ARCHIE: Yes he will.

MORRIS: I will?

MRS. MARSHALL: Yes you will!

ARCHIE: He will . . .
                     ....

ALL TOGETHER: On a wedding, wedding night
                     A little, little rape's not such a bad thing . . .

MORRIS: I won't be able to!

The song ends.

MORRIS: I won't be able to, Mommy, I won't be able to.

MRS. MARSHALL: Yes you will, my son, yes you will. *(They exit.)*

ARCHIE: *(Anguished.)* Will he?

*He also exits, rolling the wheelchair with his only remaining arm, at
the same time that the Narrator enters, happy.*

NARRATOR: At Morris's house!

*The lights change and the Red Cross logo is removed. The dollar sign is
lowered.*

NARRATOR: After the ceremony . . .

*The Narrator exits while Morris enters will Bonnie, in her wedding
dress.*

NARRATOR: *(Peeping onto the stage.)* Alone at last! *(He exits.)*

MORRIS: Bonnie . . . My wife, at last!

BONNIE:	*(Melodramatic.)* Morris, I will never be yours!
MORRIS:	But Bonnie, I love you . . . Don't you understand? I've done all of this because I love you.
BONNIE:	But I don't love you.
MORRIS:	You're cruel.
BONNIE:	I love Archie.
MORRIS:	That can't be . . . He doesn't have any money . . . He doesn't have any arms, he doesn't have any legs, he doesn't have anything.
BONNIE:	I love him. Not you. I will never love you! *(She leaves.)*
MORRIS:	Bonnie, wait! . . . She will never love me . . . I was wrong to make her marry me. It was blackmail, a vile deed . . . I was wrong, my conscience tells me this.
CONSCIENCE:	*(Entering, also dressed for the wedding.)* You were wrong.

Song: His Conscience Has Spoken to Him *(Morris and His Conscience)*

MORRIS:	My conscience has spoken to me
CONSCIENCE:	His conscience has spoken to him . . . Me!
MORRIS:	And has made me understand
CONSCIENCE:	And has made him understand
MORRIS:	That a love like this cannot be . . .
CONSCIENCE:	Like this . . . cannot be . . .
MORRIS:	I should never, never have insisted.
CONSCIENCE:	You should never, never have demanded

MORRIS:	Now she cannot love me . . . I'm just a fool I'm inhuman.
CONSCIENCE:	*(With a parrotlike voice.)* Barbarian!
MORRIS:	Heartless and irrational
CONSCIENCE:	You stupid animal . . .

. . . .

MORRIS:	My conscience has spoken to me
CONSCIENCE:	His conscience has spoken to him . . . Me!
MORRIS:	And has made me understand
CONSCIENCE:	And I've made him understand
MORRIS:	That everything has failed me . . .
CONSCIENCE:	And will fail you again;
MORRIS:	I should never, never have insisted
CONSCIENCE:	You should never, never have demanded
MORRIS:	Now she cannot love me

. . . .

	I do repent! . . .
CONSCIENCE:	That's not practical!
MORRIS:	I do repent . . .
CONSCIENCE:	That's anarchical!
MORRIS:	I do repent . . .
CONSCIENCE:	Paradoxical!
MORRIS:	I do repent . . .
CONSCIENCE:	It's not logical!

MORRIS:	I'm no longer logical.
CONSCIENCE:	No, that's not healthy!
MORRIS:	I'm no longer healthy . . .
CONSCIENCE:	It's inhuman
MORRIS:	I'm no longer . . .
CONSCIENCE:	You're no longer . . .
TOGETHER:	A good, a good American! . . .

The song ends.

MORRIS:	It's all over! *(He exits.)*
CONSCIENCE:	*(Like a homosexual.)* It's all over! *(He exits.)*
MRS. MARSHALL:	*(She enters, pushing Archie, dressed in pajamas, in his wheelchair. His other arm has been cut off.)* What insanity, boy, what insanity! . . . I don't know how Lenny could have brought you here.
ARCHIE:	Pushing the little wheelchair, Mrs. Marshall.
MRS. MARSHALL:	You cannot see Bonnie. This is her wedding night.
BONNIE:	*(Entering, in her wedding dress.)* Archie!
ARCHIE:	Bonnie!
BONNIE:	Oh, Archie! . . . Your other arm! . . .
ARCHIE:	Yes, Bonnie. All that's left is . . . my little stumpy torso.
BONNIE:	I love you, Archie! I want to marry you!
MRS. MARSHALL:	But my dear child, you're already married. Oh, these young people today! . . .
BONNIE:	*(She takes out a pistol and sings.)* I'll kill mysellllf!

MRS. MARSHALL: Bonnie!

BONNIE: How can I give it to you?

The pistol falls to the floor. Morris enters with another pistol and goes toward Bonnie and Archie.

ARCHIE: No, Bonnie, no!

BONNIE: Then I'll kill Morris.

ARCHIE: *(Macho.)* Give me that pistol. I'll kill him!

BONNIE: *(She tries to give him the pistol.)* Be careful; don't go and hurt your little hands . . . I mean, don't go and hurt yourself.

ARCHIE: *(Macho.)* Give me the pistol!

BONNIE: How can I give it to you?

The pistol falls to the floor. Morris enters with another pistol and goes towards Bonnie and Archie.

MRS. MARSHALL: No, Morris, my son!

MORRIS: I've lost my sense of what's practical. I'm dishonored. *(He aims the pistol at himself and shoots. He falls.)* I've left everything to my wife. She's my sole beneficiary. *(He dies, with a smile on his face.)*

NARRATOR: *(Entering.)* A dead body always gets in the way of a happy ending. *(He drags the body off stage.)*

MRS. MARSHALL: Did you hear what Morris said? We're the sole beneficiaries. We're millionaires! My daughter, you're a widow! You can marry the cripple.

BONNIE: Mother!

MRS. MARSHALL: I mean this young man . . . this little piece of charming young man.

LENNY: *(Entering, as he changes roles from the Narrator into*

Lenny.) So Morris finally did something worthwhile.

ARCHIE: Lenny, where were you?

LENNY: Around and about, playing at being the Conscience . . . I mean, the Narrator.

BONNIE: Archie, we can get married!

ARCHIE: Do you think so, Bonnie?

BONNIE: Of course! What's wrong with you?

ARCHIE: I only said it because of my health . . .

LENNY: What do you mean you health! The doctors have already released you from the hospital . . . There was nothing left to cut off.

ARCHIE: No, there was nothing left.

LENNY: Now don't you go catching a cold. (*He wraps Archie's pajama sleeves around him like a scarf.*)

BONNIE: Let's be optimistic, Archie!

ARCHIE: Let's be optimistic, Bonnie!

Bonnie assumes the optimistic pose, while Archie stretches his little stump-body next to her.

MRS. MARSHALL: What a moving sight!

LENNY: (*About to cry.*) What a sight! (*He exits.*)

Song: We'll Be Happy (*Archie, Bonnie, and Mrs. Marshall*)

BONNIE: We will . . . we will be happy . . .

ARCHIE: We will be happy . . .

MRS. MARSHALL: They will . . . they will be happy . . .

ARCHIE AND BONNIE:	Oh happiness, oh happiness.
ALL TOGETHER:	Oh happiness, oh happiness.

....

BONNIE:	Me in the kitchen, You in your little chair
ARCHIE:	You in the kitchen Me in my little chair, Me in the office
BONNIE:	*Me* in the office You in your little chair My love, my little love, my love . . .

....

Me in the kitchen,
You in your little chair

ARCHIE:	You in the kitchen Me in my little chair, Me in the office
BONNIE:	*Me* in the office You in your little chair, My love, my little stump . . .

....

ARCHIE:	You'll be my wife, my wife, my little, little wife . . .
BONNIE:	I'll always feed you through your little, little mouth . . .

....

Me in the kitchen,
You in your little chair

ARCHIE:	You in the kitchen Me in my little chair, I'll go to work
BONNIE:	*I'll* go to work And you'll play with the children In the cute garden of love . . .

ARCHIE AND BONNIE:	In our cute garden of happiness . . .
	....
BONNIE:	Me in the kitchen
MRS. MARSHALL:	You in your little chair
ARCHIE:	*(To Bonnie.)* You in the kitchen Me in my little chair
MRS. MARSHALL:	Me in the office
ARCHIE AND BONNIE:	*Me* in the office
BONNIE:	You in your little chair My love, my little stump . . .
	....
ARCHIE:	You'll be my wife, my wife, my little, little wife . . .
BONNIE AND MRS. MARSHALL:	I'll always feed you through your little, little mouth . . .
	....
ALL TOGETHER:	Me in the kitchen
BONNIE AND MRS. MARSHALL:	You in your little chair
ARCHIE:	*(To Bonnie.)* You in the kitchen Me in my little chair, I'll go to work
BONNIE:	*I'll* go to work And you'll only play with the children
BONNIE AND MRS. MARSHALL:	In the cute garden of love . . .
ALL TOGETHER:	In our garden of love, garden of love . . .
	....

Softly.

BONNIE: Me in the kitchen

MRS. MARSHALL: You in your little chair

ARCHIE: *(To Bonnie.)* You in the kitchen
                     Me in my little chair,
                     I'll go to work

BONNIE: I'll go to work

Beaming.

BONNIE AND
MRS. MARSHALL: And you'll play very happily
                     With the children in the garden . . .

ALL TOGETHER: With the children in the garden
                     Which will be our Eden, which will be our love
                         nest, will be our happiness, our Eden, will be
                         our love nest, will be our happiness, our
                         happiness . . .

They exit and return; reprise.

BONNIE AND
MRS. MARSHALL: And you'll play very happily

ALL TOGETHER: With the children in the garden
                     Which will be our love nest, will be our
                         happiness . . .

*The song ends. Archie, Bonnie, and Mrs. Marshall freeze, while the
Narrator speaks.*

NARRATOR: *(Entering, euphoric.)* And they were happy! And
                     they had many children!

*Curtain call music for "Archie and Bonnie." The actors wave and
dance, under the house spot, they exit.*

SCENE IX: THE GROUP

The dollar sign and the placard saying "Chicago" disappear, while the actors come back on stage, as "the group," with their scripts and still dancing. The work light is turned on.

SOPHOCLES:	Well, that's it. The reading's over. *(He closes the script.)*
BOBBY:	*(Ironic.)* so short?
CATHY:	*(Romantic.)* And they had many children!
BRIJINSKI:	Many children? So, how did we do?
LOUISE:	*(To Sophocles.)* You always did want me to be the mother-in-law.
CATHY:	The bad thing is that I don't know how to sing.
BRIJINSKI:	Me either.
SOPHOCLES:	You'll have to learn in two months.
BOBBY:	One is or one is not an actor.
SOPHOCLES:	That's it for today; let's go home. Don't forget your scripts. *(He goes down into the house.)* We start rehearsals tomorrow. Same time. I won't allow any delays.
LOUISE:	Sophocles, I wanted to tell you . . .
SOPHOCLES:	Is it about the play?
LOUISE:	*(Angry.)* No, it's not about the play.
SOPHOCLES:	Then, until tomorrow. Be on time, everybody. *(He goes out through the house.)*
LOUISE:	Sophocles . . . *(To the others, angry.)* Until tomorrow.
BOBBY:	Mr. Producer, do you have a car? Can you give me a ride?

BRIJINSKI: Can we give you a ride, Cathy?

CATHY: No thanks. My fellow is coming to pick me up . . .
                            (She exits.)

BRIJINSKI: *(Sighing.)* Cathy! . . .

BOBBY: *(Like an impatient spouse.)* Darling, I'm waiting for
                            you.

BRIJINSKI: Let's go! *(He goes out through the house.)*

BOBBY: *(Going out after him.)* I'm coming, darling. I'm
                            coming. Wait for me, my queen . . .

SCENE X: THE GROUP

*Sophocles paces back and forth, wearing Rodger's shirt and pants; he
reviews the placement of spots, the flies, the stage legs, etcetera, while a
recording is played: the tic-toc of a clock; a coo-coo sounds nine times.
The murmur of voices and comments from the public gathered in the
lobby is heard.*

SOMEONE ARRIVING
LATE: Nine o'clock!

ANOTHER PERSON
IN A HURRY: Are they going to start already?

A YOUNG WOMAN: I have an extra ticket.

A HOMOSEXUAL: They offered me a part but I threw it back in their
                faces.

A GOSSIP: They say the play's no good.

SOMEONE NAIVE: I was told that it's very good.

THE HOMOSEXUAL: Freddy, how are you?

A SNOB: Ugh! Experimental theater!

THE YOUNG WOMAN: And who did you come with?

THE HOMOSEXUAL: And I didn't even get an invitation.

THE GOSSIP: They're disorganized.

A COUNTRY BUMPKIN: Excuse me, but is this the Roxy Theater?

THE HOMOSEXUAL: Another opening; what a drag!

THE GOSSIP: I hear that they're really a disaster, a disaster.

SOPHOCLES: Come on, come on, hurry up! Who's not ready? *(He exits and can be heard off stage.)* There are people in the lobby already. Who's not ready? *(He enters.)* Hurry up. It's opening night, opening night . . . *(He exits.)*

CATHY: *(Entering, dressed as Cynthia, with Louise, who is dressed as Elizabeth.)* So soon? Have two months gone by already?

LOUISE: What is time in the theater? The blinking of an eyelid . . . I just love these old-time curtains. *(She looks out at the house through a hole in the imaginary curtains.)*

CATHY: Let's see, let me see . . . *(She looks through the hole.)* An empty house is always impressive.

LOUISE: A full house is more impressive.

They exit and Bobby enters. He has his wig on and is wearing the Counsellor's shirt and pants. He's carrying the Nanny's wig and Archie's robe. He's also carrying his script.

BOBBY: Actress Number Two's wig goes on stage leg number one . . . *(He goes towards it.)* No. Actress Number One's wig goes on stage leg number two. *(He goes there and leaves the wig.)* Little Jacovlovichovich's robe *(He kisses it.)* goes on stage leg number seven. No, on number five. *(He leaves the robe there.)* And the goddamned checkered tablecloth goes on leg number six. *(He leaves the tablecloth there and takes notes.)* Light Six B has been moved to light Six C and track Nine A hasn't been struck . . . Considering that we couldn't even afford a stage assistant . . .

LOUISE: *(Demanding as she enters.)* Hey, Sophocles, I want you to know that at yesterday's rehearsal . . . Where's Sophocles?

BOBBY: *(Without looking up from his script.)* He's around here somewhere . . . *(Louise leaves.)* I've checked my net for catching butterflies. *(He looks through the hole in the imaginary curtain.)* Doctor, if you don't come to my opening I won't have anything to do with you ever again.

BRIJINSKI: *(Entering, wearing his ridiculous Lichen underpants.)* Look, Bobby, they finished my wardrobe on time. How does it look?

BOBBY: You fool! What are you dressed as a Chondrus Crispus for? Don't you remember that you come on stage as the brother of your brother, as Abel; no, as Cain, you come in as Arthur, you fool!

BRIJINSKI: *(He leaves, running.)* I'm going to change.

BOBBY: You turned me down, baby . . . *(Transition.)* The weeg, I mean the wig of Actress . . . Bobby, not even if you were a beginner . . . Bobby, Bobby, don't get noivus, I mean, nervous . . . *(He exits.)*

LOUISE: *(Entering.)* Sophocles, Sopho . . . where is the goddamned director?

SOPHOCLES: *(Entering.)* Here I am, Louise. How are you doing for time? What do you have to do today, for example, after the opening?

LOUISE: *(Happy.)* Today? . . . Nothing, Sophocles, nothing! I don't have anything to do!

SOPHOCLES: *(Exiting with her.)* Let's go to your place.

LOUISE: I invite you to have tea. *(They exit.)*

BOBBY: *(Entering, with an imaginary microphone.)* Okay, okay, the fricking microphone doesn't work. *(He blows into it, inspects it. He turns on the switch.)* Well, yes, it does work; it was turned off. No, it's just that the debut of *la Brijinski* is driving me mad, mad, mad ... *(He exits.)*

BRIJINSKI: *(Wearing Arthur's pants and shirt, he enters rehearsing.)* I'll kill him! I'll shoot that son of a bitch of a brother! *(He changes characters and becomes Mr. Mercier.)* I know she was speaking English. *(He changes again and becomes the Lichen.)* Don't you ever call me Little Lichen again, you little whore.

SOPHOCLES: *(Entering.)* Nervous?

BRIJINSKI: *(He jumps with fright.)* No, no, not nervous at all. *(Bold, like a Conquistador.)* I'm going to take on the whole bunch of them—Elizabeth, Matilde, the maid, Bonnie, and the Alga ... and I'll be right back. *(He exits.)*

BOBBY: *(Entering.)* We're ready.

SOPHOCLES: I gave instructions that the audience be let into the house. Bobby, you give the first call.

BOBBY: I'll give the first call.

They are about to exit, from opposite directions, when they freeze.

CATHY: *(Off stage.)* They're going to give the first call.

LOUISE: *(Off stage.)* What's wrong with you? They're going to give the third call.

SOPHOCLES: Bobby, you give the third call.

BOBBY: I give the third call.

They exit, going where they were headed before. Immediately, Bobby returns and in playback, he does his routine, like a vedette, passing the imaginary microphone chord back and forth between his legs.

RECORDING: *(Bobby's voice.)* Attention, your attention please. Third call. Will the audience please be seated. Third call. The performance is about to begin.

Bobby exits and Sophocles enters, putting on Rodger's suit jacket. He crosses the stage to take his place and meets Brijinski, who enters carrying Arthur's jacket. Playfully, Sophocles startles him.

SOPHOCLES: Arthur!

BRIJINSKI: *(He's about to cry.)* Rodger?

SOPHOCLES: Good luck. *(He exits. Brijinski puts on the jacket and places the chair on stage.)*

BRIJINSKI: *(Melodramatic.)* Beaten down by life!

With the same posture as in Scene I, Brijinski collapses into the chair and is transformed into Arthur. At the same time, Beethoven's Fifth Symphony begins, the lights for "In Long Island, That Night" are turned on all at once and the bar and the chandelier are suddenly lowered onto the stage. An imaginary curtain has just been opened and the performance begins. Arthur serves himself a drink. Rodger enters.

RODGER: *(Melodramatic.)* Arthur!

ARTHUR: *(Melodramatic.)* Rodger! . . .

The music becomes louder and drowns their voices. They continue action without being heard, in a comically accelerated rhythm, while the stage lights are turned off in sections. The actors freeze. Lights out.

Note

1. For permission to stage the play, contact the author at: Aristóteles 352, Colonia Polanco, 11550 México, D.F. Tel. and Fax: (525) 545 0615.

Bibliography

Playwrights: Primary and Secondary Sources

AGUIRRE, ISIDORA

Children's Literature

Don Anacleto Avaro. (Children's play.) In *Antología* and *Cuadernos de Teatro,* ed. Rubén Sotoconil. Santiago: Ministerio de Educación, 1982.

Títeres. Santiago: Editorial Zig Zag, 1945. Also in *Teatro chileno en un acto: Obras para escolares y grupos aficionados.* Santiago: Editorial Zig Zag, 1990.

Wai-Kii. (Children's novel.) Santiago: Editorial Rapa Nui, 1948.

Novels

Carta a Roque Dalton. Barcelona: Plaza & Janes Editores, 1990.

Doy por vivido todo lo soñado. Barcelona: Plaza & Janes Editores, 1987.

Plays

Carolina o la eterna enmascarada, comedia en un acto. Santiago: Editorial Zig Zag, 1960. Also in *Teatro chileno actual.* Santiago: Editorial Zig Zag, 1966, 54–74.

Diálogos de fin de siglo. Santiago: Editorial Torsegel, 1989.

Lautaro: Epopeya del pueblo mapuche. Santiago: Editorial Nascimento, 1982.

"La leyenda de las tres Pascualas." (Unpublished.)

Los libertadores, Bolívar y Miranda. Santiago: Ediciones LAR, 1993.

Los papeleros. Santiago: Mapocho, 1964. Also Mexico City: Ediciones de Andrea, 1972 and Santiago: Editorial Torsegel, 1989.

La pérgola de las flores. Santiago: Editorial Andrés Bello, 1986.

Población Esperanza. (Unpublished, 1959.)

Los que se van quedando en el camino. Santiago: Imprenta Müller, 1970. Also in *Revista Conjunto,* 1969.

Retablo de Yumbel. Concepción, Chile: Ediciones Literatura Americana Reunida, 1987. Also Havana: Casa de las Américas, 1987 and in

Dramaturgas latinoamericanas contemporáneas (Antología crítica), ed. Elba Andrade and Hilde F. Cramsie. Madrid: Editorial Verbum, 1991, 71–111.
Y éramos entonces un pequeño género humano. (Unpublished.)

Short Stories

Ocho cuentos. Santiago: Editorial Zig Zag, 1945.

Works in Translation

Express for Santiago. In *The Best Short Plays, 1959–1960.* Boston, Mass.: Beacon Press, 1960.
Die guten Tage, die schelchten Tage. Berlin: Henshelverlag, 1975.

Criticism

Agosín, Marjorie. "Isidora Aguirre: *Carolina o la eterna enmascarada.*" *Letras Femeninas* 5, 1 (1979): 97–100.
Aguirre, Isidora. "Sobre mi teatro." *Teatro chileno actual.* Santiago: Empresa Editorial Zig-Zag, 1966, 51–53.
Andrade, Elba. "Isidora Aguirre." *Critical Survey of Drama.* Foreign Language Series, volume 1. Pasadena, Calif.: Salem Press, 1986, 31–38.
Bello, Enrique. "Isidora Aguirre define los móviles de su teatro." *Ultramar* 4 (1960): 1–9.
Bisset, Judith I. "Delivering the Message: *Gestus* and Aguirre's *Los papeleros.*" *Latin American Theatre Review* 17, 2 (1984): 31–37.
Bravo Elizondo, Pedro. "*Ranquil* y *Los que van quedando en el camino*: Dos acercamientos a un mismo tema." *Texto Crítico* 4, 10 (1978): 76–85.
Dial, Eleanore Maxwell. "Brechtian Aesthetics in Chile: Isidora Aguirre's *Los papeleros* (The Garbage Collectors)." In Miller and Tatum, 85–90.
Fernández, Teodosio. *El teatro chileno contemporáneo (1941–1973).* Madrid: Editorial Playor, 1982, 46–49 and 97–98.
González, Patricia. "Isidora Aguirre y la reconstrucción de la historia en *Lautaro.*" *Latin American Theatre Review* 19, 1 (Fall 1985): 13–18.
Hurtado, María de la Luz. *Sujeto social y proyecto histórico en la dramaturgia chilena actual.* Santiago: CENECA, 1983.
Piña, Juan Andrés, ed. *Teatro chileno en un acto (1955–1985).* Santiago: Teatro Taller, 1989.

Rodríguez, Orlando, and Domingo T. Piga. *Teatro chileno del siglo xx*. Santiago: Universidad de Chile, 1964: 97–99.

Valenzuela, Víctor M. "Isidora Aguirre: *Los papeleros*." In *Siete comediógrafas hispanoamericanas*. Bethlehem, Pa.: Lehigh University Press, 1975, 57–69.

Villegas, Juan. "Los marginados como personajes: Teatro chileno de la década de los sesenta," *Latin American Theatre Review* 19, 2 (Spring 1986): 85–93.

BERMAN, SABINA

Novels

La bobe. Mexico City: Editorial Planeta Mexicana, 1990.
Un grano de arroz. Mexico City: Seix Barral, 1994.

Plays

Bill. In *Teatro joven de México*, ed. Emilio Carballido, 123–171. Mexico City: Editores Mexicanos Unidos, 1979.

Entre Villa y una mujer desnuda. Mexico City: SOGEM, 1992. Also Mexico City: Ediciones El Milagro, 1994.

Entre Villa y una mujer desnuda, Muérte súbita, El suplicio del placer. Mexico City: Grupo Editorial Gaceta, 1994.

La grieta. Tramoya (Cuaderno de Teatro, Edición por el XV aniversario Primera y Segunda Epoca. Antología: Tomo II, Teatro Mexicano), 1990, 7–40.

Muérte súbita. Mexico City: Editorial Katún, 1988.

Rompecabezas. Mexico City: Editorial Oasis, 1983.

Teatro de Sabina Berman. Mexico City: Editores Mexicanos Unidos, 1985. [Contains *Yankee, Herejía, Rompecabezas, Aguila o sol* and *El suplicio del placer*.]

Poetry

Lunas. Mexico City: Editorial Katún, 1988.
Poemas de agua. Mexico City: Editorial Shanik, 1986.

Other Publications

Co-authored with José Gordon. *Volar, la tecnología Maharishi del campo unificado*. Mexico City: Editorial Posada, 1987.

Works in Translation

Entre Pancho Villa et une femme nue. In *Le teatre mexicain.* Veracruz: Editora del Gobierno del Estado de Veracruz, 1993.
Heresy. Trans. Tim Klinger. (Unpublished.)

Criticism

Burgess, Ronald. *The New Dramatists of Mexico: 1967–1985.* Lexington: University Press of Kentucky, 1991, 80–91.
———. "Sabina Berman's Act of Creative Failure: *Bill.*" *Gestos* 2, 3 (April 1987): 103–113.
———. "Sabina Berman's Undone Threads." (Forthcoming.)
Costantino, Roselyn. "Resistant Creativity: Interpretative Strategies and Gender Representation in Contemporary Women's Writing in Mexico." *DAI* 53 (1992): 824A–25A. Arizona State University.
Cypess, Sandra Messinger. "Dramaturgia femenina y transposición histórica." *Alba de América* 7, 12–13 (July 1989): 283–304.
———. "Ethnic Identity in the Plays of Sabina Berman." In *Tradition and Innovation: Reflections on Latin American Jewish Writing,* ed. Robert E. DiAntonio and Nora Glickman. Albany: State University of New York Press, 1993, 165–177.
———, David R. Kohut, and Rachelle Moore. *Women Authors of Modern Hispanic South America: A Bibliography of Literature, Criticism, and Interpretation.* Metuchen, N.J.: Scarecrow Press, 1989.
Gil, Lydia. "Sabina Berman: Writing the Border." *Postcolonial Perspectives* (Spring 1994): 37–55.

CASAS, MYRNA

Plays

Absurdos en soledad. In *Teatro.* San Juan: Editorial Cordillera, 1964, 7–114.
Cristal roto en el tiempo. (Pausa dolorosa en dos actos y una voz.) In *Teatro Puertorriqueño, Tercer Festival.* San Juan: Instituto de Cultura Puertorriqueña, 1961, 259–349.
Cuarenta años después. San Juan, 1975. (Unpublished.)
Eugenia Victoria Herrera. In *Teatro.* San Juan: Editorial Cordillera, 1964, 115–241.
El gran circo Eukraniano. (Unpublished.)
Tres obras de Myrna Casas. Madrid: Editorial Playor, 1987. [Includes *Cristal roto en el tiempo, La trampa* and *Tres,* which in turn contains

"Loa," "No se servirá almuerzo a Anita Milán o La historia trágica de las plantas plásticas," "Quitatetu: paseo a toda velocidad," and "Eran tres y ahora son cuatro."]

La trampa. El impromptu de San Juan. Río Piedras: Editorial Universitaria, 1974.

Anthologies

Teatro de la vanguardia: Contemporary Spanish American Theatre. Lexington, Mass.: D. C. Heath, 1975.

Criticism

Cypess, Sandra M. "*Eugenia Victoria Herrera* and Myrna Casa's Redefinition of Puerto Rican National Identity." In *Essays in Honor of Frank Dauster,* ed. Sandra M. Cypess and Kirsten F. Nigro. Newark, Delaware: Juan de la Cuesta-Hispanic Monographs, 1995, 181–194.

Panico, Marie J. "Myrna Casas: Nacional y trascendente." *Alba de América* 7, 12–13 (1989): 411–418.

Umpierre, Luz María. "Introducción al teatro de Myrna Casas." *Third Woman* 1, 2 (1982): 52–58.

———. "Inversiones, niveles y participación en *Absurdos en soledad* de Myrna Casas." *Latin American Theatre Review* 17, 1 (Fall 1983): 3–13.

Unruh, Vicky. "A Moveable Space: The Problem of Puerto Rico in Myrna Casas's Theater." In *Latin American Women Dramatists: Theater, Texts, and Theories,* ed. Larson/Vargas. (Forthcoming.)

Waldman, Gloria F. "Myrna Casas: dramaturga y directora." *Revista del Instituto de Cultura* (Puerto Rico) 21, 78 (enero/marzo 1978): 1–9.

———. "Three Female Playwrights Explore Contemporary Latin American Reality: Myrna Casas, Griselda Gambaro, Luisa Josefina Hernández." In *Latin American Women Writers: Yesterday and Today,* ed. Yvette E. Miller and Charles M. Tatum. Pittsburgh, Pa.: Carnegie-Mellon, 1977, 75–84.

MARICHAL, TERESA

Plays

Amor de medianoche. (Unpublished, 1984.)
Blip Blap. (Unpublished, 1980.)
Caos. (Unpublished, 1981.)

Cassandra. (Unpublished, 1981.)

Cortaron a Elena. (Unpublished, 1982.)

Dranki. (Unpublished, 1982.)

Las horas de los dioses nocturnos. (Unpublished, 1976.)

Jong Sang Doo Jong Sang Doo: La tierra donde los esclavos son vendidos. (Unpublished, 1984.)

Kataplum-Kataplom. (Unpublished, 1984.)

Mermelada para todos. (Unpublished, 1984.)

El parque más grande de la ciudad. (Unpublished, 1980.)

Paseo al atardecer. Revista Intermedio de Puerto Rico, Revista de Teatro Puertorriqueño 2, 1 (enero-marzo, 1986): 21–39.

Pastinote. (Unpublished, 1983.)

Pista de circo. (Unpublished, 1980.)

Prohibido hablar. (Unpublished, 1981.)

La tragedia del amor de Frankestein. (Unpublished, 1983.)

Trilogy: Divertimento liviano, Parque para dos, and *A Capella.* (Unpublished, 1979).

Vlad. In *Dramaturgas latinoamericanas contemporáneas (Antología crítica),* ed. Elba Andrade and Hilda F. Cramsie. Madrid: Verbum, 1991, 261–274.

Yo, una prisionera de guerra. (Unpublished, 1981.)

Xion o canto a la vida. (Unpublished, 1979.)

Criticism

Ramos-Perea, Ramón. "Puerto Rico: Perspectivas de la nueva dramaturgia nacional." *Tramoya* 2 Nueva Epoca (enero–marzo, 1985): 3–27.

———. "Actividad teatral en Puerto Rico (1985–1986)." *Gestos* 1 (abril 1986): 183.

RAZNOVICH, DIANA

Cartoons

Cables Pelados. Buenos Aires: Editorial Ludica, 1987.

Narrative

Mater erótica. Barcelona: Robin Books, 1992.

Para que se cumplan todos tus deseos. Madrid: Exadra de Ediciones, 1988.

Indira Gandhi, el imposible término medio. Madrid: Exadra de Ediciones, 1989.

Plays

Casa matriz. Buenos Aires: Ediciones Croquiñol, 1988.
Desconcierto. In *Teatro Abierto 1981: Volumen II*, ed. Osvaldo Pellettieri. Buenos Aires, 1992, 315–322.
Efectos personales. (Unpublished.)
Jardín de otoño. Buenos Aires: Subsecretaría de Cultura, Dirección Provincia de Buenos Aires, 1985.
Paradise y otros monólogos. Buenos Aires: Nuevo Teatro. (Forthcoming.)
Plumas blancas. Buenos Aires: Ediciones Dédalos, 1974.
Plumas blancas, plumas negras. (Unpublished.)
Teatro completo de Diana Raznovich. Buenos Aires: Ediciones Dédalos. (Forthcoming.)

Poetry

Tiempo de amar y otros poemas. Buenos Aires: Ediciones Nuevo Día, 1963.
Caminata en tu sombra. Buenos Aires: Editorial Stilcograf, 1964.
De personajes altos, imposibles. Buenos Aires: Editorial Stilcograf, 1966.
Parte del todo. Buenos Aires: Editorial Mares del Sur, 1968.

Works in Translation

Herbstzeilose. Trans. Fischer Verlag.
Konzert des Schweigens. Trans. Fischer Verlag.
Lost Belongings, in *Argentine Jewish Theatre: A Critical Anthology*, ed. Nora Glickman. Lewisburg, Pa.: Bucknell University Press, 1996.
Mater erótica. Frankfurt: Eichborn Verlag, 1992.
Oliverio Pan, Magier (Para que se cumplan todos tus deseos). St. Gallen: Edition dia, 1992.
Personliche Sachen. Trans. Fischer Verlag, 1990.
Weisse Federn, Schwarze Federn. Trans. Fischer Verlag, 1990.

Criticism

Consentino, Olga. "El teatro de los setenta: una dramaturgia sitiada." *Latin American Theatre Review* 24, 2 (Spring 1991): 31–39.
Esteve, Patricio. "1980–1981: la prehistoria de Teatro Abierto." *Latin American Theatre Review* 24, 2 (Spring 1991): 59–68.
Giella, Miguel Angel. "*Desconcierto.*" In *Teatro Abierto 1981: Volumen I*, ed. Osvaldo Pellettieri. Buenos Aires: Corregidor, 1992, 237–244.
Glickman, Nora. "Parodia y desmitificación del rol femenino en el

teatro de Diana Raznovich." *Latin American Theatre Review* 28, 1 (Fall 1994): 89–100.

Martínez, Martha. "Tres nuevas dramaturgas argentinas: Roma Mahieu, Hebe Uhart y Diana Raznovich," *Latin American Theatre Review* (Spring 1980): 39–45.

ROMERO, MARIELA

Plays

Algo alrededor del espejo. (Unpublished.)
El baile de los vampiros. (Unpublished.)
El cáncer es curable: no lo malgaste. (Unpublished.)
Esperando al italiano. Caracas: La Huella Editorial, 1988. Also in *Las risas de nuestras medusas: Teatro venezolano escrito por mujeres*, ed. Susana Castillo. Caracas: Fundarte, 1992, 65–99.
Este mundo circo. (Unpublished.)
El inevitable destino de Rosa de la noche: Obra en tres escenas. Caracas: Dirección General de Cultura de la Gobernación del Distrito Federal y Fundarte, 1980.
El juego. Caracas: Monte Avila Editores, 1977. Also in *Teatro venezolano. Tomo III*, ed. Isaac Chocrón. Caracas: Monte Avila Editores, 1982, 73–112; and *Teatro venezolano contemporáneo: Antología*, ed. Orlando Rodríguez B. Madrid: Sociedad Estatal Quinto Centenario: Fondo de Cultura Económica: Centro de Documentación Teatral, 1991.
Rosa de la noche. In *Textos teatrales.* Caracas: Centro de Estudios Latinoamericanos Rómulo Gallegos, 1982, 47–94. Also Caracas: Fundarte, 1985.
El vendedor. In *María Cristina me quiere gobernar . . . : Bilingual Anthology/antología bilingüe*, ed. Susana Castillo and Elsie Adams. Caracas: CELCIT, CONAC, 1992.

Criticism

Canale, Félix. "La actitud autobiográfica de Mariela Romero." *Escena* 9 (1976): 36–38.
Castillo, Susana D. "Fantasías textuales: el mundo dramático de Mariela Romero." In *Las risas de nuestras medusas: Teatro venezolano escrito por mujeres*. Caracas: Fundarte, 1992, 37–43.
———. "El juego: un desesperado recurso de supervivencia." *Tramoya* 20 (julio/septiembre 1980): 61–70.
———. "*El juego*: texto dramático y montaje." *Latin American Theatre Review* 14, 1 (Fall 1980): 25–33.

————, and Elise Adams, eds. *María Cristina me quiere gobernar* ... : *Bilingual Anthology/antología bilingüe*. Caracas: CELCIT, CONAC, 1992.

Chrzanowski, Joseph. "El teatro de Mariela Romero." *Revista Canadiense de Estudios Hispánicos* 7,1 (Autumn 1982): 205–211.

SEIBEL, BEATRIZ

Plays

Siete veces Eva. (Unpublished.)
El amor. (Unpublished.)
Aquí Federico. (Unpublished.)

Critical Studies

Los artistas trashumantes. Buenos Aires: Ediciones de la Pluma, 1985.
Artistas y espectáculos. Buenos Aires: Centro Editor de América Latina, 1985.
De ninfas a capitanas: Mujer, teatro y sociedad en Argentina desde los rituales hasta la independencia. Ayuntamiento de Cádiz: Fundación Municipal de Cultura, 1990.
Los payadores. In *La vida de nuestro pueblo*. Buenos Aires: Centro Editor de América Latina, 1981.
"Espectáculo teatral e inmigración en Buenos Aires." *Revista Todo es Historia* 25, 206 (February 1992): 89–97.
"La mujer en el teatro argentino en el periodo de la independencia (1810–1830)." *Gestos* 4, 8 (November 1989): 147–155.
"Mujer, teatro y sociedad en Argentina: Epoca de la colonia." *Nuevo Texto Crítico* 2, 4 (1989): 19–26.
"Teatralidad popular en Argentina: Coexistencia de múltiples manifestaciones." *Latin American Theatre Review* 23, 1 (Fall 1989): 27–36.
"Teatro y festivales en Brasil." *Gestos* 2, 3 (April 1987): 146–148.

Criticism

Itkin, Silvia. "Mujer y teatro: Historias olvidadas: Entrevista con la investigadora teatral Beatriz Seibel." *Feminaria* 2, 3 (April 1989): 35–36.
Vargas, Margarita. "From Body to Voice: Self-Realization Through Art in *Siete veces Eva* by Beatriz Seibel." *Romance Languages Annual 1991* 3 (1992): 617–621.

VILALTA, MARUXA

Plays

Archie and Bonnie. (A musical parody in one act.) In *Una mujer, dos hombres y un balazo.*

Cinco obras de teatro. Cuadernos de Lectura Popular, no. 285. Mexico City: Secretaría de Educación Pública, 1970. [Includes *Un país feliz, Soliloquio del tiempo, Un día loco, La última letra,* and *El 9.*]

Cuestión de narices. (A tragic farce in two acts.) Mexico City: Universidad Nacional Autónoma de México, 1967.

Dos obras de teatro. Textos de Teatro 17, Difusión Cultural. Mexico City: Universidad Nacional Autónoma de México, 1984. [Includes *Una mujer, dos hombres y un balazo,* and *Pequeña historia de horror (y de amor desenfrenado).*]

El barco ebrio. (A play in one act.) In *Una mujer, dos hombres y un balazo.*

El 9. (A play in four scenes.) In *Teatro I.*

El té de los señores Mercier. (A play in one act.) In *Una mujer, dos hombres y un balazo.*

En blanco y negro. Ignacio y los jesuitas. (A play in twelve scenes.) Colección Popular, Fondo de Cultura Económica, Mexico City, 1997.

En las Lomas, esa noche. (A parody in one act.) In *Una mujer, dos hombres y un balazo.*

Esta noche juntos, amándonos tanto. (A tragic farce without interludes.) In *Teatro II.*

Francisco de Asís. (A play in fourteen scenes.) Colección Popular, no. 492. Mexico City: Fondo de Cultura Económica, 1993.

Historia de él. (A play in seventeen scenes.) In *Teatro II.*

Jesucristo entre nosotros. (A play in thirteen scenes.) Colección Popular, no. 515. Mexico City: Fondo de Cultura Económica, 1995.

Le última letra. (A monologue in one act.) In *Teatro I.*

Los desorientados. (A play in three acts.) In *Teatro I.*

Nada como el piso 16. (A play in three acts.) In *Teatro III.*

Pequeña historia de horror (y de amor desenfrenado). (A play in two acts.) In *Teatro II.*

Soliloquio del Tiempo. (A monologue in one act.) In *Teatro I.*

Teatro I. Colección Popular, no. 206. 3d ed. Mexico City: Fondo de Cultura Económica, 1992. [Includes *Los desorientados, Un país feliz, Soliloquio del Tiempo, Un día loco, La última letra, El 9,* and *Cuestión de narices.*]

Teatro II. Colección Popular, no. 399. 2d ed. Mexico City: Fondo de Cultura Económica, 1992. [Includes *Esta noche juntos, amándonos tanto, Nada como el piso 16, Historia de él, Una mujer, dos hombres y un balazo,* and *Pequeña historia de horror (y de amor desenfrenado).*]

Teatro III. Colección Popular, no. 460. 3d ed. Mexico City: Fondo de Cultura Económica, 1994. [Includes *Una voz en el desierto. Vida de San Jerónimo.*]

Trío. Mexico City: Colección Teatro Mexicano, 1965. [Includes *Soliloquio del tiempo, Un día loco,* and *La última letra.*]

Un día loco. (A monologue in one act.) In *Teatro I.*

Un país feliz. (A play in three acts.) In *Teatro I.*

Una mujer, dos hombres y un balazo. (A play in ten scenes.) In *Teatro II.*

Un voz en el desierto. Vida de San Jerónimo. In *Teatro III.*

Novels

Dos colores para el paisaje. Mexico City: Libro-Mex, 1961.

El castigo. Mexico City: Editorial La Prensa, 1957.

Los desorientados. Mexico City: Ediciones Selecta, 1958, and Libro-Mex, 1961.

Short Story

El otro día, la muerte. Mexico City: Joaquín Mortiz, 1974. [Includes *Diálogos del narrador, la muerte y su invitado, Romance de la muerte de agua, Aventura con la muerte de fuego, morir temprano mientras comulga el general.*]

Plays in Translation

A Happy Country. Trans. Edward Huberman. *Latin American Literary Review* 3, 6 (Spring–Summer 1975): 113–146

A Little Tale of Horror (and Unbridled Love). Trans. Kirsten F. Nigro. *Modern International Drama* 19, 2 (Spring 1986): 25–60.

A Mad Day. Trans. Edward Huberman. *Latin American Literary Review* 1, 2 (Spring 1973): 149–158.

A Matter of Noses. Trans. Lisa Routman. Des Moines, Ia.: Drake University, 1978. (Unpublished.)

A Question of Noses. Trans. Joan R. Green. Houston, Tex.: Rice University, 1974. (Unpublished.)

A Voice in the Wilderness. The Life of Saint Jerome. Trans. Edward Huberman. New Brunswick, N.J.: Rutgers University, 1990.

A Woman, Two Men, and a Gunshot. Trans. Kirsten F. Nigro. Lawrence: University of Kansas, 1984. (In this anthology.)

As Two Pigeons, As Two Turtledoves. (Together Tonight, Loving Each Other So Much). Trans. Jan and Jana Makarius. Prague: Dilia, 1971.

Francis of Assisi. Trans. Sharon Magnarelli. New Haven, Conn.: Albertus Magnus College, 1993. (Unpublished.)

Il 9. In *Teatro latino americano, 10 atti unici di 8 autori d'avanguardia.* Rome: Instituto Italo-Latinoamericano, 1974.

La dernier signe. Trans. Mireille Pezzani. *L'Avant-Scène* (Paris, July 1964).

Le 9. Trans. André Camp. *L'Avant-Scène* 737 (Paris, November 1983).

Nothing Like the Sixteenth Floor. Trans. Edward Huberman. *Modern International Drama* 12, 1 (Fall 1978): 51–84.

Nothing Like the Sixteenth Floor. Trans. Keith Leonard, Simpson College, Indianola, Iowa, and Mario T. Soria, Drake University, Des Moines, Iowa, 1977. (Unpublished.)

Questio de Nassos. Trans. Joesp Maria Poblet. Llibre de Butxaca, Barcelona: Editorial Portic, 1973.

16 ème étage à Manhattan. Trans. André Camp. Paris, 1978. (Unpublished.)

Soliloqui del Temps. Trans. Vicenç Riera Llorca. *Xaloc* 24 (Mexico City, June 1968).

The Last Letter. Trans. Robert L. Bancroft. Amherst: University of Massachusetts, 1972. (Unpublished.)

The Story of Him. Trans. Edward Huberman. *Modern International Drama* 14, 2 (Fall 1980): 5–36.

Times Soliloquy. Trans. Edward Huberman. *Latin American Literary Review* 1, 2 (Spring 1973): 159–166.

Together Tonight, Loving Each Other So Much. Trans. Willis Knapp Jones. *Modern International Drama* 6, 2 (Spring 1973): 5–38.

Un jour de folie. Trans. Jean Camp. *L'Avant-Scène* 423 (Paris, April 1969).

Criticism

Bancroft, Robert L. Play Synopses of *Cuestión de narices, Los desorientados, Un país feliz, Soliloquio del tiempo, Un día loco, La última letra,* and *El 9. Latin American Theatre Review* 6, 2 (Spring 1973): 82–85.

———. "El teatro de Maruxa Vilalta." *El Urogallo* 3, 5 (May–June 1972): 111–117.

Bearse, Grace, and Lorraine Elena Roses. "Maruxa Vilalta: Social Dramatist." *Revista de Estudios Hispánicos* 18, 3 (October 1984): 399–406.

Boorman, Joan Rea. "Contemporary Latin American Women Dramatists." *Rice University Studies* 64 (1978): 69–80.

Gaucher-Shultz, Jeanine S. "La temática de dos obras premiadas de Maruxa Vilalta." *Latin American Theatre Review* 12, 2 (Spring 1979): 87–90.

Holzapfel, Tamara. "The Theatre of Maruxa Vilalta: A Triumph of Versatility." *Latin American Theatre Review* 14, 2 (Spring 1981): 11–18.

Knapp Jones, Willis. "*Esta noche juntos, amándonos tanto.*" *Latin American Theatre Review* 4, 2 (Spring 1971): 91–92.

Magaña Esquivel, Antonio, ed. *Teatro mexicano 1964.* Mexico City: Aguilar, 1967, 195–198.

Magnarelli, Sharon. "Esta noche juntos, amándonos tanto, de Maruxa Vilalta." *Plural* 205 (October 1988): 30–32.

———. "El gran teatro del amor: *Una mujer, dos hombres y un balazo* de Maruxa Vilalta" *Alba de América* 7, 12–13 (July 1989): 263–282.

———. "Discourse as Content and Form in the Works of Maruxa Vilalta." *Hispanic Journal* 9, 2 (Spring 1988): 99–111. [Part of this essay was translated into Spanish by Carlos David Malfavón. It appeared in *Plural* 192 (September 1987): 77–78, as "Contenido y forma en la obra de Maruxa Vilalta."]

Miller, Beth, and Alfonso González. *26 autoras del México actual.* Mexico City: B. Costa-Amic Ed., 1978, 405–418.

Morales, Gloria V. "Maruxa Vilalta: un teatro que rompe con lo tradicional." *Plural* 192 (September 1987): 72–75.

Nigro, Kirsten F. "*Esta noche juntos, amándonos tanto*: texto y representación." *Actas del VI Congreso Internacional de Hispanistas.* Toronto: University of Toronto Press, 1980, 527–529.

———. "Maruxa Vilalta." *Supplements to the Critical Surveys of Literature,* ed. Frank N. Magill. Pasadena, Calif.: Salem Press, September 1987: 373–379.

Peralta, Elda. "Entrevista con Maruxa Vilalta," *Plural* 8, 91 (April 1979): 40–46.

Quackenbush, L. Howard. "Cuestión de vida y muerte: tres dramas existenciales." *Latin American Theatre Review* 8, 1 (Fall 1974): 49–56.

Roses, Lorraine. "La expresión dramática de la inconformidad social en cuatro dramaturgas hispanoamericanas." *Plaza* 5–6 (Fall-Spring 1981–82): 97–114.

Solórzano, Carlos. "El teatro de Maruxa Vilalta." *Latin American Theatre Review* 18, 2 (Spring 1985): 83–87.

Suárez Radillo, Carlos Miguel. "La obra de la dramaturga Maruxa Vilalta a través de la confrontación de críticas y autocríticas." In *Lo social en el teatro hispanoamericano contemporáneo.* Caracas: Equinoccio, 1976, 209–227.

Valenzuela, Víctor M. "Maruxa Vilalta: *Un país feliz.*" In *Siete comediógrafas hispanoamericanas.* Bethlehem, Pa.: Lehigh University Press, 1975, 71–79.

Vásquez-Morales, Gloria. "Los personajes en el drama de Maruxa Vilalta según el modelo actancial de Greimas." Diss. Arizona State University, 1991.

Vélez, Joseph F. *Dramaturgos mexicanos según ellos mismos*. Mexico City: Compañía Impresora y Distribuidora, 1990, 59–68.

Zalacaín, Daniel. *Teatro absurdista hispanoamericano*. Valencia, Spain: Albatrós Hispanófila, 1985, 155–163.

General Bibliography

Abel, Lionel. *Metatheatre: A New View of Dramatic Form*. New York: Hill and Wang, 1963.

Arrom, Silvia Marina. *The Women of Mexico City, 1790–1857*. Stanford, Calif.: Stanford University Press, 1985.

Artiles, Freddy, ed. *Teatro para niños*. La Habana: Editorial Letras Cubanas, 1981.

Austin, Gayle. *Feminist Theories for Dramatic Criticism*. Ann Arbor: The University of Michigan Press, 1990.

Azparren Jiménez, Leonardo. *Teatro venezolano y otros teatros*. Caracas: Monte Avila Editores, 1978.

Berenguer, Carísomo Arturo. *Las ideas estéticas en el teatro argentino*. Buenos Aires: Comisión Nacional de Cultura, 1947.

Bergmann, Emilie, et al. eds. *Women, Culture, and Politics in Latin America*. Berkeley: University of California Press, 1990.

Berman, Sabina. "La mujer como dramaturgo." *El Universal*, Cultural Section (19, 20, 21 March 1988).

Burgess, Ronald D. *The New Dramatists of Mexico: 1967–1985*. Lexington: University Press of Kentucky, 1991.

Carballido, Emilio. *9 obras jóvenes: Antología*. 1985. Mexico City: Editores Mexicanos Unidos, 1987.

———. *Teatro joven de México: Antología*. Mexico City: Editores Mexicanos Unidos, 1987.

Castagnino, Raúl Héctor. *Literatura dramática argentina: 1717–1967*. Buenos Aires: Editorial Pleamar, 1968.

Castillo, Debra A. *Talking Back: Toward a Latin American Feminist Literary Criticism*. Ithaca, N.Y.: Cornell University Press, 1992.

Castillo, Susana D. *El "desarraigo" en el teatro venezolano: Marco histórico y manifestaciones modernas*. Caracas: Editorial Ateneo de Caracas, 1980.

Castro-Klarén, Sara. "Situations." *Latin American Literary Review* 20, 40 (July–December 1992): 26–29.

———, Sylvia Molloy, and Beatriz Sarlo, eds. *Women's Writing in Latin America: An Anthology*. Boulder, Colo.: Westview Press, 1991.

Cortina, Lynn Ellen Rice. *Spanish-American Women Writers: A Bibliographical Research Checklist*. New York and London: Garland Publishing, 1983.

Cruz, Sor Juana Inés de la. *Obras completas,* ed. Alfonso Méndez Plancarte. México: Fondo de Cultura Económica, 1951–1957.

Cypess, Sandra Messinger. "Dramaturgia femenina y transposición histórica." *Alba de América* 7, 12–13 (July 1989): 283–304.

———. "¿Quién ha oído hablar de ellas? Una revisión de las dramaturgas mexicanas." *Texto Crítico* 10 (1979): 55–64.

———. "Women dramatists of Puerto Rico." *Revista/Review Interamericana* 9,1 (Spring 1979): 24–41.

Dauster, Frank. *Historia del teatro hispanoamericano: Siglos XIX y XX.* Mexico City: Ediciones de Andrea, 1966.

———, et al., eds. *9 dramaturgos hispanoamericanos: Antología del teatro hispano-americano del siglo XX.* Ottawa, Ont.: Girol Books, 1979, 7–16.

Del Río, Marcela. "El Ateneo mexicano de escritoras y la Revista Ideas." *Mujer y sociedad en América: IV Simposio Internacional.* Westminster, Calif.: Instituto Literario y Cultural Hispánico, 1990.

Dreyfus, Hubert L. *Michel Foucault, Beyond Structuralism and Hermeneutics.* Chicago: University of Chicago Press, 1982.

Durán Cerda, Julio. *Repertorio del teatro chileno: Bibliografía, obras inéditas y estrenadas.* Santiago: Insituto de Literatura Chilena, 1962.

Eidelberg, Nora. *Teatro experimental hispanoamericano 1960–1980: La realidad social como manipulación.* Minneapolis: Institute for the Study of Ideologies and Literature, 1985.

———, and María Mercedes Jaramillo, eds. *Voces en escena: Antología de dramaturgas latinoamericanas.* Bogotá: Colección Teatro, 1991.

Escudero, Alfonso. "Apuntes sobre el teatro en Chile." *Aisthesis* 1 (1966): 17–61.

Esquivel, Laura. *Como agua para chocolate.* Mexico City: Editorial Planeta, 1989.

Falk, Pamela S. *The Political Status of Puerto Rico.* Lexington, Mass.: D. C. Heath, 1986.

Fernández, Teodosio. *El teatro chileno contemporáneo (1941–1973).* Madrid: Editorial Playor, 1982.

Fernández de Lizardi, José Joaquín. *La educación de las mujeres o la Quijotita y su prima.* Mexico City: Feria del Libro, 1942.

Figueroa, Alvin Joaquín. *La prosa de Luis Rafael Sánchez: Texto y contexto.* New York: Peter Lang, 1989.

Flores, Angel, and Kate Flores, eds. *Hispanic Feminist Poems from the Middle Ages to the Pesent: A Bilingual Anthology.* New York: Feminist Press and the City Unversity of New York, 1986.

Foster, David William, ed. *Mexican Literature: A History.* Austin: University of Texas Press, 1994.

Foucault, Michel. *The History of Sexuality.* Trans. Robert Hurley. New York: Pantheon Books, 1978.

Franco, Jean. *Plotting Women: Gender and Representation in Mexico.* New York: Columbia University Press, 1989.

García Pinto, Magdalena. *Women Writers of Latin America: Intimate Histories.* Trans. Trudy Balch and Magdalena García Pinto. Austin: University of Texas Press, 1991.

Garfield, Evelyn Picon. *Women's Voices from Latin America: Interviews with Six Contemporary Authors.* Detroit: Wayne State University Press, 1985.

———. *Women's Fiction from Latin America: Selections from Twelve Contemporary Authors.* Detroit: Wayne State University Press, 1988.

Giella, Miguel Angel, and Peter Roster, eds. *Reflexiones sobre teatro latinoamericano del siglo veinte.* Buenos Aires: Editorial Galerna/ Lemcke Verlag, 1989.

Gómez, Alma, Cherríe Moraga, and Mariana Romo-Carmona, eds. *Cuentos: Stories by Latinas.* New York: Kitchen Table, Women of Color Press, 1982.

González, Patricia Elena, and Eliana Ortega, eds. *La sartén por el mango: Encuentro de escritoras latinoamericanas.* Río Piedras, P.R.: Huracán, 1985.

González Cajiao, Fernando. *Historia del teatro en Colombia 1986.* Bogotá: Instituto Colombiano de Cultura, 1986.

Gorriti, Juana Manuela. "El guante negro." In *Sueños y realidades* Buenos Aires: Biblioteca de la Nación, 1903.

Greenberg, Janet. "A Question of Blood: The Conflict of Sex and Class in the *Autobiografía* of Victoria Ocampo." In *Women, Culture, and Politics in Latin America,* ed. Emilie Bergmann, et al. Berkeley: University of California Press, 1990, 130–150.

Guerra, Lucía. "Estrategias femeninas en la elaboración del sujeto romántico en la obra de Gertrudis Gómez de Avellaneda." *Revista Iberoamericana* 51,132–133 (julio-diciembre 1985): 707–722.

Guerrero Zamora, Juan. *Historia del teatro contemporáneo.* Vol. I. Barcelona: Juan Flors, Editor, 1967.

Hornby, Richard. *Drama, Metatheatre, and Perception.* London and Toronto: Associated University Press, 1986.

Hurtado, María de la Luz, Carlos Ochsenius, Hernán Vidal, eds. *Teatro chileno de la crisis institucional 1973–1980 (Antología Crítica).* Minneapolis: Minnesota Latin American Series and CENECA in Santiago de Chile, 1982.

Indice de obras teatrales. Vols. I and II. Mexico City: Instituto Nacional de Bellas Artes, 1988.

Isaacs, Jorge. *María.* Buenos Aires: Editorial Losada, 1973.

Jones, Willis Knapp. *Breve historia del teatro latinoamericano.* Mexico City: Ediciones de Andrea, 1956.

Kirkpatrick, Gwen. "The Journalism of Alfonsina Storni: A New Approach to Women's History in Argentina." In *Women, Culture, and Politics in Latin America*, ed. Emilie Bergmann, et al. Berkeley: University of California Press, 1990, 105–129.

Lavrín, Asunción, ed. *Latin American Women: Historical Perspectives*. Westport, Conn.: Greenwood Press, 1978.

Leal, Luis. "Female Archtypes in Mexican Literature." In *Women in Hispanic Literature, Icons and Fallen Idols*, ed. Beth Miller. Berkeley: University of California Press 1983, 227–242.

Lerner, Gerda. *The Creation of Feminist Consciousness: From the Middle Ages to Eighteen-Seventy*. Oxford: Oxford University Press, 1993.

Lyday, Leon F., and George Woodyard, eds. *Dramatists in Revolt: The New Latin American Theater*. Austin: University of Texas Press, 1976.

Magnarelli, Sharon. *The Lost Rib: Female Characters in the Spanish-American Novel*. Lewisburg: University Presses of America/ Toronto: Associated University Presses, 1985.

Manguel, Alberto, ed. *Other Fires: Short Fiction by Latin American Women*. New York: Clarkson N. Potter, 1986.

Mármol, José. *Amalia*. Buenos Aires: Editorial Sopena Argentina, S.R.L., 1944. Trans. Mary J. Serrano. New York: E. P. Dutton, 1919.

Martínez, Julio A., ed. *Dictionary of Twentieth-Century Cuban Literature*. New York: Greenwood Press, 1990.

Marting, Diane. *Women Writers of Spanish America: An Annotated Bio-Bibliographical Guide*. New York: Greenwood Press, 1987.

Masiello, Francine. *Between Civilization and Barbarism: Women, Nation, and Literary Culture in Modern Argentina*. Lincoln: University of Nebraska Press, 1992.

———. "Women, State, and Family in Latin American Literature of the 1920s." In *Women, Culture, and Politics in Latin America*, ed. Emilie Bergmann, et al. Berkeley: University of California Press, 1990, 27–47.

Meyer, Doris, and Margarite Fernández Olmos, eds. *Contemporary Women Authors of Latin America: Introductory Essays*. Brooklyn: Brooklyn College, 1983.

Miller, Beth, ed. *Women in Hispanic Literature, Icons and Fallen Idols*. Berkeley: University of California Press 1983.

Miller, Francesca. "Latin American Feminism and the Transnational Arena." In *Women, Culture, and Politics in Latin America*, ed. Emilie Bergmann, et al. Berkeley: University of California Press, 1990, 10–26.

Miller, Yvette E., and Charles M. Tatum, eds. *Latin American Women Writers: Yesterday and Today*. Pittsburgh, Pa.: Carnegie-Mellon, 1977.

Molloy, Sylvia. "Female Textual Identities: The Strategies of Self-Figuration." In Castro-Klarén, et al., 105–124.

Montes Huidobro, Matías. "Luis Rafael Sánchez: lengua e identidad en el teatro puertorriqueño." *The American Hispanist* 4, 30–31 (November–December 1978): 22–35.

Morfi, Angelina. *Historia crítica de un siglo de teatro puertorriqueño.* San Juan: Instituto de Cultura Puertorriqueña, 1980.

Neruda, Pablo. *Obras completas.* Buenos Aires: Editorial Losada, 1956, 73–74.

Nigro, Kirsten F. "Twentieth-Century Theater." In *Mexican Literature: A History,* ed. David William Foster. Austin: University of Texas Press, 1994, 213–242.

Ordóñez, Elizabeth. "Sexual Politics and the Theme of Sexuality in Chicana Poetry." In *Women in Hispanic Literature, Icons and Fallen Idols,* ed. Beth Miller. Berkeley: University of California Press 1983, 316–339.

Oviedo, José Miguel. "Una discusión permanente: (Renovación teatral)." In *América latina en su literatura,* ed. César Fernández Moreno. Mexico City: Siglo Veintiuno, 1980, 437–438.

Partnoy, Alicia. *You Can't Drown the Fire: Latin American Women Writing in Exile.* Pittsburgh, San Francisco: Cleis Press, 1988.

Paz, Octavio. *Sor Juana Inés de la Cruz; O las trampas de la fe.* Barcelona: Seix Barral, 1982.

Pedrero, Paloma. "Las autoras teatrales en España." Delivered at the Festival Iberoamericano de Teatro in Cádiz, Spain, 1988.

Perales, Rosalina. *Teatro hispanoamericano contemporáneo: 1967–1987.* Mexico City: Grupo Editorial Gaceta, 1989.

Pirandello, Luigi. *On Humor.* Trans. Antonio Illiano and Daniel P. Testa. Chapel Hill: The University of North Carolina Press, 1960.

Pratt, Mary Louise. "Women, Literature, and National Brotherhood." In *Women, Culture, and Politics in Latin America,* ed. Emilie Bergmann, et al. Berkeley: University of California Press, 1990, 48–73.

Prida, Dolores. *Coser y cantar.* In *Beautiful Señoritas and Other Plays.* Houston, Tex.: Arte Público Press, 1991, 47–67.

Rabinow, Paul, ed. *The Foucault Reader.* New York: Pantheon, 1984.

Ramos-Perea, Roberto. "Nueva dramaturgia puertorriqueña." *Latin American Theatre Review* 20,1 (Fall 1986): 61–80.

Rela, Walter. *Teatro uruguayo: 1807–1979.* Montevideo: Ediciones de la Alianza, 1980.

———. *Teatro uruguayo: 1808–1994.* Montevideo: Academia Uruguaya de Letras, 1994.

Resnick, Margery, and Isabelle de Courtivron. *Women Writers in Translation: An Annotated Bibliography, 1945–82.* New York: Garland Press, 1984.

Reyes, Carlos José. "Teatro e historia." *Conjunto* 61–62 (julio–diciembre 1964): 146–156.

Rizk, Beatriz J. *El nuevo teatro latinoamericano, una lectura histórica.* Minneapolis, Minn.: Prisma Institute, 1987.

Rojo, Grinor. *Muerte y resurrección del teatro chileno 1973–1983.* Madrid: Ediciones Michay, 1985.

Russ, Joanna. *How to Suppress Women's Writing.* Austin: University of Texas Press, 1983.

Salas, Teresa Cajiao. *Temas y símbolos en la obra de Luis Alberto Heiremans.* Santiago: Editorial Universitaria, 1970.

Sandoval, Enrique. "Teatro latinoamericano: cuatro dramaturgas y una escenógrafa." *Literatura chilena: Creación y crítica* 47/50 (1989): 173–175.

Saz, Agustín del. *Teatro hispanoamericano.* Barcelona: Editorial Vergara, 1963.

Silva Castro, Raúl. *Panorama Literario de Chile.* Santiago: Editorial Universitaria, 1961.

Solórzano, Carlos. *El teatro actual latinoamericano: Antología.* Mexico City: Ediciones de Andrea, 1972.

Soria, Mario T. *Teatro boliviano en el siglo xx.* La Paz: Editorial Casa Municipal de la Cultura "Franz Tamayo," 1980.

Staiff, Kive. *Veinte años del teatro municipal.* Buenos Aires: Imprenta de los Buenos Ayres, 1980.

Taylor, Diana, and Juan Villegas, eds. *Negotiating Performance: Gender, Sexuality and Theatricality in Latin(o) America.* Durham, N.C.: Duke University Press, 1994.

Torres-Pou, Joan. "La ambigüedad de mensaje feminista de *Sab* de Gertrudis Gómez de Avellaneda." *Letras Femeninas* 19, 1–2 (1993): 55–64.

———. "Clorinda Matto de Turner y el ángel del hogar." *Revista Hispánica Moderna* 43, 1 (June 1990): 3–15.

Vargas, Margarita. "Romanticism." In *Mexican Literature: A History,* ed. David William Foster. Austin: University of Texas Press, 1994, 83–112.

Vigil, Evangelina, ed. *Woman of Her Word: Hispanic Women Write.* 2d ed. Houston, Tex.: Arte Público Press, 1987.

Villaurrutia, Xavier. *Invitación a la muerte.* In *9 dramaturgos hispanoamericanos: Volume II,* ed. Frank Dauster, et al. Ottawa, Ont.: Girol Books, 1979.

Virgillo, Carmelo, and Naomi Lindstrom, eds. *Woman as Myth and Metaphor in Latin American Literature.* Columbia: University of Missouri Press, 1985.

Warhol, Robyn R., and Diane Price Herndl, eds. *Feminisms: An Anthology of Literary Theory and Criticism*. New Brunswick, N.J.: Rutgers University Press, 1993.

Wittig, Monique. "The Mark of Gender." In *The Poetics of Gender*, ed. Nancy K. Miller. New York: Columbia University Press, 1986, 63–73.

Zayaz de Lima, Perla. *Diccionario de autores teatrales argentinos (1950–1980)*. Buenos Aires: Editorial Rodolfo Alonso, 1981.

Index

Gramley Library
Salem Academy and College
Winston-Salem, N.C. 27108